CHILDREN

OF THE LAND

Studies on Successful Adolescent Development

The John D. and Catherine T. MacArthur Foundation
Series on Mental Health and Development

CHILDREN
OF THE LAND

Adversity and Success in Rural America

Glen H. Elder Jr. and
Rand D. Conger

With a Foreword by Ross D. Parke

and with the collaboration of
Valarie King, Lisa S. Matthews, Debra Mekos,
Stephen T. Russell, and Michael J. Shanahan

THE UNIVERSITY OF CHICAGO PRESS / CHICAGO AND LONDON

Glen H. Elder, Jr., is the Odum Distinguished Professor of Sociology and Research Professor of Psychology, and a fellow of the Carolina Population Center, University of North Carolina. His many books include *Children of the Great Depression.*

Rand D. Conger is professor of sociology and director of the Center for Research on Rural Family Mental Health at Iowa State University. Together Rand Conger and Glen Elder are the authors of *Families in Troubled Times.*

The University of Chicago Press, Chicago 60637
The University of Chicago Press, Ltd., London
© 2000 by The University of Chicago
All rights reserved. Published 2000
Printed in the United States of America
10 09 08 07 06 05 04 03 02 01 00   5 4 3 2 1

ISBN (cloth): 0-226-20266-6

The University of Chicago Press gratefully acknowledges a subvention from the John D. and Catherine T. MacArthur Foundation in partial support of the costs of production of this volume.

Library of Congress Cataloging-in-Publication Data

Elder, Glen H.
    Children of the land : adversity and success in rural America / Glen H. Elder Jr. and Rand D. Conger ; with a foreword by Ross D. Parke, and with the collaboration of Stephen T. Russell . . . [et al.].
        p.   cm. — (Studies on successful adolescent development)
    Includes bibliographical references and index.
    ISBN 0-226-20266-6 (alk. paper)
    1. Rural youth—United States—Family relationships. 2. Parenting—United States. 3. United States—Rural conditions. 4. Success—United States. I. Conger, Rand. II. Title. III. John D. and Catherine T. MacArthur Foundation series on mental health and development. Studies on successful adolescent development.
HQ796.E525   2000
305.235'0973'091734—dc21   99-047161

CONTENTS

Tables

Figures

A gallery of photographs follows page 126

FOREWORD

Social diagnoses too frequently represent a search for simple solutions to the complex problems of our age, such as delinquency, school dropout rates, and teenage pregnancies. Some propose divorce as the culprit; others point an accusing finger at television violence or blame feminism, communism, or father absence. In this important volume, it is refreshing to find an appreciation of the complexities of how and why youth develop as they do. Elder and Conger provide a model that could serve as an antidote to a disease of our time—reliance on binary thinking and simple answers to the complex problems of young people. It is ironic that their insights come from studying a fading way of life—that of rural Midwest farm communities.

The authors provide a rich portrait of this way of life that was once shared by most Americans. Their use of qualitative reports from members of different generations brings the era to life for readers and will be an important resource for later generations—wistful for bygone eras. However, the book is much more than an account of an older way of life; it is a story of how this way of life makes a positive difference in the lives of contemporary young people and illustrates how families adapt to economic problems, including the wrenching experience of leaving the land. An earlier volume by the authors, *Families in Troubled Times* (1994), tests important theoretical notions about how families and children cope with stressful economic change. *Children of the Land* builds upon this work by examining in more depth and with more nuance the special role that farming plays in adaptations to change and in the developmental experiences of the young. In this study, ties to the land include families that range from full- and part-time farming to displaced farm families and families headed by nonfarm parents who grew up on a farm. The authors compare each group to families headed by adults who did not grow up on a farm.

The reader can approach this volume in different ways. The most intriguing and provocative one views the work as a set of guidelines or lessons to be learned from the life experience of farm families. These lessons can help us move toward solving current social problems. History is at its best as both a documentation of our past and as a social commentary for the present. This volume aims to do both and does so admirably. Elder and Conger identify some important lessons from which we can profit.

First and foremost, the authors demonstrate unequivocally that families matter in the lives of children. At the same time, families, especially successful ones, are embedded in a network of social ties and institutional relationships which operate in a synergistic fashion to influence the development of children and youth. Not surprisingly, many familiar family characteristics emerge as desirable, such as warmth, responsiveness, the encouragement of responsibility, and the granting of autonomy.

Extended families matter too. In spite of the increased longevity of grandparents, social scientists have been slow to document the role of grandparents in the lives of our children. As Elder and Conger show, grandparents make a notable difference in the development of competence of our youth. In rural communities such as those in Iowa, children have the luxury of frequent contact with their grandparents, with 40 percent seeing their grandparents at least once a week. Elsewhere, with high rates of mobility in our society, many children do not have this opportunity due to the great physical distances that often separate the generations. The current generation is poorer for it.

Another lesson concerns the role of fathers in children's lives. It is fashionable to view fathers as rediscovered in the last several decades and to cast the "new fatherhood" as an improvement over older models of fatherhood. Elder and Conger's analysis of farm fathers reminds us that good fathering can assume a variety of forms which depend on the historical period and the context. Farming as a context promoted an apprenticeship model of fathering—a model only possible within the framework of shared daily work. Exposing children more regularly to parental work may be an idea worth revisiting. Although farm fathers bear little resemblance to the new fathers of the 1990s, they nonetheless have a major and positive impact on their children. As models of self-reliance who encourage a sense of obligation, responsibility, and shared family work, these men exert a positive and strong influence on their developing children.

The concept of social capital has only recently been introduced to social science discourse. However, farm families have embodied this concept for generations. To a greater extent than nonfarm families, adults with ties to the land are more socially embedded in their local communities, churches, and schools, which provide a rich set of opportunities for their children. These children of the land do more with their parents than do nonfarm children, who are more involved in peer culture. And farm children know more adults in the community, and more adults know them. Monitoring of children is easier and more successful, and values are more likely to be shared across levels of the social network in the community and across generations. Not surprisingly, farm youth are more academically and socially successful than their peers who are raised in nonfarm families. The challenge that Elder and Conger pose is to create contexts such as those of Iowa farm communities that will nurture and promote the development of social capital in nonrural settings.

One aspect of community influence that has been largely neglected by social scientists is the religious institution, although churches and synagogues have always played an important role in supporting and protecting families and children. This is especially evident in the farm families surveyed in this volume. As Elder and Conger discover, church affiliation is a major determinant of success among youth—academically and socially. Whether it is a belief system, a set of values, or the social capital associated with religious institutions is unclear, but it is clear that church ties are a positive element in the lives of children. The insights about the role of church and other religious institutions are reminiscent of insights about the reliance of African-American families on religious groups as a source of solace, guidance, and support.

The authors caution us against nostalgia for the lifestyle of farming communities. Farming is difficult, and small farms are becoming economically nonviable. And this way of life has its costs. While we complain about the stresses and strains of modern urban life and the demands of contemporary jobs and careers, the image of a pastoral rural life is a false one. In the observations of farm parents about the tempo of their lives, "runnin'" was often used to describe the "frenzy" generated by the social and economic challenges of farm life. No era is perfect; every period and way of life has its costs as well as its benefits.

Important theoretical and methodological insights may be harvested from this study of families with varied ties to the land. The power of the life-course perspective for organizing questions and aiding in the interpretation of findings is evident throughout this volume. Developmentalists are reminded that to understand fully the development of children's lives, we must recognize and assess their embeddedness in the lives not only of their parents, but of other generations, especially grandparents. The tracking of the multiple developmental trajectories of adult lives across generations is necessary to understand how and why children emerge as they do. Second, the focus on life transitions as important junctures for clarifying developmental patterns is evident in myriad ways throughout this volume. And the multiple meanings of transitions as both normative, or expected, and nonnormative, or unexpected, change are illustrated as well.

Perhaps the most important theoretical lesson is the reminder that a contextual view of parenting, in which parenting is not restricted to parent-child exchanges within the family, is necessary to appreciate fully the rich array of dimensions of child socialization. Parents serve as providers and restrictors of opportunities available outside the family. Not only by their direct management strategies but by their own community involvement parental influence extends well beyond the boundaries of the family system.

In the final analysis, this volume is a story of optimism and hope, not simply a tale of loss. As much as the decline of family farms can be viewed as a tragedy, the resilience of youth reared in families with ties to the land in response to their adversities is important to underscore. Most of the children of the farm crisis were adapting well to the changes it brought. This resilience of the human condition is repeatedly evident in this volume. Just as Elder found twenty-five years before in his classic volume, *Children of the Great Depression,* life trajectories are by no means determined by disadvantage of origins and subsequent misfortune. As we are increasingly recognizing, one of the most important features of development is its plasticity and capacity to recover and be resilient in the face of trauma and negative life events.

The challenge that this volume presents to us is to invent communities within communities, so that even urban environments will allow the nurturing of "small overlapping worlds" of church, school, and community. As Hillary Clinton argued, it does take a village to raise a child, or at least a successful outcome is more likely when a village is involved. Some architects, city planners, and policy makers are moving us toward these alternative views of community. African-Americans and, more recently, new Hispanic and Asian immigrants have demonstrated by their example of mutual aid and reliance on extended kin that the revival of villages may not be such a bad idea. The struggles and successes of farm families have bequeathed us this lesson as well. Let us not ignore their example. Our lives and especially the lives of our children could be enriched. This is the vision that *Children of the Land* holds out for the twenty-first century.

Ross D. Parke
University of California, Riverside

ACKNOWLEDGMENTS

The story of this book began in the 1980s, when plummeting land values and heavy indebtedness pushed a large number of Midwest families off their farms, setting in motion the most severe economic crisis for rural areas of the region since the Great Depression. To investigate the effects of this crisis, a research team at the Center for Family Research in Rural Mental Health, Iowa State University, launched the Iowa Youth and Families Project. The study included 451 two-parent families with seventh-grade children (as of 1989) in eight north central counties. The Iowa Project became longitudinal with annual follow-ups into the mid-1990s, and it was subsequently enlarged through the addition of single parents and members of the grandparent generation. With core support from the National Institute of Mental Health, the research team was headed by Conger and originally included four colleagues from Iowa State University (Paul Lasley, Frederick Lorenz, Ronald Simons, and Les Whitbeck) as well as Elder at the University of North Carolina at Chapel Hill. Elder's research was supported in large measure by the MacArthur Foundation's Research Network on Successful Adolescent Development among Youth in High-Risk Settings.

Children of the Great Depression, a longitudinal study of children who grew up during the 1930s, provided useful guidance for our rural initiative. Consistent with this earlier study, we found that economic hardship influenced children through "changes in their families." For example, hardship adversely affected the psychological well-being of children by increasing the emotional distress, negativity, and harshness of mother and father. But we also discovered evidence of resilience, and this became the point of departure for the present study, extending from 1989 through 1994.

In the midst of widespread hardship in the region, a good many youth appeared to be faring well in school, in social activities, and in matters of emotional health. Theory and literature led us to believe that trajectories of resilience were especially common among young people who grew up on a farm or who had other ties to the land, as when parents were brought up on a farm. Living on the land calls for residential stability in making a living, an intergenerational investment in community life and institutions, and an ethic of work and care that has developmental implications. This study investigates such implications and considers their relevance for social policy.

One of the distinctive features of the study is its use of diverse types of data obtained from family members, including parents, the study child and near sibling, and grandparents: face-to-face and phone interviews, questionnaires, video tapes of family interaction in the households, and public historical records. Transcripts of the videotapes and the interviews with the study child and grandparents generated rich narrative accounts of personal experiences and public events. These accounts provided valuable insight into the historical context of the families, the personal experience of major social trends, and the process by which social changes are making a difference in lives. Some of the accounts also provided explanations or rationales for life changes. The names of people in these accounts are fictitious to protect the privacy of family members. In some cases, descriptions of the same event by different respondents were composited in order to ensure this privacy.

A great many debts have accumulated across the years of this longitudinal study. The challenging task of data collection and coding was carried out most effectively by the Center for Family Research in Rural Mental Health under Conger's direction. Linda Hoyt skillfully managed data collection, and Jan Melby directed the collection and coding of videotaped accounts of family interaction in the household. We are grateful to all of the field-workers and Center staff whose diligence ensured data of the highest quality. The Carolina Population Center at the University of North Carolina, Chapel Hill, also provided a rich research environment for support of this work. Aline Christoffelsz expertly managed communications and the stages of manuscript preparation, Rick O'Hara managed the complex data file, Lynn Igoe of the Center's library ensured that all references were correct and that the endnotes followed requested procedures, and Tom Swasey brought ideas, findings, and design together in creative fashion on graphs for the book.

Research efforts like this one play an important role in training young behavioral scientists, and we in turn benefit greatly from their collaboration. In particular, four postdoctoral fellows at the Carolina Population

Center played an important collaborative role in data analysis and in the initial drafting of chapters. Stephen Russell (now at the University of California, Davis) carried out analyses of resilient and vulnerable youth for the entire project and completed data analyses for chapter 3 on ties to the land and family relations. He also prepared a write-up of the results. Michael Shanahan (Pennsylvania State University) collaborated on data analysis and on the first draft of chapter 4 concerning the work experiences of youth. Chapters on family community ties (chapter 5) and on school-community activities (chapter 8) are based on data analyses by Debra Mekos, currently at Johns Hopkins University. She prepared drafts of the chapters as well. Chapter 6 on the grandparents' significance and chapter 7 on the rural church draw upon analyses by Valarie King, now at Pennsylvania State University. She also collaborated on drafts of each chapter. An additional postdoctoral trainee from Iowa State University, Lisa Matthews (Texas A&M), contributed to the data analysis on avoiding trouble in chapter 9. These collaborators are first co-authors of the chapters in which they played a major role (followed by Elder and Conger). Elder assumed final editorial responsibility to achieve a unified theme in the volume.

As the project moved along, periodic reports were made to the MacArthur Research Network, led by Richard Jessor, and to the Iowa State investigators. This feedback strengthened the study in all phases, from design and measurement to data analysis and interpretation. Three members of the Network reviewed the entire manuscript—Marta Tienda, Richard Jessor, and Norman Garmezy—as did Sonya Salamon at the University of Illinois. Selected chapters have also been reviewed by Urie Bronfenbrenner at Cornell, and by Paul Lasley at Iowa State University. The resulting manuscript, much improved by these evaluations, represents the second volume in a series of converging studies of successful adolescent development in high-risk settings.

Labor-intensive studies of this kind cannot succeed without funding from a variety of sources. Throughout the life of the Iowa Youth and Families Project, the National Institute of Mental Health has generously provided core support (MH00567, MH19734, MH43270, MH48165, MH51361). Additional support has come from the MacArthur Foundation's Research Network on Successful Adolescent Development among Youth in High-Risk Settings, the Spencer Foundation, the National Institute of Drug Abuse (DA05347), The Bureau of Maternal and Child Health (MCJ-09574), the Iowa Methodist Health Systems, and the Iowa Agriculture and Home Economics Experiment Status (Project No. 3320). The program and review staff of federal agencies that funded the

Iowa Project have been a continuing source of guidance and support. We are especially grateful to Della Haan, Mary Ellen Oliveri, and Sheila O'Malley at the National Institute of Mental Health.

Photos were provided courtesy of the Iowa State University Extension; by Don Wishart, producer, Extension Communications, Iowa State University, Ames, IA (retired); by Ruth Book, Iowa State University, Ames, IA, and by the Iowa State University College of Agriculture Information Services, Ames, IA.

Last but not least, we are indebted to the Iowa families who have played such an important role in this study. We are hopeful that this work will underscore for everyone the heavy costs of economic conditions and agricultural policies that have accelerated the exodus of families from farming in the Midwest and High Plains. We dedicate this book to the farming families of Iowa, who rank among the best in agriculture and in bringing up children who often succeed despite much adversity.

PART ONE

Rural Change and Life Chances

Rural Iowa has been damaged the most by changing economic winds. While not broken, the rural fiber has been stretched until vacant store fronts, lost jobs, dwindling population, and decaying small towns dot the rural scene.

Editorial, *Times Citizen,* Iowa Falls, 1992

It's been hard for a lot of our families these last years and I don't see it really getting any better. Things that you want to buy take more income all the time, and the income doesn't go up. As a family, we really have to support each other a lot. And help out in whatever we do. We have plumbers, electricians. So that's a help. We do most of the building or anything like that. The community has scholarship programs for the young. And the church helps out—it's just good to know you are supported by people who care.

Older citizen, local community, 1994

CHAPTER ONE

Ties to the Land

Iowa is about the land and nature and people taking pride in
what we do with our lives.

D. Shribman, winter, 1996

As we edge closer to the twenty-first century, American families and young people continue to leave agriculture as they have during past decades. A century ago, most Americans had ties to the land through their own lives and those of immediate kin. Now only one in fifty is engaged in farming, and little more than a fourth live in rural communities.[1] This historic movement off the land has been driven by many factors, but especially by technological advances that have markedly enhanced productivity. More recently, global economic competition has reduced the profit margin of farm products and undermined rural wages.[2] The growing appeal of urban commerce is weakening the vitality of local commerce, adding more incentives for young people to seek their future in urban centers.

In these diverse ways, a new world has come to the rural Midwest at century's end, to its families and children—a world in which members of the younger generation must seek a future outside of agriculture, with few exceptions, and often in distant places. A new world foretells new lives among those who make their way in it. The story of such change, of new lives in a new world, is recorded in patterns and trends, yet rural communities continue to rely upon the resourcefulness of a small number of farm families, their leadership, social involvement, and economic resources.

Are resourceful pathways for rural young people associated in any way with the social resourcefulness of families, especially of families still engaged in farming? To answer this question, we focus on rural Iowa, a region that suffered mightily in the Great Farm Crisis of the 1980s. The state lost a higher proportion of its citizens through outmigration than any other midwestern state across the decade. The number of farms has declined significantly since the 1960s, and the average surviving farm has grown in size. Most Iowans in the last century operated farms. Today little more than one-tenth run farms, though most rural Iowans have some connection to agriculture. Despite this change and the correlated economic hardship of rural communities, Iowa's children continue to rank among the very best on school success indicators compared to children in other states.

The historic economic problems of family farming were magnified by the 1980s Great Farm Crisis that hit the American Midwest with a force that will long be remembered. It was, indeed, the Great Depression all over again. By the mid-1980s, the Iowa landscape was littered with the casualties of this crisis, symbolized at times on courthouse lawns by a white cross for each lost farm. Across the countryside, seventy-five banks had closed, plus several hundred retail stores, and some fifteen hundred service stations.[3] By the early 1990s, the construction industry was still down by 40 percent from the late 1970s. Businesses had boarded-up windows, and "for sale" signs appeared on the main streets of towns across the state. Good jobs and employment of any kind were difficult to find in small towns. Prompted by such limitations, people began leaving rural counties at a rate as high as 20 percent during the decade. The entire state lost nearly 5 percent of its population during the 1980s. Everyone knew someone who had left for other places, but especially young people.

Population losses of this magnitude posed drastic consequences for rural communities. The economic cost was most obvious in terms of declining jobs, sales, and taxes. An Iowa businessman noted that he had "watched business after business after business go out. We've lost industry. There hasn't been anything left unaffected by this."[4] Mounting social costs also threatened the quality of community life, as in the breakdown of families, a reduction of students for the local school, and the loss of parents to provide leadership in civic, church, and school associations and functions. Many rural communities had to abandon local schools through consolidation and experienced the financial crises of local stores, churches, and social services as well. As in other times and places, the young people who left home were typically among the most able.

These economic and social costs are particularly evident in the departure of farm families, the economic and social foundation of rural life. Farm families generate the critical social capital, the relationships and working arrangements, that make communities desirable places in which to live and raise a family.[5] They are typically characterized by shared goals and common activities. Parents and children in farm families do more activities together, in the family and centered in the community, than do urban families. Farm children are also counted on to a greater extent—they are more involved in activities that other family members value and rely upon. Children and young people on family farms are expected to do their part. Such an environment is likely to produce the discipline and competency necessary for a successful life.[6]

Farm families in the Midwest frequently assemble in community associations to achieve common goals, such as a stronger school system, an effective youth group, or improved roads and health care. The typical farmer belongs to several voluntary associations or cooperatives.[7] Leadership for the common good is a responsibility of farm families, in particular, and such actions satisfy norms of social obligation and stewardship. In these rural farm communities, effective social relations among people who have contact with children represent social capital that fosters personal qualities of competence.[8] Adults with working relationships of mutual trust can share observations about children and enforce norms and goals. Social engagement for community goals is especially common among farm families such as those of German ancestry in which generational succession is important,[9] a prominent cultural theme of rural midwestern communities.

With these qualities in mind, some observers question whether rural depopulation will alter our national character. "What about the beliefs and value systems that have been associated with life on the land? Will Americans be able to establish an acceptable value system that rests on life in cities, perhaps symbolized by concrete and neon lights?"[10] Is the rapidly shrinking number of farm families symptomatic of a great transformation in which social resources are becoming scarcer in the lives of children?[11] Are there fewer people in rural America who care for children in nurturant families, who know their friends and the parents of these friends? This loss means that social control is less effective in children's lives, reflecting an absence of adult consensus on things that matter. These questions have special relevance when we note the striking decline of two-parent farm families over the past century and a corresponding increase in the prevalence of divorce and one-parent households (figure 1.1).

The decline of families with ties to agriculture threatens the survival of an accustomed quality of life in rural communities that dot the open countryside, for young and old, children, parents, and grandparents. However, the quality of life at the community level may be placed at even greater risk when industrialized farming takes over. The long-term effects of this economic system tend to "limit future economic potential wherever it is found."[12] Low wages, impoverished schools, and civic passivity are coupled with a siphoning of local wealth. Industrialized agriculture in the San Joaquin Valley of California has degraded the environ-

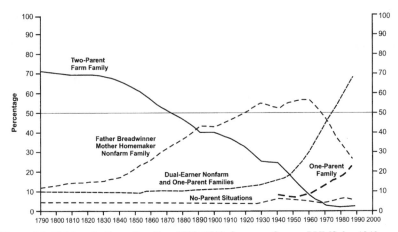

Figure 1.1 Children in Farm Families, 1790–1789. Sources: Census PUMS for 1940–1980, CPS for 1980 and 1989, and appendix 4.1 in *America's Children*. Note: Percentages are plotted for children aged 0–7 in father-as-breadwinner families and in dual-earner families; estimates are for 10-year intervals to 1980, and for 1989. Reprinted with permission from Donald Hernandez, *America's Children,* © 1993, Russell Sage Foundation, New York, NY

ment, and its practice of recruiting imported labor "has tended to weaken and impoverish communities and to divide them along class and ethnic lines."[13] In Iowa, industrialized farming in the form of corporate contracts is most evident in hog factories that pollute the water, soil, and air.

This book is based on the rural life experiences of Iowa children who were born at the end of rural prosperity in the postwar era, a time that extends up to the late 1970s. They grew up in the north central region, experienced the Great Farm Crisis of the 1980s, whether through their own families or others, and now face a world transformed. We focus on children with family ties to the land, ranging from full-time farming to farm-reared parents and parents without a farm background. With an eye on routes to life success rather than failure, we investigate the extent to which successful development is linked to the social resources or capital of families with ties to the land. The study follows children in these families from the seventh grade through junior high school to high school graduation, a time of important life decisions on employment, further education, and social relationships.

We view the proposed sequence of family ties to the land, social resources, and adolescent competence within a framework of generational succession and the life course. The sequence involves key social roles that are played by parents, grandparents, and the adolescents within the last six years of secondary school. As applied in this study, life-course theory[14] locates all of this within a particular historical time and place, stresses the role of parents and children as agents in working out options in their lives, brings sensitivity to the social timing of lives, and locates families in a matrix of linked relationships. The vitality and quality of this matrix provides the social resources or capital for human development.

This research problem emerged through interaction between the Iowa Youth and Families Project,[15] a panel study that was launched in the late 1980s to investigate the continuing socioeconomic effects of the farm crisis on families and children, and the MacArthur Foundation Research Network on Successful Adolescent Development among Youth in High-Risk Settings.[16] Research conducted as part of the Iowa Project has shown that rural families were adversely influenced by the farm crisis and that the emotional and behavioral responses of parents affected the competence and adjustment of their children.[17] Lower income and indebtedness increased feelings of economic pressure. Such pressures over time eventually led to depressed feelings and marital negativity. These factors undermined effective parenting and the perceived competence of children.

Moving beyond the legacy of economic hardship, we ask how rural youth manage to succeed in a disadvantaged region through the assistance of family, school, and civic groups. What are the resourceful pathways to greater opportunity? *Children of the Great Depression*[18] led to questions of this kind for Americans who had grown up in the 1930s, and such questions have become more compelling with each new level of inequality in American society. These issues shaped the long-term objectives of the Iowa Youth and Families Project and the research mission of the MacArthur Foundation Research Network on Successful Adolescent Development among Youth in High-Risk Settings.

The Iowa Project and the MacArthur Network were joined in 1988 when Elder became a member of the latter and encouraged its efforts to develop a common focus on the pathways that enable youth to surmount their disadvantaged backgrounds. Economic decline in the rural Midwest had become a chronic condition of disadvantage by that time, defining the setting as a high-risk environment. Families with ties to the land, from full-time farming to a farm childhood, theoretically possess social resources that could establish an important bridge to life opportunity for Iowa young people. These resources feature engagement in the community and the shared activities of the generations.

Before turning to the Iowa Project and its life-course approach, however, we describe the contrasting worlds of childhood that are represented by the study region, which is only fifty miles away from Des Moines, the flourishing state capital.

Two Worlds of Childhood:
Rural Decline and Urban Prosperity

Rural America presents two faces to the larger society, the appeal of agricultural life, especially for children, and a portrait of chronic, debilitating poverty. Today, children who grow up amidst poverty in rural America are as common as in our inner cities.[19] Rural hardship and urban opportunities have fueled rural outmigration, linking the problems and prospects of countryside and metropolis.

The inequality of rural and urban America has widened appreciably over the past decade, generating a contrast that is strikingly apparent as we place the study region in context after the farm crisis and compare it to Des Moines, the largest metropolitan area in Iowa. Des Moines, Iowa's state capital, has become a diversified center of government, finance, transportation, and high technology. Before turning to this comparison, we note some general trends on rural population decline, urban growth, and the steady expansion of farm size. The study region of eight counties (figure 1.2) lies due north of Des Moines. Webster, Hamilton, Hardin, and Marshall counties make up the lower tier; Humboldt, Wright, Franklin, and Butler comprise the upper tier.

This rich agricultural region, with land values above the state's average, lost half of its farms between 1950 and 1990, as did Iowa as a whole, and the decline in other parts of the country was comparable. During the same period, farm size nearly doubled for the study region (up to 361 acres, 1992), as it did in the state and nation. The study region's population declined by 12 percent over this forty-year period, and virtually all of the

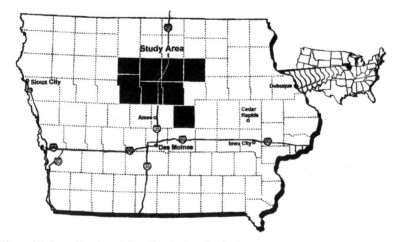

Figure 1.2 Iowa Youth and Families Project Study Area

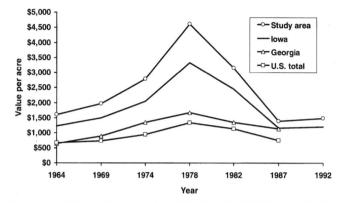

Figure 1.3 Average Value of Farm Land and Buildings in 1992 Constant Dollars per Acre. Source: U.S. Census of Agriculture

loss occurred in the farm sector. Two counties lost nearly a third of their mid-century population over this period. At the same time, the state population grew by 6 percent, mainly in rural nonfarm and urban areas, despite a net loss for the 1980s. As might be expected, Des Moines was the principal beneficiary of this growth—an increase of nearly 50 percent.

How did the study region fare in the Great Farm Crisis when compared to the state and other regions? Consider the value of farm land and buildings, which rose sharply in the 1970s and then declined just as abruptly. We calculated the average values from 1964 through 1992 in constant dollars for the study region and for Iowa, Georgia, and the United States. The state of Georgia was included to provide a regional contrast for the Midwest. It is the site of an ambitious 1980s study of farm families and farm operations in crisis.[20] Figure 1.3 shows that the growth in value was most rapid up to 1978 for the study area and the state of Iowa; it declined just as rapidly from 1978 to 1987, and then stabilized to 1992. By comparison, Georgia and the country as a whole show little if any change. Though declining profits and inflated prices threatened the survival of farms in all regions at the time, the midwestern grain states suffered the greatest loss in land values, owing partly to an embargo on grain sales to the Soviet Union.

Two additional economic indicators—housing units authorized by building permits and retail sales—enable us to compare the study region with trends in Des Moines and the United States (see appendix table E1.1). In each case, we used 1977 (= 100) as the baseline to assess the percentage change. The number of housing units authorized by building permits is a sensitive barometer of economic growth and decline. For example, in the four upper-tier counties, officials authorized the con-

struction of more than nine hundred housing units from 1977 through
1980. By 1985–88, this figure had dropped to only fifty-one. New construction over these four years had literally disappeared. By graphing
the data in figure 1.4, we find that authorized building units declined
sharply both in Des Moines and in the study region through 1982, and
then the economies of the two areas followed different trajectories. Des
Moines's construction picked up substantially and matched the U.S. level
by 1990, whereas construction activity in the study area continued to fall
until 1986 and then stagnated through the early 1990s at less than 20
percent of the 1977 activity rate.

This contrast in the economic health of rural Iowa and Des Moines,
from the doldrums to prosperity, also appears in figures on retail sales,
as constant dollars. The Great Farm Crisis undermined the economic
health of small-town stores, and many were eventually forced to close,
leaving boarded-up buildings lining the main streets of rural communities. Despite the appeals of local merchants, families in the study region
increasingly shifted their shopping to the malls and stores of the large
cities, particularly Des Moines. Total retail sales had declined by 23 percent across the eight counties by 1987, a year when sales in Des Moines
were slightly greater than they were in 1977. The health of Des Moines
was matched by figures on the Midwest as a whole and exceeded the
prosperity of the South Atlantic region. Most striking, the economic gap
has continued to expand. By 1992, sales for the study region were still
down by 26 percent, whereas Des Moines had actually gained this same
amount in retail sales. A grandmother in the study observed (1994) that

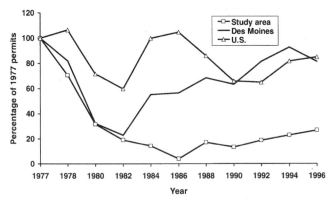

Figure 1.4 Building Permits Issued in Study Area, Des Moines, and the United States
(1977 = 100). Note: Percentages add up to more than 100 because targets could provide more than one response (up to four); $N = 358$.

It's been hard for a lot of our families these last years, and I don't see it really getting any better. Things that you want to buy take more income all the time, and the income doesn't go up. As a family, we really have to support each other a lot. And help out in whatever we do. We have plumbers, electricians. So that's a help. We do most of the building or anything like that. The community has scholarship programs for the young. And the church helps out—it's just good to know you are supported by people that care.

The farm crisis affected farm operations initially, but this impact was soon felt across farm and nonfarm communities alike. Most everyone shared the hardship. The two worlds, farm and nonfarm, were linked together through the misfortunes of families that lost their farms. We refer to them as "displaced." By the 1990s, more than sixty study families had lost their farms, a loss that proved almost impossible for the men to accept—to give up a farmstead that had been a part of family history for generations.[21] Nearly half of the men succeeded in finding jobs that used their skills, such as truck driving.

One man who had lost his farm ten years earlier still felt "terrible" about it. It is hard, as another displaced farmer put it, to "watch others come in and pick it up and take it over. Things you've worked hard to preserve and carry on, to see that crushed and gone." Another Iowan vividly recalled the bitter struggle during bankruptcy proceedings and the awful pain of seeing "them come and take the farm away and not know what you were going to do." That was "the hardest thing we've ever faced." He turned to alcohol as a way of dealing with the bitter memory, but soon managed to pull himself together with the help of his wife.

During our first visit with these families, the men were less accepting of the loss than the wives, who typically envisioned an improvement in the economic well-being of the family. Their men, however, could not readily put aside the loss and turn to another life, no matter how practical this action might seem. Their farming past remained alive because they couldn't think of another job where they could run their own affairs. In the midst of a farm loss, one young man still hoped that he could get back into farming "and just be a success for once." In most of these displaced families, parents recognized the effect of their troubles on the children. A displaced farmer, for example, thought his troubles were responsible for the problems his son was having at school. "Our frustrations really bother him and make things more difficult," explained the boy's mother.

At the time of this visit, families still engaged in farming could be defined as survivors of the farm crisis across the 1980s. However, we find no persuasive evidence that the displaced families and farmers were somehow different from the full-time farm families in life history and personal functioning. Judging from financial reports, however, there is reason to believe that survival was associated with a conservative management style in which the operator "avoided debt, preferred direct control over farm tasks, accepted a more modest standard of living, and expected hard manual labor and personal attention to detail."[22] For most farming families in the study, the crisis did not end with the loss of a farm, but persisted through the declining profitability of farming. Pressures "to leave the land" rose accordingly.

Clearly, the rural America sampled by the Iowa Youth and Families Project is a distressed region; a social world in which the economic prospects for young people have faded over the past decade. Though virtually all farm parents in the study, as of 1990, still considered farming a "good way of life," 40 percent are concerned about the survival of their farming operation, and over a fifth would leave this occupation if they had an opportunity to do so. Most study parents believe that the economic distress of their region has much to do with the Great Farm Crisis of the 1980s. Nearly nine out of ten parents on farms felt they were adversely affected by the farm crisis as of 1991, a conclusion also drawn by two out of three parents who had no direct connection to farming.

The Iowa Project and Approach

A small pilot study of families in 1988 provided a foundation of instruments (survey and observational) for launching a panel study of 451 two-parent families in 1989, the Iowa Youth and Families Project. Each family included a seventh-grade child and a near sibling, either younger or older. In this first year of the study, 140 families were engaged in farming, and over 60 families had lost farms since the 1970s. The men in farming grew up on farms, but one in six married a woman with a nonfarm background. Nearly 150 nonfarm families were also headed by parents who grew up on farms. A farm background thus applies, in one way or another, to nearly three out of four children.

The families were contacted for data collection across a six-year period. Annual collections were arranged in 1989 through 1992, and again in 1994 when the study child was in the twelfth grade. A phone interview was scheduled in 1993. In each follow-up year, the parents and children were surveyed on family experience, personality, social development, and socioeconomic hardship or conditions. They also participated in a series of four videotape sessions, one for both parents, one for the siblings, and two for the family as a whole. The videotapes were coded by using a set of behavior ratings from a number of earlier coding systems.[23] In the 1994 follow-up, we interviewed the adolescents and also collected interview and questionnaire data from as many as nine hundred grandparents. *Families in Troubled Times*[24] used typescripts of the family videotapes to obtain verbatim observations by members of the sample families. Some of these quotations are used in this volume; however, the vast majority are drawn from the 1994 interviews.

The grandparents were typically born between World War I and the mid-1930s, and the parents between the beginning of World War II and the end of the Korean War. Over half of the grandfathers served in World War II, and two out of five of the fathers served in the Vietnam War. When the Iowa Project began, the fathers averaged thirty-nine years of age; the mothers were two years younger. The families averaged three children at the time and varied in social position from the upper middle class to the working class and lower, with a total family income of approximately $33,000. One-third of the fathers were engaged in farming, either full or part-time, and slightly more than one-tenth had actually lost a farm over the past decade or so. Another one-third of the fathers had grown up on farms but were not now living there. Only one-fourth of the fathers had no contact with farming, neither through parents nor through their own working lives. Most of the mothers were employed in a paid job, even among families on a farm.

With few exceptions, the grandparents grew up on farms in the Midwest and actually farmed at some point in their lives. Over half of the grandfathers were still engaged in farming at the end of the 1980s. The older grandfathers, in particular, experienced hard times as children and adults, during the 1920s and 1930s, but they also enjoyed a lengthy period of prosperity following World War II. These men typically launched their farming careers in the 1940s and 1950s, a time when land values were low and prices were high and relatively stable. Shaped by the hard times of the prewar years, this generation pursued a relatively cautious management style that avoided heavy indebtedness while relying upon family labor.

The sons of this generation faced a different world, one initially seductive to those inclined to expand and then devastating as the economy lowered land values abruptly. One-fourth of the men had a college education, compared to fewer than 4 percent of their fathers. A good many had degrees in agriculture and training in agribusiness techniques, but they were not immune to the widespread decline. A third of the sons of the grand-parent generation actually entered farming, usually in the late 1960s and 1970s, but only two out of three were still in business by the 1990s.

Ecological Niches and Social Resources

As seen across the generations, these Iowa families occupy different "ecological niches"[25] in relation to agriculture and family farming. At the end of the 1980s, 20 percent of all families in the sample were still fully engaged in farming: the husband defined himself as a farmer, and most income came from the land or livestock. Another 10 percent found themselves in and out of farming—men from this group did not regard themselves mainly as farmers when they were asked, and they, along with their wives, were typically employed off the farm. We describe them as part-time farmers. Slightly more than 10 percent were unsuccessful in continuing to farm during the crisis of the 1980s—they represent displaced farmers and families.

Another third of the families was headed by men and women whose sole contact with farming occurred in childhood. They grew up on a farm, in a family life distinguished by interdependence and collective goals, by shared activity and nonmaterialistic values; and then embarked on a career apart from farming. They are now employed in jobs that range from professional and managerial to semiskilled. The remaining families, about one-fourth of the sample, were literally generations removed from farming. Neither husband nor wife in these families had even spent a childhood on a farm. To sum up, the families are distributed as follows:

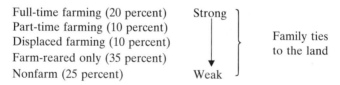

Full-time farming (20 percent)   Strong
Part-time farming (10 percent)
Displaced farming (10 percent)   Family ties
Farm-reared only (35 percent)   to the land
Nonfarm (25 percent)   Weak

Each of these ecological niches can be arrayed in terms of involvement in farming and the cultivation of crops, what we call "family ties to the land." The influence of farm culture and history may be expressed through all of them. To assess this influence, we compare families in each of these family niches to nonagricultural families on the basis of "resources" that have important implications for successful development in adolescence.[26] These resources include the following:

- Family relations, especially the social-emotional bond and joint activities linking parent and child.

- Productive roles and values for children, involving both unpaid chores and earnings.
- Family connections to community institutions, including the church, school, and civic organizations.
- Children's ongoing social relations with grandparents and with age-mates and adults in school, church, and community.

These resources apply both to relationships and activities *within* families and to those that *connect* families to other households, organizations, and institutions. In this regard, resources are a form of social capital that is found in social organizations and generates something of value for people. Involvement in social organizations or relationships provides access to particular opportunities and developmental experiences. Activities of this kind empower; they encourage shared beliefs and interpersonal trust. The accumulation of social capital is most likely to occur among people who are embedded in relationships with people who know each other and share values, a bounded network that is common in rural communities. Two out of three of the Iowa children from farm families (full-time) attended small, seven-grade schools (with fewer than fifty students in a grade), compared to less than half of the nonfarm youth.

Farm-reared children, in particular, live in "small worlds" of such networks, worlds of overlapping spheres—family, school, church, and community.[27] As in the Catholic urban parish with its primary school,[28] these overlapping spheres define functional communities through activities that link people with shared values, norms, and understandings. Parents, friends, and relatives frequently appear in the activities of farm children. They are part of a common universe of meanings and upbringing. Social control and constraints provide essential behavioral guidelines. One boy claimed that he liked the recognition he had in his village, but not the visibility, a level of surveillance that enabled his mother to know his activities before he "even got home from school at night."

This type of community is characterized by the closure of social networks that involve a child and at least two adults. As Coleman observes, closure occurs only when the adults have a relationship, when they are able "to observe the child's actions in different circumstances, talk to each other about the child, compare notes, and establish norms. The closure of the network can provide the child with support and rewards from additional adults that reinforce those received from the first and bring about norms and sanctions that could not be instituted by a single adult alone."[29]

Talented adults do not ensure social capital for children, a point that Coleman makes by using the example of a human development triangle. Human capital is located at the nodes of the triangle. The links between the nodes symbolize social capital. Human development requires substantial human capital at the nodes and social capital in the links. Single-parent households and discordant marriages thus represent a loss of social capital for the development of children. By contrast, the joint activity pattern so characteristic of farm family life ensures greater social capital, as do the multiple connections between farm families and community institutions, church, school, and civic organizations, such as Future Farmers of America (FFA) and 4-H clubs. Within each of these institutions there are many adults who know both parent and child.

Connections of this kind are part of the strategies by which parents maximize the developmental options and experiences of children. These strategies apply to family interactions within the household, as in patterns of encouragement and praise, as well as to the external world beyond household boundaries, as in the placement of children in special school programs and community athletic leagues.[30] Both types of family strategies are favored by the collective weave of household members in farm families. Farm operations bring family members together in a common enterprise; and they require, along with cultural traditions, certain community investments in children's lives. Shared activity of this kind has declined in rural America because of the mounting obligations of farm parents to nonfarm employment.[31] The pace of farm life has become more frenetic.

Competence and the Life Course

In theory, social resources that enhance opportunities and competencies in youth are concentrated among families with ties to the land. These competencies can be thought of as age-graded forms of successful development—the process of doing well according to one's age (e.g., a seventeen- or eighteen-year-old in the senior class of high school).[32] Success in academic work is one such dimension, as reported by the adolescent and by others. *Academic competence* creates future opportunities and raises aspirations. It provides evidence of desirable qualities for adult roles, a disciplined life style, industriousness, and standards of excellence.

A second dimension is *social competence or success,* as reflected in positive relations with age-mates, teachers, and parents. Socially competent youth are likely to be involved in school, church, and community activities that advance their sense of competence. School activities range from athletic teams to student government, music competitions, and dramatic arts. These youth are also likely to be seen by parents and other adults as socially mature, as young people whose judgment is worth knowing and trusting.

A third dimension centers on *self-appraisals* of academic competence, self-esteem, and mastery. Successful youth generally score high on these positive aspects of self, though positive regard may not always be high for youth who are doing well in academic tests, owing to an unusually critical self-view. As a rule, however, competence or success fosters more of the same along with greater self-confidence. The fourth and last dimension concerns the *avoidance of problem behavior,* such as confrontations with teachers and classmates, rule-breaking behavior, and heavy use of alcohol and drugs. Competence may be expressed in antisocial and prosocial ways. Street-life, for example,[33] can entice highly talented youth into deviant associations and rule-breaking activities. The moral constraints of prosocial activities may effectively counter such incentives, as in school and religious groups.

Theory and empirical studies lead us to expect that successful development across the preadult years has much to do with resourceful pathways. Such pathways refer in particular to the presence and quality of linked social relationships that make up the life course. Typically, farm children in our study region are involved in relationships with parents and siblings that are part of a broader network of social ties with uncles, aunts, and grandparents who live nearby. At least some of these relatives may be part of their local church and may even participate in their civic organizations, such as the 4-H. Also potentially influential are neighbors who are members of their church and community residents who teach or coach in the local school and often provide leadership for youth groups.

A resourceful pathway may be distinguished by the presence of a number of significant others who provide affection, the disciplines of accomplishment, and moral guidance. Strong family support would buffer the social disappointments and rejections of school and peer activity. To a lesser extent, resourcefulness applies to a pathway in which children with troubled family relations can turn to a supportive grandparent, teacher, or sibling. One significant other is known to make a difference in the lives of disadvantaged children. However, a child's problems with a troubled family situation are compounded when the family is also isolated from significant community roles. Life-course theory underscores the relevance of these social connections for human development.

Family Ties to the Land and Resourceful Pathways

Four concepts define a way of thinking about resourceful pathways to adulthood: (1) the sequence of experiences and events that links family ties to the land to children's success, (2) the social and cultural properties of these families, (3) modes of family strategy, and (4) cohort histories.

Linkages, such as community ties, constitute a microtheory of agricultural influences in children's lives. The social and cultural properties of farm families provide answers to why they are likely to be resourceful in ways that enhance children's development and life chances. Examples include the collective nature of farm family life and children's roles of social responsibility.

The response of families to changing socioeconomic and regional conditions includes changes in economic roles and community ties. Some of these responses or family strategies may generate social resources for children, such as off-farm employment and the renewed involvement of parents in threatened community institutions. To place children's pathways in context, we use the concept of cohort histories to bring sensitivity to the particular historical time of the Iowa parents and their children as they approach the end of this century.

Linking Farm Origins to Children's Success

This study is based on the premise that access to social capital or resources plays an important role in shaping the life chances and developmental accomplishments of youth in disadvantaged settings. The greater the access, even in a local world of declining attractive options, the greater the prospects for academic and social success among young people in high school.

Drawing on theory and empirical evidence, we expect youth with ties to the land to have the greatest access to these resources through the embedded social life of their families in agricultural counties of north central Iowa, a region that has lost substantial economic standing over the past decade. This is not an either/or expectation; rather, it is framed in terms of probabilities. In theory, youth with ties to the land are more likely to have access to such resources. However, not all farm families are resourceful. In addition, we expect youth who have other family ties to the land (part-time farm, displaced farm, and farm-reared) to resemble farm youth in access to resources compared to young people in nonfarm households.

Ironically, the risks of economic dislocation and failure in the region are directly experienced by many of the families whom we depict as more endowed with the social capital and other resources that facilitate an ability to bounce back or return to normal—families with ties to the land. Farm families more rapidly and directly felt the impact of plummeting land and property values during the farm crisis of the 1980s, and a substantial number were unable to recover. However, cycles of adversity in agriculture are central themes in rural life, and farm families acquire ways of accommodating to them over the years. The adage "next year will be better" is generally affirmed by climate and market changes.

In short, risk and resilience go together in this drama of family ties to farming and movement off the land. As in the case of middle-class families who entered the Great Depression, productive Iowa farms and their families before the 1980s crisis brought social capital to hardship that increased their chances of an early recovery and enhanced the life prospects of their children. They are likely to be resilient,[34] implying that youth at risk in this rural population may not be saddled with an enduring handicap. By contrast, Iowa families that entered this crisis era with few social ties in the community were at greater risk than families with multiple social ties and obligations.

Our challenge in the following chapters is to answer the question as to whether families with ties to the land are endowed with social capital to a greater extent than other rural families. Our second question asks whether aspects of social capital—from relationships within the family to the community ties of both children and parents—make a difference in the likelihood of adolescent success and failure. We hypothesize that family ties to the land make a difference in adolescent competencies through correlated social resources or capital.

To put this formulation to a test, we construct analytic models that specify linkages between family ties to the land and child behavior, beliefs, and expectations.[35] What is the process by which these ties have implications for a developmental trajectory of self-confidence and accomplishment? Answers to this question address the meaning of a family's "farm" or "nonfarm" status. The implications of a farm status assign particular meanings to the category itself. In theory, then, linkages provide answers as to why farm origin and more distant ties to the land should matter for children's lives. They provide an interpretation of the relationship, an account of the mechanisms by which a declining farm population could influence social life, human character, and life chances.

To illustrate the construction of conceptual linkages, consider the hypothetical relation between parents in full-time farm and nonfarm families and the child's regard for them across the secondary school years. Knowledge of the male-centered kinship system in farm communities suggests that the son's and even the daughter's regard for the father would be stronger in farm than in nonfarm families, especially when the father is better educated and more successful. To identify the consequences of children's positive regard for academic and social competence, we convert it to more specific and concrete manifestations, such as emotional attachment, value identification, and desire to emulate. These processes, in turn, have implications for self-confidence and maturity in late adolescence, for social success with peers, and for academic competence. Successes of this kind may be self-reinforcing and cumulate over time, just as failures initiate downward spirals of personal efficacy.

This is an analytic process for tracing childhood experiences over the life course across subsequent events and outcomes into adolescence and the adult years. As a general rule, the greater the time-spread between behavioral events, the lower their correlation, but this low correlation does not mean that the early event does not have relevance for later life. On the contrary, the event may set in motion a cascade of changes or transitions that have long-standing effects, as in the cumulation of advantages or disadvantages. Some changes have opposing influences, as when athletic prominence among boys increases their status among conventional *and* antisocial peers. By specifying "chains of influences," we identify contingencies as well as linkages which modify how and if the chain makes a difference. Thus, parental influence is likely to be greatest when all parents of an adolescent's friends know each other and share values.

The analysis is organized along the lines of a multistaged design, beginning with an assessment of the most immediate, proximal effects, and correlates of family ties to the land and agriculture (chapter 2). Proximal effects refer to different ways of providing social capital in children's lives—their family relationships, productive roles with others, family ties to community institutions, children's ties to grandparents and religion, and to social roles in the community and school. Each of these proposed linkages represents a "microtheory" of why and how family ties to the land make a positive difference in the developmental experience of children. The study concludes by linking these aspects of social capital to measures of adolescent success and trouble at the end of high school (see part 2 of this book), such as measures of academic competence, a sense of mastery, peer-group involvement and prominence, social maturity in the eyes of parents, and avoidance of behavior problems.

The most general formulation defines family and individual resources as linkages between family ties to the land, along with socioeconomic influences, and successful development among rural youth. Chapters 3 and 4 examine social and individual resources *within* the family. First we consider family relationships involving emotional attachments, parental identification, social independence, and shared activity between parents and adolescents, including productive roles. The meaning of farm origins for these relationships is likely to depend on prospects for continuity in farming.[36] In subsequent chapters we investigate linkages *between the family and the larger world* of church, school, peer group, and community associations. Parents with more extensive "connections" are likely to have children who are similarly involved in their respective communities.

Social involvement in both generations tends to favor adolescent success in the high school years and a constructive transition to careers after high school.

In the course of this study, the concept of linkage will remind us that an association between variables at two widely separated points in time merely represents a point of departure for research that seeks greater understanding. Construction of a sequence of experiences and events builds an explanatory theory of the process that has developmental implications for the adult years.

Farm Families: Their Social and Cultural Properties

Farm families in different systems of agriculture may well differ on characteristics, and yet, as John Bennett notes, "Farmers the world over, and at all levels of national development have much in common."[37] He refers to decisions about production in relation to resources, the balancing of options against constraints, and the management of risk. However, the differing priorities of ancestral cultures, whether on farming as a business or as a valued way of life, may be expressed in different styles of farming.

In the Midwest, for example, farm families of German origin tend to stress generational continuity more than do families of English background. Families with a German heritage "are bound by a meaning for the land that links the generations through shared obligations. Parents help by passing on land in a manner that enables children to repeat the process."[38] English origins favored a view of the farm operation as primarily a business enterprise. Since more than four out of five families in the Iowa Project are of German origin, with nineteenth-century roots extending back to Mecklenberg and Upper Saxony, we fully expect generational continuity in farming to be prominent in the culture of the study families.

The concept of *generational continuity* is driven more by a preference for farming as a valued way of life than by monetary gain, though effective perpetuation of family farming across the generations depends on the successful management of the farm operation. Farming success is valued, but not merely the goal of money-making and great wealth. Success is measured by doing well as a farmer. In farming households of German ancestry, one can well imagine midwestern fathers who counsel sons against a monetary motive for entering the farming enterprise. Indeed, in our first meeting of the Iowa families, several farmers expressed this sentiment in family conversations. A large-scale farmer in the region wanted his sons to follow in his footsteps, but "they have got to learn to do without a lot of material things if they want to farm."[39]

Keeping the family farm in the family may involve the employment of only one son, usually the oldest, but generational continuity in farming within the "larger family" is achieved nevertheless as a "gendered" sequence. By and large, farm management in the Midwest is a male-oriented career, though women can and generally do play essential roles in the farm operation.[40] The choice of succeeding one's parents in farming and the agricultural lifestyle is typically an option for young men, though a good many women marry into farming. All of the farm families in this Iowa Project have men as the primary farmer. Rules of inheritance permit the family land to be divided between brothers, with each plot usually supplemented by rented land. Typically, the actual transfer of land from father to son occurs late in the father's life, in his mid-sixties.

The male orientation of this intergenerational transaction ensures a distinctive pattern of lineal ties among farm families. It is biased toward the male line in terms of social intensity and positive affect; sons who get along with their fathers are most likely to go into farming. By contrast, city and nonfarm families generally have stronger ties to the wife's side of the family.[41] Unlike most urban youth, farm children see their paternal grandparents in the daily routines of life. They are literally part of their world. Shared experiences extend across church, school, and civic functions.

With this interweaving of lives across the generations, we expect grandparents, especially on the paternal side, to play an important role in the lives of grandchildren who are on the farm, as listeners, companions, supporters, and mentors. They could step into crises and provide tangible as well as intangible support. Some of these grandparents may become "bridges to maturity" for their more disadvantaged grandchildren. All of this depends, of course, on the existence of positive relations between parents and their parents. It also depends on the grandchild's relation to his or her parents. Weak ties lessen access to grandparents.

Whether moving across the generations to grandparents or into the future, gender differentiates the life experiences and chances of farm children. Boys have a plausible and potential future within the farm operation or community, while girls learn early in life that a promising future generally requires either marriage to a local boy or advanced education and the prospects of leaving home permanently. In this manner, pathways to success lead in different directions for boys and girls. Among boys, in particular, the pathway involves close ties to fathers, and such ties may strengthen their aspiration to be like their fathers and to farm. No such connection is likely among girls, though supportive relations with parents can be a powerful force in doing well amidst adversity.

Another distinctive feature of farm families centers on the collective nature of family life and children's roles. Farm families are characterized by a web of interdependence that relates members to family goals, whether business or other. This contrasts with the greater individualization of activities in urban families, as expressed in the self-orientation of children.[42] Children are brought up in farm families to consider family business needs—labor, time, or financial. Particularly in planting and harvest seasons, the farm takes priority over everything. During these periods of mobilization, children experience the heightened expectations of interdependency, of being needed and counted on. What they do and do not do has real consequences for other family members.

Because their enterprise often relies upon the labor of household members, farm families generally expose children to the realities and obligations of economic life and success through chores and voluntary assistance. This informal system resembles some aspects of an apprenticeship that provides a sequence of progressively more difficult, adultlike tasks. In southern rural communities of Illinois, Salamon found that parental "recognition of a child's contribution to the farm and the awareness that their labor is depended on has consequences for a child's development."[43] This involvement reinforces a child's sense of personal responsibility and significance. "Children as young as six spend summers 'walking beans,' checking the rows for weeds and volunteer corn, aware that what they do is needed and has economic worth."[44] With these observations in mind, we expect Iowa farm children to be more involved in activities with their parents and to rank higher on a belief that they are counted on by their parents and family, that they are "significant" in this sense.

By comparison, children in urban or nonfarm families are seldom part of a common economic venture with parents, and they are less apt to be viewed as partners or co-workers. Apart from family-owned businesses in the cities, these children have less of a social role within the family that provides a sense of personal significance.[45] In contrast to the more collaborative farm family, nonfarm youth are positioned in a relatively hierarchical family system that may prolong dependency. Lacking compelling social responsibilities and access to adultlike roles, these youth are more likely to spend their earnings on themselves and to find local peer groups especially attractive.

The final point on families with ties to the land, noted earlier, centers on their distinctive social involvement in the affairs of church, school, and community. Consistent with the German estate of farming and its ethic of stewardship over the land, we expect Iowa families with ties to the land to rank well above nonfarm families on their social involvement and leadership involving church, school, and civic functions. Social involvement is a form of family adaptation to social change, and it also represents a potential social resource for creating success and even high achievement among rural boys and girls.

The residential stability of farm families over the life course and the generations is another source of their community ties. Stable families are more involved in church, school, and community life. But this involvement is played out within a backdrop that deserves comment: the civic culture of the state. One of the more distinctive examples appears every four years in the Iowa precinct caucuses,[46] which typically occur on a Monday night, "usually in stinging cold and under cover of snow." They are a "combination of church fellowship dinner, cattle auction, quilting circle," among other things. On this occasion, "neighbors get together in fire halls and basements, talk about their preferences, declare one another bloody fools or Communists, separate themselves into corners and vote by ballot." The collective experience of precinct caucuses brings to mind the early days of settlement and farming, when "whole communities got together for threshing dinners prepared at harvest time."

Family Strategies of Survival and Success

The resourcefulness of farm families and their contributions to community life and to the future of their children have been challenged across the decades by the declining profitability of farming. In the 1970s gross farm income increased significantly, but so did the costs of farm production in equipment, fuel, feed, fertilizer, and pesticides.[47] The margin of profit became smaller, placing greater priority on farm expansion and efficiency. But expansion placed farm operations in heavy debt, a burden which became too heavy for many to address in the 1980s farm crisis.

When we visited families for the first time at the end of the 1980s, the smaller farms as well as the very large farms were in very difficult straits. The capital expenses of running a small farm of two to three hundred acres matched those for larger, more productive farms, but the small farmer could not approach the gross income of these operations. The steady loss of operating farms in the state has largely come from the smaller, more marginal operations. The wife of one of the young farmers with only a hundred acres to farm despaired over finding a way to pay their heavy debt and remain on the farm. As she put it, "So our biggest concern is 'How are we going to be coming out of this?' "[48] Their response—a strategy of off-farm employment—is especially common in dismal economic times. The wife acquired a clerical job in the nearby town, and her husband found employment as a local trucker.

Most farm families at the end of the crisis decade, the 1980s, were engaged in this strategy. Ninety fathers defined themselves as farmers at the time and a substantial number held at least one paid job off the farm. The average acreage for their farms exceeded 650. Forty percent of the families were headed by men who only farmed (Type I), although some of their wives were employed up to thirty hours per week. Only a tenth of their family income came from nonfarm sources. Another 46 percent of the families were characterized by extensive off-farm employment of both spouses (40 percent of the men, 77 percent of the wives— Type II). Nearly 30 percent of family income came from nonfarm activities. In the remaining farm families (Type III), all husbands and wives were gainfully employed off the farm, and three-fifths of all family income was derived from this activity. All of the smaller farm operators held full-time jobs off the farm.[49] Thus, Type I families include 40 percent of the original farm families; Type II, 46 percent of the original group; and Type III, 14 percent of the families.

Off-farm employment presents a number of implications for the differentiation of farm and nonfarm households. In some respects, it tends to minimize the difference. With little if any employment off the farm, farm couples tend to engage in shared activities within and outside the household. The necessity for such employment generally means less shared time, especially with both spouses employed. A young father in this predicament recalled that "when we were first married it wasn't so bad because we weren't each working a job in town and then trying to farm." Most likely off-farm employment would also minimize opportunities for joint work and social activity between parents and children. The important question is whether off-farm employment has increased since the 1980s, and how it has influenced family life and the life chances of rural youth.

In difficult times, family farms have frequently relied upon the greater use of family labor to replace paid help and services. At the end of the 1980s, Iowa families with gainfully employed mothers were more likely to have children who helped out with chores at home.[50] The longer mother's work week, the greater the likelihood of this pattern of assistance among boys and girls. The labor needs and economic difficulties of farm families also increased the chances of paid work or earnings among youth, particularly boys. In the context of farming, these earnings typically came from projects, like raising a steer or a flock of chickens. Farm girls were most likely to use at least some of their earnings for family needs, in covering school expenses, for example. Among farm youth in general, the new economic realities suggest that they may be more involved in productive roles than nonfarm youth, but the off-farm employment of their parents has reduced the scope of shared work and family time for them.

Another family strategy to consider in these changing times is the involvement of farm families in the affairs of community life, church, school, and civic functions. Some of these involvements are directly linked to economic interests, as in rural cooperatives, but all institutional connections bear upon their general interests. Off-farm employment represents a community link among farm families, providing information and other useful social resources through workmates, although employment of this kind often requires long commutes to other communities. Presumably, long-distance commuting reduces local involvement, including the time to participate in the school, church, and community activities of children.

On balance, the family strategies of survival and success in this declining region work against the distinctive qualities of families with ties to the land, those that enhance the development and achievement of children. Whether or not off-farm employment and various economies ensure the survival of families on their farms, the adaptive process itself may produce greater similarities to urban or nonfarm families in terms of social resources for children.

Cohort Histories

The Iowa children were born in the late 1970s, and consequently they share a common history. The farm economy was on the verge of its greatest decline since the Great Depression, a collapse that persisted across much of the 1980s and even into the 1990s for rural residents. Not all families were directly involved in farming and its risks, although the costs of farm losses had repercussions for all families.

Farming is the principle industry in the area, and thus sharp alterations in farm prices and land values send powerful waves throughout the economy and local population. Lacking a diversified economy, "agriculturally dependent communities were swept along in the flood waters of the farm crisis of the 1980s."[51] Despite these interdependencies, Iowa rural families were unevenly affected by the economic decline and, more generally, by the declining profitability of farming. Slightly more than 25 percent of the families were engaged in farming, 10 percent had lost their farm in recent years, over 30 percent of the parents had grown up on a farm but were not now farming, and another 25 percent were several generations away from farming.

This variation within a single cohort generates a key analytical feature of the study. The story is largely based on social differences *within* the cohort. Full-time farm families provide the very best test of a distinctive mode of social and cultural life, especially when compared to families in which the parents neither grew up on a farm nor currently manage one. Apart from income level and parental education, we expect farm families to be characterized more by shared activity between the generations. Collective priorities should be more pronounced in these families than in other households, which are more distant from the land.

By definition, part-time farm families are locked into the worlds of both farm life and nonfarm employment. The commercial values and individualism of community life may well be part of their perspective. From this vantage point, they should be less apt to differ from nonfarm households in social life and culture. Adults in displaced farm families and those Iowans who grew up in the world of farming undoubtedly maintain ties to this world, to family and friends, but they are not likely to match the full-time farmers in these respects.

In an agriculturally dependent economy like Iowa's, the farm operations of families have historically been the engines of growth, and the farm families themselves tend to be among the better off in communities. In 1988, full-time farm families had a median family income of $40,076, compared to the low thirties for all nonfarm households. By 1993, this income had declined into the mid-thirties, closely matching the total income of other families. Characteristic of the cyclical nature of agriculture, however, farm income returned to and even exceeded earlier levels by 1996 and 1997. In theory, farm families are better endowed with social capital of relevance to children's lives than other families. From this angle, farm families are the "haves" in an economically declining region. However, they also remain at risk for the social changes and stresses of the time.

Approximately sixty families lost their livelihoods in farming, and so we have only the survivors in farming, but we find nothing in the early life history of these survivors that distinguishes them from the displaced men. Studies suggest that a risky or conservative managerial style may be the most important factor.[52] Episodes of severe emotional depression during the farm crisis were most often reported by adults in the full-time farm families and in displaced families.[53]

Iowans in these different ecologies have different stories to tell about the Great Farm Crisis as well as different lessons to offer their children. At the beginning of the 1990s nearly four out of five fathers in the study who were farming at the time claimed that friends were ruined financially by the crisis (figure 1.5). This compares to half of the farm-reared men and a third of the men with nonfarm occupations. A much smaller percentage of men felt that they would not recover from their financial

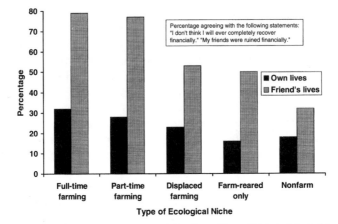

Figure 1.5 Continuing Economic Effects of the Great Farm Crisis in Men's Lives and in Friends' Lives: Report of Iowa Men in Different Ecologies, 1991

losses, but the percentage increases steadily with involvement in agriculture.

Despite this legacy, over 80 percent felt that the spirit of their community was still intact, if not stronger, in the face of generalized hardships and that they had come through without lasting emotional scars. A much larger proportion of the men in farming even concluded that they had become stronger as a result of "surviving the crisis"—between 40 and 50 percent of the farmers and displaced men. The latter had lost their family farms, but they had come back to much better incomes as a whole. They had survived with something to spare. Their wives held similar views, although they were more critical of what farming puts families through in uncertainty and material hardships. Whatever the difficulties, including the severe drought of 1987 (the worst since the 1930s) and the endless flood of 1993, which produced another "great lake" in Iowa, many farm families appear resourceful and even resilient, having bounced back from setbacks of one kind or another that typify the fortunes of the farm economy.

There are similarities between urban middle-class families who suffered economic losses in the Great Depression and stable farm families who were hard hit by the farm crisis in rural Iowa during the 1980s. Urban middle-class families brought more human and social resources to the Great Depression crisis, compared to other families, and the same applies to farm families in the 1980s. Economic threats and setbacks were commonplace in the experience of farm families, and this no doubt prepared them to adapt to recurring belt-tightening conditions.

By comparison, urban middle-class families are especially vulnerable to the status losses of joblessness. They are likely to "overestimate the hardships which they define as threats to their social position and aspirations of their children."[54] This vulnerability has also been noted among farm families,[55] but these families have life histories of exposure to economic and social reverses. Men and women in farming families have always had to come to terms with cycles of good times and bad times.

Hard-pressed middle-class families in the 1930s tended to recover more rapidly from their losses, when compared to working-class families, and their children seemed to do at least as well as children from more privileged middle-class homes.[56] Will this life trajectory also apply to boys and girls who have grown up in contemporary farm families? Though beset by a rural economy that favors "leaving the land" for other livelihoods, do children in these families at least match the accomplishments of other children? And to what extent does social capital make a difference in their developmental paths?

Across each of the generations, the economic decline and farm exodus of the 1980s carries different meaning. Each generation is characterized by the historical rationale and shared experience of growing up in a different time period, and by the correlated activities, resources, and options of their life stage. Especially in eras of rapid change, individuals who share a common historical time are thought to acquire a distinctive outlook from the historical world, defined by their birth date, a view that "reflects lives lived interdependently in a particular historical context."[57] In terms of these differences, the *principle of life stage* asserts that people of unlike age will be differentially influenced by social change. People age in different ways because they experience different historical times.

For the young, a life of farming is not likely to be popular, but neither are the prospects of leaving home. Farming parents were threatened not only by the loss of the farm but also by the loss of a family legacy, the homeplace. The grandparents, some still engaged in farming, had more in common with their grandchildren in terms of hardship and the future than with their parents. Each generation is both distinctive and similar in cohort history. The common ground includes war as well as economic hardship. A number of the grandfathers served in World War II, a good many of their sons served in Vietnam, and some of their grandchildren are now contemplating a military future.

Studying Lives in Changing Times: A Cautionary Note

There is usually a disparity between problems that motivate a study and the data at hand. This gap is understandable when a contemporary project draws upon historical data that were generated with other questions in mind. But disparities also arise as soon as the data are collected. The important task is to achieve the best possible fit between research question and data.

This goodness of fit also depends on an awareness of the study's limitations and their implications. Consider the Iowa Youth and Families Project. This panel study was originally designed to investigate the response of rural families to economic stresses resulting from the farm crisis of the 1980s, with emphasis on the family dynamics that connect economic hardships to the lives of children. Thus, measurement focused on experiences within the family, on family relationships and interactions, parenting styles and parental mood, and on the perceived family experiences of children. Concerns of this kind restricted our initial coverage of family embeddedness in the larger community and of the communities themselves.

This study of rural economic hardship was patterned after an earlier study of children of the Great Depression,[58] including the selection of children from the seventh grade who were living with both parents. The study children also had to have a near sibling, a brother or sister within four years of age. Last, as a study of the legacy of an agricultural crisis, the project made every effort to maximize the number of farm families in the total sample. Over a fourth of the families were engaged in farming, though a smaller number defined themselves solely in terms of this occupation. When considered as a whole, these specifications meant that sample recruitment would require a large area, though not so large that the costs of data collection would be exorbitant. Our videotaping of family life made data collection labor-intensive and placed a premium on minimizing the travel time to families.

We ended up with 451 families and children scattered across more than thirty school districts, all within an eight-county region in north central Iowa, where the farmland ranks among the best in Iowa. The region is relatively homogeneous on social, economic, and cultural dimensions. With very few children in any particular school, we were unable to explore their social networks or obtain stable measures of school climate. Nevertheless, the school districts have much in common on measures of student success and problem behavior. Virtually all of the variation is from differences between families and children, not between school districts. Hence, distinctive school and community-level influences do not present themselves as a prime consideration in this research. By its own right, the study region can be viewed as an ecological niche in the socioeconomic changes taking place in rural America.

In the ways noted, these Iowa parents and children do not constitute a representative sample of the rural sector of the state or of the Midwest.

As we have seen, the farm crisis hit Iowa with particular force and largely bypassed other regions. However, the generalization boundaries of this project are historical as well as geographic. The study sample includes children who are members of a single birth cohort, the late 1970s. Children born in the 1960s experienced more prosperity, while those born in the late 1980s entered a rural society in chronic distress and decline. Ultimately, replication of the study will be a decisive criterion for determining the boundaries of empirical generalization. But in the absence of genuine efforts to replicate, we shall draw upon the results of other studies to evaluate our findings and place them in context.

Our principal aim is to identify the "chain of influences" by which a family's status relative to farming makes a difference in the relative success of youth in rural Iowa. Success includes academic competence, self-confidence, maturity, social status among peers or classmates, and the avoidance of problem behavior. The linking process is defined largely by social resources or capital, ranging from the quality of social ties to parents and grandparents to the community involvements of parents (see figure 1.6). Given the study's aims, we are interested in the developmental implications of exposure to life in a farm family, no matter how potent or weak the effects may be. As in any study of social change, we must trace the sequence of influences that link change to specific behavior and developmental outcomes.[59]

Amidst changing times, new worlds give birth to new lives. Over the past century rural America has been losing population, especially from the farm sector. Assessments of this decline for communities and their young people have emphasized the economic consequences. This loss is critical, but we emphasize the loss of human and social capital. At century's end, generations of young people in rural America face a local future with scarce and declining options. This volume charts their life course through high school, identifying resources and constraints that make a difference in their journey.

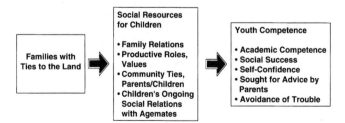

Figure 1.6 Resources of Families with Ties to the Land: Their Developmental Implications

CHAPTER TWO

Families and the Generations

The farm is "a special place. No one would stay . . . if they didn't
love the land."

Middle-aged farmer, 1995

The Great Farm Crisis of the 1980s placed many Iowa families in precarious circumstances. Over a third of the fathers who were farming during
the early 1990s still felt that they would not be able to recover financially
from their losses, and a fifth made similar claims about their lingering
emotional distress. Nevertheless, virtually all remained committed to the
belief that "farming was a good way of life," and most of their wives
shared this appraisal. In large part, farming was good for family life and
for children. The farmstead represented a place where children acquired
sound values, where freedom meant responsibility, a place where the
generations worked together.

When traced across the generations, belief in the virtues of a farm
childhood clearly has elements of a romantic image of the past, a "world
in which children can run and play freely, safe from the problems and
threats of the city."[1] Yet many Iowans in the study embraced this view,
ignoring the high accident rate among farm children. Over a fourth of
the grandparents stressed the close-knit relations of farm families, while
others mentioned a responsible work ethic, the ease of parental supervision and control, the experience of nature, and constructive things for
children to do. Their grandchildren shared these sentiments, particularly if they came from farms. For example, over two-thirds of the boys
described a farm as the best place for a child, compared to fewer than
13 percent of the boys from nonfarm households.[2]

In theory, some of these virtues of a farm childhood represent qualities
that make farm families resourceful pathways to adulthood for children.
Three domains have special significance:

- The embeddedness of farm families within the larger community through kin ties and connections to social institutions, especially the school, church, and civic organizations

- The interdependency of farm family life, as expressed in joint work and social activities between the generations, and in collective commitments that subordinate individual interests to family considerations
- Values of responsibility, industry, nonmaterialistic attitudes, and family commitments.

As discussed in chapter 1, each of these domains constitutes potential connections between Iowa families with ties to the land and the behavioral competence of their children. Thus, the first question to answer is, Are families with ties to the land more embedded in the larger rural community when compared to families with no such connections to agriculture? Are these families characterized by more shared activity among grandparents, parents, and child, and by a stronger sense of family? Is the civic engagement of parents also mirrored in the lives of their children, in church functions, school activities, and community associations? And, last, Are families in farming more likely to expose children to values of responsibility, industry, and nonmaterialistic sentiments?

Iowa families, as we have seen in the study sample, vary widely on ties to the land, ranging from the ecologies of full-time and part-time farming to the displaced who lost their farms, the farm-reared parents who grew up on a farm but are not now farming, and nonfarm households. The parents in nonfarm families have no farming experience, either in childhood or in the adult years. We use this category as our comparison in a series of analyses that estimate the effect of ties to the land. Depending on the outcome, we contrast each ecological group with the nonfarm, adjusting for socioeconomic influences. Though some families changed their ecological niche over the course of the study, we focus on the typical placement of the Iowa families when their study children were in the seventh through tenth grades.

We begin this chapter on the theme of kinship ties and family continuity in agriculture, an intergenerational transition in which farm sons succeed their fathers or are launched by them with newly acquired land. Mark Friedberger tells the story of an Iowa farmer who managed to launch nine of eleven sons in farming between the economically depressed 1930s and the 1960s.[3] He did so by working out low-interest loans for run-down property with the Farmer's Home Administration or Land Bank, and then proceeding to sell the land to his sons on contract well below the market value. Family continuity on the same land and homestead understandably requires opportunity as well as motivation,[4] such as access to an economically successful farm and good relations with father.

Nearly 70 percent of the Iowa parents have fathers who once farmed (the study child's grandfathers), but only a third were engaged in farming at the end of the 1980s. We first identify socioeconomic and family factors that made a difference in the paths followed by young men in the G2 generation (fathers of the study children), and then compare the life histories of farmers in the two generations. This provides a social and cultural context for understanding the social capital of farming generations in the lives of children, the second part of this chapter. Social capital refers to the web of ties between grandparents and parents, and the interdependence of farming parents and children.

Farm families are distinguished by a collective interdependence that relates members to family goals, whether business or other. Children are brought up in farm families to consider family business needs as family needs. Especially in planting and harvest seasons, the farm takes priority over everything. During these periods of family mobilization and the routine cycle of farm life, children experience heightened expectations of interdependency. Salamon points out from her Illinois study of farming communities that "involvement in farm activities conveys to children, from an early age, their importance to the family enterprise."[5]

Kinship ties and the interdependence of farm families are important components of the social embeddedness of farm children. Another component involves the community connections of parents and children. In the second part of this chapter, we turn to the civic, school, and church ties of parents, and to the social activities of their children in school and community. The residential stability of farm life favors social investments in local institutions, as does the German farming heritage of most families in the sample. Accordingly, we expect such involvement to be most characteristic of both generations in farm families as compared to more mobile nonfarm households.

Our concluding section centers on values that distinguish family life in farming. These include a sense of responsibility, a work ethic, and nonmaterialistic goals. If Iowa farm youth are more involved in activities with their parents than nonfarm adolescents, as observations suggest, they would rank high on a belief that they are counted on by parents, that they are responsible. Family-based farming has also traditionally subordinated consumption to the priorities of successful farming and its way of life. In her study of family-based farming in Georgia, Barlett interpreted the intrusion of materialistic goals of consumption as a threat to the financial survival of family farms.[6] With these observations in mind, we expect farm parents and youth to be less oriented toward materialistic objectives in life when compared to nonfarm families.

Family Continuity in Agriculture and Kinship

Iowa sons (G2) of farmers in the grandparent generation were born during the prosperous postwar era (1945 and after), and a third of them went into farming. In the 1989 follow-up, we asked the Iowa parents (G2) who grew up on farms about their early family life and the socioeconomic standing of the family and farm operation. Using thirteen different measures, we compared men who entered family farming to men who did not.[7] Both the early family environment and socioeconomic circumstances had something to do with transitions into farming. Those who continued in farming differed in predictable ways from men who left their farm families for alternative careers.

First, the men (G2) who entered farming came from families that were more invested in farming. The fathers of these men were more involved in agriculture and had spent more years farming than the fathers of nonfarm offspring. They were more likely to own and operate their farms, as opposed to leasing or laboring on farms. Second, the fathers with sons who entered farming were better educated and more stably employed, and they provided a higher standard of living when compared to the fathers of nonfarm sons. Third, they faced less competition from brothers for a career in agriculture. They were more likely to have no more than one brother.

The fourth and last factor involves family ties. Farm men tended to come from a more harmonious family when compared to nonfarm men. The remembered quality of early family experiences may express present-day feelings as well as childhood realities. For our purposes, we focused on memories of parental unhappiness and quarreling, depression, hostility, rejection, and harsh parenting. Parental unhappiness and conflict are least characteristic of the families of men who entered the world of farming, compared to nonfarm men. No other family influence made a difference, but the evidence suggests that family continuity in agriculture did not occur under conditions of family strife.

All of these influences are statistically significant. A discriminant function analysis arranged the predictors in order of magnitude, beginning with farm involvement and continuing with years farmed,[8] standard of living, unemployment, marital conflict, number of brothers, and education. As a whole, the model accounts for one-fifth of the variance in the farm/nonfarm choice, and correctly classifies three-fourths of the men. Recollection of the past has limited usefulness in tapping adolescent or young adult relations with father, and thus we can only infer from the evidence that a positive relation between father and son was a decisive condition for generational succession in farming.

From this vantage point, the generational succession of farm families resembles a process of evolutionary adaptation. Effective farms survive, even prosper, and are led in the next generation by sons who have good relations with their fathers. Salamon found family continuity to be espe-

cially common among farmers of German ancestry,[9] a nationality represented by four out of five families in the Iowa sample. More marginal
units are abandoned by the younger generation in favor of nonfarm employment and may be taken over by other farm operators.

It is important to note that the two farming generations of men encountered different historical conditions as they launched their careers.
The grandfather generation typically began farming with some independence during the 1940s and 1950s, a time when land prices were relatively
low and commodity prices were stable and high.[10] The farm crisis of the
1980s had little effect on these men because their land was paid for as
a rule, their debts were low, and their capital resources were high. They
benefited in many ways from a long phase of uninterrupted prosperity
from the end of World War II to 1974. The offspring of this generation
experienced a very different world. Born in the 1940s and early 1950s,
more of these young men had college degrees in agriculture and training
in agribusiness techniques, but they were not immune to the widespread
decline of farm land values and farm incomes during the 1980s. Many
plunged heavily into debt and eventually lost their farms. Indeed, one-
third of the Iowa men who entered farming in this generation had to
leave the field by the end of the 1980s.

Continuity in farming is coupled with dramatic change in family patterns that reflect what Hernandez terms the revolutionary changes of
the twentieth century in children's lives, particularly a declining size of
family, the rising level of parental education, and the sharply increasing
proportion of women in the paid labor force.[11] Table 2.1 compares the
life histories of parents and offspring in these generations. The left-hand
columns of the table present the life histories for parents and son, the
paternal side of the G2 family. The right-hand columns focus on the
maternal lineage, comparing the life histories of mothers and daughters.

Most members of the grandparent generation are still living, and appear to be in relatively good health. Seventy-five percent of the grandfathers and 85 percent of the grandmothers are living, and approximately
two-thirds of these parents are described as having good or excellent
health. Their median age is sixty-nine; most have not reached the age
when health declines become commonplace. Nearly all (95 percent) of
the grandparents maintain independent residences. About a fifth of the
grandmothers are living alone, compared to fewer than a tenth of the
grandfathers.

Graduation from high school was still uncertain for members of the
grandparent generation and college was almost unknown in their life
histories. But by the time their children had come along, secondary education through high school was the rule. The goal shifted to higher educa-

Table 2.1

Comparison of Grandparent (G1) and Parent (G2) Farming Generations Belonging to Same Family Lineage

Social Factors	Paternal Grandparents Father N = 272		Maternal Grandparents Mother N = 200	
	PGF/PGM	Father	MGF/MGM	Mother
Birth year median	1918/1922	1949	1921/1924	1950
Education				
% high school graduate	53.6/81.9	98.2	57.5/73.5	98.5
% college graduate	3.3/2.9	24.3	2.0/1.5	21.0
Relative education				
% wife more	46.7	30.1	42.5	29.0
% husband more	13.6	29.8	18.0	31.0
Family size				
median	6	5	6	5
range	3–16	4–14	3–16	4–9
Farm activity				
median years farmed	31	—	34	—
% currently farming	53.9	45.2	59.5	37.5
Women's employment				
% employed	19.5 (ever)*	86.0 (current)	27.0 (ever)*	87.5 (current)

Source: Based on Table 2.1, p. 38, Glen H. Elder Jr., Laura Rudkin, and Rand D. Conger, "International Continuity and Change in Rural America," in *Adult Intergenerational Relations: Effects of Societal Change,* edited by Vern L. Bengtson, K. Warner Schaie, and Linda M. Burton, © 1994, Springer Publishing Company, Inc., New York 10012. Used by permission.

* Percentage of G1 mothers ever employed during G2's childhood (ages 5–16).

tion and the completion of four years of college. Over a fifth of the G2 men and women completed college. Reflecting perhaps the increasing knowledge and skill demands of modern agriculture, educational gains across the two farm generations are most striking for men and their educational status in marriage. Better educated than their fathers, men in the G2 generation are more likely to have as much education as their wives or even more. This declining educational disadvantage is consistent with a growing educational priority among farm sons, and the importance of advanced education for employment out of agriculture.

During the first half of the twentieth century, farm wives typically worked on their own farms, managing enterprises such as poultry.[12] Fewer than 30 percent of the grandmothers were ever employed in paid jobs. This is a rough estimate, since recollections of farm women's off-farm employment leave much to be desired on accuracy. However, by the middle years of their daughters and daughters-in-law, nonfarm employment for women had become an acceptable necessity in response to the eroding profit margin of family farming. Nearly nine out of ten of the farm wives were employed, and many were working a forty-hour week. A notable decline in rural wages is also a factor in the work schedule of these women. They are working more hours and earning less per hour than rural women in the 1960s and 1970s, but their jobs add up to an essential boost for hard-pressed families through earnings *and* benefits—health and retirement.

Intergenerational continuity in farming is coupled with substantial change in the roles of women, and this change applies to the G2 generation as a whole, regardless of whether they have farmed or entered nonfarm careers (see appendix table E2.1). The men typically married at age twenty-three and their wives at age twenty-one. Children came along two or three years later. The educational advantage of farm women still holds to some extent, although the difference is too small to be significant. Both groups reported total family incomes that approached $40,000, on average, by the end of the 1980s. The similarity of these groups ends when we turn to the nearness of kin (parents and in-laws) and the frequency of contact, whether face-to-face or by phone and letter. Eighty-five percent of the men on farms live within twenty-five miles of their parents, compared to approximately 60 percent of the nonfarm men and women. Proximity makes frequent contact more possible, and farm families are more likely to make contact with grandparents every week compared to other families. The differences range from 22–30 percent and suggest that farm generations, compared to nonfarm, are more embedded in a field of kinship ties and patterns of reciprocal assistance.

Proximity has its costs, however, such as more frequent intrusions in family affairs and efforts to control what a son or daughter does. Indeed, we find that parents and in-laws are a prime source of demandingness among farm families. Farm men are most likely to perceive their parents as too demanding, when compared to nonfarm parents, and the cause of the problem, as they see it, involves the unwanted exercise of authority by parents who reside nearby. However, only a fourth of the farm couples describe the husband's parents as sometimes or "often demanding." Neither this problem nor evidence of conflict eroded a sense of emotional ties and support across the generations.

Influential Grandparents in Farming Families

Perceptions of emotional support from the grandparent (G1) generation (perceived appreciation, always there to be depended on) were equally common among families in different ecological niches, farm as well as nonfarm.[13] This emotional tie between the generations paves the way for children of the parent generation to know and interact with their grandparents. Among the Iowa children, for example, we found access to be severely limited when the tie was weak or conflictual. Men and women who were at odds with their own parents were likely to keep them at an "arm's length" from their own family. They did not initiate contacts on a regular basis, and they discouraged their parents from visiting.

Farm parents did not feel closer to their own parents when compared to nonfarm families, but they lived closer to the husband's parents and had frequent contact with them. Distance proved to be a substantial barrier to contact between grandparents and grandchildren in earlier times. As one Iowa grandparent observed, "I think grandparents of today are more important because we see more of each other."

Greater longevity is partly responsible for such contact, since contemporary grandparents are more likely to live to see their grandchildren marry and have children of their own. Another factor is the greater ease of travel. Judging from their comments, Iowa grandparents think nothing of driving many miles "to be there" for a public performance of a grandchild. A grandmother who lives near Des Moines noted that they would drive up to South Dakota for her granddaughter's "science project when she shows it off."

Proximity may not matter as much as it once did in determining opportunities to be with relatives, but greater proximity and frequency of contact are expressed in stronger social ties between Iowa farm youth and their grandparents, compared to other young people. In interviews with grandparents in 1994, we asked them how frequently they saw their grandchildren in the study, how close they felt to these children, and what they did with or for the children. We averaged the responses of husband and wife to produce scale scores for the maternal and paternal side of the family. The various rural ecologies made a significant difference *only* in the salience of paternal grandparents.

These grandparents were most likely to report frequent contact with and a close relationship to children who were growing up in families with ties to the land—full-time, part-time, displaced, and farm-reared, each compared to the nonfarm group (appendix table E2.2). They were also more likely to claim that they enjoyed the companionship of their grandchildren, frequently attended their activities, engaged in mentoring, and provided tangible support at times. These significant effects are especially strong among youth from full-time farm families and remain strong even with adjustments for the influence of the grandparents' age, gender, education, income, and health. Grandparent reports did not vary in relation to granddaughters and grandsons.

The prominence of paternal grandparents in the lives of grandchildren who live in families with ties to the land is based solely on the reports of grandparents. Does this pattern also emerge when we take the perspective of grandchildren and ask them how close they feel to their grandparents? We asked this question in their senior year and found that perceived closeness is uniquely associated with boys and girls who live on full-time farms. Perhaps reflecting proximity and frequent contact, these farm youth are significantly more likely to feel close to their paternal grandfather and grandmother (average beta = .28, $p < .05$), as contrasted to adolescents in nonfarm families. No other ecology produced a significant effect.

The closeness of farm youth to their paternal grandparents does not mean that other young people do not have significant grandparents in their lives. Maternal grandparents may be more salient for them. Three out of five youth in the study describe at least one significant grandparent, and we find that there is no difference between nonfarm and farm youth on the likely presence of this kind of person. Paternal grandparents are more salient to farm youth through their connections to the land and farming, but significant grandparents are equally common in the lives of village young people.

One such grandparent observed that "grandparents can be of assistance to young people by letting them know they will always be there for them, and letting them know how much they love them." With deep appreciation for what a grandparent meant in his early years, an Iowa grandfather observed that "being involved with them on everything makes a big difference. The kids are more proud of what they do. You know if you don't have anybody coming to see you, why you don't care whether you do what you're supposed to do or not. If you've got backing from Dad and Mom and Grandpa and Grandma, why it all makes a big difference."

When asked what she would most like to pass along to her grandchildren, a grandmother with farming experience thought a moment and then centered on "that love for each other that grandparents and grandchildren should have. I think it's important in your life to love each other, and to be there for each other. There are rough times when maybe you don't agree, but during those times we have always been able to get together. I think that is the way it has to be." Over the past few years it has been "hard for a lot of our families," and "I don't see it getting any better. . . . As a family, we really have to hang together."

Up to this point, we find evidence of family continuity in the succession of farming from one generation to the next, in ties linking farming generations, and in patrilineal connections between grandparents and grandchildren in farm families. These connections suggest that farming families are more engaged in practices that assemble relatives than other families. Examples include annual reunions of one side of the family or another, the assembly of near relatives for family anniversaries, and family gatherings during holidays.

Family reunions can bring the generations and family units together, and interviews suggest that young people play an important role in maintaining them. One of the Iowa grandparents in the study observed that her mother's side of the family has had reunions for as long as she could remember at summer places on a nearby lake: "We all get together with our extended families and we spend the day and swim and talk, show family videos and laugh." Her entire family would go up there for a week with her mother. "We have thought about putting an end to these gatherings, but our children tell us, well if you don't want to do it, we are going to do it. So keep it up. They love it." Over 40 percent of the families reported recent attendance at a family reunion. But only full-time farm families were significantly more likely to participate than non-farm households ($p < .05$). On other family rituals (the celebration of holidays, family events such as birthdays with kin), we find no difference between farm and nonfarm families.

Within the Family: Shared Activities and Closeness

Is the kinship embeddedness of farm families matched by strong ties within the family? These ties include the social relationships of parents and children, brothers and sisters. Strong family ties may emerge from the work experience of children who live on farms, both unpaid, in the form of chores, and paid through wages and the sale of stock; from the joint efforts of parents and children on the farm, as during the harvest season and the daily rounds of labor; and from the shared community life of each generation, expressed through 4-H clubs or a local organization of the Future Farmers of America.

Labor needs on working farms involve children in productive roles at an early age. With this in mind, we asked young people in the Iowa Project whether their families counted on their help, and whether they worked for their parents and had a lot to do. To determine the interdependent nature of this work between parents and youth, we asked the adolescents how much work time they spent with their parents. Joint activity between the generations also applies to youth-group activities in the community. We asked them how often they participated in such activities with parents.[14]

As expected, farm boys and girls are notably more engaged in family work than nonfarm adolescents, especially boys. Compared to girls, boys are also more likely to claim that they work on the family farm. When interviewed in the eighth grade, most farm boys and girls reported that they were working for parents, though only the work activities of farm boys tend to involve parents as well. This gender difference may reflect in part the greater involvement of girls in unpaid chores within the farm household.

Farm boys in high school were likely to describe their working relationship with fathers as apprenticeships—they learned about farming and the required skills by doing things with their fathers. One youth from a 600-acre corn and hog farm felt that a working relationship with his father had convinced him of a future in this field. The most rewarding part of his experience was "working with the animals and getting to work with my Dad. . . . Dad taught me everything he knows, which is quite a bit, and it will probably affect me for the rest of my life."

If children who grow up on farms are more engaged in activities with parents, compared to other youth, is this involvement reflected in more positive evaluations of parents? In the eighth grade, the adolescents were asked about the warmth of their parents, and they were also asked how much their parents were valued guides and examples in their lives. The perceived warmth of each parent was measured by four highly related questions, each with responses that ranged from "never" to "always." Valued guidance was tapped by an "identification" index composed of five interrelated questions, including a question on "wanting to be like the parent."[15]

Farm youth are more positive toward mother and father when compared to nonfarm youth, but the contrast is not as large as it was for shared activity. Farm status appears to matter most for feelings about father in the case of girls and boys, a difference that is consistent with the centrality of fathers in the world of farming. The preference for father is most noticeable in terms of identification. Farm boys and girls are more likely to be identified with father than with mother, who tends to be more dissatisfied with life on a farm, especially the material side. During the farm crisis of the 1980s, mothers were more critical of farming and less attached to the farm than were their husbands, especially women who did not grow up on a farm.[16] Among families that lost their farms, men were more likely to remain attached to the hope of farming once again, while their wives generally sought a new life off the farm that would offer more advantages for home and children.

Some of these differences between men and women can be viewed in terms of changing circumstances. Consider couples in full-time farming, part-time farming, and displacement from farming in the four years from 1988 to 1991.[17] Economic conditions worsened for the farm families; the part-time farm couples managed to hold their own in large measure by increasing their off-farm employment, and the displaced families experienced an improvement in family income. Between 1988 and 1991, farm wives became more disheartened by the financial adversity of farming, more so than their husbands, while wives in displaced families were buoyed by the positive change in their financial status. They were more likely than their spouses to move away from the depressed outlook they held at the end of the 1980s. Couples in part-time farming followed a middle course across these years. The more negative response of wives to adverse financial conditions in part reflects their concern for the well-being of their children.

Farming links the generations around common tasks, but it is clear that this social organization of family life does not ensure emotional advantages over other families. Farm youth are only slightly more attached to their parents, when compared to youth in nonfarm families. The story of such ties extends well beyond the boundaries of farm life. Some farm families rank well above average on these ties, while others rank below. We shall gain more understanding of these differences when we consider the link between ties to the land and family in chapter 3. But more understanding can also be gained by exploring the relations between siblings who have grown up on farms and those who have lived in small towns.

In the open country of Iowa farming, the distances between farmsteads increase the mutual dependence of brothers and sisters. They often serve as peers or friends. A young girl who once lived on a farm observed that "you get to spend a lot of time with your family. I mean, your basic friends are your sisters and brothers." If siblings on farms have less opportunity to pursue activities with nonfamily peers, do they develop stronger bonds than siblings in nonfarm households? To put this question to a test, we identified three types of sibling pairs in the sample: two sisters, two brothers, and mixed gender. In all cases, the pairing involves the target child and a near sibling who are both in the project. We did not have the sample size to distinguish between age variations in sibling relationships. Both full-time and part-time farm families define the farm subgroup, since we needed to have as many cases as possible. The nonfarm contrast included all of the families who were not engaged in farming at the time.

The target child was asked three types of questions about the sibling in 1989 and 1990. The first question dealt with feelings of satisfaction with the relationship, the second set of questions indexed admiration for the sibling, and the third set tapped affection or caring. As expected, farm youth, boys and girls, generally report more positive sentiments toward their siblings than do adolescents from nonfarm households and communities (appendix table E2.3). This difference is not statistically significant, but it extends across relationships involving children of the same or different gender. The weakest contrast involves siblings who differ in gender.

However, the only consistently significant difference in this direction involves brothers. Brothers on farms appear to have a more positive relationship than brothers in nonfarm households—the study child feels more satisfied with the relationship, is more likely to admire his brother, and is more likely to care for him. The strength of the male bond in farm families generally parallels the strength of the male bond across generations engaged in farming. Several years later, in the tenth grade, we observe similar differences in the amount of time spent with the near sibling. Farm brothers are much more likely to spend time together at this age than brothers in nonfarm households, and the difference also applies to sisters and even cross-gender pairs. The overall contrast is statistically significant (3.7 vs. 4.2, $p = .04$), but the number of cases is too small to produce reliable differences among brother pairs.

Sibling relations may be ruled by other emotions, ranging from competition and envy to hostility. The latter is likely to occur in families where parents are at odds with each other and behave in a punitive way toward their children. This type of family is less common among farming households, but any explanation for the harmony of near-age brothers in farm families must include a normative emphasis on cooperation in the culture of farm families. Children are socialized into the family cooperative, a superordinate cultural theme in which family members work together to enhance the collective welfare.[18] They learn to appreciate the interdependence of their family world and are rewarded for carrying responsibilities at an early age.

The strength of ties between brothers in farm families has functional significance in perpetuating the family's role in farming from one generation to the next. Though only one son usually takes over the family farm, fathers frequently make arrangements for other sons who want to farm. They purchase additional land, for example, and help with the initial investment. By renting land, a family can provide the basis for multiple farms or a partnership involving two or more brothers. In the study region, a number of partnerships link brothers in farming enterprises that exceed fifteen hundred acres. The Great Farm Crisis brought additional land into the marketplace for the expansion of farms by farmers who had the resources to rent and even buy parcels. But as we shall see, the farm crisis and the declining profit margin in corn-belt agriculture also made this enterprise far less attractive to Iowa youth as a way to make a living.

Social Ties in the Community

The inheritance of family farms across the generations ensures a measure of involvement and leadership in community life among farm families. In the north central region of Iowa, continuity in farming has become more problematic since the farm crisis of the 1980s, but it remains a powerful ideal and reality, as symbolized by "century farms" (in the family for one hundred years or more) and an abiding attachment to the land. The farm of Robert Heinz, for example, has been in the family since the late 1800s, and his family has long played an important role in the local community and its Lutheran church.[19] His wife, a bookkeeper for the local feed mill, currently serves as president of the PTA, just as his mother did when he attended the high school.

Heinz sits on the boards of a farmer cooperative and regional development council, supports the local FFA by attending functions with his two sons, and serves as a church trustee. His energetic role in the community is mirrored by the activity of his boys. Both are involved in high school athletics—track and basketball—and student government; they are active in the church's lively youth group and take part in a school-sponsored organization of the Future Farmers of America. The boys have learned to count on the presence of parents and grandparents at their athletic events. Most nights of the week find some member of the family engaged in a community affair of one kind or another.

Do we find a concentration of this pattern of involvement among farming families? To assess parental involvement, we focused on civic ties and leadership, church attendance, and participation in PTA meetings of the local school. In each of four years from 1989 through 1992, we asked the parents how many clubs and organizations they belonged to and how frequently they attended the meetings. The number of groups was multiplied by the frequency of meeting attendance to obtain a score for each of the four years. The scores were then averaged to produce a single index for each parent. On civic leadership, each year we asked whether the parents were currently officers, board members, or committee members for any organizations they belonged to. We summed the "yes" responses to form the index. For a measure of church attendance, we computed the average attendance frequency across the four years. Lastly, attendance at meetings of the Parent-Teacher Association was averaged on a five-point scale across the four years.

Churches have been prime movers of civic engagement within the rural midwest. Settlement of the region brought new churches and the new congregations soon established schools, if they were not already available. Reading skills were essential for the practicing Christian in Bible study. Today congregations offer small, sociable gatherings that extend the long arm of a caring people.[20] As a rule, they strengthen awareness of human need as well as the community attachments that make outreach compelling. Ammerman describes "congregations as connected communities" through the affiliations of their members and the community of churches.[21] They build social trust and shared communication, essential elements of social capital. She notes that

> congregations are both sacred places, making claims for the power of a transcendent Other in the midst of this world, and civic places, mobilizing all sorts of resources for the sake of the community. . . . In congregations, we voice collective grievances, envision solutions, seek divine sanction, gather material goods, build networks, invest time and energy. As an ongoing institutional presence in the community, congregations provide the stability within which cultural traditions are preserved and sometimes created anew.[22] (370)

Three types of rural ecologies are especially relevant to an Iowa family's connections in the community: families in full-time farming, families with farm ties (includes part-time farm families, displaced families, and farm-reared parents), and families with no link to agriculture—the nonfarm households. The middle group includes families in transition between worlds. They are less stable than farm families and are more likely to be pressed for time, owing to the requirements of multiple careers. Even with adjustments for income and parental education, the most involved parents are concentrated in full-time farm families (appendix table E2.4). They are more involved in civic life, in their church, and in the local PTA, compared to other parents, including those who have more distant ties to farming. However, we also find that families with any link to farming are significantly more engaged in community roles than nonfarm parents. Gender matters also; women with ties to farming are more engaged in church and community life than men.

The strong involvement of farm families makes sense in terms of their stable presence in the community over the decades. Such connections help to ensure the quality of life from generation to generation. But it is less clear why any tie to farming is reflected in more community ties. One plausible interpretation involves the experience of growing up on a farm and learning the value of social participation through childhood observation. Presumably the parents of these adults established a high standard of civic engagement. Related to this point is the possibility that social ties in childhood are carried into the adult years, especially for the young who settle near their family of origin. This continuity from childhood to adulthood is likely to be most evident among daughters and mothers.

The middle group of families with farm ties includes a wide range of life experiences, from the multiple roles of parents in part-time farming to loss of the family farm and a farm background. Are these differences expressed in community ties? For example, loss of the family farm might entail residential changes that sever ties to local civic groups. Likewise, parents who are managing farm and nonfarm jobs may not have the time to participate. These two groups of parents do not rank as high on civic involvement as the farm-reared, but the difference is statistically significant only among women ($p < .05$). Moreover, the groups do not differ at all on civic leadership, church, or PTA attendance. Overall, then, we find more evidence of resemblance than dissimilarity among parents with some farm ties.

This approach to community ties tells us how each parent relates to community institutions. Since the actions of each spouse are related, the data also describe family variability. We constructed an index of this variability by using all four measures of involvement from both parents. In the first step, we divided the sample into three categories (scored 0 through 2) on each of the four domains, from civic participation to PTA attendance.[23] Using the distribution of cases and the substantive meaning of the scores, we identified three levels of community ties across the first four years of the study: highly involved, involved, and isolated. The category of "highly involved" included 71 families with scores of 6 to 8; isolated families were indexed by scores of 0 to 2 (97 families). The remaining families were placed in the middle. The distribution of highly involved and isolated families by farm status (figure 2.1) corresponds with the results on each parent.

Do children follow their parents in leading an active life of social participation? Are farm youth also more engaged in church, civic, and school-based activities? Table 2.2 compares three rural ecologies on time spent in the community, on attendance in church, and on extracurricular activities and unsupervised time spent with peers. All of these measures apply to grades 8 and 9. The general pattern of involvement among Iowa youth tends to match findings on parents. The greater the involvement of parents in farming, the more involved they and their children are likely to be in community life, the church, and school.

Youth on farms report spending far more hours per week on community activities than other adolescents. Judging from the joint activities linking farm generations, some of this community time is spent with father and mother. Farm youth are also significantly more involved in church life and extracurricular activities. Both of these activities depend

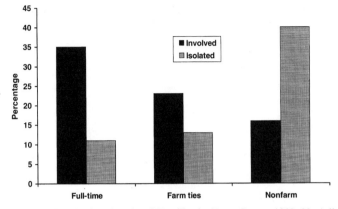

Figure 2.1 Highly Involved and Isolated Families by Farm Status, 1988–90: Adjusted for Mother's Education

in part on the encouragement of parents and their help in providing transportation. Subsequent chapters explore how farm youth depend more on sponsorship and promotion by their parents, owing to the transportation challenge of long distances in open farm country.

In his book *From Generation to Generation,* Eisenstadt identifies two regimes for the adolescent years that have special relevance to our study region, north central Iowa: adult sponsorship and a spontaneous peer culture.[24] High levels of interaction between the generations favor a type of adult sponsorship in which adults represent a vital and continuing force in the development of young people. Rural societies, like the agrarian Midwest, are often characterized by integration across age groups and an adult sponsorship of child socialization. We find this integration concentrated among families that are engaged in farming. It is least evident among families that are generations removed from the land.

Cross-age and cross-generational ties are expressed in the prevalence of joint work and youth-group activity among young people and parents on the farm and in the local community. Farm boys, in particular, are more likely than other boys to work with their mothers and fathers. In many cases, their parents participate with them in youth-oriented organizations, such as 4-H and the FFA. A greater involvement of farm youth in the life of local churches also represents a form of socialization under adult control and sponsorship.

Rural churches bring the generations in families together, from grandparents to grandchildren, and often involve older children in sponsored organizations, such as the teenage world of the youth group. Children's peers are a key part of this world, but they are selected and monitored

Table 2.2
Eighth and Ninth Graders' Civic, Church, and School Involvement by Farm Status, with Average Annual Income and Parental Education Controlled, in Means

Type of Involvement (Eighth-Ninth Grades)	Full-Time Farmers	Farm Ties[a]	Nonfarm	Significant Differences
Community				
Hours per week spent in activities	6.6	4.5	4.8	Full-time vs. others: $F = 9.4$** Non-farm vs. others: $F = 1.3$
Church				
Attendance, weekly frequency (1 = low, 5 = high)	4.3	4.1	3.8	Full-time vs. others: $F = 14.2$*** Non-farm vs. others: $F = 9.6$**
Schools and Friends				
Extracurricular activities: number	9.8	9.0	8.1	Full-time vs. others: $F = 5.5$* Non-farm vs. others: $F = 5.9$*
Unsupervised time with friends (summed score)	14.2	15.5	17.8	Full-time vs. others: $F = 7.2$** Non-farm vs. others: $F = 10.0$**
N	79	255	80	

[a] Includes part-time farm, displaced, and farm-reared parents.

* $p < .05$; ** $p < .01$; *** $p < .001$

by the social institutions of adult sponsorship—the family, church, adult-directed youth groups, and schools. An adult-sponsored regime is fueled by the resources or capital that make social institutions effective.

Spontaneous peer associations are a natural part of the developmental process, but they can place children at risk of failure and antisocial events when they flourish in the absence of adult nurturance, investment, and supervision. Parents who are not engaged in activities with their children and remain aloof from their social worlds of community and school establish conducive environments for antisocial peers. Few truly large schools exist in the study region, but they are most likely to experience the adversarial role of antisocial peers and culture. From a variety of directions, then, spontaneous peer relations are apt to become deviant influences in the lives of youth who lack resourceful environments that are marked by high levels of interaction with caring adults.

The networks and cultures of Iowa farming communities are at odds with the development of antisocial peer cultures. Age-mates are mobilized in the adult-sponsored regime for accomplishments that enrich the community, such as service work. For example, eighth-grade boys and girls with farm ties reported significantly more time devoted to school and community service projects than other youth. Moreover, highly involved parents were more likely than less involved parents to participate with their children in community volunteer activities (see chapter 5). Consistent with these differences, we find in table 2.2 that youth on full-time farms were most likely to be involved in extracurricular activities during the eighth and ninth grades. They were also least involved with friends in unsupervised situations.

Observers at the end of postwar prosperity, the late 1960s and early 1970s, came to a startling conclusion: that to an unparalleled degree, America's children were growing up without adults. They were isolated from adults in school and neighborhood, and time demands had limited their contact with parents. This theme was highlighted by Urie Bronfenbrenner in *Two Worlds of Childhood*,[25] a comparison of the United States and the Soviet Union.

Twenty-five years later we see confirmatory evidence for this assessment in the continuing dissolution of marriages and families through hardship, personal instability, homicide, and incarceration. Bronfenbrenner noted the loss of learning experiences in family and work, both moral and skill-based: "While the family still has the primary moral and legal responsibility for the character development of children, it often lacks the power or opportunity to do the job, primarily because parents and children no longer spend enough time together in situations in which such training is possible."[26]

Iowa families with ties to the land provide a different view of children's developmental experience. More than families who live and work in small towns and cities, parents in these families are engaged in community institutions and in the lives of their children. The two forms of involvement are mutually reinforcing. Involved parents in civic life are empowered to do more for their children, while involvement in children's lives underscores the importance of playing important supportive roles in school, church, and civic organizations.

In all of these ways, a good many families with ties to the land have established resourceful pathways to adulthood for their children, even in a time of scarcity and diminished alternatives in rural America. From 1989 through 1994, for example, families engaged in full-time farming became more dependent on nonfarm employment to pay the bills. The average percentage of income from farming declined from 70–79 percent to 55–59 percent. Despite such changes, families with ties to the land continued to provide pathways to opportunity. A final example of these resources comes from the realm of values, the preferred options that guide decisions and actions, such as the devaluing of materialism and a consumer lifestyle.

Values to Live By

When parents and children talk about the virtues of living on a farm, they invariably mention basic values of this lifestyle—those of hard work or industry, self-reliance and a sense of responsibility, a commitment to family life, social trust and a value system that is not devoted to money and consumerism. People who depend on each other must learn to trust, as on farms and in small towns. The work ethic of farm life is valued for the confidence it provides young people who are thinking about themselves and the future, and what they can do with their lives.

One boy who lived on a farm told the story of how he gained such confidence by being given tasks that he mastered, even though they seemed overwhelming at first. His boss, the farm manager, would lay out the day's work, and he would think to himself, "I can't do that—it is too much." But by breaking large tasks into small sequenced parts and working hard, he often managed to surprise himself. He even completed the assignments before time ran out. Mastering the challenge showed him that he could handle major challenges in his life. A work ethic became valued through the rewards of such mastery experiences. The exuberance of such mastery is expressed in a high-school boy's pleasure at what he could achieve in work: "It has given me a great work ethic." We discuss this important topic again in chapter 4.

If family life underscores views of the "desirable," as in the unconscious patterning of behavior, then one might expect youth in farm families to place considerable value on two future identities: becoming a community leader and a religious person. They are likely to have parents who exemplify this lifestyle. During the eighth and ninth grades, boys and girls in the study were asked a three-response question about whether they wanted either of these identities. We averaged the two years to produce single measures. We first assessed the effect of each rural ecology (full-time farm, etc.) and then asked whether parental roles explained it. Gender, family income, and parental education were taken into account in the analysis.

Youth from full-time farm families were most likely to embrace the goal of becoming a community leader (beta = .14, $p < .05$); no other rural ecology provided support for this objective. Youth who held this goal were also likely to have parents in community leadership roles (beta = .22, $p < .01$), and this parental example accounted for nearly half of the effect of farm status. Our results are similar on the desire to become a religious person. However, in this case, youth with any farm tie were likely to express this desire, when compared to the nonfarm (beta = .14, $p < .05$). Parental religious attendance predicts this value orientation among youth in the sample (average beta = .51), and entirely accounts for the influence of farm status. All of the influence of farm life on young people's desire to become a religious person occurs through the greater religious involvement of their parents.

A core value of family farming within the tradition of German ancestry takes the form of antimaterialism.[27] Farm children in many Iowa homes are brought up to value farming as a way of life, not primarily as a way to make money and acquire material possessions. When sons express interest in farming, their fathers are likely to stress the importance of getting their values straight. Hard times had persuaded some fathers to discourage their sons' interest in farming.[28]

In the second year of the study, we asked the parents whether the following statements described their child: "never happy with the amount of money we have," "never satisfied with things we buy them," and "thinks money grows on trees." The five-response items on each question are highly correlated. As shown in appendix table E2.5, these statements were least likely to be seen as descriptive of children among parents who are engaged in full-time farming (average beta for parents = .31, $p < .01$). The reports of parents who are farming part-time or are displaced rank next on rejection of the description, followed by the farm-reared. Likewise, we find that children who had some experience with life on a farm were significantly less likely to view "money as a life goal" in the seventh and eighth grades when compared to nonfarm youth (beta = $-.40, p < .01$). One-fifth of this effect is explained by the nonmaterialistic sentiments of parents. Neither parents' education nor income made a difference in these results.

Beyond farming, children of higher-status families are least likely to be described by parents as materialistic. But socioeconomic position does not meaningfully alter the stronger effect of farm status. This background is far more important than the education and income level of parents. It is also more important than the materialistic outlook of parents. Whether parents prize a well-paid job for children or not has little importance for how they describe their children's relation to money. Farm mothers, for example, are most likely to express a disinterest in financial success as a goal in its own right. This success represents a by-product of doing well in an occupation. However, the more materialistic mothers were least satisfied with farming as a way to make a living.

Farming that is not coupled with a materialistic culture has greater adaptability when economic reversals occur. These events have occurred in virtually every year since the late 1980s—dismal prices for farm products, drought, damaging storms, and floods have combined to make life exceedingly difficult for farmers in the region. "Making do" is often the requirement for survival from one year to the next. Family and individual needs may have to be postponed for farming families to survive a bad year of heavy losses. This same outlook can serve farm children well when they attempt to complete their schooling and enter a job market where the opportunities are scarce. They may have learned to have patience about living conditions from parents in difficult times. Their home ownership might be delayed until they achieve financial well-being or security.

At the other end of the industrialization continuum, the transition to postindustrial life, Inglehart concludes from surveys that Americans and Europeans have shifted from a heavy emphasis on physical security and material well-being toward more emphasis on the quality of life.[29] The change results from a decline in scarcity during the childhoods of current adult generations. Enduring value priorities, he asserts, are shaped by exposure to conditions of abundance or scarcity during the early years. Consistent with this account, we find that children from high-status homes are not seen as materialistic by their parents, compared with more economically pressured children (note income effect). But even with adjustments for income and education, the children of farm families are least apt to be seen as materialistic.

Farm families are most likely to embrace values of hard work, community service, religious practices, and a devaluation of material goods as an end in themselves. Farming generations, parent and child, are also more engaged in community social institutions, and in the world of kinship. At the other extreme, social isolation is concentrated among families that have no ties to agriculture. This isolation may extend to kinship relations as well and weaken family options for survival in difficult times. Such contrasts point to differing developmental outcomes among children by the end of high school. Do we find differences between the academic and social success of youth who have grown up in farm and non-farm households?

Resourceful Families and Children

Iowans typically have academic and social success in mind when their children are doing well. This description applies to Jim Beichler, the twelfth-grade son of a large stock and grain farmer in the north central region. His teachers and parents report an outstanding record in the honors track, and they note also his role as captain of the football team and leader of his church youth group. He is popular with classmates and has the self-confidence to flourish in leadership posts. Family represents a major source of his support, and his parents frequently seek his advice on major issues involving the farm.

Age-appropriate standards represent a basic criterion of successful development in this appraisal of Jim's status. Pathways to adulthood are marked by successive standards of age-appropriate behavior. These standards include expectations that rule out certain behavior up to a specific age, such as alcohol consumption, and they also involve norms that prescribe behavior after a particular age, such as school. Age-appropriateness by the end of high school includes an academic record that ensures graduation, and perhaps social acceptance by classmates, a positive sense of self in self-esteem and mastery, and a recognized maturity by parents that enables them to seek their children's advice.

When combined with standards of excellence, norms of age-appropriate behavior define competencies for adult life. Jim's excellence has been expressed in academic accomplishments and student leadership. With these distinctions in mind, we emphasize four domains of adolescent success: academic, social life, self-confidence, and the young person's social maturity and judgment in the eyes of parents. The social risk along this developmental path comes from the appeal of age-inappropriate behavior that represents what Stinchcombe has called "early claims on adult status": heavy drinking, drug use, early sexual intercourse, and so on.[30] In chapters 9 and 10 we investigate the process by which the success and social resources of young people enable them to "avoid trouble" and realize their goals of adult status and a rewarding career.

Academic competence is indexed each year, from grade 7 in 1989 to grade 12, by three interrelated components (see appendix B). The first is average grades for the year, as reported by the adolescent and his or her mother. The second component, only available in the twelfth grade, involves reports of achievement-oriented behavior by mother and teacher, such as "How well do you think your child keeps up with his or her classes?" The eight teacher items include "Learning school subjects is easy for her." The third component taps "perceived achievement." Examples of questions include, "I don't do well in school" and "My teachers think I am a good student." The three components were standardized and averaged to form a single scale. Social success was indexed by three questions that were asked of teachers in the twelfth grade: "She is one of the more popular kids in her school," "She hangs out with the popular kids at school," and "Compared to people the same age, how well does the student make new friends, meet new people, get along with others?" In addition to this teacher account, we asked the adolescents whether their parents considered their judgment by listening to the child's ideas, considering such ideas, asking for the child's opinion, and listening carefully to his or her point of view. Last, self-confidence was measured by two scales: self-esteem and personal mastery.

Despite the economic reverses of the past decade, Iowa farm families tend to have successful children. Even with adjustments for family income and parental education, these youth in the twelfth grade are more likely to be successful in grades (beta = .23, $p < .01$) and social life (beta = .19, $p < .05$) than youth from families with no ties to the land—the nonfarm households. The effects are slightly larger for girls than for boys. The advantage of farm families extends even to those with some ties to the land—to the families that once lived on a farm but lost it and to parents who grew up on a farm but now work in other areas of the economy. The children of these families were also doing better in academics and social life than the offspring of nonfarm households (average beta = .12, $p < .10$), apart from differences in family income and education. However, neither farm life nor more distant ties to the land made a difference in how youth viewed themselves, whether self-confident or not, or in their maturity status with parents, on the basis of advice-seeking. Farm parents were not more likely to seek the advice of their sons or daughters.

The full story behind these variations and similarities will emerge as we turn in subsequent chapters to family relationships, work experiences, kin and community roles, and youth activities in church and school. An example of this appears as we consider the plans of youth in chapter 3 and how they influence family relationships. Future plans give meaning to relationships in the family and to connections with the larger community. Youth who intend to stay may invest more in family and community ties, while the act of leaving or preparing to do so may produce greater interpersonal distance between the generations.

Another example of variations among farm and nonfarm youth involves the mastery experience of their work. On farms, this work is often joined to the efforts of father and siblings, and the contribution of each participant becomes critical to the completed project or task. Doing something well under these circumstances has immediate payoff and may reinforce a sense of personal efficacy. However, youth work in a different context could weaken feelings of competence or expertise. Unpaid chores may have such effects, reinforcing dependency and resentment among older youth.

As we turn to the relation between ties to the land and family, we do well to keep in mind the socioeconomic distress that persists. The formal end of the farm crisis did not bring closure to the hardship chapter of families. The poverty rate in Iowa has continued to rise (up to 14 percent in 1996), with the heaviest concentration in rural areas. Looking across the region, an older Iowan who has a grandchild in the study saw little chance of young people making it in farming:

> It is just hard to make a living unless you can farm lots and lots of acres. The profit margin is getting so small now . . . there isn't much for young people here, and especially for young women. For a man, there is a little window factory and a grain elevator that does a feed, seed, and fertilizer business. But employment is just so limited.

PART TWO

Pathways to Competence

A grandfather reflects on a grandson who grew up on his farm: "We were tickled to death it was a boy. [He] grew up out there on the farm and he was under my arm and on my tractor" at a young age. "Just kinda grew up that way . . . he was a little devil, just like his grandpa. Liked to learn everything. If I was working on the combine or something, he'd be under there with me, you know. All eyes. And when I would be driving the tractor, he'd have his eye on that all the time. He was a great pleasure to us, and we've been quite close."

Grandparents attended his school activities, "every one. Very seldom missed anything they did. . . . I think being involved with them on everything makes a big difference. The kids are more proud of what they do, you know. If you don't have anybody coming to see you, why you don't care whether you do what you're supposed to or not. If you got the backing from Dad and Mom and from Grandpa and Grandma, why it all makes a big difference."

CHAPTER THREE

Ties to Family and Land

We work together and support each other.

Young boy, about family, Iowa

Times have become harder for many Iowa families, yet most young people have coped well with the adversity. This is true for both farm and nonfarm youth who have experienced family hardship and limited opportunities for local employment. For the most part, conditions of adversity did not impair the academic success and well-being of boys and girls whose families had ties to the land. Does the explanation for this accomplishment involve social ties and resourcefulness? In this chapter we begin to address this question by examining the role of intergenerational ties to family and land, with emphasis on relations between parents, particularly fathers, and children.

Ties to family and farming form a system of interlocking social domains. As noted, farming is a family endeavor in the Midwest, and farm families are distinguished by stronger ties between parents (particularly fathers) and children compared to families who are not farming. Sons in farm families are more likely than other boys to work with fathers and to enjoy their company in youth groups, such as 4-H and Boy Scouts. Farm boys are generally more identified with their fathers than boys from nonfarm households; girls are also more involved with their fathers in farm families than in other households. Less variable by farming background are the ties of boys and girls to their mothers; farming makes little difference in the realm of mother-and-child relationships.

These strong intergenerational ties make a great deal of sense when farm youth envision a future organized around agriculture—when they aspire to life on a farm. By contrast, ties with father have no relevance to a farm lifestyle among youth who do not live on a farm, owing to the family inheritance of farms. In farming, shared activities with father

This chapter was written in collaboration with Stephen T. Russell.

through work and community activities enable the young to learn the trade and emulate their father's way of managing things. Joint activities of this kind can be thought of as an apprenticeship for farm living. One boy on an Iowa farm noted that work with his father had convinced him that he wanted to farm as well. Such activity can nurture strong family ties and attachments to farming as a way of life.

We assume that the successful development of farm children in the midst of adversity has much to do with intergenerational ties to family and land. It does so through intergenerational continuity that favors the developmental influence of families on children's academic and social competence. Such continuity invites parental investment in successive generations. Farm fathers have much in common with sons and daughters who share their commitment to this life. Mothers in farm families may have more significance, in themselves and in relation to fathers, among children who envision a future outside of agriculture. Young people have less reason to be invested in farming as an occupation and as a way of life today, especially in view of its declining standard of living.

Our point of departure centers on family continuity and change, including boys' and girls' views of farm life in the future and the family ties of youth who are living in different family circumstances relative to farming. We then enquire whether these factors contribute to an understanding of youth's academic and social success. Do family status and ties make more of a difference among youth who prefer a farming lifestyle in the near future?

Family Continuity and Change

Ties to family and future goals have particular relevance and meaning among farm youth within a framework of cultural continuity across the generations. Such continuity is expressed in the beliefs and priorities of families who view farming as a way of life and not primarily as a business. Despite the extraordinary trials of the farm crisis and a declining margin of profit, approximately nine out of ten farmers and wives in the study concluded at the end of the 1980s that they were satisfied with "farming as a way of life."

The collective nature of farm life is a cornerstone of intergenerational continuity. "An interdependence prevails between the farm and the farm families: business decisions are intimately connected with the life course of family members and household management."[1] As one example, children's chores on the farm are frequently carried out with parents. An Iowa boy whose family lost their farm in the 1980s crisis recalled that the "biggest thing" that farm life gave him was "a sense of my family

... a strong bond with my brothers and sisters and my mom and dad. . . . I'd say I have pretty good memories of growing up on a farm."

Families that farm usually have an agricultural tradition that stretches back in time, often over more than three or four generations. The century farm is an especially visible form of this continuity, a transfer of property and land across descending generations. Three out of four of the farmers studied grew up on a farm, and the remainder typically acquired land from the wife's family. In 1991, the median size of a farm was 650 acres, four out of five wives were employed off the farm, and yet most family income was still obtained from farming.

As we have seen in chapter 2, the decline of total family income from farming has made this occupation less appealing as a livelihood to young people who now live on farms. This recoil from the "down" side of farming appears even among agriculture majors at Midwest universities. One survey found deep anger, resentment, and frustration over the "long hours, great risk, and small financial returns involved in farming. They're bitter, and they're not going back."[2] However, the full story of generational succession in farming will not be known until the young reach middle age. Retirement of the father clarifies realities and can lead adult offspring back to the family farm to bring up their children.

In the Iowa Project, very few boys thought well of farming as their future occupation, a sobering development in light of the wisdom that farmers are born, not made (table 3.1). They are typically born and raised in a farm family. Each "new" generation of farmers tends to be drawn from the pool of children of the last generation. Being raised on a farm, then, is as much about learning a future career as it is about growing up.[3] Fewer than 20 percent of the boys from farm families report that they want to farm, regardless of their prospects for this future. The figure is only 5 percent among boys who did not live on a farm. Girls seldom thought about the possibility. Only one girl (from a nonfarm household) claimed that she wanted to be a farmer. These aspirations were reported in the eighth, ninth, and twelfth grades (years 1990, 1991, and 1994).

Why did some farm boys favor farming, while others did not? From prior studies, we know that a future in farming is more common among boys who live on a prosperous farm and who have relatively few brothers.[4] One might also assume that agricultural prosperity during childhood would be a factor. A great many Iowa farm children were exposed to the stresses and perils of farming during the 1980s, and the lessons from this experience clearly discouraged some from wanting to make a living by farming. A large number want the lifestyle of a farm, but not the economic stresses of the occupational role. Consistent with notions

Table 3.1

Adolescents' Views of a Rural Future—To Farm and/or Live on a Farm

Farm Status by Gender	N	Aspirations	
		To Farm[a] (1989–92) %	Live on a Farm[b] (1990, 1991, 1994) %
Boys	196	8.2	51.0
Farm (full, part-time)	53	17.0	67.9
Nonfarm (displaced, farm-reared, nonfarm)	143	4.9	44.8
Girls	228	0.4	38.6
Farm	57	0.0	54.3
Nonfarm	171	0.4	33.3

[a] In the first four years of the study, youth were asked to choose a desired future occupation. If the youth chose being a farmer at least two of the four years, he (or she, in one case) was classified as wanting to be a farmer.

[b] In grades 8, 9, and 12 (1990, 1991, and 1994), youth were asked how important it was to them to live on a farm (5 = very important). They were considered to have a farm preference if they scored "somewhat important" or higher in 1990, 1991, or (not and) 1994.

of selective migration,[5] boys who do not want to farm tend to rank higher on achievement test scores in the seventh grade.

Though most farm boys do not want to farm themselves, this does not mean that they intend to leave rural life behind and pursue their futures in urban settings. Even though economic conditions are leading them to other occupations, half of the boys and over a third of the girls report that they want "to live on a farm" when they settle down. This gender difference reflects the greater agricultural opportunities for boys. It may also reflect the mate-selection opportunities for young women in the city or on a college campus.

Contrasts between the farm as a place of work and as a place to live are noted by the son of a successful farmer. "I've kind of steered away from . . . just coming home and farming outright. I think I'd like to live on a farm and maybe do some livestock farming but yet have a . . . job on the side other than having the main source of income [be] the farm." He came to this view from observing the emotion-draining financial struggles of his parents across the 1980s and 1990s. In his view, the farm was definitely not a good place in which to make a living.

A majority of youth from full-time and part-time farm households desire to live on a farm in the future (see figure 3.1). This is a popular option even among youth who do not live on a farm, and it does not vary according to the farm background of their parents. Through a variety of experiences, these young people have come to know the farm as a good place in which to bring up a family. For example, a son of parents who grew up on a farm claims he values the shared work experiences of farm parents and children. He also thinks farm life "makes you want to achieve more of your goals." Firsthand exposure to farm life, as among displaced farm families, produced the strongest preference for living on a farm among youth in nonfarm households. Over half (53 percent) still want to settle on a farm. A girl with this life history felt that it was important to raise her "family in the country." Others noted the close-ness of family life and the experience of working together for something of value.

This value of "working together" was expressed most often by farm youth. When asked about the benefits of growing up on a farm, the son of a farmer who actually plans to farm emphasized his sense of responsibility: "I've done chores all my life. . . . I get up every morning, and I come home at night, and I do my chores. . . . I've got my own chores to do, plus I help Dad. It's helped me develop responsibility, patience." The boy's productive role in farm operations and his shared work with father gave him a sense of significance, a belief in himself as a person who matters and has a purpose in life. Productive roles are considered more fully in chapter 4. Here we take a brief look at work with parents, which, for some farm boys, represents an apprenticeship, a time of prep-aration for the day they will move into the family business.

Not surprisingly, boys spend more time working with their fathers than do girls (figure 3.2). When asked if there are advantages to growing up on a farm, a boy cited the things he learned from his father. "I'm a

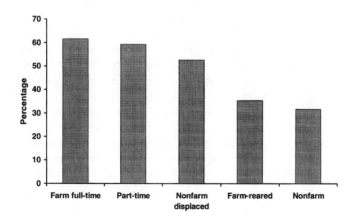

Figure 3.1 Percentage of Iowa Youth (Grades 8, 9, and 12) Who Want to Live on a Farm by Family's Relation to Agriculture

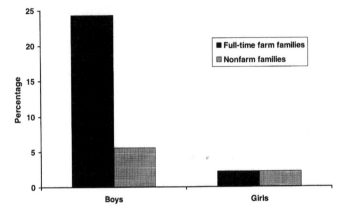

Figure 3.2 Percentage of Youth (Grade 10) Who Spend Half or More of Their Work Time with Their Fathers by Farm Status of Family

lot more mechanical than most of my friends because of things I learned from my Dad, and you know, I just help. I think I work a lot more and work harder, probably." Beyond responsibility and a work ethic, other farm youth contrast farm labor and its "required helpfulness" with the absence of this incentive in urban families. One boy from a large livestock farm noted that in the city "it's just a matter of getting up, cleaning up the room. On a farm, you have to get up, get outside, and do something . . . out in the field. That's where you learn hard work and labor." Another farm boy made the same comparison. "I learned more what work is all about than my friends who live in the city."

Joint activities between the generations also extend to community events and organizations among farm youth and their households (figure 3.3). Farm parents set an example of this involvement, and they also run the transportation system (the family car) that initially enables farm youth to get involved in civic organizations and activities. Farm parents have to do a "lot of running" between home and school, as one mother put it. We asked how often the adolescents participated in youth-group activities with each parent, such as 4-H, FFA, and Scouts. Youth on farms participate with fathers more often than those who do not live on farms, and boys who participate are more involved than girls.

Farm boys are most active with fathers, both at work and in the community. By contrast, activity with mothers does not vary by farm status, and neither boys nor girls were likely to report shared work with them, though most acknowledged at least an occasional joint activity in community organizations. This gender contrast reflects the prominent role of father in farm family life, and differs strikingly from one portrait of urban fathers—men who are absent, ineffective, or uninvolved. Farm fathers typically play a central role in the social development of their sons, and we suspect that this is most true when boys want to follow in their father's footsteps.

Joint activities in work and community represent a potentially influential form of social capital in human development. They are also basic to the proximal processes, the "engines of development," in Urie Bronfenbrenner's terminology.[6] In a proximal process that matters, children engage in an activity with significant others or with symbols and tasks; but the activity must take place on a regular, recurring basis to enable it to become more complex over time. Within the family, joint activities in work provide children with the emotional and skill resources that are likely to enhance such development in academics and social life. Beyond the immediate family, joint civic engagements establish access to social opportunities with peers and adults for young people.

Joint parent-youth activities make a difference in children's ties to the land and family, and they are particularly relevant for sons when they involve work with fathers. Both work time with fathers and time spent with them in a community youth group tend to enhance the ties of young people to a rural way of life (appendix table E3.1). These ties also provide more time with father in situations of mutual influence. Nearly one-fourth of the boys who spend work time with their fathers want to be farmers, as compared to only 6 percent of the other boys. The findings are most dramatic if we look only at farm boys, where the option is more realistic and meaningful. Over 40 percent of those who worked with fa-

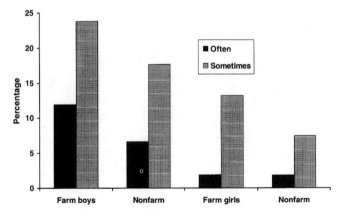

Figure 3.3 Percentage of Youth (Grade 9) Engaged in Group Activities with Father. Note: Activities include, e.g., 4-H and Scouting. Farm group includes full- and part-time farm families; nonfarm includes all others

thers want to be farmers, compared to fewer than 5 percent of the other boys. Shared work is an influential form of socialization into farming. In like manner, farming is desired more by boys who spend substantial time with their fathers in youth-group activities. And, again, this is particularly true for boys from farming families (20 percent).

In the farming community, work time with father is coupled with the desire to live on a farm, to identify with father, and to perceive his warmth. Among girls as well as boys, work with father is coupled with aspirations for settling on a farm. Indeed, virtually all of these workers (92 percent) hold this view, in contrast to little more than half of those who do not want to live on farms. Shared work might be required by the circumstances and prompt hard feelings or resistance, but we find just the opposite tendency. Work with father is linked to identification with him and to perceptions of his warmth.

"Working with Dad" on the farm represents a family apprenticeship for young boys in agriculture. Looking back on such experience, a twelfth-grade boy noted that "something related to agriculture" is what he will probably do "because I know a lot about it. Dad taught me everything he knows, which is quite a bit, and it will probably affect me for the rest of my life." The rewards involve getting "to work with the animals and getting to work with my Dad. It is kinda neat picking out a hog when it was a baby and watching it grow and finally selling it." He thought he might "get more respect" because he's second in command out here, "even over Mom, because I know how to do a lot more things outside than she does."

The experience of joint social activity with father also appears among youth who favor life on a farm and report strong ties to him. Reports of this activity were obtained for only one year (1991), but there is good reason to assume that shared activity and ties to father and agriculture are mutually reinforcing lines of action. Shared activity can strengthen such ties and be reinforced by them. Adolescents with close ties to their fathers would choose to do things with them, and this would strengthen the father-child bond. Since joint work and social activities have the same correlates in future aspirations and ties to father, we tried to combine them in a single index, but without success. Their correlation is virtually zero. They are clearly not tapping a general form of association, though both contribute to our understanding of the father-child bond and life plans.

All of these patterns involve activities with a father who is central to farming, along with the emotional sentiments of this relationship. By contrast, relations with mother tend to generalize across types of farming. There are few differences between farm and nonfarm families in the degree to which youth identify with and perceive warmth and support from their mothers. Most report moderate levels of identification and high levels of perceived warmth. These patterns apply to both boys and girls.

The connection between ties to father and agriculture is most vividly expressed when we take current status on a farm and the preference for life on a farm into account (figure 3.4). The strongest ties to father in the sample of farm and nonfarm adolescents appear among farm youth who envision living on a farm during their adult years. Their future is consistent with residence on a farm, and fathers are bound to play a key role in establishing a bridge between this present and future. Joint work and social activity with father favor such a bridge and maximize their shared experience. As one farm boy put it, "I'm sure Dad wouldn't like it as much if I wasn't interested in farming. He likes that I'm out there working and I help him and stuff because that's his thing."

Neither farm status nor farm aspirations are relevant to the father relations of youth from nonfarm households. This group occupies the middle ground, neither close nor distant. By comparison, farm youth who seek a different future have the weakest ties with father. These young people have little in common with their fathers, either in shared activities or in interests. But their desire for a life outside of farming may also convey something more than lack of shared experience. It may be seen by fathers as rejection of a cherished way of life that has been part of the family for generations.

The farm fathers of youth who embrace different futures hold remark-

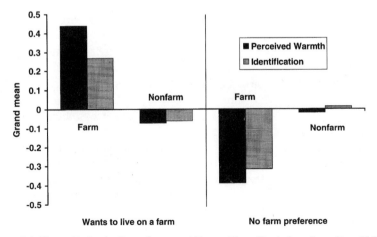

Figure 3.4 Ties to Father by Farm Status and Future Plans, Deviations from Grand Mean

ably similar views of farming. After the farm crisis (1991), we asked men and their wives about farming as a way of life, as a means of earning a living, and as an occupation they would prefer to leave. Men with farm-oriented sons were most satisfied with farming as a way of life, followed by its value as a way to make a living and the desire to leave farming if the opportunity were available. The only group difference involved satisfaction with farming as a way of life. Men with farm-oriented children were more satisfied than were other fathers ($p < .05$). This picture changes, however, when we turn to the wives' attitudes and their discontent, a disenchantment observed in the early twentieth century as "the woman problem on the farm."

As one midwesterner put it, "My mother wanted my father to leave the farm and move to a college town where the children would have 'a better chance.' "[7] Nearly eighty years later in north central Iowa, a wife voiced the same sentiment when she expressed dismay over her husband's lasting attachment to the South Dakota farm that was lost in the 1980s.[8] "The farm still influences us today because you don't like it here and want to go back. Yet we left there to have a better life. It is hard for the kids and me because we don't understand why you want to go back." A better life for children, both as living standard and future, stands out prominently in women's contemporary disenchantment with Iowa farming, but their concerns also extend to the hard life, long hours, and inadequate economic returns for everyone in the family.

Farm mothers of children who did not want to live on a farm were much less satisfied with farming than those with farm-oriented children.[9] This appears in their evaluation of farming as a way of life and as a way to make a living. They were more likely than husbands to express some disenchantment with farming. Indeed, their attitudes were significantly more negative than the attitudes of their husbands. By contrast, none of the spouse differences were statistically significant among parents of farm-oriented youth. Only a fourth of the women in the latter group said that they would leave farming if they could, compared to half of those with children who want a different life. The social and economic discontent of mothers clearly represents a noteworthy influence on the goals of rural farm girls and boys.

But even with attitudes and economic conditions favoring a life beyond farming, it is important to note that a good many farm youth remain on good terms with their fathers. In some cases, disinterest in farming centers on a realization that he or she is "really not an outdoors farm-type person," as noted by the son of a prosperous farmer. He expressed special pleasure over helping out his parents in harvest season and claimed he got along well with his father and respected him for what he does, but he had no interest in farming.

With these attitude variations in mind, one might expect to find differences in value orientation and in shared values across the generations. Among farm youth, the intention to live on a farm is likely to be coupled with more agrarian values compared to other life plans. To put these comparisons to a test, we focused on five "values" that were presented to mother, father, and adolescent (1992): having a job that pays well, a college education, being a community leader, devaluing money as a life goal, and being a religious person. In chapter 2, we found that farm youth were most likely to embrace the last three values. Each question was rated on a five-point scale. We first calculated the average rating for each group (farm preference or not) and then a measure of intergenerational agreement—a correlation coefficient.

The first two values represent a general value orientation regarding life achievement that extends across farm-nonfarm cultures, and indeed we found no difference between the two groups on parent and adolescent scores. However, the groups differed as expected on the other three values. Farm-oriented youth ranked themselves significantly higher on being a community leader and a religious person than did adolescents who favored a different future. They also placed themselves lower on "money" as a core value. All of these differences are statistically significant at the .05 level and reflect parental values to some extent. Value agreement between the generations is more common in farm-oriented households,[10] but the differences are small.

Among youth who live on farms, boys and girls have much stronger ties to father when they want to live on a farm than when they prefer a different lifestyle (figure 3.5). Deviations from the grand mean on ties

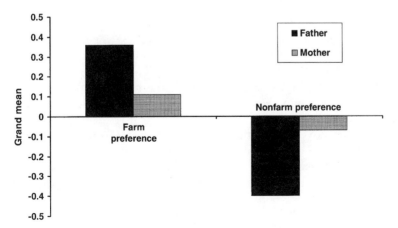

Figure 3.5 Ties to Father and Mother among Farm Youth by Future Plans, Deviations from the Grand Mean

to father vary significantly by the desire to eventually settle on a farm. There is no gender difference. By contrast, this desire is unrelated to the strength of ties to mother among girls and boys. The deviations hover around the grand mean.

The modest differential status of mothers on the two pathways of farm youth corresponds with their relative educational advantage in marriage. Mother tends to have more education than father among farm adolescents who seek a future outside of farming compared to the parents of farm-oriented boys and girls. In motivation and resources, then, these contrasts reveal meaningful sources of intergenerational continuity and change. They also tend to conform to the known sources of extreme social mobility and social stability among the young. Postwar studies of extreme upward mobility generally identify mother as the distinctive influence.[11]

Up to this point, aspirations for life on a farm or in other places have been viewed in terms of a single perspective across the adolescent years. What can we learn about the family and perceptual changes that occur as residential aspirations change? We know that the goal of living on a farm declines from the eighth to the eleventh grade (45 to 30 percent). What developmental experiences might account for such change? Three experiences come to mind. First, the goal might lose meaning through an increasingly troubled relationship with parents. The decision to live on a farm is based on positive social ties with parents. Second, school achievement tends to acquire more significance for future life prospects during the high school years. Thus, academically successful youth may find the prospect of life on a farm less desirable. Third, awareness of a dismal job market in the local community is likely to increase with age and breadth of knowledge.

A series of multivariate explorations provide considerable support for these explanations.[12] First, an increasing awareness of poor job prospects clearly has a dampening effect on aspirations for life on a farm. By the end of high school, more youth are aware of the very few good jobs in the local community. This growing awareness makes farm living impractical to a good many. Second, declining relations with father and even mother over the adolescent years make a local residence near parents far less attractive. Third, the desire to live away from home tends to gain importance among the brighter, more accomplished youth as they approach the end of high school. Individual development along with awareness of local conditions and family changes combine to produce the trends we have noted.

We find that each pathway among farm youth is resourceful in distinctive ways, when compared to the situation of nonfarm youth. Father stands out in the lives of farm youth who want to live on a farm, and we find that kin figure prominently as well. We asked if they had relatives or other adults that they could talk to about problems and worries. Among farm youth, approximately three out of four of those who want to live on farms claimed that they had a relative that they could talk to about their problems, compared to only half of those who want to live elsewhere. The latter, by contrast, are more likely to report that teachers are important as advisors.

Mothers, teachers, and possibly college-going friends make up the distinctive social world of farm youth who plan to leave home for a more distant realm of education and work. Fathers and relatives, who may include the father's brothers in farming and grandparents, are more prominent in the lives of farm youth who plan to live on farms. Do these variations matter for their academic and social accomplishments? What does the centrality of teachers and a greater distance from relatives tell us about youth who plan to leave the region? We approach such questions by asking whether the meaning of success varies across such pathways.

Pathways to Success in High School

Farm youth who plan to make their lives on farms and those who intend to leave home and community follow paths that have different implications for success in high school. The decision to leave home for college or work links opportunities to a solid, if undistinguished, record of accomplishment in academics and social leadership. Future possibilities depend on a record of achievement. A productive life in modern agriculture also calls for such credentials, especially when college is involved. Young people from farming families are more committed to service as community leaders than youth who plan to leave home, and they are less invested in money as a goal in life. Ideals of this kind may be expressed in social status among classmates and in academic success.

Nonfarm youth who plan to follow their parents in pursuing a future out of agriculture may well resemble the "farm leavers" in school achievements of all kinds. A bright future in general depends on doing well in schoolwork and student activities. Whether desired or not, a life in farming is unrealistic for boys whose parents are not farmers, and we have found very few such youth who want this kind of future. Far more common is the desire to live on a farm and work elsewhere, perhaps in an urban setting. Family life on a farm is much desired by Iowa youth who have any connection to the land, but this desire may represent a less competitive and stressful life-goal for town or village youth.

Consider two behavioral dimensions of success, academic and peer prominence, along with feelings of self-confidence and the maturity recognition of being asked by parents for advice—what we call "advice-seeking." Our general index of academic competence for the twelfth grade includes three components: grade point average reported by child and mother, the child's sense of academic accomplishment, and the child's academic achievement in the eyes of mother and teacher. The scores for each component were standardized and averaged. We use the general index since our results did not vary across the components.

Peer success or prominence is indexed by a summation of three items from teachers on popularity and acceptance during the twelfth grade. Youth self-confidence in the twelfth grade is measured by an average of scores for self-esteem and mastery. Last, advice-seeking by parents provides an index of the perceived social maturity of the adolescent. We use only the measure for father because he is most central to issues of farming and family continuity.

Studies consistently indicate that girls out-perform boys in school, while boys tend to score higher on self-confidence than girls.[13] This gender difference may be especially large among youth who seek to leave the farm. Also, we expect fathers to be more active in seeking advice from sons than from daughters, particularly in a rural setting in which farm life and its family economy is tied to the father-son relationship. Across the four pathways, father's advice-seeking should be most common among farm-oriented boys who live on farms. Appendix table E3.2 shows the mean scores for the four subgroups and gender, with statistical adjustments for parents' education, residential change, and family income level.

Four themes emerge from the pattern of group means across the pathways. First, farm youth rank well above their nonfarm counterparts on academic and peer success. These achievements are especially noteworthy among youth who plan to settle elsewhere. Success in making a good life depends on a record of accomplishment. By contrast, academic and peer success is least characteristic of *nonfarm* youth who want to settle down on a farm, especially boys. They don't want to work the farm, only to enjoy its lifestyle.

In many respects, these young people resemble the "people left behind" in a fast-changing society; they are least able to compete in a world of high technology and demanding skill requirements. Out-migration streams typically select the most able sectors of the young adult population in a declining region. These are the achievers in our sample, boys and girls who are seeking their fortunes away from home. They will leave behind both able youth in agriculture and another group that may lack the skills and motivation to compete effectively in urban labor markets.

A second theme centers on gender differences in success. As many studies have shown, girls rank consistently higher than boys on academic competence. This advantage applies to farm youth who want to live on a farm, but it is greatest for those who plan to live elsewhere. The daughter of parents who lost their farm during the Great Farm Crisis of the 1980s noted that she is "real determined to get away from the farm. I'm going to go to college. . . . I'm moving . . . to a larger city right afterwards. (The farm loss) just made me more determined to do well in school." In recorded commentary on high school life, we find that "building a record of achievement" was on the minds of most youth, but especially girls, who looked to college and urban employment for a path out of rural America.

These gender differences are expressed with regard to peer success as well. Farm girls who want to leave the farm rank very high on peer success, significantly higher than boys who also have this plan. This activity mirrors the traditional civic leadership and involvement of farm parents. Finding the right mate could also be part of this life story. College-bound girls undoubtedly looked forward to meeting new people on their future campus. Girls were also less likely than boys to be "unsuccessful" in academics among nonfarm youth who aspired to life on a farm. This difference partly reflects their greater opportunity. Unlike boys, they could enter farming through marriage to the son of a local farmer.

A third observation involves self-confidence. Though farm youth are most accomplished in high school, they appear less sure or confident of themselves than adolescents from nonfarm families and communities. The differences are consistent, though modest in size, and bring to mind the costs of achievement demands. By and large, farm youth who plan to live on a farm have done well in school work and peer popularity, but they do not match the self-confidence of youth who plan to leave the farm or of nonfarm adolescents generally. The difference may reflect pressures to achieve as well as lack of exposure to the world beyond home, church, and local community. If less knowledgeable of this larger world, they may feel less assured of their chances.

The fourth conclusion centers on fathers who acknowledge the social maturity and wisdom of their teenage children by seeking their advice. In this last theme, fathers were most likely to seek the advice of sons and daughters who were following a path that matched their own. They had more in common. The pathways are defined by farm youth who want to live on a farm, and by nonfarm adolescents who seek a nonagricultural route. In both cases, fathers were just as likely to turn to daughters as to sons.

Among farm boys who plan to leave the world of farming, fathers remain highly responsive in terms of advice-seeking, despite relatively weak emotional ties. The boys do not view their fathers as people they would like to become, and they are least likely to see them as warm and empathic. The emotional bond is relatively weak. Nevertheless, these fathers are perceived by sons as recognizing their maturity by seeking their advice. Daughters who aspire to a less traditional (nonfarm) path do not perceive this support. In fact, they place father lowest as "a significant other"—in terms of identification with him, perception of his emotional warmth, and of his seeking their advice. This is the only group in the sample where gender differences are large and statistically significant. A good many fathers on farms appear to have little in common with their daughters.

Goals that define each pathway determine partly the meaning of family relations, such as emotional ties to father, and the significance of school accomplishments. High grades and peer recognition are consistent with the ambitions of farm youth who intend to find their way in the world beyond farm and local community. Success and failure in school also determine the salience of certain options, such as the attractiveness of life on a farm for youth who are not doing well in classroom and peer group.

Goals and Their Meanings

Let us turn now to a broader consideration of the meanings associated with farm and city ambitions. Does preference for life on a farm in adulthood diminish academic influences compared to the goal of leaving home and community? Relevant influences on ties to family and land include the ecologies of farming (farm, displaced, etc.), relations with father, joint work and social activities with father, and parenting styles, such as inconsistent or harsh discipline. Parental education, family income, and residential moves or change are included as established influences on children's competence. Parental education and income index achievement models and resources, whereas residential change weakens the social integration and support of families and children. The disruption of social ties "brought on by a family move is associated with negative life outcomes that extend into early adulthood," according to a recent panel study.[14] Our family lens is focused on father because of the distinctive nature of the father-child relationship in farm families and its link to the perpetuation of this way of life across the generations.

To assess the influence of each rural ecology, we used nonfarm families as a reference category for all other ecologies—for farm families (full and part-time), displaced families, and the farm-reared,that is, parents who grew up on farms but never farmed (appendix table E3.3). The nonfarm families are headed by parents who have never farmed and did not grow up on farms. By using these families as a contrast group, we are able to determine whether an ecology's effect is the result of its proximity to full-time farming. Though some families changed status across the six years of the study, we classified each one in terms of our best judgment about its status over this time.

Parental education combines the education of husband and wife. Family income level was averaged across four years, using 1988 dollars (1989, 1990, 1991, and 1992). Paternal identification/warmth represents an average of these two scales for 1991–92. Our measure of inconsistent parenting provides an index of erratic discipline. An index of harsh punitive parenting was not included in the analysis because it is too highly correlated with paternal warmth. The analysis also includes time spent working with father and youth activities with father.

We begin with academic competence, then take up peer success, and conclude with self-confidence and father's efforts to seek advice from his teenage son or daughter. Overall, family influences tend to be stronger among youth who aspire to life on a farm, but the differences are not reliable for the most part. The set of influences matters most for academic success and least for self-confidence, with peer success and father's advice seeking in between.

Youth with at least some connections to the land through their families are doing better at the end of high school on academic success than other adolescents; this is least true of the displaced—the children of parents who experienced the distress of losing a family farm (see column 2, appendix table E3.3). The loss often involved wrenching changes in family residence and school, and for many the event continues to reverberate as a source of distress and hardship up to the present. Considering these changes, it is especially noteworthy that children from displaced families are actually doing better academically at the end of high school than the children of nonfarm households.

Farm origin matters even when it only appears in the lives of farm-reared parents who are now living in small towns. Their children are doing better in school than the children of parents who have never known farm life, regardless of education, income, and residential change. The discipline and values of farm life may be part of their socialization. A capacity for hard work is another legacy that may be expressed in these results. All categories of farm culture are most consequential for the academic achievement of youth who want to live on a farm, as one might expect. However, the difference in this small sample is not large enough to be statistically reliable.

The capacity to work hard is a recurring self-observation among youth who have grown up on a farm or who have parents with this background. This account frequently came up when we asked all study members what they learned from their jobs and chores. A farm boy who raises cattle referred to his work ethic: "I'm hard-working and motivated, self-motivated to do chores and everything." Another boy whose parents grew up on a farm noted that after he has put in a hard day's work (as a car mechanic), he can "relax and feel good, not sit there and [feel] I'm never gonna do anything with my life. Well, now I know I can do something with my life. Not afraid to work."

Educated parents, a reasonable level of economic well-being, residential stability, and parental consistency also play important roles. But what *fails to make a difference*, surprisingly, is the involvement of fathers in the lives of their children. Youth who report working with father and sharing social activities are not more successful in school. Likewise, positive emotional ties to father contribute little to academic success. However, the influence of farm background and relations with father are most potent when youth expect to settle on a farm. This is the cultural ideal in farming communities.

Rural farm ecologies are a positive force in social popularity, and this is especially true when youth prefer to settle on a farm, although the difference is not statistically significant. Unlike academic success, parental education and male status are generally less consequential for social success in school than the ecologies of farming, displacement, and farm-rearing. Social success is more common among youth who have strong ties to father (beta = .12, $p < .05$), but no other family activity matters, including inconsistent parenting and joint activity with father.

The self-confidence of youth and the value of their advice to their fathers have much to do with the quality of relations to their fathers (see appendix table E3.4). For both girls and boys, strong ties to father and consistent parenting are predictive of self-confidence at the end of high school (beta = .25, $p < .01$; and .13, $p < .05$, respectively). Joint activities with father are not relevant, however, as was the case for academic and social success. All of these findings were obtained with parental education, income, and residential change controlled.

Youth were more likely to feel self-confident if they came from residentially stable homes and had educated parents ($p < .05$). Though girls generally report lower levels of self-confidence than boys, we find this to be true mainly for youth who are headed for an urban future. By contrast, farm girls and boys who plan to live on a farm reveal no difference in self-confidence.

How do we explain this result? Farm experiences may be a factor. One girl from a farm family felt she had become more independent than her friends through her experiences on the farm. "In some ways I'm more independent. A little bit more mature I think. I'm not real sure if that has to do with being on a farm, however." Another farm girl felt that the experience enabled her to "understand life more. It's made me appreciate it. You have to work for what you want, . . . on the farm you have to do a lot of work. And it's made me respect my parents." The girls' self-confidence is apparent in the way that they view the importance of having grown up on a farm.

In the case of recognition by father as being worthy of giving advice, the significant influences are limited to strong ties to father (beta = .46, $p < .001$), residential change ($-.14$, $p < .01$), and male gender (.09, $p < .10$). One might assume that youth who do more with their fathers, in work and social activities, would have more occasions in which to offer advice, but we find no such effect. Joint activities may, of course, vary greatly in the accompanying *quality* of relations between father and child, and this factor seems to be essential for understanding developmental outcomes. It is also clear that the meaning of joint activities with father has much to do with youth's plans. Time spent with father on work has apprenticeship value for boys who plan to farm, but it may be actually detrimental to the academic and social success of adolescents who intend to leave the farm and hometown.

Goals of future residence and work clearly matter in terms of the relative success of Iowa youth on school achievement and relations with classmates at the end of high school. The desire to live on a farm applies to competent farm youth and to the least able from nonfarm families and communities. A preference to live elsewhere describes the most achievement-oriented boys and girls who have grown up on farms, and to a lesser extent the sons and daughters of nonfarm parents. Each of these goals identifies different future pathways to adulthood. They differ in terms of significant parents and adults and in terms of shared values.

Despite such meaningful differences, family influences have basically the same effect on academic and social success across the different paths. Family ecologies and processes (family relations, parenting) matter for the high school academic and peer success of these young people. Of special relevance are the culture of farming, parental education, and family stability, and to a lesser extent strong ties to father. Only the latter is a major predictor of self-confidence and father's advice-seeking.

In all analyses up to this point, we have explored father's influence at the end of high school. Relations with father and academic success represent a plausible sequence of mutual influences from early childhood until the completion of school. Academic success could elicit praise and encouragement from a nurturant father, which in turn would reinforce the son's or daughter's identification with him. Supportive relations with father would promote greater effort by the child in schoolwork, establishing conditions that favor more paternal encouragement. To put this dynamic to a test, we constructed identical measures of ties to father and grades for each grade level, from 8 through 10 and then 12. Using a hierarchical linear model, we investigated the relationship between grades and ties to father with a number of covariates, such as parental education, farm status, residential moves, and child's gender.

Across all trials, we found no reliable evidence of a developmental, interactive relationship between grades and positive ties to father. This may be so in part because relations with father have different meanings for youth who are growing up on farms. Boys who plan to live on a farm feel relatively close to their fathers, but they are not doing as well academically as boys who plan to leave home for other destinations. In fact, their future in managing the family farm does not require high academic achievement if college is not part of the picture.

Developmental Risks and Success

Behavioral continuity from childhood and early adolescence to the adult years has drawn much attention in recent years. In theory, good homes operate to the advantage of these youth, while family disadvantages are reproduced in the lives of other children. But even in the bleakest circumstances, some children from disadvantaged families manage to rise above the limitations of their high-risk environment. In theory, they do so in part with the help of protective factors that minimize the adverse influence of risks. Norman Garmezy concludes that "comparatively little is known about persons who escape those too frequent cycles of disadvantage."[15] We describe "doing better" than expected as a trajectory of resilience. Doing "worse" than expected, on the other hand, entails greater potential exposure to developmental risks, such as deviant peers and the abuse of alcohol, drugs, and sex. This trajectory involves increasing vulnerability.[16]

We have not observed a developmental impact of family relationships that is linked to youth's ties to the land and residential plans, particularly ties with father. Family relations as measured here have little to do with their academic and social achievements in high school. The principal effects involve self-confidence, but the quality of relationships may be most consequential for youth who are doing "better" or "worse" than one would expect, given particular family circumstances.

We estimated the effect of these circumstances during early adolescence on measures of successful development in the twelfth grade (presented in appendix B). Relevant background factors included parental education; family income; family debt-to-asset ratio; residential moves; unstable work; family and parenting resources, such as parental depression, marital hostility, and inconsistent and harsh parenting; and the youths' intellectual ability as indexed by the Iowa Test of Basic Skills.

Using the results of these regression analyses and their residual scores, we formed groups of resilient and vulnerable youth on each developmental outcome. Resilient youth were defined as adolescents who ended up above the seventy-fifth percentile on residual scores, while vulnerable youth were identified below the twenty-fifth percentile. Resilient youth did better on academic competence than one would expect in terms of personal and social background, whereas vulnerable youth did much worse than expected. In a series of logistic regression analyses, we estimated the odds of youth with particular attributes (such as strong ties to father) doing better than expected or doing worse. Factors with coefficients of 1.0 or higher indicate a higher likelihood of being in the resilient or vulnerable group as scores increase. Coefficients with values below 1.0 identify factors that lessen the chances of being in the vulnerable category or in the resilient group.

Consider first the overall classification of resilient and vulnerable youth. Using our four measures of prosocial competence, we assigned an adolescent to the resilient group if judged resilient on three or four of the outcomes. We followed the same procedure on vulnerable youth. For both resilient and vulnerable status, the logistic regressions estimated the effect of gender, residential preference, paternal identification-warmth, time spent working with father, and youth activities with father. Strong ties to father are a significant factor in the overall resilience of Iowa youth (2.14, $p < .01$), and they also play an important protective role in reducing the chances of vulnerability (.63, $p < .05$) (figure 3.6).

Resilient youth follow a course of increasingly stronger ties to father from the eighth to the twelfth grade, as indexed by their identification, while vulnerable adolescents show greater antipathy toward father over this time period (figure 3.7). The "identification" gap between these groups expands substantially over the adolescent years.

Unlike our prior analysis, identification with father and the perceived warmth of father emerge as notable influences for youth who are doing better and worse than expected in terms of personal and social background. No other factor is worth noting, except that work time with fa-

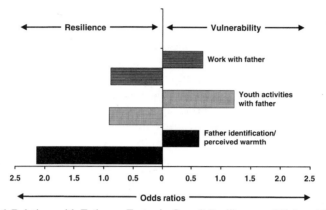

Figure 3.6 Relations with Father as Factor in Overall Resilience and Vulnerability of Iowa Boys and Girls

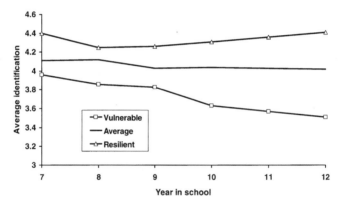

Figure 3.7 Trajectories of Paternal Identification among Resilient and Vulnerable Youth: Mean Scores

ther may produce greater vulnerability. It is not statistically significant, but this outcome is worth noting among youth who are not going into the world of farming. Without this future, joint work is not an apprenticeship.

This developmental cost appears more clearly when we turn to specific outcomes (appendix table E3.5), such as academic and social success. On both modes of success, joint work with father increases the likelihood of vulnerability ($p < .10$). Excessive time devoted to work with father might be a factor here as well as a pattern of accelerated entry into the world of work, whether coupled with dependence on parents or not.

Involvement of this kind would necessarily diminish investments in schoolwork and student social life. Since shared social activities with father do not have an adverse effect (or a positive effect) on youth, the issue appears to be rooted in the work experience itself.

Emotional ties with father turn out to be the most important source of resilience and vulnerability relative to self-confidence and the advice-seeking efforts of father. Youth who are doing better than expected are distinguished by strong ties to father, while those doing worse tend to have weak ties. These findings are consistent with the importance of strong ties to father for feelings of worth and mastery, and for affirming relations with father. However, joint work with father appears not to be a positive influence, overall, on the competence of boys and girls.

Clearly, the quality of relations with father have important consequences for Iowa youth who find themselves doing better or worse than expected late in high school, compared to family origins and circumstances. Thus, boys and girls whose self-confidence exceeds expectations based on their background tend to have supportive, caring fathers in their lives. Not having such a person significantly increased the likelihood of a vulnerable self, of personal insecurity, and low self-esteem.

In this rural society, why are risks linked to involvement with father on work projects, a risk expressed through diminished success in academic achievement and relations with peers? This is so even though positive relations with father are coupled with such activity. Possibly joint work with father on farms turns youth away from the social world of adolescence to the incentives of adult work. Just as realistic work among boys in the 1930s oriented them toward work at an early age,[17] joint work with father may have a comparable effect on farms. Do youth with such experience enter full-time work roles at an early age? This outcome will be known in detail as we follow their lives into adulthood.

Conclusion

In north central Iowa, youth's changing ties to family and land are recasting their lives in notable ways. One change involves the declining profitability of farming and the continuing movement of families out of agriculture and rural areas. This includes the displacement of households during the 1980s and the increasing amount of off-farm employment by parents. Changes of this kind and growing economic inequality in rural America have fueled a second development that is intergenerational in nature: the declining appeal of farming and a farm lifestyle among the younger generation. However, as noted, this appeal may be enhanced when youth leave school for work and family.

Both changes diminish the significance of father to children, and his role in fostering their competence through the adolescent years. Strong ties to father among boys and girls are consistent with productive farm operations and with a future life on a farm. Adolescents in farm families who want this lifestyle are more identified with father and perceive warmer relations with him than do youth in other households. They are also more involved with their fathers in joint activities, including work projects and civic organizations, especially the boys.

This family pattern applies mainly to the experience of farm youth who wish to settle on a farm. The salience or attractiveness of father is greatest among these youth, along with the mentoring role of relatives, and both parents share a commitment to the farming way of life. Farm adolescents who seek their future away from family and community tend to find their mothers especially important, along with other adults such as teachers. These mothers are generally better educated than their spouses, and they are more dissatisfied with farming and its hardships than other women. Youth in this group have stronger ties to mother than to father, who symbolizes the world they are leaving. Nonfarm adolescents are neither as close to their fathers as farm-oriented youth, nor as distant as farm youth who plan to make their lives in urban America.

Each of these projected routes to adulthood has developmental implications. By the end of high school, farm-based adolescents fare better than other youth on academic achievement and social success with peers. Consistent with selective outmigration, however, achievements are greatest when youth are headed away from home to employment or more education. Such youth are more talented, but they also need a stronger record for entry into college and labor markets. This statement applies as well to nonfarm adolescents. Those who choose to live on a farm are least accomplished on school achievement and success with peers. Important influences on success generalize across these diverse pathways.

The academic and social success of youth have more to do with the socioeconomic resources of families than with their social relations, as we have explored them. Well-educated parents, adequate income, and a stable residential history prove to be important factors. However, strong ties to father and his involvement in joint activities made little difference, positive or negative, except through aspirations to live on a farm and their association with lower academic achievement. By contrast, high-quality relations with father are a major influence on feelings of self-confidence and on father's willingness to request advice from his children, an action that affirms their maturity. The education and income of parents did not have consequences for these behaviors.

Not all youth prosper, as one might assume, or match common expectations. Some do better than expected, based on family origins, while others do worse. Family relations enabled us to take one step forward in understanding why children end up on these different pathways. Using residuals from a series of prediction equations, we identified resilient and vulnerable youth for all developmental outcomes. Strong emotional ties to father proved to be an important predictor of resilience and vulnerability. The presence of strong ties played a significant role in resilience, while their absence helped to make youth vulnerable. This relationship had particular significance for self-confidence and social maturity.

Many questions remain about the developmental significance of productive activities for Iowa youth. Some jobs involve joint contributions with parents, but virtually all involve some contact with adults. What is it about such work experiences that leads to positive or adverse consequences? We turn to questions of this kind in the next chapter.

CHAPTER FOUR

Always Work to Do

The job comes first, before friends.

Teenage boy, Iowa

"Always work to do" represents a defining theme on family farms; the workday is never done. Children's labor is typically part of a collective effort that benefits the family, and young people derive satisfaction and personal significance from making these contributions. Farm youth generally claim that they have a lot to do, that their families count on them, and that they frequently work for and with parents. Some of this is paid work, as in the sale of managed livestock, and some is unpaid (e.g., household or farm chores). In either case, productive labor involves young people in nonfarm as well as farm settings, though it varies in meaning.

Farm children are brought up to view what they do in terms of their families. They are counted on, and this nurtures a sense of significance.[1] The family suffers if a child does not come through on an assignment or task. By comparison, young people who live off the farm and in small communities are more able to make individualistic and discretionary choices in work and spending matters, though some also work on farms. In Iowa, rural farm youth are more likely to give a portion of their earnings to family needs and savings than youth in a metropolitan area.[2]

Are experiences of this kind developmental? Are there developmental advantages from productive labor? Observers of family farms believe that children learn enduring disciplines from their labor. For example, there is the belief that "growing up in farming is learning the value of work and money, accepting responsibility as a contributing member of the family business, and sometimes making the first steps toward . . . [a] future career."[3] From productive labor, children learn that they can do hard work and do it well. Other attributes include the

This chapter was written in collaboration with Michael J. Shanahan.

delay of gratification for the achievement of larger goals, clarified priorities, and skills in working with people. These developmental benefits may also stem in large measure from children's labor off the farm, in the countryside, and in small communities.

Chores may not provide the benefits of paid employment, even though some payment is expected in support for college, employment, or in terms of the farm itself. Chores represent responsibilities that are part of family membership, and we shall use this term to refer to work that is not directly coupled with earnings. Some families expect children to clean their rooms and to do their part in the larger household. Among farm families, this expectation generally extends to the farm operation itself, especially through the routines of daily chores, such as feeding animals. As one farmer put it to his sons, "This farm is yours, you know," implying that routines of this kind amount to working for oneself. However, parents remain the decision makers. To the extent that chores place young people in a prolonged dependency role, under the direction of parents, they are less likely to develop a sense of personal efficacy and accomplishment.

Paid work, by contrast, offers more recognition of the transition to self-direction and maturity. On a farm, this income may come from the sale of stock as well as from a weekly salary. The earnings of a young person are likely to signify behavior that is valued by others when a job is well done by meeting or exceeding expectations. Valued behavior includes industry, responsibility, punctuality, careful attention to detail, and emotional control. Service jobs, in particular, place a premium on workers who get along with customers.

Children's earnings thus represent, for parents and the larger community, a tangible index of success in the adult world. Paid work entails "a contractual exchange based on established procedures for monetary compensation, eliminating the personal nature of children's relationships."[4] By depicting children as more mature and responsible, such work calls for less supervision and more involvement in adult decisions.

However, substantial earnings might encourage less investment in the developmental tasks of adolescence, reducing academic motivation and accelerating early claims on adult status through cars and sex, drinking and drugs.[5] Paid work could be pursued as an attractive alternative to academic troubles as young people try to escape failure by investing in jobs that provide income. When this occurs, adolescent work promotes pseudomaturity, the superficial ability to assume adult roles without depth of judgment and character. Instead of developing the skills of adult competence, involvement in paid work may actually postpone or sidetrack maturity.

These negative consequences of adolescent work seem least likely among farm youth who are enmeshed in meaningful relations and incentives; they are needed, and in feeling needed they are connected to the adult culture of rural life. This connection applies to earnings on farms and to the delayed payments for chores, as in college support. A sense of "mattering" to parents is important to adolescents, as they begin to assume adult roles and responsibilities. Rachman's discussion of "required helpfulness" also suggests an important relationship between helpful acts and competence.[6] Successful acts of required helpfulness promote long-term developmental changes in the helper through new skills. Parents who need the assistance of children in the household, owing to work hours and other commitments, may turn chores into maturity demands that enhance practical skills, responsibility, and feelings of belonging.[7]

To address these developmental implications, we turn first to the maturational meanings of productive labor, and then explore the circumstances under which youth are most involved in such work. For example, the household assistance of children seems most likely when labor and time pressures increase—when family size is large and the mother is employed full-time. Economic pressure in the household is a plausible antecedent of children's paid employment, as during the 1930s.[8] Economic hardship and large families prompted youth to assume more chores in the home and obtain paid work in the community. Are economic and time pressures a factor in the chores and earnings of Iowa youth?

What are the developmental implications of successful involvement in productive labor, particularly in paid work? A greater sense of mastery seems likely for both farm and nonfarm youth. Self-efficacy increases when *challenging tasks* are done well.[9] The children of the Great Depression felt empowered by their ability to do work that was needed by the household.[10] Paid work and earnings can also be viewed as a means of gaining respect and recognition. Related to this developmental outcome is the personal gratification from learning how to do hard tasks and the resulting work ethic, industry, and personal responsibility. A second type of developmental implication involves changes in relationships toward greater equality and adultlike status. Paid work in particular may reduce a youth's time with family but the resulting earnings could promote greater parental recognition of maturity, as expressed in seeking a son's or daughter's advice.

Some Developmental Meanings of Work

Even in seventh grade, Iowa youth generally take their responsibilities seriously. They were asked to indicate how important it was that they do their daily and weekly chores. Most said either very or extremely important. This rating was higher for farm youth than for adolescents from other families, and for girls than for boys. However, the uniform importance attributed to these responsibilities is noteworthy. When asked in an open-ended interview (twelfth grade) what made work important, youth focused on three points: (1) being counted on by others— the experience of linked lives, of being interdependent; (2) feeling that work is part of a larger, lifelong exchange—assisting now may enable the family to be more helpful later; and (3) acquiring a sense of adult status from evidence of autonomy that is socially responsible.

"Being counted on" comes from an experience of social connectedness in doing chores or completing a paid job. Expectations of chores "performed" well reflect the obligations of social bonds within the family. They also indicate a commitment to something larger than the self. A young boy on a farm noted how the chores he did helped the family as a whole "instead of just getting a set wage." "If I help the family, it saves the family money as a whole. So we can take the money we save . . . and apply it to maybe . . . a new truck." Paid jobs also placed youth in situations where they felt needed and obliged to meet the expectations of others, even under adversity. Delivering groceries in inclement weather is a case in point. A boy with such a job noted that "even if the road's got three-foot drifts across, you've got to do your best to get there."

Family events may increase the need for children's assistance through the obligations of linked lives, as when a parent becomes ill, when fathers work multiple jobs, and mothers take on part-time or full-time jobs. Mounting time and labor pressures create new productive roles for children. An Iowa girl noted that her "mom and dad both work. Sometimes I am expected to help make supper and to clean up. And to take care of my little brothers while they are gone." Changes in parental employment are linked to the household role of children.

Care-giving jobs in the community also placed youth in positions where they had to help on occasion or simply encourage patients to learn to manage by themselves. A young girl with a caregiver role in a facility for the mentally handicapped noted that her work had made her more aware of how much her parents needed her help at home. "Now I realize that everything has to be done. You always have to help your parents."

Another quality of work that enhances its importance to young people involves the realization that it is part of an exchange or developmental process that allocates resources as necessary across the life course. A boy on a large stock farm noted the exchange between his unpaid work now and his father's paying for his college education: "[Dad's] going to help me in financing college." Farm chores had become part of a family effort to achieve goals within a system that ensures distributive justice in the long-run. However menial chores may seem at the time, they acquire added meaning as a path to valued status in young adulthood.

An aspect of this lifelong payoff takes the form of acquired resources with benefits in adulthood. A part-time car mechanic felt that he gained the self-assurance that he could do something with his life. He is no longer "afraid to work," as he put it, and he knows what he wants to do in his life. Another payoff is a sense of competence in relating to adults. A part-time cashier now feels comfortable amidst adults. "I think it's easier to make conversation with people older than me now. You have to make conversation at work." A girl working as a bank clerk after high school valued her exposure to prominent people in town who knew her and the kind of work she did. These people might serve as references or provide information about jobs that would advance her career.

An additional set of developmental meanings involves the conferral of adult stature and maturity. Youth eventually realize that even menial chores are done by adults. In this sense, youth perceive themselves as competent substitutes for adults, a perception that enhances their status when confirmed by adults. One girl alluded to such substitution in comments about her mother's employment. "I know I'm helping my mom out when she doesn't have time—so she doesn't have to work all of the time." Similar observations were made by girls engaged in child-care and other domestic tasks.

Employment in a paid job generally represented a step along the path to adult status. Local employers were likely to retain employees who were responsible, reliable, and did a good job. This work standard might entail effective relations with customers and a good-quality product. Children who maintained paid jobs were frequently perceived by parents as more mature and trustworthy. They were more grown-up. A girl who worked as a waitress observed that her parents trusted her more and had given her more freedom. They felt she was responsible with her own money.

These observations suggest that chores and paid work may be instrumental in the development of competence because they heighten a sense of mattering. They are often a part of a generalized exchange system that extends across the life course and promotes the achievement of goals, and they enhance integration into adult roles and self-conceptions. At the same time, the characteristics of chores are more indicative of childhood than of adulthood. Paid work is contractual, more impersonal, and standardized. Chores do not provide independent income to the worker, and money may be provided by parents when needed—it is not earned in the marketplace.

These observations imply that chores may enhance competence early in adolescence when they possess a more adultlike meaning. This seems likely when children experience a reasonable level of autonomy and see their contributions as integral to family life. Even in ideal circumstances, however, youth will attempt to disengage from chores and contribute to the family by way of earnings as they become older. Is this life pattern observed among Iowa youth who consider chores so important? We turn now to the ecologies of their chores and work.

The Ecologies of Children's Labor

The turning seasons of the year are marked by different activities on farms, from the planting weeks of spring to the harvest of summer and fall, and the fallow months of winter. Farm children have a role to play in the work of all seasons, though perhaps less so in the winter months. By the end of middle school, nearly all of the Iowa boys reported that they had a job during the summer, compared to three-fifths during spring and fall, and slightly less than half during winter. In this very limited sense, we do find a cycle of involvement, though it is not as great as we expected. The peak involvement time is summer for girls as well, but 60–70 percent reported paid jobs during the remainder of the year. Girls were more likely than boys to work during the winter because they were less involved in farm or outdoor work.

This cycle of activities, marked by the passing seasons, appears most descriptive of children's lives on farms, and yet we find no reliable difference between farm youth and adolescents in small communities. In part, the similarity reflects the tendency for small-town youth to work on farms or in some form of agriculture. Farm youth tend to work for parents, as expected, while nonfamily adults and friends are more prominent in the nonfarm group. In the rural Midwest, a male world in many respects, we expected more boys to be employed in paid jobs than girls, but the evidence shows just the reverse. Slightly more than a third of the boys at the end of middle school reported jobs, compared to about half of the girls. This difference reflects to some extent the greater tendency for boys to be involved in farm work.

From a developmental perspective, one might expect a transition from chores to paid employment as children mature. Doing chores for parents can place youth in a dependency role, whereas earned income symbolizes autonomy on a path to adulthood. A farm boy who raises steers for sale and is paid an excellent price is likely to be admired by friends and family. He has succeeded in the competitive marketplace, and *not* just because he is a son or relative. Youth are well aware of this difference, of getting compliments from an employer who is not a relative and of getting one from an uncle "just because he wants me to feel good."

Paid work is commonly indexed in terms of work hours. From the eighth grade to the twelfth grade, youth reported how many hours they devoted to chores each week on average. Earnings tell us about work experience over a year. Youth were able to report how much they earned over the past year, and the earnings themselves indexed accomplishments. The reported income figures for each year were transformed into constant 1988 dollars. The type of chore also has special relevance in tapping the gender and age relevance of work. We come back to type of chore when we turn to its developmental influences.

Chore time tends to decline between the eighth and twelfth grades for boys and girls (appendix table E4.1), farm and nonfarm, but the trend is not uniform or linear. By the eighth grade, farm boys in particular were working more hours than other youth. However, this involvement declined thereafter and then increased by the end of high school, perhaps in response to greater adult responsibilities on the farm. By comparison, earned income follows a more substantial and consistent upward path to the twelfth grade.

This earnings upswing is substantial for boys and girls in farm and nonfarm settings (see figure 4.1). The rate of gain is greater for boys than girls, and for nonfarm than farm youth. The male advantage in level and rate of earnings gain may reflect wage discrimination as well as the value placed on certain types of employment in rural areas. Farm boys tend to make more money early on but then fall behind the earnings of nonfarm youth. They appear to take on more unpaid responsibilities at

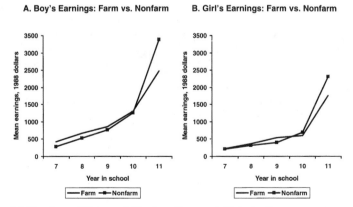

Figure 4.1 Earnings of Farm and Nonfarm Boys and Girls, in Constant Dollars

this time, while nonfarm youth are free to increase their earnings in any way they can.

The striking increase in earnings during high school among youth who live off the farm could reflect a number of developments. Some youth experienced a loss of their family farm, others had parents who knew farming through their childhood, and still others had no ties to the land. The psychology of these groups is likely to differ significantly. For example, deprivation might well have reinforced the desire for economic self-sufficiency among displaced youth. They grew up amidst a traumatic family loss, and their mothers frequently voiced a desire for more of the material benefits of life.[11] These women were more bitter than their husbands about the family's economic misfortune.

This circumstance brings to mind the lives of children in hard-pressed families during the Great Depression.[12] A large percentage found odd jobs in the community that enabled them to help their families, but underlying all of this was the aspiration for a better life and for more recognition of their personal worth. Most also realized that family misfortune had placed more responsibility for their accomplishments on their own shoulders. They sensed that if good things were to occur, they could only happen if *they* made extra efforts.

This refusal to accept misfortune as a personal verdict also appears in the psychology of displaced youth in the Iowa Project who have survived the emotional trauma and economic hardship of losing their farm and heritage. The desire to regain their social standing shows up in scattered comments across interviews conducted in high school. We have work and earnings records on 61 boys and girls who were displaced from family farms. As a group, they do indeed stand out on earnings relative to all other subgroups. Even with adjustments for gender and family income, displaced youth in the twelfth grade averaged more than $3,400 for 1993. This compares to approximately $2,500 for other nonfarm adolescents and around $2,000 for farm youth ($t = 2.91, p < .01$). Weekly hours devoted to chores do not vary across these groups.

Loss of the family farm creates economic pressures for adolescent chores and earnings. To what extent have youth responded to family hardships and needs by taking on additional responsibilities? In the seventh through the tenth grades, we asked each adolescent whether he or she performed more chores and earned more in response to family need. General economic conditions in the region had not improved significantly over this time period.

Between one-half and two-thirds of adolescents claimed that they had taken on more chores in the seventh grade (appendix table E4.2). The percentages dropped to the twenties or so late in high school, a decline that may reflect the changing standards and expectations of maturity and age status. However, the percentage who earned more money in response to family hardship did not change over this period, remaining in the sixties for the most part. This stability could reflect a different pattern of influence over time. Economic factors might become more important as youth get older, in comparison to time and labor pressures.

A more thorough test of economic factors is provided by the effect of family indebtedness on chores and earnings. To this measure, we added other ways of indicating family pressures that could increase the responsibilities of youth. These include the time and labor demands of the household as indicated by the number of hours a mother works each week, the size of household, and farm status. Labor pressures increase in farm families and in larger households, whereas both factors and the work week of mother add to a household's time pressures.

To assess the effect of these pressures, we needed to take into account the productive roles of youth under changing circumstances. Youth devote varying amounts of time to chores and earnings from year to year, and yearly changes in family indebtedness, mother's employment, and household size are also likely. A hierarchical linear regression model[13] enables us to examine how factors that change through time, such as mother's employment hours per week, affect the time adolescents devote to chores.

We find that more chore time is observed among youth who live on farms, who are members of large households, and who have mothers who work long hours (appendix table E4.3). Size of household and mother's work time are very important factors. Family indebtedness does not promote more time on chores across the secondary school years, though it does indicate whether youth are likely to take on more chores because of family need. Pressures of all kinds, except those of the family farm, are associated with more chores: indebtedness, larger household, and mother's work hours. In addition, girls are more likely than boys to respond to such needs.

Three major factors affect the earnings trajectories of youth: age or maturity, gender, and economic conditions. Earnings increase sharply in the high school years, and the gains are mainly experienced by boys and by youth who come from economically needy families—those that rank high on indebtedness as measured by the debt-to-asset ratio. But efforts to earn more in response to family need (appendix table E4.3) are linked only to gender and household size. Girls are more apt to respond in this fashion than boys, and large households are most predictive of this activity overall. The time pressures resulting from mother's long work hours are not directly linked to the earnings activities of children, most likely because they do not unambiguously tap economic pressures. Families do better with mothers in the workforce, whereas large households point to greater time and economic pressures.

This picture of work involvement across the adolescent years acquires additional meaning from information on the *kinds of chores* managed by younger and older youth, and spending patterns, whether on leisure or nonleisure items and activities. Though involvement in chores tends to decline with increasing age, the adultlike responsibilities of some chores should be carried out more by older youth.

From an exploratory factor analysis, we identified three main clusters. One cluster includes masculine types of chores, such as yard work, farm work, and fixing things. A second includes chores that are appropriate for younger as well as older youth, such as cleaning the house, cleaning up one's room, taking out the garbage, and setting the table. The third cluster includes responsibilities best suited for older children, such as doing the laundry, shopping, or planning and preparing a meal. Factor scores were computed by averaging the values from items in each cluster. As expected, Iowa youth spend less time by grade level on the "younger" chores and more time on the "older" chores from the eighth to the twelfth grade (table not shown). No age trend appears for the masculine set of chores, though boys are more involved in such tasks throughout adolescence.

In efforts to clarify the social meaning of earnings, we note that the *use* of money has important implications. In this sense, a distinction between leisure and nonleisure spending should tell us something about the meaning of work and its developmental significance. Nonleisure spending refers to expenditures that are not strongly related to one's immediate gratification. Examples include giving money to the family, spending money on education, using earnings to cover the expenses of chores or clothes, and putting money into savings or investments. This form of spending signifies the acceptance of more adult responsibilities, along with a sense of independence and concern for others. We find that rural Iowa youth are more likely to report such spending than adolescents in a midwestern metropolis, St. Paul, Minnesota.[14] A third of Iowa youth in grade 10 claim that they gave or loaned money to their families, in contrast to fewer than a tenth of the urban adolescents.

Does nonleisure spending become more or less common with age among Iowa youth? To explore these issues, we summed up the types of nonleisure expenditures for each grade from the eighth to the twelfth. The index provides an indirect measure of nonleisure spending, with a range of 0 to 4. We find that the diversity of such expenditures increases across the years—a significant main effect for grade level. Iowa youth use some of their earnings in two forms of nonleisure spending in early adolescence and they increase this diversity significantly up to the twelfth grade.

Overall, the productive activities of youth correspond in many respects to theoretical arguments about the developmental significance of work. Earnings tend to increase across the adolescent years, while time devoted to chores or unpaid work generally levels off or declines with age. Economic need in the family is a significant source of this earnings gain, and youth from larger households are most likely to try to earn more under conditions of family need. The dramatic earnings increase among displaced youth may reflect both this need as well as a strong personal need for self-sufficiency. But contrary to expectations, life on a farm does not make a difference in earnings by the end of high school. This may reflect the involvement of older farm youth in farm chores and operations as well as the greater time for paid jobs among youth in non-farm communities.

Time and labor pressures motivate youth's chore involvement, and this kind of employment is greater on farms than in nonfarm communities. Girls are more likely than boys to respond to family need by doing more chores. Chores commensurate with the skill level of older youth tend to increase over time, while chores that are manageable by younger children become less common with age. Do these chores with greater maturity demands and earnings foster a stronger sense of mastery among adolescents? Do they make resilience more likely in trying circumstances?

Work Paths to Competence

Work roles come with certain expectations and performance standards. A high school boy recalled the time he forgot to feed the livestock, noting the painful discovery when he returned home after a ball game that his father had done his work. Now he speaks of the responsibility of work and the maturity he gained from the experience.

Whether the job is cooking at a fast-food restaurant or working on a farm, most youth believe that the work they do has contributed to their competence and maturity. At the beginning of high school, we asked all employed youth whether six abilities were developed by their job: following directions, getting along with others, being on time, accepting responsibility, managing money, and learning things that will be useful. Most boys and girls with jobs felt that their work helped to develop these abilities—they replied either "some" or "a great deal." Three abilities were ranked more positively by farm youth—following directions, ac-

cepting responsibility, and learning useful things—but the only significant difference involves boys on learning useful things ($F = 8.18$, $p <$
.01). Farm work for boys resembles an apprenticeship in which things
are learned that are useful in a life of farming.

An important developmental gain from challenging work is the sense
that one can do hard tasks and succeed—it is the personal knowledge
of mastery in tough, demanding situations,[15] the feeling that "I've been
there before, and know I can do it." A high school boy who works under
a manager on a large hog farm told a story of how he gained this sense
of mastery. His boss would give him his work list for the day, and at first
it seemed overwhelming. "I'd look at it, and it is a huge list, and I'm
feeling, that's impossible. I can't do that. I'd die if I did that. But I end
up getting it done two hours before I'm supposed to get it done. Now
I look at that and I'm not afraid to try anything. . . . I'm not afraid
because I know that I can do something if I try my hardest."

We need to know more than we do about productive roles to be able
to identify work successes in challenging circumstances, but there is good
reason to believe, as noted, that paid work may recruit and develop
mastery-oriented youth. We focus on two versions of mastery: a general
perception which is indexed by our measure of personal mastery (one
component of self-confidence along with self-esteem) and the perception
of academic success or achievement. Personal mastery taps a generalized
perception of self-efficacy, whereas perceived achievement refers to
mastery only in the arena of education. These two scales, along with
earnings, are available from the seventh grade through the tenth grade,
and then in the twelfth grade.

Do these perceptions of mastery and academic success vary over time
in relation to youth's earnings? Hierarchical linear regression models
enabled us to assess the interplay of these multiple trajectories. Statistical controls include age and gender, farm status and parental education,
total family income, residential moves, and preference for life on a farm.
Prior analyses suggest that the effects of earnings will vary by age and
gender. Hence, we included such interactions in the equations. The
skewed distribution of earnings led us to use its natural logarithm, as
shown in appendix table E4.4.

Consistent with expectations, the increasing earnings of Iowa youth
tend to enhance their sense of personal mastery. The effect is significant
at the .001 level and tends to be most pronounced in early adolescence.
Earnings do not enhance or diminish the perceived achievement of
youth. We find no evidence that earnings are a negative force in the
academic record of boys and girls. The time youth devote to chores appears to be irrelevant to their sense of mastery and school achievement.

Does this picture change when we focus on chores for older youth and more masculine chores? The answer is no, at least for personal mastery. Chores have no effect on mastery feelings, no matter what the type of work may be. The reason may involve the variable autonomy demands and performance standards of chores. Children do not lose an assignment when they fail to do the work, but they can lose a paid job by failing to show up once or twice.

However, we find that chores for older youth and more masculine chores do have different effects on perceived achievement. Masculine chores turn out to be a significant positive force in perceived academic achievement (.25, $p < .05$), whereas domestic chores for older youth tend to have just the opposite effect: $-.39, p < .05$ (not shown in table). Domestic chores may indicate a dependency arrangement. In any case, the negative effect becomes more negative over time and underscores the possibility that productive activities can have adverse developmental effects. More information is needed on the process by which chores make a difference in children's development. Chores may be coupled with low academic expectations, or they may be linked to achievement standards.

The significance of mastery beliefs among youth with paid jobs may be understood in part by the way parents view maturing sons or daughters. Young people with paid jobs may be considered more mature and capable of sound judgment. Were parents more likely to seek their advice? In each year of the study, parents were asked whether they sought their children's advice, and the latter were asked the same question. We found that such advice-seeking within Iowa families did increase with the earnings of youth.[16] Farming families did not differ in this respect, although the collective nature of family life may account for the strength of shared communication and bonding. The effect of youth's earnings on advice-seeking is especially striking for boys in relation to father and mother.

The importance of rural culture in these developmental patterns is suggested by a corresponding study of young people in a midwestern city—St. Paul, Minnesota. The earnings of city youth did not enhance their relations with parents,[17] perhaps because they reinforced individualism and broadened differences between the generations. Their earnings activities undoubtedly entailed more freedom that could be used to undermine the authority and wishes of parents. These urban adolescents were also more likely to spend their earnings on items that had little value for the family as a whole.

By contrast, Iowa youth were engaged in work and spending patterns that had genuine value in the family. In this cultural context, their earnings help the family; they symbolize doing one's part as a member of the family. A high-school girl noted how much her parents respect her and what she does, now that "I do have a job. That's very important to them . . . that I am making my own money."

Linking Paid Work and Competence

A sense of mastery refers to feelings of competence that might be expressed in any number of specific domains—schoolwork, athletics, and meeting the public. We turn now to some processes by which a paid job enhances competencies of various kinds. Urie Bronfenbrenner would include these processes under his concept of a *proximal process.*[18] The process refers to complex reciprocal interactions between the individual and persons, symbols, and objects or tasks in the immediate environment. Interactions of this kind take place over a long period of time on a regular basis.

To gain insight regarding the proximal processes of work, we asked all twelfth-grade students with paid jobs what, if anything, they learned from the work they were doing. Their observations mentioned the abilities that we included in our survey, such as *accepting responsibility* and getting along with people, but they also provided insights on how youth have adjusted to the demands of a work role. Consider the responsibility of a paid job with undesirable hours, such as delivering pizzas at night. A boy with such a job reflected on its hours:

> Working at night, to 10 o'clock on weekends—its kinda bad. All your life you've grown up not having to do anything at night, and now you have to settle down and realize that you've got to get your priorities straight . . . the job comes first, before friends. I'm getting older now, so I really have to start to learn what it's like to have a job. It's going to be good in the future.

Getting one's priorities straight involves knowing what employers expect. A boy employed at a car parts store thought his work was most rewarding when he was asked to do more than the usual on a particular day or weekend. The extra work made the job more satisfying because it tested his abilities. In the process of doing additional work, he was perceived as more competent by supervisors.

Mastering the challenges of work on a local farm produced many lessons and personal insights for a boy who once thought he couldn't handle the load. He learned what people expected of him, and he learned that he could do it. As he observed,

> I've learned that it's not easy; you've got to put a lot of effort into it. Some days are good days, and some days are bad, but

the good make up for the bad. [The job's] affected my schooling plans, because I know that I'm going to have to work hard in school. I don't want to be working for $5 an hour for the rest of my life. . . . [Concerning my family, the job's been a good thing] because now I buy all my own clothes, and that helps out with the family.

Learning to accept responsibility typically requires *social skills in working with diverse kinds of people,* whether adults in general or the mentally handicapped or children. In her role as a dental assistant, a middle-class girl describes the once-daunting task of working with people she did not know or like and conversing with them for fifteen minutes or more. In her words, she has to "talk to patients while they are waiting" for the dentist. "I've really had to learn to talk to people I don't even know. . . . It's challenging and makes you have to think of things to talk about."

For other youth, just working around adults made them feel "more comfortable" in their presence. A young woman who answers the phone at her father's lumber business marvels at her competence with adults. "I can work with older people. And I actually understand what they are talking about more than I thought I would." Perhaps the most vivid account of work with older people comes from a young woman who does housekeeping in a nursing home. "I'm not afraid to go into a nursing home anymore. I'm getting to know people there. That's a real plus because there are negative feelings about it. I used to be scared to death of them."

Childcare, nursing, and people-oriented jobs in general provided valuable lessons in reaching out to people who seem very different. A cashier at a fast-food establishment noted how much her job enabled her to overcome the disadvantages of acute shyness. "Work kind of showed me that I could talk to lots of people. . . . You've got to talk to people you don't know, and it's helped me deal with different kinds of people. I used to be afraid of truck drivers and that kind of thing, different kinds of people. You realize that they are not really that different." Exposure to different people through employment enlarges a youth's social perspective, just as travel expands the range of knowledge and contacts. In this sense, the workplace introduces young earners to greater social pluralism and the ideas associated with it.

Skill in getting along with others was mentioned more often than the ability for appropriate *self-regulation, particularly of emotions.* This ability was noted most often in managing relations with people who are different. A waitress thought she gained most in learning "how to be patient, how to be nice to people you don't want to be nice to, . . . [learning to] adjust to different people and how to act in relation to different people, what to say and what not to say." A cashier stressed many of the same challenges: "how to be nice to [customers]. No matter how rude they are to you, you have to be nice to them. I guess you don't have to do that the rest of life, but when you're working you do." A boy with a summer job as county park ranger noted that he learned on duty to get along with "nasty people. You learn to kind of swallow your pride and . . . be calm with them. They're your customers."

Self-regulation skills, especially of the emotions, are part of the more general task of what Erving Goffman calls self-presentation;[19] presenting a culturally approved self to others.[20] Job qualifications spell out some of these desired qualities. In response to norms in local workplaces, the faces of workers may change from scowls to pleasure as they approach an obligatory gathering. A waitress notes that "when you are at work you have basically got to have a smile on your face and be happy even if your life is in the dump. You have got to say that this is the best day I'm having in my entire life." Management of one's emotions is a key part of this self-presentation—managing one's temper, remaining patient, holding one's tongue when talking to a supervisor or manager.

A final process linking work and competence involves the *clarification of goals and aspirations.* Paid work may provide work experiences and exposure that crystallize vocational ideas and concepts of self. Babysitting is a common job for younger adolescents and often sharpens the confidence of young women in their ability to be good parents. As one girl put it, "I learned ways to help a kid and how to understand him. I think it will be a lot easier when I have my own kids." Work in a dentist's office, with its demands and rewards, focused a girl's plans on medical school.

Many of the young people who are working on farms used this experience to clarify their plans regarding farming. An instructive example of the relevance of work experiences for the future appears in the life of a young man who found school difficult and irrelevant. Work provided "experience . . . school doesn't substitute for experience." This line of work directed him to agriculture as a future occupation and shifted his attention at school to "shop and 'ag' classes."

These proximal processes—accepting responsibility, learning social skills and self-control, and the clarification of goals—provide ways of thinking about how productive labor can promote competence in young people, on farms, and in small communities. In this developmental process, young people engage successfully in more adultlike roles and in more complex settings. To be sure, not all productive labor brings such benefits, though even work viewed as monotonous and devoid of intrinsic interest can be exciting and novel at first exposure. In one respect, paid work experiences are probably not unlike chores; their developmental benefits may dissipate with continued employment. Nevertheless, these accounts of work are suggestive of the developmental potential of employment in the rural Midwest.

Work Experience, Resilience, and Vulnerability

Valued work experiences enabled some adolescents to become more competent than one would expect from their family backgrounds. As noted in chapter 3, groups of resilient and vulnerable youth were identified on each measure of competence, from academic and social success to self-confidence. We focused on personal mastery, since work experience is most relevant to this view of self. Resilient youth scored in the upper quartile of residuals from an equation predicting a mastery orientation in the twelfth grade, and vulnerable youth scored in the lowest quartile.

To determine whether work experiences played a significant role in the resilience or vulnerability of youth, we estimated a series of logistic regression equations with gender and farm status controlled. The first two equations for resilience and vulnerability focused on earnings (log) from grades 7–12, the second set assessed the effect of hours devoted to chores per week, and the third set included measures of older and younger domestic chores and masculine chores (all scores averaged for grades 8–10).

We know that youth who increased their earnings from employment across adolescence tended to perceive themselves as more mastery-oriented. But does the mastery experience of paid work identify youth who have a more positive view of self than one would expect from their background? We call this the resilient group. Or do earnings protect youth from feeling more vulnerable about themselves than one would expect—what we term the vulnerable group?

Earnings do not make a difference in the likelihood of resilience among youth, *but they do lessen the prospects of being vulnerable on self-mastery* (odds ratio = .79, $p < .05$). Vulnerable youth in this sense are less likely to have had substantial earnings through paid work experiences. This protective influence is consistent with the meaning of paid work for a number of Iowa youth. Over and over again they refer to the greater confidence their work has given them—the confidence from having fulfilled the work expectations of a demanding employer, from producing an order in time, and from conquering apprehensions. In their beliefs at least, they think they are more competent today because they met the responsibilities of paid employment.

Productive Work Empowers

The productive activities of rural youth include the work experience of chores and paid employment. Chores are part of the household economy, and they convey to children a sense of being needed, especially among families that have ties to the land. They are also most likely to be carried out by children when family pressures are intense—the pressures of scarce labor, time, and income. However, chores can resemble the dependency regime of family life in which the young are subordinated to the supervision of parental authority. Consistent with this view, youth tend to spend less time on chores as they grow older, whether living on farms or in small communities.

Paid work is more connected to the adultlike realm of self-direction and personal responsibility. Money is exchanged for certain goods or products within a framework of expectations. With few exceptions, Iowa youth have worked for pay by the end of high school. Their earnings increase by grade level, especially in high school and among young people who do not live on farms. Most notable in this group are the children of displaced farm families. Their earnings increased most strikingly over the high school years, motivated perhaps by the keen desire to become economically self-sufficient. Economic need plays a modest role in motivating paid work in the sample as a whole.

Children are frequently involved in family chores before adolescence, and these responsibilities may be most developmental at this age. Quantitative indications of the developmental benefits of chores are elusive. Youth speak about learning to handle family responsibilities and feeling that their contributions do matter for the well-being of the family. However, in accounts of what they have derived from the work they do, most are speaking about the challenge of managing a job that has an economic payoff, either now in earnings or later on in college support or in the prosperity of the farm that will eventually be theirs. Not all jobs are viewed in this positive way, but most youth acknowledge that even menial jobs offer important lessons, such as cooking or selling in a fast-food restaurant. Young workers claim that their jobs facilitate the skills of autonomy and the effective management of responsibilities, the learning of social skills and self-skills. The earnings of youth enhance feelings of personal mastery across the adolescent years.

Productive labor is clearly an important part of young lives in families that have ties to the land. This is certainly true of the daily routine of chores on farms, and we assumed that it would be true of paid work as well throughout the adolescent years. However, we find that the boundary between farm and nonfarm is blurred by work opportunities and interests. A large number of farm youth work off the farm in small communities, while many youth who do not live on farms nevertheless work on farms. In any case, paid work has increased their feelings of personal mastery, and it has minimized the risk of fatalism or hopelessness among youth who have come to paid jobs with a troubled history.

In debates over the meaning of the rural-to-urban transition, the topic of productive labor among farm youth has posed questions about the work ethic of Americans. Will it decline in the years ahead as the farm population continues to decline? As Henry Wallace once observed (1963) in the *Des Moines Register*,[21] "Farm folks are used to working. . . . I shudder at the fact that only eight percent of our children have the kind of background where you have to get the hay in if it's going to rain—to meet a problem, no matter what." The evidence from this sample of Iowa youth provides some assurance of the work ethic's vitality, even among young people who have no ties to the land. "Getting the hay in before it rains" is not the only moral imperative experienced by rural youth, whether farm or nonfarm.

To achieve greater understanding of resourceful pathways that are linked to families in agriculture, we turn to the community ties of families. Farm youth are more embedded in the community ties of parents, as we have seen. Is this connectedness a positive force in their lives?

CHAPTER FIVE

Bridging Family and Community

You know everybody. If something happens, you can interrupt someone at their house. . . . Most likely they know your parents or you know them.

Boy in senior class

Generations of farming families in the Midwest reveal a distinctive pattern of civic engagement in their rural communities. What does this tell their children? Do civic-minded parents bring up children who are more likely to succeed socially, compared to other parents? In this chapter we test the proposition that successful development is enhanced when parents build social bridges between family and community. Networks of parental engagement link children to people and experiences outside the home, widening their worlds and opening doors of opportunity as they make their way to adulthood.

Community influences on families and children occur in large part through the social ties and mutual obligations that provide family members with a sense of belonging and shared responsibility, especially in times of crisis. Two mechanisms are relevant. One involves the extent to which community members interact with each other on a regular basis, within and across the generations. For example, a father who is very active in his son's Boy Scout troop will develop relationships with his son's friends and their parents, widening his social contacts and, more important, melding his social relationships with those of his child. This melding occurs through the joint involvement of farm parents and children in community organizations, church, agricultural groups, and school.

The other mechanism is value consensus, the extent to which community members share a set of norms, values, and expectations.[1] Families who belong to a Lutheran church are likely to share and mutually reinforce a particular set of beliefs about morality and a good life. In communities characterized by intergenerational closure and value consensus,

This chapter was written in collaboration with Debra Mekos.

families are better able to safeguard their children from risk because the moral education and well-being of youth becomes the responsibility of adults in the community and not merely of individual parents. Parenting thus represents a community enterprise. Active engagement in the institutions that directly affect children—the school, the church, and community youth programs—enables rural parents to monitor their children's social contacts and experiences outside the home, protecting them from dangers and risks, and promoting a value orientation that emphasizes academic success and responsibility to self and others.

The conceptual model of this chapter identifies two pathways through which parents' community ties have a potential developmental effect on adolescent competence. One pathway involves family processes within the household.[2] They are defined in terms of parental investment to enhance children's skills and competencies. Examples include parents who help with homework, who encourage and praise achievement, and who discuss school and educational issues. The other pathway involves parental efforts to link children into after-school or summer enrichment programs, as well as parental involvement in church and civic organizations, and the child's extrafamilial contacts, including relations with peers, teachers, and other adults, such as close neighbors and recreational league coaches.

Parents structure their children's peer relationships by placing them in organizations that are selective of certain personal qualities—Scouting, 4-H, or church youth groups. This structuring is particularly common among parents with ties to the land who are involved in an adult-sponsored form of upbringing. They are the principal actors in structuring the lives of these adolescents, and they do so through their joint involvement in recreational and school organizations. We distinguish between the child's peer network and their adult mentors in school and community. The latter endorse the core values of the community, whereas the peer group may or may not do so.[3]

The model illustrates how parents' community ties influence competence, directly through their participation in social institutions that affect children and indirectly through their efforts to involve children in the organizational life of the community. This in turn brings them into contact with other caring adults. Linkages of this kind strengthen and build on each other from preadolescence to late adolescence, and it is this aggregation of advantage provided by adult-guided socialization that places youth on a path to competence.

The first step in our analysis of civic ties is motivated by the question of family variation in community roles. Families with ties to the land are more socially engaged than other families, but are there other factors that matter, such as the education and economic resources of parents? How important are residential changes and the commuting distance for rural parents? We begin, then, by asking about key factors that distinguish among families with strong, average, and weak social ties to community groups and institutions. In this study, social ties refer to involvement in groups, not to social ties to particular people, as in Granovetter's (1973) innovative account of the "strength of weak ties."[4]

This portrait of social differences provides a context in which to assess the influence of such ties on the lives of rural young people from different backgrounds. Are youth from engaged families more successful in academics and social life than young people from uninvolved households? And are parental investment strategies an important part of the explanatory picture? In the concluding part of the chapter, we ask whether the civic ties of families explain why some children at the end of high school are doing better or worse than expected in terms of family background.

Community Ties in a Rural Ecology

Strong community ties, defined in terms of the active participation of parents in school, church, and community organizations, typified Iowa families with ties to the land, especially those engaged full-time in farming. Weak ties were characteristic of nearly half of the nonfarm households that claimed no farming experience or history. This variation in community involvement may be quite common in rural areas. For example, in an ethnography of Illinois farming communities, Sonya Salamon found distinct barriers to civic involvement, especially in areas with a high concentration of German ancestry.[5]

The farm families in these Illinois communities tended to be extremely close-knit, joined together by a set of cultural norms and a commitment to preserve them. Yet other families in the region that had no generational ties to the land were made to feel isolated and alienated because of their outsider status and perceived threat to community norms and values. Salamon observes that "integration rests on the commitment of community members to maintaining group norms. Therefore, when a community is tightly integrated, an outsider finds the atmosphere decidedly unfriendly. Barriers are erected because people are wary of intruders, and gossip is used as an effective social control mechanism.[6] In discussing one farming community's response to the invasion of urban commuters establishing residence in their rural area, Salamon writes, "The new residents are called 'strangers'; they do not farm. Explained a fourth-generation farm wife, 'The real way we tell them apart from everyone else is because they're not related to everyone here, like the rest of us.' "[7] Later Salamon adds, "So effective is the yeoman church at reinforcing ethnicity and integrating families that community boundaries are considered tight, both internally and by non-Germans from neighboring communities. Germans in all the communities are suspicious of newcomers. A non-German middle-aged woman who married into Heartland recalled, 'For three years I went to church and not one person came up to talk to me. Well, I just came home and cried and cried.' "[8]

Our own sample, which is mainly German in ancestry, does not allow a test of whether the practice of social exclusion in close-knit communities explains why some parents, especially those not engaged in farming, are marginally involved in civic life. Yet the distinction is an important one. Despite the existence of strong social cohesion in rural areas at the community level, not all families and children will have equal access to the social resources their community provides.

This raises a critical question—are families with weak community ties able to compensate for their lack of social capital through greater access to human skills, such as education and income, or to other forms of social resources such as close kinship ties? To explore this question, we compared families with weak, average, and strong community ties on a number of social factors using multinomial logistic regression. To take advantage of sample size, separate models were run for demographic factors on the entire sample, and for geographic and social network factors that were not available on twenty families who did not participate in the 1991 follow-up.

Lower levels of education and a shorter length of time in the community distinguish families with weak ties from other families (appendix table E5.1). While mothers with weak ties tended to work longer hours, there were no differences in fathers' work hours or family income. The absence of income differences is important to note, since income is a potentially important source of social involvement. Families with weak community ties are likely to be doing as well financially as families with strong ties.

Families with weak ties also appear to be more geographically isolated than other families (see appendix table E5.2). Specifically, mothers and fathers traveled longer distances to work and lived further away from their child's school, even after adjusting for the fact that nonfarm parents by definition live further from their workplaces than full-time farm parents do. This geographic isolation, and the greater time spent traveling to and from work and school, may explain in part why these parents are less integrated in their community.

Families with weak ties also displayed a consistent pattern of social isolation with respect to friends, immediate family, and their extended kin, compared to families with average or strong community ties (see appendix table E5.3). The women in these families reported less support from friends and more conflict with their extended families. Usually less involved with relatives, men reported more conflict and less contact with kin, despite living as close to relatives as other parents did. Moreover, men and women in this context reported doing fewer activities together as a family.

What stands out is the pervasive lack of social resources among families with weak community ties. Except for household income, these families have not compensated for their lack of community capital with other personal and social resources. Is their marginality a reflection of the communities in which they live? Our data do not allow a direct test of community characteristics on parents' participation. Yet an examination of the towns and counties in our sample revealed no differences in the distribution of families with weak or strong community ties.

What is interesting is that despite living in the same area, parent evaluations of community strengths and resources by these groups are quite different (see appendix table E5.4). Parents with weak ties viewed the local economy as more dismal, the local schools as poorer in quality, and the churches and community residents as less supportive of families in need. These family differences were obtained even after adjusting for the lower levels of education and shorter length of residence characteristic of parents with weak ties.

Consider two families as an illustration. Both have lived in the small farming community of Allison (pop. 1,000) for over a decade, yet one farm-reared family we will call the Gordons is very active in community affairs, while the other, a part-time farm family we will call the Drakes, contributes little time to school, church, and civic functions. How do they rate Allison as a place to live and raise a family? When asked whether they agreed or disagreed with statements about their community, Mrs. Gordon disagreed that many families were having financial problems and claimed that teachers in the local schools really cared about kids and that one of the nice things about Allison was that everyone was friendly and helpful.

Mrs. Drake's opinions could not have been more different had she lived on the other side of the state. When asked the same questions, she strongly agreed that many families faced financial difficulties and took issue with the belief that teachers cared about kids and that Allison residents were friendly and helpful. When asked whether they would like to remain in Allison, both Mr. and Mrs. Drake strongly stated that they would move elsewhere if they could. It is difficult to say whether the Drakes' negative views are a cause or result of their community isolation; more than likely they are a combination of both.

Engaged Families and Successful Children

Now that we have a better sense of how families with differing community ties vary on other resources, we can begin to explore the implications of parents' civic participation and leadership for youth competence. Through the multiple roles and relationships that emerge out of networks of engagement, parents become more knowledgeable of programs and services for their child, more versed in the educational policies and practices within their child's school, and more aware of their child's peer network and social activities outside the home. As in many areas of life, knowledge leads to empowerment.[9] Thus, parents who are more knowledgeable are also in a better position to shape the institutions and social networks of which their child is a member. In this way, parents construct bridges between home and community, ensuring that the values and expectations their child experiences in the family are reinforced by those espoused in his or her peer group, school, and neighborhood.

Building bridges between home and community may be especially important in parenting *adolescent* children, since this developmental period involves the formation of an identity apart from the family.[10] In the search for autonomy and a more individuated sense of self, young people spend increasing amounts of time away from home and the watchful eye of parents, and more time in the company of peers. While interactions with peers are central to healthy social development, they may also produce a greater risk of involvement in antisocial behavior, particularly as precocious claims on adult status—drinking, sexual experience, and fast driving.

Parents with strong community ties are better able to monitor their teenager's social activities outside the home because they are part of a larger network of community adults. While they may have little direct knowledge of their child's activities with peers on a given day, chances are they know a parent, teacher, or other adult who does have this knowledge and is in a position to redirect antisocial activities into more prosocial experiences, such as an uncle or a neighbor on a farm. In the words of one full-time farm mother, "We're proud of them keeping busy with outside activities. We feel those activities will help make them a better person and they won't have idle time. Idle time can sometimes get a child into trouble."

To examine the links between family-community ties and adolescent competence in the twelfth grade, we carried out a series of two-phase multiple regression analyses. Ties to the land, parent education, and child gender were entered first, and then two dichotomous variables to represent the contrasts between (1) families with strong and weak ties and (2) those with average and weak ties. This procedure allowed us to determine the extent to which community ties account for the greater competence of youth with ties to the land. Models were estimated separately for school grades and perceived achievement on the premise that community ties may matter more for objective indicators of school success than for adolescents' perceptions of their academic ability.

Two key findings are evident (appendix table E5.5). First, parents' community ties are more strongly associated with objective measures of competence—school grades and peer success as rated by teachers—than with our subjective measures—the children's *perceptions* of their academic competence, self-confidence, and acknowledgement of social maturity by parents (advice sought from children). Only the results for grades, perceived achievement, and peer success warrant presentation (see figure 5.1).

The second notable finding is that the community ties of parents explain at least half of the effect of connections to agriculture—growing up on a farm or having parents who grew up on farms—on peer competence. Community ties also accounted for about a fourth of the effect of farm and farm-reared status on school grades. In other words, socially engaged parents are one important reason youth with farm or farm-reared parents are succeeding socially and academically. These effects do not vary by gender of child.

Some of our families with strong community ties were devoting large

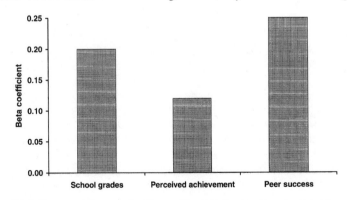

Figure 5.1 Influence of Community Ties on Youth's Grades, Perceived Achievement, and Peer Success in Grade 12: Strong versus Weak (Beta Coefficients). Note: farm status, parent education, and gender of child are controlled

amounts of time and energy to civic commitments, particularly full-time farm families, who one could argue have significant work demands and little discretionary time. How do parents view their civic involvement? The little qualitative information we have on this question suggests that parents are torn between the obligations they feel to their families and to their communities. One of the more active parents, a full-time farm wife, is quite eloquent on the subject:[11]

> Just finding the time is a problem because we are so committed to different things. We have different committees, each of us, and the fact that our kids are very involved in things, that makes us very involved going to all their activities, which we enjoy, but we rarely have an evening all to ourselves. This year when our family comes home during the summer, my goal is to spend time doing fun things with them, and to say no to some of the everyday things like committees and meetings. We're just going to have to say no, we can't come tonight because our family is home and we're doing things with them. That's what I'd like to do.

This same farm wife goes on to talk about her ambivalence regarding her children's participation in community activities:

> There is a lot of conflict about how much money—it seems to take a lot of money for the children to be involved in things they want to be in at school. It also seems to take a lot of time, and sometimes we disagree about how much of that is necessary. I have a hard time sorting that out, because it seems like a good thing that they are involved in so many things, but they don't have time for jobs. It costs to be involved in all that stuff because there's a lot of traveling back and forth when our school is fifteen miles away. It leaves less time for them to help here with chores. And you get stressed out with that, because you think you've got more than you can do now, and they're not here to help.

Yet other parents take a more balanced view regarding the costs of involvement. In the words of a farm father, "What's enjoyable is doing things with the kids, going to their school activities, that's what's most enjoyable to me." His wife noted that, "It's not such a terrible problem not having the time to spend together now." Indeed, as a father put it, "Because we enjoy the time with our kids and their activities, I can't think of anything I'd rather do than go to things with the kids."

The rewards of involvement are also echoed in the exchange between a couple who had lost their farm some years ago. The father explained that "we really haven't had any difficulties in raising our kids. I guess living nine miles from town probably helps a lot." But the mother quickly added the costs of "runnin," a colloquial term for transportation in the countryside: "That's probably the biggest difficulty!! Having to run back and forth to town every day to pick them up from school activities." The father stressed the advantages of knowing where the children are: "But it saves problems knowing where they're at. They can't roam the town and get in trouble." His wife agreed, "Yeah, there isn't much to do. We usually know where they're at."

Though parents on the whole derive great satisfaction and pride from their children's activities and achievements, there is the sense that they are making large sacrifices as couples to maintain their civic ties and serve as bridges between home and community for their children. But in what ways and through what pathways do parents' civic participation and leadership confer benefits for their children? This is the question we turn to next. Since the community ties of parents were not significant predictors of self-confidence and advice-seeking by parents, the remainder of this chapter focuses on school grades, perceived achievement, and peer competence.

Building Bridges between Home and Community

Youth who grow up in families with stronger community ties are more socially and academically competent, but *how* does parent involvement foster the development of competence in children? Parents are better equipped to direct their children into competence-promoting experiences and relationships through contact with people and programs that play a role in their child's life outside the home, as well as the content of youth programs and peer activities. Parents with stronger community ties can influence their child's experiences outside the home directly, through monitoring and participating with the child in school and community activities, and indirectly, through the child's contact with other community adults—teachers, coaches, neighbors—who can serve as mentors.

Several types of social resources within and outside the family were used to examine this question, as drawn from prior studies in the MacArthur Network on adolescence and other research.[12] The dimensions tap three general domains: parents' involvement in youth programs, parents' investment in their child's schooling, and the child's extrafamilial contacts. Measures of youth-program involvement include parents' awareness of community youth programs, efforts to improve youth programs in the area, efforts to organize after-school tutorial and athletic activities for children, and joint participation with children in community youth groups and volunteer work. Investment in schooling refers to parents' monitoring of children's activities and contacts outside the home, discussing school with children, helping a child with homework and school projects, and knowing and contacting the child's teachers. Extrafamilial contacts include the child's report on the amount of unsupervised time spent with peers, and the number of school mentors such as teachers, community mentors such as neighbors, and older peer mentors such as adult friends they can go to for support and advice.

In view of our interest in youth competence by the twelfth grade, all measures of social resources were obtained from data collected in the seventh to tenth grade. Some items were only available at a single wave, while others were available at all waves of the study; when the latter occurred, the scores were averaged. Parental investment was also constructed separately for mothers and fathers (see details of measurement in appendix B).

Except for child monitoring, the indicators of parental investment are only moderately correlated with each other (r's ranged from .03 to .28) and between mothers and fathers (r's ranged from .18 to .39). Consistent with Coleman's theory, they appear to be conceptually distinct forms of social capital within the family. Similarly, the number of school, community, and older peer mentors is modestly correlated with the amount of time spent with peers (r's ranged from .01 to 17). Yet types of mentors were significantly correlated with each other (r's ranged from .22 to .44), suggesting that children with access to adult mentors in one context are more likely to have mentors in other contexts as well. This association may reflect the initiative of youth as well as their talents or needs.

Do parental investment efforts and extrafamilial contacts differentiate families with weak and strong community ties? A series of analyses was carried out with comparisons between families with weak and average ties and those with weak and strong ties. They were carried out separately for youth-program involvement, parental investment in schooling, and extrafamilial contacts, and separately for mothers' and fathers' investment strategies (see appendix tables E5.6 and E5.7). Child gender differences and interactions between child gender and community ties were also examined, and are reported when significant. In addition, parental education and length of time in the community were included as controls.

Overall, mothers and fathers with strong community ties are more engaged in parental investment strategies than are parents with weak ties. They are more aware of and active in community programs for their children, even after adjusting for their higher levels of education and longer time in the community. They are also more likely to enroll their children in after-school programs, and they spend more time participating with their children in community youth groups and volunteer work. Thus, in many ways parents with stronger community ties are actively building ties between home and community and opening doors of opportunity for their children.

Not surprisingly, parents with strong community ties are also more active in monitoring their child's activities outside the home and spend more time discussing affairs at school with their child.[13] The differences between families with strong and weak ties are greatest for monitoring among *daughters* and for discussing school among *sons*. However, these families do not differ in time spent helping with homework or contacting the child's teachers. This result may reflect the meaning of these strategies when assessed in the ninth grade. Relevant aspects of parental investment for children's academic achievement may vary by age.[14]

Specifically, helping with homework and contacting teachers may be coupled with better school performance among younger children, while discussions about school are more consequential in the high school years. By mid-adolescence, parents' attempts to help with homework and contact a child's teachers are likely to be more a reflection of the child's school failure rather than a strategy to ensure their child's success. Talking about school, on the other hand, reflects a genuine interest in a child's experiences outside the family, displaying an attitude of caring that engaged parents are more likely to possess.

Another way in which parents can involve their children in competence-promoting experiences outside the home takes the form of limiting the amount of time they spend "hanging out" with friends. This form of social control is consistent with the monitoring activities of socially engaged parents. Indeed, the risk of peer involvement in unsupervised activities is greatest when parents are not socially engaged in the community. These parents, as we know, seldom monitor their children or set standards. The stronger the social engagement of parents and parental contact, the lower the risk of children's unsupervised involvement with peers (figure 5.2). However, the children of engaged parents are not more likely to seek the support of nonfamily adults, such as neighbors, teachers, and coaches, possibly because they have little need to do so. They are getting along well without such assistance.

This result is potentially important because it suggests that there are multiple avenues in which youth form relationships with significant adults outside the family and benefit from their support and guidance. In families with strong ties, children's contact with adults in the community may evolve as needed. They have the social connections, but may

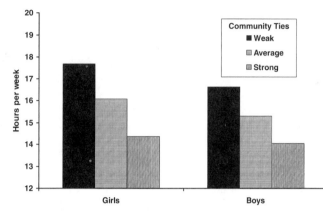

Figure 5.2 Unsupervised Time with Peers by Strength of Parents' Community Ties

be less in need of adult guidance outside the family, compared to youth from isolated households. Young people in isolated families may need redoubled efforts to make the best of opportunities. Whatever happens to them in positive ways may require strong initiatives by other adults in the community.

Do Parental Investments Matter?

Do investment efforts or strategies among parents help to explain the impact of community ties on children's competence? To address this question, we estimated a series of regression analyses (not shown). We first explored the effect of parental ties on youth competence at the end of high school: grades, a sense of academic success, and the social success of youth among age-mates (model 1). These are the only modes of success that were influenced by the community involvement of parents.

The second analysis (model 2) focused on strategies of parental investment which are linked to community involvement. What role do they play in explaining the effect of parental ties? Do the investment efforts of mother and father actually reduce the influence of family connections or ties? In the third model, we include evidence of extrafamilial contacts with teachers, coaches, and others. These contacts apply to integrated and isolated families, but in either case they should provide valuable insights regarding the social resources of Iowa families. In all cases, the linking processes are similar for boys and girls.

Overall, parental investment strategies contribute very little to an understanding of youth's grade achievements, perceived achievement, and peer success, and they also do not take us far in accounting for the developmental benefits of parent social ties. Three investment efforts were included in the analysis: the monitoring of child behavior, the parental enrollment of children in community programs, and the discussion of school by parents. In monitoring, we tap the extent to which youth reported that parents have structured their behavior by knowing where they are and by setting rules and restrictions. Program assistance refers to the involvement of parents in getting children into community activities and programs.

Monitoring is the only significant influence on grades, and it contributes very little (beta = .09, $p < .10$), especially when compared to the much larger impact of parents' civic engagement. Youth who felt competent as students were most likely to experience some monitoring by parents and school discussions with their fathers. These factors come through as significant influences, though still modest (beta = .11–.12, $p < .05$). In combination, they reduce the effect of community ties to insignificance.

In the case of peer success or prominence, we centered on the assistance strategy of parents and their joint involvement with children in youth and volunteer groups. Monitoring is not especially relevant to this mode of competence, and neither is a discussion of school affairs. However, father's assistance or program initiatives make a difference in the likelihood of peer success (beta = .19, $p < .01$). Boys and girls who are successful with peers tend to have socially involved fathers. Father assistance accounts for only a small part of the effect of parental ties and adds little to the explained variance.

The third analysis examined the potential influence of peers and significant adults outside the family. We explored the consequences of unsupervised time spent with peers and of interaction with adult mentors. This time refers to hours spent with peers after school and on weekends. School mentors, such as teachers and coaches, are relevant to academic achievement, and involvement with older peers can function as a vehicle for social success or deviance. Time spent with peers and access to older peers have no detectable effect on the social success of youth. However, both make a difference in academic success. Unsupervised time with peers significantly increases the risk of academic troubles, while access to school mentors diminishes this risk. Together they add notably to the prediction of academic grades—about a fourth of the variance.[15]

Overall, it is clear that the "investment" efforts of Iowa parents do not tell us why strong family ties to the community make such a positive difference in accomplishments. By and large, boys and girls from socially engaged families do well regardless of whether parents discuss school events, monitor their behavior, or promote their involvement in school programs. How can we explain this lack of connection between behaviors that fit together in a theory of family capital? Socially engaged parents are investment-oriented as parents, *but the timing of the most critical investment may occur much earlier, perhaps in the grade-school years.*

There may be prior windows of opportunity in which to achieve benefits from the parental management of social and academic opportunities. By the time children enter the middle years of adolescence, a large part of their social pattern has been established. Indeed, other studies have argued persuasively that the connections between families, community, and child competence are complex, and that greater attention must be given to the connections that are important at different life stages and contexts.[16] We shall return to these issues after examining the relevance of community ties for resilience and vulnerability in adolescence.

Doing Better or Worse Than Expected

Community ties and parental investment strategies enhance the life chances and accomplishments of Iowa youth. Are they also defining elements of young people who are doing better or worse than one would expect in terms of their family background in the seventh grade? One might argue that they are most consequential for youth who have risen above the social and economic limitations of their background. More family support is needed under the circumstances. If not forthcoming, one might expect children to do worse than expected, unless they gain the support of nurturant adults outside the family—such as a close neighbor or a caring teacher and coach. Coleman and Hoffer found that social connections or resources outside the family mattered most for the school success of children who lack resources of this kind within the family—for example, among children from single-parent households.[17]

As noted earlier, we have identified groups of resilient and vulnerable adolescents who were doing better and worse in their senior year of high school than predictions based on their social and economic status in early adolescence. Using residuals from prediction equations, we defined the upper fourth as "resilient" and the lower fourth as "vulnerable" relative to each of the developmental outcomes. Social resources are relevant to success and failure in two ways. First, we ask whether variations in community ties make a difference in the success of resilient and vulnerable youth. They matter generally, but do they play a special role in the unusual successes and troubles of these youth?

The second approach uses odds ratios from logistic regressions to compare resilient and all other youth on parental community ties, investment strategies, and extrafamilial contacts. We also compared vulnerable youth on these factors—those doing worse than expected. Coefficients above 1.0 indicate that the factor is predictive of resilience or vulnerability, while smaller coefficients indicate just the opposite.

Community ties predict academic and social competence at the end of high school, and they also predict whether youth are doing better or worse than expected on social competence. This is the only outcome that emerged with significant findings from the analysis. As shown in figure 5.3, over 40 percent of the socially vulnerable youth are members of families with weak ties to the local community, while fewer than 30 percent are members of families with strong ties. Only 15 percent of socially resilient youth came from families with weak ties, compared to 30 percent or more of the other adolescents.

To elaborate this finding, we examined the extent to which parental investments and out-of-household contacts account for the influence of parental ties on social resilience or vulnerability. In the first logistic regression equation, child gender and an index of parental community ties were entered, followed in the second equation by the investment strategies of each parent and extrafamilial contacts. The investment strategies of fathers, along with the community involvement of parents, predict social resilience and vulnerability (appendix table E5.8). The results do not vary by gender.

Youth are likely to be socially resilient in popularity and leadership among classmates, relative to their family background, if they have strong family ties to the community as well as fathers who promote their involvement in community programs and discuss school matters with

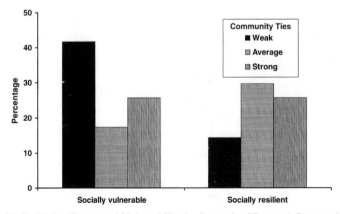

Figure 5.3 Social Resilience and Vulnerability by Strength of Parents' Community Ties

them. These activities partly account for the effect of family community ties, suggesting that they have particular relevance for the success of youth from disadvantaged circumstances. Conversely, the vulnerability of youth to low status among peers has much to do with the lack of paternal involvement in such activities. As in all analyses to date on the investment strategies of parents, it is noteworthy that the father's activity is clearly more important than the mother's for minimizing the vulnerability risk of Iowa youth. This difference does not vary by gender and may reflect the salience of male status in rural America.

Resilience and vulnerability in other respects—academic achievement, self-confidence, and advice-seeking from parents—are not predicted by the investment strategies of parents or by their social ties in the community. What does matter, and mainly for school achievement and self-confidence, is the extent to which youth have access to significant mentors beyond the family and do not experience much unsupervised time with peers. Appendix table E5.9 shows the extent to which gender, time with peers, and three types of mentors (school, community, and older peer) differentiate resilient and vulnerable youth on academic success and self-confidence. In the domain of academic achievement, resilient youth tend to report more school mentors and less unsupervised time with peers, whereas the opposite conditions increased the risk of vulnerability. Access to significant mentors is also important on feelings of self-confidence. School and community mentors significantly increase the chances of youth for ranking higher on self-confidence than expected in terms of family background.

Within the limits of our data, we find that key sources of youth resilience and vulnerability have much to do with parental social ties and actions that occur outside the household and link it to community institutions. Youth who are doing better than expected on peer success in terms of family background are likely to differ from other youth on socially engaged parents. Those who are doing worse rank low on these social connections. In the realm of academics and self-confidence, school and community mentors turn out to be most important for the resilience of youth.

This analysis also suggests that the explanatory significance of parental investment strategies is restricted to particular circumstances—such as "when extra assistance or support is needed." For example, the investment efforts of fathers account for some of the effect of community ties on social resilience. Likewise, family isolation accounts in large part for the social vulnerability of adolescents, and much of this effect occurs through the lack of parental investments. Access to social resources *out-*

side the family may counter the lack of social resources *within* the household.

The Socially Embedded Family

In theory and practice, Iowa parents who are involved in their local communities establish a resourceful environment for their children. They are more engaged as parents in a variety of domains. Socially involved parents tend to know where their children are, and they make extra efforts to open up social opportunities for them through community programs. The children of engaged parents are likely to have grown up on farms in a social world that is adult-sponsored. They do more social activities with their parents than the children of less involved parents. The latter spend more time with peers in a world that lies beyond the supervision or awareness of parents.

Parents with strong ties to the local community have numerous advantages over other families. They are better educated, have closer relationships with friends and family, and report stronger connections to the land over multiple generations. In farming communities, where historical continuity is paramount, ties to land and kin have special meaning and status. The advantages of farm families and those with strong community ties cumulate over time, as do the disadvantages of nonfarm families. As such, it is not surprising that farm youth are more academically and socially successful than nonfarm youth. Much of their success stems from family access to community resources.

But community involvement is not free of costs. Some of our most involved parents talked at length about the high price they paid to meet civic obligations and support their child's participation in school and civic activities. They refer in particular to the lack of time for family activities. Being a church elder or school board member, running a church fund-raiser or helping to organize the school's annual homecoming celebration, chauffeuring children from one youth activity to another—these and other activities compete for scarce time and energy with household work and paid jobs. Some of the parents are managing two jobs and commuting a substantial distance to each. It is not overstating the case to refer to this rural life in terms of "frenzy"; social and economic changes in the Cornbelt have brought worrisome time pressures to many families.

Parents often use the term *runnin'* in talking about the constant transportation of children among home, school, and community destinations. Runnin' also brings to mind a continual effort to cover all the bases in a very busy life. In his ethnography of a small, rural town in Illinois, Peshkin observed that being part of a small community has its costs—everyone has a role to play.[18] When people belong, they feel a sense of responsibility for what happens, a feeling of obligation that can interfere with responsibilities to the family. This sense of civic obligation is continually reinforced by the expectations and messages of other community residents, whether stated or implied, placing pressure on families to participate. Given the economic and temporal demands of rural life, it is notable how involved farm families, parents and children, are in the organizational lives of their communities.

But not all parents have the time to participate actively in the community. Some parents work many miles away in another city, others live away and return on weekends, and still others simply work very long hours. Thus, the isolated family is not necessarily a family that lacks an appreciation for contributions to community life—one that is largely wrapped up in personal problems. In an effort to identify the different kinds of nonparticipatory families, an exploratory study examined two other routes to youth involvement.[19] One entails a warm, nurturant family; the second involves direct encouragement of social activities. Interestingly, neither of these practices made a difference in youth activity when parents were socially involved. However, both contribute significantly to youth social activity when parents are not engaged in the community.

Parent involvement is a prime mechanism of historical continuity for communities in the rural Midwest, but how do the social ties of parents affect the competence-building experiences of their children? Initially, we assumed that the socialization or investment strategies of parents would provide one answer. For the most part, however, they do not account for the influence of community ties. This may be because of the relevance of these strategies for younger children. Program involvement may have great developmental significance for children who are heavily dependent on parents, but it becomes far less relevant for older teenagers. If there is a developmental sequence of parental behaviors that matters most for children at different ages, this may also apply to the investment strategies we have explored in rural Iowa. By late adolescence, when many youth are making their own money and driving cars, parental efforts to guide their activities and social contacts are bound to be less effective.

These strategies may also be especially important in preventing problem behavior and in accounting for resilience. Studies have investigated the process by which community cohesion and parental investment strategies combine to minimize youth involvement in delinquency and street gangs.[20] We shall explore this possibility in chapter 9 when we come to protective factors in minimizing the risk of antisocial behavior. At this point, we know that the investment strategies of fathers make a significant difference in the likelihood of social resilience and vulnerability. Beyond the family, adult mentors in the community emerge as consequential factors in the resilience of youth on academic achievement.

Perhaps extrafamilial strategies gain potency under deprivational circumstances in the family. Children in families with strong community ties are surrounded by developmental influences. They have warm, supportive parents, so that we find little benefit to be gained in competence from extra efforts to monitor behavior and participate in cross-generational activities. These youth may also have supportive relatives nearby. In all of these ways, we may speak of a "socially redundant" environment. There are backup systems to cover needs if one or more family members cannot help out owing to illness, separation, or death. If a parent is not available, other adults can be counted on to step into the role. There is indeed "a village" to bring up a good many children in this region.[21] By contrast, children from conflicted or isolated families have fewer advantages in the way of parental guidance or support and should be more strongly influenced by the benefits of extrafamilial mentors.[22]

Access to mentors is the social resource in this analysis that does not vary by the strength of community ties among families. This suggests that community mentors gain importance when parents are impaired or when family hardships are severe and limiting. Children of advantage may pursue opportunities that emerge out of their parents' participation and leadership in community organizations. We find that the efforts of fathers play a central role in defining this pathway to success. In other more deprivational circumstances, such opportunities are likely to occur through caring teachers, coaches, and neighbors.

These potential explanations for children's advantages in socially engaged families center on the behavior of parents, but there is a more direct link through the social accomplishments of their children, in church, community, and school. Do socially active parents establish a standard of behavior which their children adopt? Rural communities have survived over the years through the civic engagement of successive generations. Is this continuity expressed through the family and, more specifically, through farm families? We turn to this question in chapter 8 with its focus on the lessons and opportunities associated with youth activities.

North Central Iowa

A Farmstead in North Central Iowa (courtesy of the Iowa State University College of Agriculture Information Services)

Hard Times in Baltimore City, Iowa (photo: Ruth Book)

A Father–Son Team Filling the Corn Planter (photo: Don Wishart)

Corn Planting on a "No Till" Field (photo: Don Wishart)

Always Adjustments to Make: Cultivating the Corn (photo: Don Wishart)

Mom and the Boys Bring Lunch to Dad, Who is Cutting Hay (photo: Don Wishart)

Fair Time Arrives: A 4-H Girl Shows Her Well-trained Heifer (courtesy of the Iowa State University Extension)

Much Time and Effort Are Needed in Preparing Animals for Competition (courtesy of the Iowa State University Extension)

A Winning Combination in the Judging Ring (courtesy of the Iowa State University Extension)

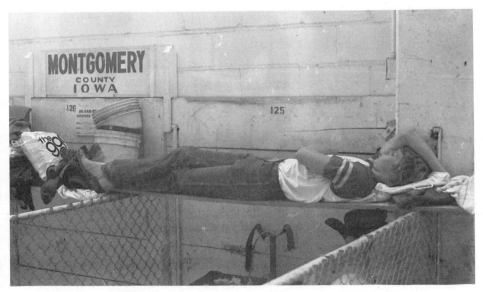
After a Long Day at the Fair (courtesy of the Iowa State University Extension)

A Fall Harvest of Soybeans (photo: Don Wishart)

Preparing to Transfer Corn to Truck and the Storage Bin (photo: Don Wishart)

Corn in Harvest as Far as One Can See (photo: Don Wishart)

Tractor Work at Harvest's End (photo: Don Wishart)

Weather and Farm Prices—Two Conversational Certainties (photo: Don Wishart)

Hauling a Large Hay Bale to the Farm Animals (photo: Don Wishart)

CHAPTER SIX

Wisdom of the Ages

Grandparents . . . [are] living evidence that human beings can adjust.

Margaret Mead

Parents with ties to the land are socially engaged in ways that offer many advantages for their children—from church to school and civic organizations. They are also engaged in the lives of their own parents, members of the grandparent generation. What relevance does this older generation have for the young amidst scarce opportunities in the rural Midwest? They have lived across historic decades of good and hard times, accumulating much wisdom about survival, "right living," and success. Do they represent a bridge to maturity for grandchildren through their wisdom, support, and moral guidance?

Grandparents "make the past real, as they describe something they actually saw, rode in, marched in, or participated in."[1] They are historians in their autobiographical accounts of lives and times. But they also can make the future seem possible and inviting, even in the midst of a traumatic family crisis. After all, they have lived through difficult times and managed to do reasonably well at that. When everything looks bleak to the young, grandparents can point to light at the end of the tunnel.

Iowa youth in this study typically have access to grandparents, even within their local community. Only 3 percent reported no living grandparent when they reached the twelfth grade. A third still had four living grandparents, and another third had three surviving members of this generation.[2] The tendency for men to marry younger women and to have a shorter life span accounts for a lower percentage of surviving grandfathers, about half on the paternal side of the family and two-thirds on the maternal side.

In this chapter we ask what roles grandparents are playing in the lives of their grandchildren and the extent to which "close relations" enable

This chapter was written in collaboration with Valarie King.

these young people to succeed in life. We begin with the views of the grandparents themselves on what it means to be a grandparent.[3]

Ways of Grandparenting

Grandparenting and *grandchildren* have widely shared meaning among Iowans in the older generation (G1). During 1994 we presented each grandparent with six value statements about the meaning of grandparenting and grandchildren. Nine out of ten concluded that grandchildren enable older people to feel needed and that they ensure a measure of immortality for the individual and the family (see appendix table E6.1). Three out of four agreed with the notion that grandchildren, in some sense, belong to grandparents just as they belong to parents. Last, most believed that it was important that grandparents' views influence family members (69 percent). All of these perspectives are intercorrelated (average $r = .42$), showing a high degree of consensus on the nature and meaning of relations between grandparents and grandchildren.

When asked about positive experiences as a grandparent, the older generation was most likely to cite events or activities that represent "vicarious enjoyment"—enjoying the opportunity to see the children grow up, do things, and achieve (33 percent). One noted the pleasure of seeing his grandchildren "get what they want out of life." Another expressed "the joy of watching them grow from young to old." The next most common source of pleasure (29 percent) involves the joys of a "shared life"—being together on holidays, the closeness of family life, the rewards of just spending time together. As one grandmother remarked, it's "a good feeling when they come home for the holidays." For some, the addition of grandchildren to the family made it seem "just like having your own children back again" (see figure 6.1).

A fifth of the grandparents cited the special rewards of providing "active support" in the lives of their grandchildren—helping and encouraging them, attending their events, celebrating their accomplishments, and taking them on trips. Another fifth stressed the love and support of their grandchildren; as one grandfather recalled, "They write you a little note and tell you you're number one." A grandmother spoke with great pleasure about her granddaughter who would "run in the door and come for a hug and kiss."

There are down sides to relations with grandchildren, though half of the grandparents could not cite a single negative experience. Thirteen percent mentioned "problem conduct," both disappointment when the child fails to use his or her talents and concern about the child's problem behavior—bad language and friends, getting pregnant, heavy drinking.

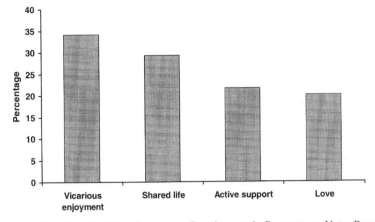

Figure 6.1 Most Positive Experiences as a Grandparent, in Percentages. Note: Percentages add up to more than 100 because grandparents could provide more than one response (up to three); $N = 765$.

Some of the grandparents talked about the frustration of not being able to do anything about such problems. Grandparents may feel a sense of responsibility to help their grandchildren along the road to maturity and success, but they have little if any control when grandchildren leave home.

Conflict between the generations proved to be rare—only 5 percent mentioned this problem. Another infrequent problem is physical distance. Rural Iowa grandparents tend to live close to their children, and therefore geographic separation is not a common problem. Only one out of ten were troubled by the lack of contact and great distance. For the most part, both grandmothers and grandfathers reported similar positive and negative experiences, although grandmothers were more likely to mention the positive experiences of a shared life and expressions of love.

These central themes are based on each grandparent's experience with grandchildren in general. Some grandparents have only one grandchild, whereas others report more than ten. Grandparents who visit grandchildren often are more likely to establish a strong relationship with them compared to those who rarely visit their grandchildren. But contact and pleasurable time do not describe what actually takes place in this relationship.

We first asked about the relationship itself: frequency of contact, participation in activities that involve the grandchild, being a companion and friend, and quality of the relationship. Forty percent of the grandparents see their grandchildren at least once a week. Only one-fourth have physical contact less often than once a month, with 3 percent reporting no contact at all in the past six months.

Involvement in the grandchild's activities is relatively common. Seventy percent of the grandparents reported that they had attended an event (a play, game, or musical performance, etc.) in which their grandchild was involved, and a third actually did projects and activities with him or her. The activities included touring a museum, seeing an art exhibition, going to an athletic event, and shopping. Joint projects ranged from repairs and cooking to farm tasks and building a house. The three types of involvement were combined to form a single index of shared activities.

Many grandparents were involved in a variety of shared activities with their grandchildren. As one grandfather observed, "I think being involved with them makes a big difference. The kids are more proud of what they do." A grandmother remarked how she and her husband often took her grandson fishing and on trips when he was younger, and that he would often help them on their farm. When their grandson entered high school and became involved in sports they became active supporters: "We went to every basketball game—we loved to watch him play. And his friends too, we knew so many of them." This grandmother also attended his football games even though "I don't know football . . . but I pretended that I know." Distance did not prevent such involvement, though it did reduce the frequency.

Another dimension of the relationship entails companionship and friendship. We asked each grandparent how often he or she played such roles. A third claimed that they often did so, and most were engaged in various intergenerational projects or activities. As might be expected, they felt that they had a very satisfying relationship with their grandchildren. Three out of five judged the relationship as excellent; nearly half claimed to be very close; and three-fourths felt that they were much loved by the child. They spoke of times when grandchildren "just dropped by" to see how they were or when they came over to talk about a personal problem. We summed responses to these items to form a scale on the emotional quality of the relationship.

The grandparents were also involved in two explicit forms of assistance, mentoring and tangible aid. Most grandparents reported that they offered solicited and unsolicited advice to their grandchildren, occasionally served as voices of wisdom and experience on a troublesome issue, shared tales from their own childhoods, and talked about family traditions, stories, and history during visits and family gatherings. We summed responses to these expressions of mentoring to form a single index. Three types of aid were combined in a tangible assistance scale: financial aid, helping the child learn skills, and finding a job for the grandchild. Many of the children were too young to be looking for a major job, and only 13 percent of the grandparents reported such aid. However, most recalled times when they assisted with money and the learning of skills.

Many factors bear upon the significance and function of these Iowa grandparents. For example, we know that farming makes a difference, with proximity and other circumstances favoring the paternal line—from the children of farmers to the parents of these men who typically live nearby. Other relevant factors include education and income level, age and health, gender and geographic distance. Age and health tell us something about the ability of grandparents to travel and do things with their grandchildren. Historically, grandmothers have been more engaged in kin activities than grandfathers, but again this may not hold in farming communities where the male line is strong. The kinship implications of distance are more straightforward: the greater the geographic distance, the lower the prospects for grandparent contact with grandchildren.

Life-history attributes also influence the nature of relations with grandparents. Consider involvement in the collective life of rural churches. Members of a particular family, as a kin network, are likely to meet at local church gatherings. Children often see their grandparents at church on Sunday mornings, and some are known to be driven to youth meetings by grandparents on Thursday nights. We view current reports of church attendance as indications of a life pattern or lifestyle.

Recollections of competence as a parent have direct relevance to grandparenting. Memories of incompetence may be expressed in the hostility of adult children and their efforts to restrict their parents' access to their children. Such incompetence may also be expressed in attitudes of indifference to child care. In both cases, memories of this kind are symptomatic of weak intergenerational ties.

One of the most important constraints on an elderly person's involvement with grandchildren is the sheer number of grandchildren who are close at hand. The greater this number, the more limited is the interaction with each grandchild. Just as parents may be indulgent toward their only child, grandparents may "spoil" an only grandchild. One of the study girls acknowledged this special treatment by her grandmother. "She sends me cards and everything all the time and she's so proud of everything I do, even though it's not that big a deal. My brother and I are the only grandchildren, so she spoils us."

When we included all of these potential influences in an analysis of reported ties to the study grandchild, seven emerged as most important (see appendix table E6.2 for complete details). In addition to the significance of farm status on the father's side of the family, strong relations are predicted by grandmother status, proximity to grandchildren, involvement in church, memories of competence as a parent, good relations with adult children, and a small number of grandchildren. In a nationwide sample (National Survey of Families and Households), Uhlenberg and Hammill obtained similar results on frequency of contact with grandchildren.[4]

These factors are statistically significant across most dimensions of grandparenting, but they do not take us far toward understanding the differences in grandparenting. Except for frequency of contact and its strong connection to physical proximity, we account for less than a fourth of the variation in grandparent ties to grandchildren. The education and income of the grandparents as well as their age and health add little to the picture. Gender of the grandchild also adds little. However, we find some evidence from an exploratory study that the personality of grandchildren influences the responsiveness of grandparents.[5] Whether from lack of initiative or an unpleasant personality, grandchildren who score highest on emotional depression are much less likely to report a close relationship with their grandparents. An irritable, explosive personality would seem to produce the same kind of weak or nonexistent relationship.

Up to this point we have viewed the significance of grandparenting from the perspective of rural grandparents. Most members of this generation feel blessed by the experience of grandparenting. They see grandchildren as an assurance of continuity across the generations and individual lives, one that provides a sense of purpose and meaning. Positive experiences with grandchildren, from shared activities to vicarious enjoyment and feelings of being needed, far outnumber negative experiences. Grandparenting is expressed in a variety of ways, and we have identified some aspects of this role. A substantial number of grandparents participate in activities with their grandchildren, serve as companions and friends, maintain positive relations, engage in a variety of mentoring activities, and help out occasionally in tangible ways, financial and other. Grandparents with ties to farming tend to maintain active relations with grandchildren, as do those who more generally live close by, attend church, get along with adult children, feel competent as a parent, and do not have many grandchildren.

Within this context, we turn now to the grandparents who are identified as significant adults by the study children, their grandchildren. These grandparents are people whom the grandchildren believe "they can count on when they need help." They feel loved and appreciated by them.

Grandparents in Young Lives

Grandparents have much at stake in their relations with grandchildren and generally accentuate the positive aspects of this relationship.[6] Virtually all of the grandchildren also feel close to their grandparents. We asked the grandchildren (1994) whether they could depend on their grandparents and whether they felt appreciated and cared for by them. Responses to these items were so skewed toward the positive end that we chose to define a "significant" grandparent as one who was described as providing support "a lot" (a score of 4 on both items). This measure of significance is available on each grandparent. We summed across all grandparents to determine whether a child had at least one close or significant grandparent.

Over a third of the youth with paternal grandparents feel especially close to them (39 percent for grandfathers, 37 percent for grandmothers). This percentage increases to 44 percent for maternal grandfathers and to 52 percent for maternal grandmothers. Overall, 60 percent have at least one especially close grandparent. Father's parents are less likely to be living, but, as was demonstrated in chapter 2, the survivors are especially important to grandchildren who live on farms.

Farm life brings the generations together. As one adolescent remarked about his paternal grandfather, "When I was young, he was always the one that would be out in the field. And he would be the one that would let me drive the tractor. . . . He kind of spoiled me, but he also taught me some things on the farm." His grandfather still serves as a role model. He is someone the boy turns to whenever he needs help or has a question.

To measure "the perceived strength" of the relationship, from weak to strong, we added three additional items to the measures above with their responses from one to four. They assessed the grandchildren's perceived happiness in the relationship, the extent to which the grandparent helps them in significant ways, and how close they are to the grandparent compared to other grandchildren. Responses across these four category items were averaged to produce a total score for each grandparent (alphas ranged from .75 to .79), with a rank order on mean strength of bond as follows: maternal grandmothers = 2.99, maternal grandfathers = 2.86, paternal grandfathers = 2.78, and paternal grandmothers = 2.76. For our purposes, the grandparent who received the highest score represents the adolescent's closest grandparent. The average score for such grandparents is 3.11.

The two indexes provide different views of a consequential grandparent. The dichotomous index identifies the existence of at least one significant grandparent, while the other scale estimates the *strength of the bond* to this person (closeness). Despite these differences, the two scales are highly correlated ($r = .67$). By using the adolescent's perception, we are able to include grandparents who were unavailable for their interview, whether because of illness or refusal. We find a modest association between grandchild reports of closeness/significance and grandparent reports of involvement. The dichotomous measure is correlated less strongly with the multifaceted aspects of grandparenting (such as companionship or mentoring) than the "strength of bond" measure; average correlations of .24 versus .36.

The importance of grandparents in the lives of these adolescents also appears in their twelfth-grade interviews. They were asked a series of open-ended questions about one of their grandparents. The grandparent chosen for the open-ended questions was based on the following protocol: If the grandchild admitted to having a favorite grandparent (which 59 percent of them did), then that grandparent was chosen. If there was no favorite, then the grandparent they saw or talked to most often was chosen. Some grandchildren only had one living grandparent and they were, of course, chosen. In a few cases where the boy or girl named two grandparents as favorites or saw them equally often, the same-sex grandparent was chosen.

What Grandchildren Like Best

What did children like best about relations with their most significant grandparent? As figure 6.2 shows, the most common response (40 percent) had to do with sharing similar interests and activities—doing things together, getting along very well, and talking a lot. Some youth lived in the same community as their special grandparent. As one girl remarked about her maternal grandparents, "I see them all the time, and they're at most of my special things in life. Like, they always go to concerts or games, or they're always here for my birthday and holidays. I go to the same church as they do, so I just see them more."

Thirty-two percent thought their grandparent was a particularly good person. In discussing his grandfather, a grandson remarked, "He's so friendly and outgoing with people. I think I really admire that. . . . I rarely see him mad. Mom said he wasn't always like this. . . . Sometimes after you get rid of your children and move on to grandchildren you

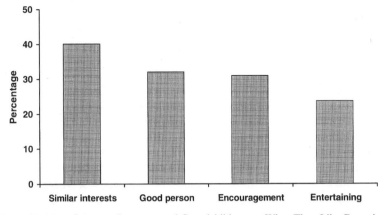

Figure 6.2 Most Common Responses of Grandchildren on What They Like Best about Chosen Grandparent, in Percentages. Note: Percentages add up to more than 100 because adolescents could provide more than one response (up to four); $N = 363$.

change a little." Almost as commonly cited is emotional support—the grandparents were people who gave them encouragement or advice, listened to them, understood them, and were always there for them (31 percent).

Some grandparents enable their grandchildren to feel special, as though they mattered: "Well, she just thinks I'm great. . . . She's a lot like my mom. I have a feeling I'll end up a lot like both of 'em." In the words of another girl, "My grandmother always talks to me about what I want to do in the future and how I'm doing in school. And she tries to encourage me in doing everything I want to do . . . she tells me 'I believe in you, you're so smart.' She just makes me feel like I belong some place in this world and [that] I'm going to make something of myself."

In other cases, grandparents became significant others when support was lacking from parents or other key people. One girl who shows horses and loves working with them found a supportive ally in her maternal grandfather: "He really understands what I want to do. . . . [My] other grandparents haven't a clue on what it is, and my dad thinks it's a waste of my time, but my grandpa, he's really cool about it all." Similarly, a grandson counted on his supportive grandfather: "I guess he's always been supportive of me, wanting me to go in the Air Force. My parents got on my back for getting Bs and Cs. He said just, 'Good job kid. Good work.' "

Another reason youth were attracted to their grandparents had to do with their good nature. They were often funny or fun to be with, or had a lot of spirit (24 percent). A granddaughter described her grandmother as "kind of older, but, she's young. She really enjoys life and doing things and getting out with people, and she doesn't like to be a homebody."

Living in close proximity helped to foster the grandparent-grandchild relationship, just as a great distance made it more difficult. A boy remarked that the best thing about his relationship with his paternal grandmother was that "she's close. She only lives a mile up the road, so a lot of times if I want a snack, and she always has goodies to eat, or a can of pop, [I] go up there and talk to her, and make sure she's getting along all right . . . [it's] a good, nice place to meet with the relatives, and it's just somewhere you can go and watch TV for a little while."

A similar theme was echoed by a girl about her grandmother: "Well, she lives right behind the high school and she's close. If we ever needed anything she was the one we called so we just kind of grew up thinking if mom's not home, grandma's there." As noted, children who live in farm families are most likely to live near their grandparents. In reference to his father's father, a farm boy observed that "I've known him my whole life because he helps out on the farm. I see him every day. . . . He's really smart. He knows what he's talking about and is funny. Just good to be around."

What Grandchildren Have Learned

Grandparents can be important role models for their grandchildren and, as we have seen, a good many participate in mentoring activities. Most study members report learning important lessons from their grandparents (see figure 6.3), with more than one-third mentioning developing

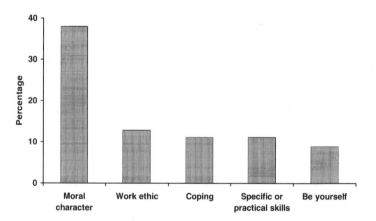

Figure 6.3 Most Important Things Learned from Chosen Grandparent, in Percentages. Note: Percentages add up to more than 100 because youth could provide more than one response (up to four); $N = 358$.

moral character and values in particular. When asked to identify the most important thing he had learned from his grandfather, a twelfth-grade boy thought it was "the basics of life probably. How to be a good person, how to be a gentleman and all of that. He helped bring me up better than most people." A boy from a working-class family concluded that "probably the most important thing would be church. She's [grand-mother] always encouraging me to go to church and Sunday School and youth group, and to be a Christian."

Other values that children learned from their grandparents reflect family priorities. One boy's grandmother stressed that "it's good to stay close with family. I realize that now that I'm out of high school, a lot of people I was around in high school are not going to be there for me, . . . [but] family are going to be with you for a long time." This sentiment is echoed by a young woman who noted that her mother's mother taught her "that your family is the most important thing to you, and that you should always stand by them no matter what."

Related to such values is the importance of a strong work ethic and of trying to do one's best, mentioned by another 13 percent. The son of a displaced farmer observed that he learned never to "stop learning even when you're older." In reference to his paternal grandfather, a farm boy recalled that "he taught me that you need to work hard if you really want to get somewhere. He's probably a perfect example of it. He still works hard today. Trying to keep his farm looking nice."

Another major domain is learning how to cope with adversity and making it through tough times (11 percent). Youth often learned this by example, with grandparents serving as important role models. As one girl put it, grandmother "taught me that even if horrible things happen to you, you can still survive. One of her daughters died when I was just two, and her husband died when Mom was sixteen, and her mother died. Her grandmother died. I mean, she's just had a lot of things happen to her that I think would be like the end of my world, but she's still here."

Helping Strategies

Three-fourths of these young people said their grandparent helped them do things (see figure 6.4). Proximity and good health enabled "helping" activities to occur. Grandparents were not seen as "helping" when they simply lived too far away for occasional contact, or when they were sick and thus unable to do things.

The most common "helping" response (38 percent) involved projects or teaching episodes. One girl singled out her mother's father for special

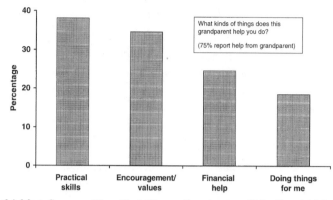

Figure 6.4 Most Common Ways That Chosen Grandparents Help Grandchildren, in Percentages of Grandchildren. Note: Of the 265 who said "yes," 260 had valid responses for the follow-up. Percentages add up to more than 100 because youth could provide more than one response (up to four).

praise. In the 4-H club, "if I have wood or finishing projects that I do, I always go down there and he helps me out." Similarly, another granddaughter talked about her mother's mother: "Every fall she takes all of us grandkids out on a nature hike. That's always fun. . . . Once she took us gliding in an airplane. She always has interesting things for us to do. It's just different every time with her."

Thirty-five percent of the study members also mentioned that their grandparents helped them out by giving advice and support on matters ranging from academic projects and sports to car repairs. A granddaughter noted that her mother's mother "advises me on a lot of things. She's real supportive of me, like if I sing at church, she'll come and watch." A significant number of grandparents (25 percent) provide financial support so that grandchildren can buy things that they want or need. Some youth were convinced that their grandparents will take an active role in helping them through college: "If I need money, he's there for me. . . . He helped me buy a car this year, . . . and he'll probably help me out with college too."

Grandparents as Confidantes

In theory, grandparents can serve as a resource for grandchildren in terms of helping them with problems they might be having, people to whom grandchildren can turn in times of need. But do grandchildren actually turn to grandparents with their worries or concerns? Many grandchildren in the sample claim they do. Only 18 percent did not (see

figure 6.5). A girl who had experienced the loss of her family's farm felt
that she could not discuss her family problems with her grandmother,
in large part because she feared that the discussion would find its way
back to her parents. Confidences were not easy to preserve. The precarious health of grandparents kept some youth from sharing much with
them. One boy thought that if he did bring up his problems, his grandmother would "probably get more worried than I would. It's not good
for her health." Others concluded that their grandparent couldn't and
wouldn't understand.

If faced with serious family problems, a number of youth thought they
would turn to either their friends or grandparents. As many as one out
of five talked to grandparents about problems with friends of either sex,
and a similar percentage talked more generally about "anything in their
lives." The confidante the study children turned to in situations of this
kind seemed to vary by the problem itself. A twelfth-grader offered her
philosophy by stating that "it all depends. Probably if something's real
deep, I'd go to my friends, but stuff that we can work out I'd probably
tell grandmother. If its problems like boys or something in school you'd
go to your friends. If it's a problem with your family or something you'd
go to your grandparents."[7]

It is not surprising in this age of divorce that family difficulties are a
common topic with grandparents. One-fourth claimed they were able to
talk to grandparents about problems they were having with parents, and
to get advice on what to do about them. A young granddaughter noted
that "in the past I've had a lot of problems with my mom and dad. I can

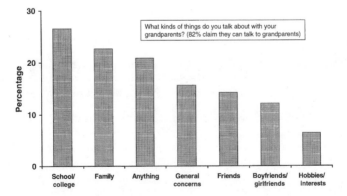

Figure 6.5 Grandchildren Who Say They Can Talk to Chosen Grandparent about
Their Problems: The Most Common Problems They Talk About, in Percentages. Note:
Of the 296 who said "yes," 282 had valid responses for the follow-up. Percentages add
up to more than 100 because youth could provide more than one response (up to four).

talk to grandfather about that. And my siblings too. If I have a problem with them, he's got a pretty good view of how to solve problems like that."

Times of marital discord led a working-class girl to ask her maternal grandmother "if she would talk to Mom or if she knows a way that I could say something to her without hurting her feelings about it." Even after a divorce, another grandparent tried to keep her former son-in-law in the grandchild's world. Members of the family "invite him to family things and still buy him Christmas presents."

These observations describe special grandparents. Over three out of five adolescents claimed they had a favorite grandparent, one to whom they felt particularly close over the years. Favorite grandparents were not always on the side of the angels, however. They could be intrusive and "pressing" as one young boy put it. "She feels she's got to know everything" about me.

Favoritism from the perspective of grandparenting is a family problem that typically ends up on the doorstep of parents. As one child put it, "Why does grandmother only pay attention to my brother?" Her mother's mother was her favorite "because she isn't always expecting something." In another girl's life, her father's mother tended to play favorites. She "really likes [my little sister] because she's tall and skinny and in basketball. She is always telling me, 'You need to lose some weight, you have to do this, you have to do that.' " Her other grandmother doesn't do that. "She loves me for what I am."

Overview

As these voices attest, a three-generation network can serve as an important resource for young people. Rural grandparents frequently represent significant others in the lives of their grandchildren. They can provide the means for youth to cope successfully with the stresses of contemporary life by providing a measure of support and guidance:

> Grandparents function as a family resource by bridging the past, present, and future for younger generations, giving a sense of security, aiding in ego development, and offering a vision of the future . . . grandparents expand the age range and number of available adult role models, . . . providing children a resource beyond their parents with which to identify and to learn about loving relationships.[8]

Our findings are consistent with accounts of the important roles that grandparents can play,[9] including helping parents become more understood by their children, serving as arbitrators in conflicts between parents and children, buffering stress when family members experience a crisis, providing family history and bridges to historical times that grandchildren never knew or have trouble understanding, and playing a listener role while offering assistance and attention.

Kornhaber and Woodward argue that a good many of these functions have been taken over by surrogate providers (peers, teachers, media) who have no personal or lasting commitment to children.[10] However, grandparents are still key providers of most of these functions in rural Iowa. More generally, the rising level of divorce and single parenting suggest that grandparents are becoming more consequential in the lives of children. Indeed, demographic changes have only recently made the grandparent role a common and lengthy one.

Nevertheless, there is great diversity in the grandparent experience of young people in north central Iowa. Some report no meaningful grandparent or only negative experiences, while others vary widely in perceived closeness to their grandparents. These variations appear to make a difference in the developmental experience of youth, but do they emerge as a key influence? To answer this question, we consider different family arrangements and scenarios.

Significant Grandparents and Successful Development

Grandparents who truly matter in the lives of children are commonly thought of as people who become parents for grandchildren who lack them. These grandparents often represent "the last resort" when the father is absent and mother is ill or disabled, for example. They may resist parenting young children,[11] but they typically relent under pressing circumstances—when they discover that there is no one else. By contrast, significance in the rural Midwest is often acquired by grandparents in healthy, nurturant families. They have strong emotional ties to their adult children and partly because of that to their grandchildren as well.

In both family systems, grandparents can be thought of as a backup for the rearing of children. A backup system of this kind is in place for the troubled family when the grandmother takes the place of her daughter and former son-in-law as a social parent of their children. Lacking such a surrogate, some children might be placed in foster care. As such, the grandmother's contribution to the development of her grandchildren reaches a maximum. In the other world, rural grandparents add much to the richness of children's experience, but their contribution typically reinforces a "developmental" environment. They are unlikely to have an influence beyond that of the parents and immediate family. In this sense, they are "socially redundant" and add mainly to existing strengths.

But social redundancy may be more descriptive of the rural family in some areas than in others. Grandparents, we have noted, do some things that parents don't do. They are confidantes for problems with parents, and they can serve as unconditional supporters. Social redundancy may also be limited by the more sporadic nature of contact between grand-parents and their grandchildren. Even among farm youth who see grand-parents every day, their contact does not match the constant interaction with parents. As in much of the world of kinship, grandparents tend to make their primary contribution at points of crisis. They appear most fully when needed.

Keeping all of these issues in mind, there is one other distinction that has special relevance to the influence of grandparents: the age or life stage of the grandchildren. When are grandparents most likely to make a difference? Consistent with the primacy notion of human socialization, we might expect the impact to be greatest during the child's early forma-tive years. As a rule, the older the age, the lower the impact of socializa-tion and new experience. By the adolescent years, basic dispositions and patterns have been established, and family socialization is likely to have a reactive cast. Parental harshness and arbitrariness may be elicited by the behavior of an aggressive teenager. Iowa young people are in this age category and consequently may be an especially important factor in determining relations with their grandparents.

These accounts have little empirical foundation since studies have sel-dom even asked questions about the developmental influence of grand-parents in children's lives. For the most part, grandparental influence has been viewed as peripheral to the family's role. Grandparents are entertaining, but they are not a core factor in children's development. The studies that have been done are difficult to compare, owing to dif-ferences in samples and in measures of grandparenting and grandchild behavior. Nevertheless, it is instructive to note that most studies of grandparental influence have found positive effects, especially in early childhood. Thus, greater grandparental involvement has been linked to grandchildren's secure attachment as infants and young children; to higher placement on mental and physical development; and to fewer behavior problems and more coping skills among children of divorce.[12]

Note that all of these findings, except those pertaining to children of divorce, are based on early childhood. Cherlin and Furstenberg's (1986) national study found that grandparent involvement (closeness, contact, and style of grandparenting) was not associated with level of problems or distress at home or in school among older children.[13] In some cases, the sign of the relationship was negative, suggesting that grandparents were more involved when grandchildren were having problems. This is the interpretation Cherlin and Furstenberg prefer—grandparents tend to help out more when children and grandchildren are having problems. They also note that such children might be doing even worse if grandparents were not helping out.

As a whole, these studies do not tell us how grandparent involvement affects the well-being of grandchildren. An important unexplored path may involve parents in the middle generation. Grandparent involvement could be mediated by the behavior of parents and it may also be contingent on this behavior. When grandparents do not have close relations to their children, they have little chance of close relations with their grandchildren. Do these relations add anything beyond the impact of parental nurturance? The functions of grandparenting (e.g., companionship, mentoring, and financial support) are suggestive of explanatory pathways.

Another limitation of studies to date involves the tendency to focus on one or at most two grandparents, even though the same child may work out different relations with each grandparent. A strong relationship to one grandparent may be all a child needs developmentally, and this could be overlooked if the study only takes into account one set of intergenerational relationships. Our measure of grandparental significance takes into account the child's relation to all living grandparents.

To assess the developmental effects of closeness to grandparents (a five-item index), we used a sequential regression analysis for grade point average, perceived achievement, peer success or competence, feelings of self-confidence, and advice-seeking by mother and father. We distinguished between grades and perceived achievement because the latter is more likely to be influenced by positive relations with grandparents, especially in adolescence.

The first model includes full-time farm status and farm ties (part-time, displaced, farm-reared) in relation to nonfarm status, parental education, gender (male), and closest grandparent. The second model adds the perceived warmth of parents in the senior year (average of five-point ratings of each parent, 1994) to determine whether this factor accounts for the impact of the closeness to grandparents (see appendix table E6.3). Chapter 3 shows that the perceived warmth of father played a noteworthy role in the youth's concept of the future and social competence, especially with regard to self-confidence and father's recognition of the child's maturity through requests for advice.

Looking at results from the first model, we find that grandparental closeness makes a positive, though modest, difference in the lives of grandchildren. Having a close grandparent does not matter for the grandchild's grades in the twelfth grade, as one might expect, but it is linked to how positive students feel about their academic competence (beta = .12, $p < .05$). Consistent with reports of unconditional support from grandparents, youth do regard themselves as more competent in academics when they have a close grandparent in their lives. With the exception of peer success, grandchildren who have a close grandparent are doing significantly better on measures of personal and social competence, of self-confidence, and of maturity in giving requested advice to parents. The effects are statistically significant, with an average beta coefficient of .13, $p < .05$. All of these effects are modest, however, and they generally become insignificant for boys and girls when the perceived warmth of parents is added to the analysis.

Closeness to a significant grandparent provides little additional understanding of the successes and failures of youth through high school *when they have warm, supportive parents.* Well-educated parents were far more consequential for youth's academic achievements. But grandparents can be thought of as playing strategic roles of support when crises arise or when problems arise. They do not match the influence of their children as parents, but perhaps their efforts can prevent problems from arising or promote success in the midst of adversity, when all else fails. Some of the grandparents impressed upon their grandchildren the importance of family, of sticking together through thick and thin. The family, as one put it, "will be there when you need it."

To explore the notion of strategic help or influence, we focused on youth who were doing better at the end of high school than one would have predicted in terms of social background, and on those who were doing worse. We have referred to the former as resilient and to the latter as vulnerable. Using residual scores derived from prediction equations (appendix D), we identified both groups in relation to academic competence (includes grades, perceived achievement, sense of achievement), peer success or competence, self-confidence, and advice-giving from youth to parents. Resilient youth scored above the seventy-fifth percentile, and vulnerable youth scored in the lowest quartile. Boys and girls who were placed in the resilient category across three of the four measures were assigned to a general category. We followed the same procedure on vulnerability.

In relation to the general categories of resilience and vulnerability, we asked whether the presence of a close grandparent increased or decreased the likelihood of membership in each group. Controls included two types of farm status: full-time and farm ties or other (compared to nonfarm); male status; and parental warmth. Odds ratios show the prediction of membership in the resilient and vulnerable groups. Ratios above 1.0 indicate that the factor in question increased the likelihood of membership. Lower ratios identify factors that reduced the chance of membership.

Youth who were doing better than expected in the overall classification (the resilient adolescents) are distinguished only by the perceived warmth of parents. Adolescents with warm, supportive parents were nearly four times as likely to be doing better than expected, when compared to youth with low scores. The presence of a close grandparent is not a factor in this group, but it is an important barrier to doing worse than expected—the vulnerable youth (ratio = .50, $p < .05$, with parental warmth in the analysis; appendix table E6.4). A close grandparent, warm parents, and being female significantly reduced chances of becoming vulnerable and at-risk in high school. At least in our general classification of youth resilience and vulnerability, a strong family (supportive grandparents and parents) played a key role in lessening the chances of vulnerability.

A close grandparent also proves to be a protective influence on vulnerability relative to academic achievement (see appendix table E6.5). Adolescents with a close grandparent were less likely to become vulnerable ($p < .10$), while being male increased the risk significantly. Boys were less apt to do better than expected on academics, the only factor to make a significant difference ($p < .05$). The presence of a close grandparent also lessened chances of becoming vulnerable on self-confidence and advice requests from parents, but this effect proved to be insignificant with parental warmth in the analysis.[14]

When and How Grandparents Make a Difference

Though parents represent a key resource in the successful lives of adolescents, nurturant grandparents also play important roles at strategic points, especially when grandchildren are having difficulty with school, friends, and parents. It is noteworthy that youth are less apt to be at risk or vulnerable when nurturant grandparents are part of their lives.

Let us take another look at potential examples of grandparent contributions. For example, when parent-child relationships are weak, can a strong bond with grandparents make a positive difference? Can they make up for the loss of parental support, or do they merely minimize the consequences? The most straightforward way to investigate this proposition is to determine whether grandparental closeness makes the greatest difference in children's competence when parental warmth is below average.

Looking across all measures of academic and social competence, we

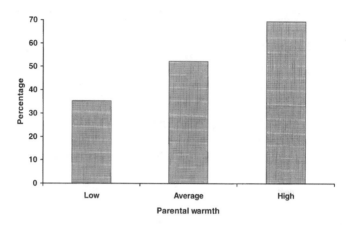

Figure 6.6 Percentage of Youth with a Close Grandparent by Parental Warmth, 1994

find no evidence that grandparents do have more of an influence under such circumstances. One reason for this outcome is the very small number of families in which parental warmth is low and the child has access to a close grandparent. To a very significant degree, grandparents become important when parents are nurturant to them and to their own children. Most of the adolescents fit this category. Of those who have poor relations with parents, two out of three also lack a single "close grandparent" to turn to in time of need.

By comparison, nearly three-fourths of the adolescents who have warm relations with parents also have a close grandparent (see figure 6.6). Only 18 young people come from homes where they have a close grandparent and nonsupportive parents. This compares to 33 families in which youth lack both supportive parents and grandparents, and 73 families where both parents and grandparents are very supportive.

The critical comparison involves two groups that are below average on parental warmth (appendix table E6.6). The only difference between them involves the presence of a close grandparent in the second group. Using all of the developmental outcomes from grade 12, group comparisons typically reveal the expected difference, suggesting that grandparents are consequential, but the difference they make is too small to reach statistical significance. However, we gain insight into these different family situations through the commentaries of youth who were interviewed in the twelfth grade.

The Nonsupportive Family

In nonsupportive families, young people describe their parents as below average on parental warmth and do not mention a grandparent to whom they feel close. Indeed the most notable feature is the lack of commentary on grandparents. Several young people noted that their grandparents lived too far away and that they did not have very much contact with them. They rarely felt that they could discuss personal problems with them or that the grandparents were receptive to helping.

Consider the Cole family. Donna, the daughter of a displaced farm family, rated her parents low on parental warmth, and all three of her living grandparents received scores indicating their below-average status in response to how much they made her feel loved and how much she could depend on them. She scored below average on every outcome except grades. She was also in the vulnerable groups for advice-seeking by parents and peer success. Donna did not have a favorite grandparent, so she was interviewed about her maternal grandmother, whom she saw most often.

When asked what she liked best about their relationship, she replied "I don't know. I just don't see her all that often." She did not feel that she learned anything of importance from her grandmother or that she could talk to her abut her problems. The interviewer noted that Donna appeared to have little interest in herself or her life. Her defiant attitude added to the problems her parents were having in dealing with their own personal and material difficulties following the loss of their family farm.

Possibly resulting from the farm loss, the child's paternal grandparents played a peripheral role. They were not people to whom Donna could turn when problems arose. This situation changes dramatically when youth have access to caring grandparents.

Making a Difference

Our interviews highlight the importance of a responsive, caring grandparent for youth who lack such qualities in relations with parents. All of these families rank below average on parental warmth, but the study child has one or more close grandparents to turn to in time of need. Youth described their close grandparent as "like a parent," "a friend," someone who "understands me," is "nonjudgmental," and "a good listener," someone they can talk to, and a person "who makes me feel good." In the senior high interviews youth viewed many of these grandparents as very special figures in their lives, even though this is not clear from the quantitative analyses.

Sally Greene and her family are a typical example. Though not involved in farming themselves, the Greenes have farm backgrounds. When she was in the ninth grade, Sally's parents divorced after years of marital problems. She placed her father extremely low on parental warmth and her mother somewhat higher but still below average for mothers. She did not have a very close relationship with her paternal grandparents. However, she had developed a significant relationship with her mother's parents. She rated them high on dependability and love.

Sally chose her maternal grandfather as her favorite and describes a relationship in which she receives much love and guidance. The best part of their relationship is that grandfather is her "mentor" who is "always there for me, no matter what." She describes him as a "very Christian man" who gives her much biblical advice. Despite her many family problems, Sally repeatedly stressed the importance of family and expressed a determination to have a strong marriage and family of her own someday. Her grandfather's guidance was important in this commitment. "He just kind of taught me that family are always there. He's . . . been like the head of the family. . . . As he put it to me, 'Your family will always be there for you.' "

Sally's grandfather has always been a stable force throughout her life, someone with whom she used to spend her weekends with while growing up: "I always helped on the farm. I loved doing chores, and I'd get my boots on and I just thought that was the greatest thing. In the summer I'd get on the tractor with him and we'd bale hay." Here was an adolescent who could turn to a caring grandparent whenever she needed to. Whenever she felt down, "I'd call him up. It only takes one phone call, just to hear his voice. Then I go on with my life."

Notwithstanding all of this support, Sally scored below average on every outcome except grades. She was academically resilient, doing better than expected, but was also in the vulnerable group on advice-seeking by parents. Her parents were less likely to seek her advice relative to expectations based on her background. The troubled marriage and eventual divorce of her parents continued to distress her, as did the coldness of her mother and father. Her grandparents provided some compensation for the failures of her parents' marriage, but they could not fully make up the deficit. Grandfather, in particular, provided a safety net that kept his granddaughter from falling into a vulnerable group by the end of high school.

Family Strength and Social Redundancy

Family strength and social redundancy exposed youth to a richness of relationship that gave them the assurance of "their family being present when needed." If something happened to a parent, such as illness or hospitalization, other members would step up to fill the void. Sometimes these other members were grandparents. Social redundancy provides a fail-safe family environment for children in a time of great uncertainty from one season to the next.

Grandparents were a popular topic for nearly all of the adolescents in this group. They saw their grandparents as being involved in their lives, as seeing them often, and as being able to talk to them. Interestingly, a few did live far away but were nevertheless able to maintain strong ties. Other youth talked to their grandparents about family fights that troubled them or family problems, despite having parents who scored extremely high on warmth.

Phyllis Thomas and her family best illustrate this family system. She described both her parents as warm and caring people, giving them the highest score on the scale. She also felt close to all four grandparents, but especially to her mother's mother. When asked what she liked about the relationship, she replied that she "could talk to her about anything. She is easy to relate to if I have a problem, and she likes to do things." Over the years Phyllis had learned many things from her grandmother, but especially about "how important your family is and closeness. Our family is really close. I want to raise my kids like she raised my mom because I think my mom did a good job raising me. She learned that from her mom."

This grandmother helped her on school projects and provided what she termed "an understanding heart" when she was having "a fight with her mother." Often she found herself sharing thoughts about the future. "She wants me to go to college after school and then get a good job. I want to be an accountant, and she's glad about that. Thinks it will be a good job for me." Beyond this special grandmother, Phyllis also had very positive relations with her other grandparents. She would consult with them at times and always felt much supported by their interest in her activities and achievements.

Across these types of family circumstances one gains an appreciation for the genuine contributions of grandparents to the successful development of their grandchildren, *and* an awareness of their limitations. Proximity is clearly an important factor in whether certain grandparents will become significant in the lives of grandchildren. However, proximity is not the determinant of intergenerational relations. Other important factors are part of the calculus.

In the upper tier counties of Iowa that are part of this study, grandparent involvement is typically embedded in a strong, effective family system. In many cases, this involvement reinforces the strengths of the family unit, enhancing nurturance and moral structures that tend to place young people on paths of academic and social success. Phyllis Thomas not only has two loving parents to turn to, but four caring grandparents who are very much a part of her life. The social resources of this family (the Thomases are also engaged in their local community) ensure an abundance of developmental support and a plentiful supply of social insurance for difficult times.

Involved grandparents support the striving for excellence by their grandchildren, as seen in their frequent attendance at plays, PTA meetings, class performances, and athletic contests. This support may add up to an important difference in some families, but it generally reinforces the positive contributions of parents and siblings—they are one part of the support team and clearly a most important part for some youth. However, the distinctive grandparent contribution appears to be that of a "safety-net" that keeps certain young people from becoming children at risk. One way grandparents play this role is through their local church and religious faith. We see this influence played out among youth who are part of church youth groups and their Thursday night meetings.

CHAPTER SEVEN

Church, Family, and Friends

Thursday night was church night—everyone went to their youth groups.

High school boy, small town

The communal life of farm country and small-town Iowa is organized in large measure through the rural church, with its notable place in young people's lives. Though some congregations are aging rapidly as the young move away to find jobs, and some church memberships have fallen dramatically, rural churches continue to bring people together in ways that make a difference in children's lives. These significant others include grandparents, parents, and friends. Churches offer an activity program in which the parents and friends of youth meet and interact around common objectives. We view this world as an adult-sponsored community where parents and peers function as moral allies rather than as adversaries.

Iowa children most likely follow the church involvement of parents and their adult friends, first through Sunday school and later into the youth-group meetings of Thursday night. In theory and reality, the choices that lead youth along this path establish a selective functional community that upholds standard community values. The protective nature of this community of like-minded people is commonly noted by parents who seek worlds of this kind for their children.[1] Examples include the near total institution of a Catholic parish, its school, and its youth organizations.

When successive generations settle nearby, churches become meeting grounds for the "larger family" and its religious culture. As noted in the last chapter, children grow up in the midst of their grandparents, beginning at birth or shortly thereafter. The latter attend significant religious events, such as confirmation and baptism, and claim that they frequently talk to their grandchildren about matters of religion, including the power

This chapter was written in collaboration with Valarie King.

of prayer. As one grandmother put it, faith can help these young people manage tough situations. She tells her grandchildren that sometimes "you wonder if it'll ever work out, but it will."

The older generation's presence on Sunday morning adds an element of social control and stature to church-going. Grandparents speak of looking for their grandchildren each Sunday and recall the disappointment when they do not come. Not surprisingly, the decision on whether to attend may entail some concern about "what Grandmother will think if I don't show up." Such questions signify a culture of elder authority and respect that grandparents bring to the rural church.[2] When grandchildren are expected by grandparents to participate in the life of the church, they are more likely to do so.

In addition to this multigenerational culture, the rural church fosters a network of parents and children who know each other and possess a common culture. Teenage friends who attend the same local church generally have parents who know each other and share common moral values. With its program of service activities, entertainment, and religion, the church youth group draws religiously involved adolescents into active membership during early adolescence, producing a shared culture on issues that matter. Religion "gains the power to alter behavior when it is supported by attachments to others who accept the authority of moral beliefs that religion teaches."[3] Given this selectivity and reinforcement, it is not surprising that children in religious groups are more successful in avoiding problem behavior than other youth.[4] Their religious involvement significantly lowers the risk of drug and alcohol abuse. This involvement also reduces the risk of problem behavior and emotional depression, while promoting competencies for later success, as in greater academic success.

Religious involvement can be thought of as a "public" and collective expression of religion.[5] When parents and children attend church, they participate with others in a collective expression of religious music, ritual, and teachings. In this chapter, we focus upon church attendance and participation in the church youth group. Prayer and religious beliefs represent a private side of religiosity. While religious involvement tends to foster academic success and the avoidance of problem behavior, some religious beliefs may discourage intellectual inquiry and academic excellence. Belief in the infallibility of biblical scripture is one example.[6] These beliefs were not measured in this study, and we do not consider potential connections between such beliefs and intolerance. The social capital dimensions of religious life are at the core of this chapter.

We first consider the extent to which Iowa families pass along their faith through religious practices and then turn to the meaning of religious activity among friends in church and youth group. We close by asking how the religious involvement of youth matters for competencies at the end of high school.

Passing on Religion

Religion has particular salience in the midwestern rural culture of young people. Rural midwesterners rank at the top on church attendance among Americans, and rural families are generally more involved in church life than urbanites.[7] They are most likely to form relationships with members of their congregations. Given such practices and the religiosity of Iowa parents, it is not surprising that many young people in this study are involved as well.

During the eighth grade, for example, nearly four out of five adolescents attended church at least weekly, while only 5 percent never attended. By the twelfth grade, weekly attendance had dropped some, to 46 percent, though other church activities (such as choir and youth group) had become more attractive (from 31 to 58 percent). The Thursday evening youth group, ranging from grade 8 to 12, was the primary activity for over 80 percent of the adolescents who were doing things in the church. In addition to religious instruction, youth groups organized discussions on matters of common interest, carried out service projects in the community, and planned social events or trips. One group helped flooded communities during the great summer flood of 1993 when the midsection of Iowa resembled another great lake. Only 12 percent were involved in the choir, and even fewer reported activities such as organist, council member, usher, and Sunday school teacher.

To index the religious involvement of youth each year (eighth, ninth, tenth, twelfth), we summed church attendance with involvement in church activities.[8] A total measure averaged across the four time points has scores ranging from 0 to 3 ($\overline{X}$ = 1.94). Youth with high scores were consistently involved in weekday church activities and the Sunday service, while those who scored lowest were consistently uninvolved. Three out of four adolescents are Protestant, mostly Lutheran, Methodist, and the United Church of Christ (a merger of Evangelical and Reformed and Congregational Christian churches), while the remainder include Catholics and a small number who report no affiliation. Critical points of involvement extend from the eighth grade to the end of high school.

As shown in figure 7.1, the unusual involvement of farm parents in the religious life of their communities is matched by the involvement of their children. Farm families played a leading role in the establishment of churches, and they continue to be well-represented in socializing

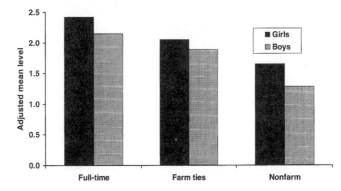

Figure 7.1 Religious Involvement by Farm Status among Girls and Boys, Adjusted Mean Levels. Note: Means adjusted for parent's education and family per-capita income (1989)

youth for a community of like-minded adults, a functional world in which parents know each other and share values. An elderly grandmother, who once farmed, recalled a story passed down across the generations about her family's role in setting up first churches and then schools in the region "so children could learn to read the Bible."

Beyond farming, well-educated parents tended to have children who are involved in the church, and economic well-being appears to matter very little (appendix table E7.1). The least stable families in residence are also least likely to have active children, and boys are less involved than girls. But the important factor is the religious practice of both the mother and father. Parents who attend church on a regular basis have children who are involved. Parental influence explains more than two-thirds of the effect of farm status along with the influence of education, residential change, and civic ties.

Parents who are actively involved in the church establish a culture of church-going and practice that provides standards and incentives for youth.[9] Speaking perhaps for others, a young girl reported that her parents had "made her go" to church, though now she was taking an active role in the youth group. Another boy describes the natural progression that occurred in his life. "My mom and dad went every Sunday. It's kind of like your choice, but I go because of my family. That's where they grew up and I grew up around the church." Transportation in the family car played a role as well for youth who lived on farms. Going to church provided a way to get off the farm and see friends.

Are grandparents an influence on the church-going of grandchildren apart from parents? Qualitative interviews underscore the importance of religion in forming a link between grandparent and grandchild. Some youth report that their grandparents have attended their church events, such as choir performances. On occasion they encouraged their grandchildren to become more involved. One grandmother helped her granddaughter with the catechism. "I'd always go there [to Grandma's house] to spend the afternoon, and she would help me with all that." Another girl noted that her grandfather had given her "a lot of Biblical advice." More than anything, he wanted to "pass on spiritual values which seem to be missing in much of today's generation. We are a religious people and have strong spiritual and moral values."

The importance of passing on one's faith to grandchildren is stated in many different ways, from the desire to have them become "very good Christian people" to the notion that this standard is the most important inheritance for the next generation. We do not have adequate information on the grandparents to put intergenerational transmission to an adequate test, but we could determine whether church-going grandparents made a difference in the religious practice of grandchildren, even apart from the practice of parents. We averaged the church attendance of all grandparents as well as the attendance of both parents. Actively involved grandparents are likely to have involved grandchildren (beta = .27, $p < .01$), and this effect remains significant, though diminished, even with parental attendance in the analysis: a coefficient of .07, $p < .05$. One out of four families rank high on church attendance (at least once a week) across the three generations. Only 5 percent of the three-generation families were uninvolved in the church—they attended less than once a month or never.

Religiously active youth are likely to come from a family of churchgoers, but the increasing popularity of church-sponsored youth activities through the adolescent years underscores the importance of age-mates or friends for continued involvement. Meetings of the youth group bring young people together for activities they enjoy, unlike "the deadly boredom of a church service," as one young boy explained. He probably "would have lost total interest in the church" had it not been for his "youth group and Sunday school." But in other ways, these groups embrace family values and control, defining a network in which the boy's parents know the parents of his "youth-group" friends.

From Church to Youth Group

Entry into a church youth group during the eighth grade can be thought of as a rite of passage, marking greater opportunity for self-direction and autonomy, a place where youth have more say about their activities than they had before. In the midst of friends with common values, members of a youth group generally feel comfortable talking about such issues as religion, sex, and problem teachers. As a boy put it in the twelfth-grade interview, it is good "knowing that basically everyone agrees with me." When he says something, they reply "Yeah, we understand." It is easier talking about "being teenagers" when "I'm with my friends."

Youth programs are less available today as rural churches decline in size. An elderly grandfather spoke with great pain about the loss of his church and the lack of social programs for young people. There is "nothing for them to do" socially. "It seems like today all the young people want to go somewhere else. Our attendance got down so low that we just couldn't keep it going financially." Another grandparent noted that "we're going to lose a lot of our youth programs. Even our little rural church will go before long. We don't have little children growing up in our neighborhood like we used to."

In their senior year of high school, some members of a church youth group stressed its popularity. A middle-class boy from one of the larger towns in the study region observed that "it was kind of a popular thing to be a member of your church youth group. Thursday night was church night, and everyone went to their youth groups. At the time it was just what all your peers were doing." Though actively supported and occasionally chaperoned by parents, the popularity of youth group had much to do with its program of appealing activities, especially in communities that had little else for young people to do together. They enjoyed bowling, roller skating, sledding, and pizza making, as well as the pleasure of doing something together to benefit others, such as fund-raisers for worthy causes and volunteer efforts on behalf of the institutionalized elderly.

During the ninth grade, we asked youth whether their friends would think the following activities were "cool": athletics, school activities, working hard to get good grades, community activities, and church activities. "If you had done one of these things, what do you think your friends would say if they knew about it?" Adolescents who were not involved in the church and youth group (the lower third on index) were most apt to rank athletics in first place and school activities in second. The religiously involved (upper third on index) tended to place church activities more highly, as one might expect, along with school activities. Perceptions of peer values by religious involvement differ most among the boys (figure 7.2). Involved boys were more likely to believe that church and school activities were "cool" things to do among their peers, compared to the uninvolved.

For a more specific account of the social norms of the youth-group community, we asked youth whether their friends encouraged deviant behavior and were involved in such activities themselves. "Sometimes

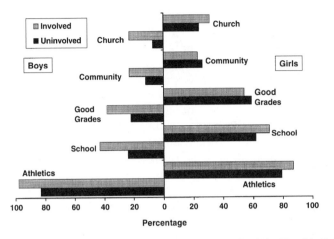

Figure 7.2 Percentage of Friends Who Say Activities Are "Cool" by Youth's Religious Involvement

your friends may want you to do things that could get you into trouble at school. How often do your friends encourage you to do the following things?" The encouragement scale included thirteen types of behavior, ranging from "cheating on a test" to "drinking beer" and using "illegal drugs." Responses range from "never" to "often" (scores from 1 to 4) with an overall alpha coefficient of .89 for the tenth grade. As one might expect, the more involved youth were least likely to describe friends who encouraged such behavior ($r = -.21, p < .01$). Involved boys were not different from girls in this perception of friends.

In the same grade, we also asked the students how many close friends had done any of the listed problem activities over the past year. The fifteen activities ranged from "joyriding" and "hitting someone" to skipping school, stealing, and the use of drugs. Scores varied from 0 to 14 (alpha = .78). Girls were less likely than boys to report such peer activities, but in both cases these reports were less often made by adolescents who were involved in the church and youth group. The overall correlation is identical to that reported on friend encouragement.

These differences, though modest in size, fit a general pattern that represents support for the moral values of the rural community and its parents. In the tenth grade, we find that youth who are involved in the church are most likely to claim that they respect their parents, especially their mothers. They believe "other people" also respect their parents.[10] Religiously involved youth are less inclined to see friends that their parents object to. Though nearly half of the adolescents felt they would see their friends even if parents had objected to them, this was not as likely to be the sentiment of those who were involved in the church and youth group (a 12 percent difference). Last, the involved adolescents were also actually less apt to spend time with friends during the week and on weekends.

Such perceptions of friends are consistent with the study members' values in the church and youth group. In the tenth grade, these youth were more likely than other adolescents to consider a college education and career success as very important in their future.[11] They were also more likely to want to become religious people, to improve the world, and to achieve good marriages. Beyond simply keeping them off the streets, or as one boy put it "cruising up town trying to find trouble," the church community gave them people to turn to in time of trouble and pointed them in the direction of worthy goals and moral standards. In many cases, the minister was someone young people could talk to if they "had problems at school or something."

Youth programs in church recruit young people with such values, but they also reinforce and sustain them among contrary forces. Service values, for example, are reinforced by volunteer activities and their rewards—"helping out and having fun at the same time," as an active participant noted. A farm boy with many responsibilities at home explained how much satisfaction he received from helping people "in retirement homes and making them feel comfortable with themselves." Leadership values were strengthened by the experience of running the youth group. For a young farm girl, this effort proved to be a way of "getting other people involved in it" and enabled her to put religious beliefs into action. Such leadership efforts also strengthened her self-confidence.

Though youth groups recruit young people and are age-segregated in this sense, the age range extends from eighth to twelfth grade, and members are linked to adults through various church functions, such as putting on a play for the congregation. This larger community exposes the young to achievement models and lessons that reinforce success goals. The college preparation and plans of older youth are part of the group experience for younger adolescents. Some of these influences are noted by Sanders,[12] who found that involvement in the black church made a significant difference in the achievement of young people. Regular participation in church services and programs strengthened self-concepts of academic achievement, work habits, or discipline. Within the church, young people found guidance and encouragement from congregation members with whom they established strong ties.

As a whole, these features of youth in a religious community provide insights into why they generally succeed academically and socially, according to most reports. The disciplines of achievement are reinforced by community themes of hard work, responsibility, and integrity. In families that are connected to church members in the community, involved youth tend to know more about opportunities and are likely to believe in their ability to build upon them. Guided by parents, adults, and peers, these young people are less apt to associate with youth who regularly break the law. Advantages cumulate along a path that invites more adult support.

We turn now to the competence of involved youth. How much does it matter that some youth are involved in the rural church and youth group, while others are not?

Religious Ways and Competence

The developmental relevance of church and youth-group activity involves three issues that center on selection and personal change. The first concerns religious activity at the very beginning of adolescence and the notion that active youth are most likely to be drawn into the youth program. The effect of involvement may partially reflect this selection process.

A second issue concerns involvement over time. Other things being equal, the young person who remains involved is most exposed to the experience. Change in religious involvement through the high school years thus has particular relevance for the development of competence in academics and peer relations.[13] Seniors who are doing well in school and with peers are likely to have more exposure to the disciplines and objectives of church and youth group, and also to classmates who subscribe to them.

The third issue focuses on developmental change in competence from early to later adolescence—the eighth to the twelfth grade. Here we distinguish between competence as status and competence as developmental gain. Does increasing religious involvement (a difference score between eighth and twelfth grade) enhance the likelihood of even greater academic and social success by the end of high school? Which youth are doing better in grades and relations with peers by the time they leave high school? In addressing this issue, we include religious involvement at the beginning of adolescence to appraise the importance of selection and evidence of increasing religious involvement.

All three issues find empirical support in a set of regression analyses (appendix table E7.2). A youth's religious involvement in the eighth grade is generally predictive of his or her competence by the twelfth grade, especially on grades and peer success (model 1). Second, adolescents who *become more involved* religiously by the end of high school (model 2) tend to rank higher on indicators of competence, from academics and peer success to self-confidence and relations with parents. Model 3 includes measures of religious involvement and competence for grade 8 and shows very similar results. Farm status, parental education, and the adolescent's gender are controlled in all outcomes.

Consistent with most studies, religiously involved youth tend to stand out primarily in terms of academic competence. They do better on grades and tend to see themselves as more competent. This connection applies especially to youth who remain involved up to the end of high school. Not surprisingly, initial activity in the church tells us less about this competence than an increasing pattern of involvement, which is most predictive of an increasing level of academic competence. We do not have religious beliefs in this analysis, but even if we did, they are unlikely to show a different picture. It seems that fundamentalist beliefs (such as the inerrancy of the Bible) dampen aspirations for advanced education, according to recent studies,[14] though religious beliefs in this cultural region broadly favor education.

We have assumed that the direction of influence flows from religious involvement to competence, though a case can be made for reciprocal influence as well. Some youth who are successful in academics and social leadership may become active members of a youth program, and participation in such groups would, in turn, enhance achievement. However, the primary flow of influence seems likely to move from religious activity and socialization to individual competence in academic achievement.

Students who are singled out by teachers as successful with their peers in the twelfth grade are likely to have been involved in the church and youth program. This connection may well reflect the social and leadership skills acquired in youth programs. However, we find no evidence that *greater* involvement across the adolescent years actually enhances their status with peers. That is, greater activity does not predict a developmental gain in peer success. This may reflect the stability of peer popularity from middle school or early adolescence to high school, as well as our use of reports by parents in measures of change. Teacher ratings were not available during early adolescence, and thus we have to rely on the peer-status reports of parents. Presumably teachers know more than parents about the peer relations of students in school.

A number of the most active young people in youth programs spoke about how their self-confidence had increased as a result of their group experiences. We find some empirical evidence for this assertion in appendix table E7.2. The more involved young people were likely to hold more positive views of self in the twelfth grade, and they were likely to have become more self-confident over time, compared to other adolescents. The effects are not large, but they are consistent.

Greater self-confidence tends to arise from mastery experiences and from affirmations by others, including peers, teachers, coaches, community leaders, and parents. Young people who demonstrate the ability to manage difficult situations and carry responsibilities are generally sought for advice. We see evidence of this in the perceptions of parents by actively involved youth who tend to respect mother and father. They are also more likely to report that parents seek their advice. Fathers, in particular, are more likely to ask their advice, compared to the uninvolved adolescents. Increasing religious involvement clearly predicts greater advice-seeking by father.

A history of religious involvement represents an important factor in the development of competence among rural adolescents. The more youth remain engaged through high school, the stronger the influence. Does this influence enable some young people to do better than expected in terms of their early background? And does it prevent some from doing worse? We use the term *resilient* to describe adolescents who are doing better than expectations based on their background (see appendix D)—they are in the highest quartile on residual scores. *Vulnerable* youth scored in the lowest quartile. These groups were generated for each of four outcomes: academic competence, peer success, self-confidence, and advice-giving. For an overall classification, we identified youth as resilient if they were so described on at least three of the four measures. The same procedure was applied to a classification of vulnerable youth.

Odds ratios from logistic regressions indicate the extent to which eighth-grade religious activity and increasing involvement significantly identified resilient and vulnerable youth. Factors with ratios above a score of 1.0 increased the likelihood of membership in the resilient or vulnerable group. Lower ratios indicate lower prospects of group membership.

Overall, we find that youth who became more religiously involved over time significantly increased their prospects of doing better than expected: the resilient group (see appendix table E7.3). Initial religious activity did not make a difference, and neither factor significantly affected the risk of doing more poorly than expected.

As in our general models, more religious involvement sharply increased a youth's chances of doing better than expected on academic competence, and it also reduced prospects for vulnerability ($p < .01$ for both cases). This is also the case for peer success, self-confidence, and advice-giving. In addition, more religious involvement protects youth from becoming less popular or successful with peers than one would expect from their background.

By bringing together all of the threads in this account of religious activity, we can identify young people for whom religion is central to their family culture and life concept. Consider the case of Marie, the daughter of a part-time farmer with German and Norwegian ancestry who grew up on a farm outside of Marshalltown, Iowa. Marie's mother is working full-time; consequently Marie helps out at home whenever she can. Her two brothers also assist with household chores. The family belongs to the Lutheran church in their community and generally attends services at least once a week, as do the grandparents.

Marie is close to her parents and claims to be very close to her grandparents, especially on her father's side of the family. They still farm nearby. "They're just neat people," she says of her grandparents. Her paternal grandmother almost represents a second parent. With faith and practice the cornerstone of their life, these grandparents became an example that was not lost on her thinking. She admires them for the kind of people they are—enjoyable to be with, always supportive but firm. If possible, she does not want to live far from home. Family means too much to her.

When asked about important activities in the twelfth grade, Marie immediately pointed to her youth group, which she ranked as the most important activity in her life. "I believe in church. Just going to church has influenced my beliefs. I'm sure that the person I become will be basically because of things I got from church." She was active in the local church as early as the third or fourth grade, and attributed this to her parents' insistence. She became president of the local youth group, along with many other activities in school and church. By the end of high school, Marie was putting much of her time into school, church, and peer activities, and she placed well above average on academics and peer popularity.

The significance of young people's involvement in a religious community is mirrored by its importance as a legacy from their grandparents. When asked what they would most like to pass on to their grandchildren, they frequently come back to religion and the faith that has served them well over difficult times—loss of farm, health, family members; the cycles of flood and drought. Faith should be at the heart of life. With it all things are possible.

A grandmother who had survived a troubled year urged her granddaughter to "have faith in the Lord" during a time when her family was losing their farm and her parents were struggling. Some days later she paid a return visit and said, "Oh, Grandma, you helped me so much." In the grandmother's words, "it made me feel good to think that I could tell her these things that were very important in my life . . . you just have to have help and you can't do it alone." Iowa families, especially on farms, play a central role in equipping children with the moral values and beliefs that will nurture and structure their lives. Grandparents are an important part of this transmission.

In another family, a grandfather explained that spiritual and moral values are "something that I hope our grandchildren are learning from us." The rural church is part of this transmission through the congregation of believers and the shared culture of parents and friends. The co-involvement of adolescents and their friends in church youth programs establishes a culture that supports personal integrity, the virtues of civic life and civility, and an ethic of achievement. Their friends are allies of the adult community of parents. In perception, they do not encourage rule-breaking activities or problem behavior; and they favor investment in school, service to others, and cooperation.

Surrounded by adults and peers who care about worthy accomplishments, religiously involved youth tend to score higher than other adolescents on school achievement, social success, confidence in self, and personal maturity acknowledged by parents, but especially by fathers. They are more likely to surpass expectations of competence that are based on early background than are uninvolved adolescents. And they are less at risk of doing more poorly than this background would predict.

The importance of religious life in this region of Iowa reflects its general prominence in the rural Midwest[15] as in the South. Among small communities everywhere, civic life has much to do with the vitality of local churches. This may be especially true for children and youth, and their social life. Nancy Ammerman[16] refers to these church communities as the seedbed of civic life and humanitarian efforts. Religious communities may also inhibit innovative thinking and tolerance for different beliefs and groups. Such influences deserve more attention than they have received in the present inquiry.[17]

With family, church, and peers in the picture, we turn in the next chapter to the social experiences of school in an effort to explore the developmental significance of athletics, clubs, and leadership. These worlds are often small, but we have seen that the social resources of farm youth have much to do with membership in small worlds that offer many social options.

CHAPTER EIGHT

Lessons from School

Sports "made me realize how hard you have to work if you want to get somewhere someday."

Boy from displaced farm family

Adult-sponsored activities in Iowa schools and communities are a central feature of young people's lives, and athletic events, clubs, and leadership experiences are especially common among youth from farm families. This chapter asks whether civic life of this kind reflects the example set by parents and the participation pressures of small schools. Social participation and responsibility are imperatives of life in "small" communities and schools.[1] Kathleen Norris writes about the "frantic social activity in small towns" of the High Plains.[2] By addressing such issues, we examine the developmental potential of social participation and leadership. In theory, social activity promotes competence and feelings of personal efficacy, even among youth from hard-pressed backgrounds.[3]

The social involvement of young people typically entails challenges in mastery learning that resemble the mastery experiences of youth with work roles. Young people may be attracted by a game or a dramatic arts production, yet lack the required skills. To acquire such skills, they enter situations in which they have less control than they had before. This prompts efforts to regain control over their lives. The entire process may be thought of as a "control cycle" in the life course.[4] Enhanced by feelings of personal efficacy,[5] efforts to restore control may require some adjustment of expectations and resources. Equilibrium is achieved when expectations match reality or the resources available. Once expectations are fulfilled, they may be raised again, setting in motion another round of efforts to achieve control. In this manner, the activity involvement of young people fosters competencies and motivation.

Rural communities in the study region generally offer a range of social opportunities for their young people, including church groups, 4-H clubs,

This chapter was written in collaboration with Debra Mekos.

school clubs, and athletic teams. Looking at this variety, an older Iowan bemoaned the "hurriedness of life" in keeping up with many activities:

> Monday nights have many school functions. Tuesday night it is usually a ball game. Wednesday night it's probably something else. Thursday night is church night. Friday night it's another ball game. A lot of school events are scheduled for Saturday, and there are Sunday night activities for the children at church. So where is time for the family?

Some family time occurs when parents and children participate in the same activities, a common event among farm families. Transportation to each child's social activity, "running back and forth" as one parent put it, is also family time. Life is clearly very busy for Iowa parents who are heavily engaged in their careers, in their children's experiences, and in their communities.

We begin this chapter with a descriptive account of activity patterns across the adolescent years, junior high and senior high, and of how these differ by farm family status, community ties, and school size. From the seventh to the twelfth grades, only a fourth of the adolescents remained in the same school. The remainder made the transition to high school after the eighth grade, except for thirty-four youth who made the transition after the ninth grade. We turn next to the consequences of youth involvement for competence, and end with an account of how extracurricular participation fosters resilience in adolescents at risk.

Throughout, we stress the developmental relevance of adult-sponsored activities as they provide youth with the kinds of life challenges that enhance prospects for success in adulthood. They do so by establishing opportunities for self-direction, social responsibility, and leadership within a network of relationships to peers, teachers, and community adults.

Activity Patterns through Adolescence

Boys and girls in the study were asked to list all school and community-based activities in which they were involved during the eighth, tenth, and twelfth grades. These activities, presented in appendix table E8.1, were classified according to three general domains: (1) school sports, such as track and basketball; (2) school and civic clubs, from drama and math clubs to 4-H; and (3) school leadership roles, such as president of the class, co-captain of the football team, and editor of the school newspaper. We summed the activities in each domain for each year.

Membership in a youth organization is clearly the rule rather than the exception among young people in north central Iowa. During junior and senior high, over four out of five participated in some type of sport, three-fourths were involved in at least one school or civic club, and slightly fewer than half occupied at least one leadership role. A number of youth were engaged in multiple activities. In the eighth grade, a third played on at least four different athletic teams, one out of ten belonged to at least five different school and civic clubs, and a fourth held leadership positions in at least two organizations by the twelfth grade. Across the secondary school years, the typical adolescent devoted some 14 hours each week to school activities and another 4.5 hours to community organizations or functions.

This civic life is especially characteristic of young people who grew up on farms. Two groups of young people had ties to the land in their own lifetimes: those who *now live on farms*, whether full or part-time, and those who grew up on farms that were subsequently lost or left by parents—the *displaced.* The nonfarm adolescents had no direct exposure to farm life, although their parents may have lived on farms through adolescence. Youth from farm and displaced families rank well above the nonfarm group on leadership, even with adjustments for parental education and residential change, though not on sports and clubs ($p <$ .05; appendix table E8.2). These differences persist across the adolescent years. Consistent with the literature on sex-typed activities, girls are more involved in social clubs than boys are, but we find no difference by gender in athletics. One of the central themes of rural culture is the increasing prominence of girls in athletics.

We found no reliable difference between the leadership of farm and displaced youth, even though the latter experienced more severe stresses and dislocations in the agricultural crisis of the 1980s. Their fathers lost the family farms on which their living was based. At the end of the 1980s, displaced youth ranked well above farm and nonfarm youth on severity of emotional distress, perceived indifference from parents, and economic hardship.

How, then, can we explain their accomplishments in the midst of so much hardship? The daughters of displaced parents in the twelfth grade, for example, are more socially prominent through student leadership than girls from farm as well as nonfarm families. Boys in displaced families also rank high on social leadership, equal to the farm boys and well above the nonfarm group. The experiences of American children who grew up in the Great Depression may offer some explanation.[6] Especially in the middle class, adolescents from deprived families were observed to be more socially prominent than youth from more privileged families. The economic hardship and status deprivation of heavy income losses in the 1930s seemed to spur these children of the Great Depression "on to greater efforts in the household economy and on their own behalf in relations with members of their own age group."[7] Hard-pressed children did not accept poverty as a definition of their status, but worked doubly hard to make something of themselves, to achieve social recognition and acclaim on their own.

In a revealing portrait of himself, a boy had this to say: "You have to have ambition—you just can't have ability and personality; you have to work."[8] This outlook appears frequently among Iowa youth who have some ties to the land. In the aftermath of the Great Farm Crisis, displaced youth may have expressed comparable sentiments. They may have tried very hard to become people of worth on their own merits. Some of this ambition probably came from the paid work that was motivated by family need. For a young boy who worked on a hog farm, the realities of hard work told him that life would not be easy and that "you've got to put a lot of effort into it." He has also learned that he "can do anything" he sets his mind to. "I know I can do something if I try my hardest."

A senior girl from a displaced family claimed she had matured "a lot faster" through her many leadership roles—captain of the basketball team, vice president of her class, and so on. We shall meet other young people in this chapter who have come out of difficult circumstances and made something of themselves through social opportunities and activities.

To show how involvement changed in adolescence by farm status, we designed a set of graphs based on appendix table E8.2, beginning with sports (see figure 8.1). The tendency to participate on a number of sports

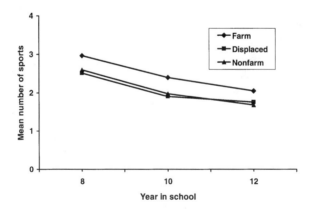

Figure 8.1 Sports Activity of Youth from Grade 8 to 12 by Farm Status

teams declined across the secondary school years. Increasing specialization and level of expertise may be one explanation, along with the discovery of personal talents. School culture in the seventh grade encourages widespread exploration of sports as a way of finding one's talents.

Involvement narrows to one or two sports over time, in response to greater competition from other discovered talent or a special relationship with a coach. This kind of story is told by a boy from a displaced farm family who ended up as captain of his high school varsity basketball team. He played all types of sports in the seventh grade, including wrestling and basketball, but a teacher and coach largely accounted for his continuing involvement in basketball: "I like him, he was my favorite. He coached us all the way up to our sophomore year. It's by far the best sport. We've been excellent, only lost fifteen times in seven years."

In contrast to the declining pattern of sports involvement, participation in clubs increased over time, especially among girls (figure 8.2). The overall pattern is typical for youth from all ecologies, farm, displaced, and nonfarm. Part of this increase may reflect the greater number and variety of clubs and interest groups typically offered to adolescents in high school as opposed to junior high school.[9] In any case, the upward trend no doubt also reflects a growing awareness of college-bound youth that membership in school and community activities is a crucial prerequisite for acceptance to a good university. Indeed, some mentioned this as the primary reason for joining an organization.

Consider the experience of a farm boy who became involved in Future Farmers of America in the ninth grade: "I got involved at first because I thought it was an organization I could get into that looked good on resumes and stuff. [But then I really started] enjoying it and ended up

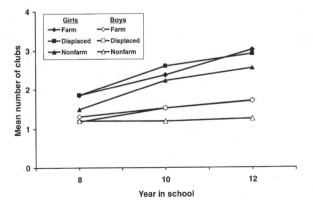

Figure 8.2 Social Club Activity of Youth from Grade 8 to 12 by Farm Status and Gender

in contests every year. I was treasurer, then vice president, and now president. This year I went down to Des Moines and got second place in the public speaking contest."

Impressive résumés can be a particularly useful resource for Iowa youth who plan to settle elsewhere. But do social activities reflect their goals? To address this question, we divided farm and nonfarm youth according to whether they wanted to settle down on a farm or live elsewhere. Farm youth who aspire to life outside their region rank at the top on school achievement, as noted in chapter 3. Those who want to live on a farm are next on achievement, along with youth in nonfarm communities who prefer living in another part of the country. Nonfarm youth who aspire to life on a farm, though not in terms of farming, are doing least well in school. These differences in goals are expressed in social activities.

The most involved adolescents, defined by number of club and civic group memberships, are those from farm families who plan to live elsewhere. Boys average two membership groups, and girls three and a half. These youth are college-bound and possess activity records to match. All other groups score much lower. Apart from this distinctive subgroup, the analysis shows that girls are far more active than boys ($p < .001$), that adolescents on farms are more involved than nonfarm youth, and that residential preferences matter ($p < .05$). Nonfarm preferences are associated with significantly higher levels of club activity. These differences are not as pronounced for athletic involvement or for leadership.

Explanations for the striking gender differences are less apparent, although they may be tied to the gender disparity in social roles and economic opportunities in farming communities. Earlier chapters have stressed the notion that pathways to success may lead in different directions for boys and girls, especially in the world of farming, where incentives for taking over the family business are far greater for sons than for daughters. If girls are educated early on to view their futures in terms of leaving home and pursuing higher education, then it is possible that their growing involvement across the high school years in organizations like Future Teachers of America, the speech/debate club, and math/science fairs reflect efforts to increase their options after high school. One girl expressed sentiments of this kind on her involvement in the Girl Scouts. "It has shown me different areas of life, different things I can do with my life. Like if I want to be a scientist or something, I can do that."

In student leadership we find yet another pattern of change over time, with significant declines between the eighth and tenth grades, followed by significant gains up to the twelfth grade (figure 8.3). This curvilinearity, which applies to all rural ecologies and gender groups, may have

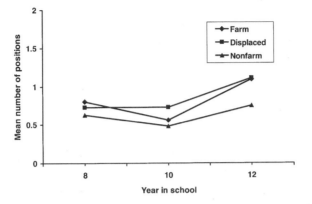

Figure 8.3 Student Leadership from Grade 8 to 12 by Farm Status

little substantive significance. In early adolescence, most leadership opportunities in athletics involve the role of captain of a team. By the tenth grade, the decline reflects pressures toward specialization in sports with reduced opportunities for leadership. In any case, leadership gains from the tenth to the twelfth grade most likely reflect the ascendance of students in the school's status hierarchy, and the greater number of organizations that have student leadership roles.

The leadership gain may also reflect the efforts of some youth to put into practice their striving for autonomy and social recognition as mature people. Consider the case of an enterprising farm girl who organized a student-run theater board for her high school in April 1993:

> A couple of years ago we had no say in what play we did, and it was horrible. We all hated it. I just thought I'd never let that happen again. So we kinda decided to overthrow the spring play director, and we offered the Shakespearean production as an alternative to the spring play. And then I started the theater board. Now we hire actors and actresses to come in and conduct workshops, and we're getting ready for our spring play.

Getting Involved: The Influence of Family and School

Why would farm youth be involved to a greater extent in the civic life of school and community? Part of the answer may lie in the example and guidance of their parents' social ties and leadership experience. Farm parents establish a social pattern and a model that can become the lifestyle of children, particularly during their dependence on parent transportation.

As noted in chapter 5, farm parents tend to embrace a stewardship ethic on care for the land and community. They are more active than other parents in social institutions that directly affect their children. They are more engaged in sponsoring and organizing youth programs, in serving as youth-group leaders, and in joining their children in church and civic functions. This round of activity tends to ensure continuity of adult support and guidance from home to school. Active parents demonstrate how problems can be solved and communicate through their experience the value and rewards of social responsibility to children. Their networks of engagement widen children's social worlds far beyond the immediate family, bringing them in contact with other caring adults.

A second explanation emphasizes the social imperatives of schools that farm children are likely to attend. Nearly half attended small schools in the eighth grade, schools that average fourteen to thirty students per grade. Little more than a fourth of displaced and nonfarm youth attended such schools. Consistent with arguments against school consolidation in the Midwest, a small school must draw upon the talents and energies of most students to field athletic teams and run clubs.[10] Opportunities call young people to participate, and these opportunities are especially great for student leaders. A third explanation links the competence of farm youth to the pursuit of student leadership and social activities. Competent youth tend to get involved.

In a classic study of big schools and small schools, Barker and Gump found that students who attended high schools of 150 students or fewer experienced particularly strong pressures to become involved and contribute in meaningful ways to the life of the school, regardless of gender, ability, or social class.[11] This involvement produced dividends for personal development in terms of inner confidence and mastery. As for the larger schools, student clubs and leadership roles were dominated by a handful of students. And the percentage of uninvolved students increased markedly. Assuming that this account applies to Iowa, social opportunities to become active in school and to assume leadership roles would be greatest for those who attended small schools. This should apply especially to youth who are living on farms across the north central region.

How important are socially active parents and small schools in the activities of Iowa youth? Turning first to the social connections of parents, we find that they significantly increase the likelihood of children's involvement over the secondary school years, as shown by the repeated measures analysis in appendix table E8.3. Within each level of parental involvement, from weak to strong, and across all domains (sports, clubs, and leadership) student activities up to the twelfth grade increasingly reflect the social ties of their parents. The greater the involvement of parents, the greater the involvement of children.

The community involvement of parents plays an important role in the athletic and leadership careers of their children. As noted earlier, involvement in sports tends to decline over the adolescent years, but it declines most notably when parents *are uninvolved in community affairs.* These less involved parents are more residentially unstable and have less education than other parents, but lack of community involvement by parents continues to have a dampening effect on children's athletic activities when these factors are taken into account. Student leadership, which was largely nonexistent in the eighth grade, tends to follow the same pattern over time. The sons and daughters of actively engaged parents increase their leadership experience from junior to senior high, while the children of less engaged parents lose status and leadership experience by the time they reach the twelfth grade.

Club activities show a striking pattern of gender differences. As prior analyses indicate, girls are far more involved in these activities than boys, a difference that increases over time. But this trend also depends on the community involvement of the same-sex parent. The data suggest that the involvement of the same-sex parent may be a stronger influence on a boy's or girl's social activities than their gender and related ideology.

The activity level of the father establishes the pattern for boys, whereas the mother's actions present an example for girls. Note that boys from families with strong parental ties, who by definition have highly engaged fathers as well as mothers, more closely resemble girls on their level of heightened involvement, while girls from families with weak ties, who by definition have minimally engaged mothers as well as fathers, more closely resemble the inactivity of boys.

Parental involvement emerges as a major factor in the activity patterns of Iowa young people, but the effect of this example may be constrained by social opportunities in the local schools. As mentioned, small schools offer more opportunity of this kind than large schools. At the time of our study, the consolidation of small high schools in north central Iowa was still in its early stage; thus nearly half of all study members were still enrolled in schools with fewer than fifty students in the graduating class. Furthermore, a fourth of the schools had a seventh-to-twelfth-grade structure in which students of all ages shared the same school building and staff. This design ensures a degree of student continuity that is relatively unusual in the American educational system.

We assigned youth in the study to one of three school sizes, based on student enrollment in the eighth grade: small schools with 14–29 students per grade ($N = 144$); medium-sized schools with 30–69 students per grade (N = 148); and large schools with 70–300 students per grade (N = 132). We chose to focus on the eighth-grade figures on size of school because the activity involvement of students is launched during these middle years.

Some students moved to larger high schools, but school size in the junior high period represents the critical context in rural Iowa schools. This is where activity patterns are established. Continuity of school size is the dominant pattern in any case. For example, over four of five students from small schools in the eighth grade were still in small schools by the tenth grade. Fewer than 10 percent had moved into large schools, as we have described them. Likewise, students who began in large middle or junior high schools were typically still in such high schools—nine out of ten.

We find no evidence that the effect of family civic ties varies by size of school. However, consistent with theory and expectations, the activity involvement of youth is inversely correlated with school size on all grade levels (appendix table E8.4). Students in each category of school size were arranged by level of activity across the three grades (eighth, tenth, and twelfth), and all mean scores were adjusted for parental education and residential moves. Regardless of grade, *students in small schools ranked at the top on sports involvement, clubs, and student leadership* ($p < .05$). They were also more likely to be involved across time. In the case of clubs and civic groups, students in small schools gained more on club activity up to the twelfth grade than youth in larger schools. A similar trend appears in student leadership, but it is not statistically significant.

In theory, access to leadership opportunities increases as organization size declines, and we do find evidence of this effect. Among the three types of activity, the likelihood of becoming a student leader is most strongly influenced by school size. With fewer students competing for participation and leadership posts in small schools, more students from these schools occupy multiple roles, especially in sports (see appendix table E8.4). Clearly, students in the smaller schools believe that in a larger school they would not, as one girl put it, "have the opportunity to participate in music, sports, and drama, as I do."

Another image of the small school features an all-consuming preoccupation with athletics.[12] Ethnographies depict rural communities in which high school football and basketball games become a focal point for social interaction and a primary source of pride for residents.[13] If accurate, this portrait suggests that students in small rural schools are motivated more by athletics than by doing well academically, providing, of course, that small schools are large enough to afford an interscholastic sports program. "Smallness" does, in fact, restrict such programs, but students in small schools at the eighth grade do not place significantly more or less value on sports (see appendix table E8.5).

What they do value more is schoolwork. When asked about the time they devote to schoolwork, students from small schools reported more hours on weekdays and weekends than youth in large schools. Consistent with this priority, they also claimed to spend far less time with friends over the week. Both differences were significant beyond the .01 level. Time devoted to school activities is slightly higher among students in the large schools, but the difference is not reliable. Similar commonality appears on time spent with family.

Do students in small schools believe they have more caring and involved teachers? Do they respect them more? Some comments from the twelfth-grade interviews suggest that they do. For example, a senior boy from a small school felt that he received "more personalized attention from teachers." Students in small schools do have more responsibilities, and they may feel more a part of things as well, though even our study's large schools would not qualify as large in urban America.

From the eighth-grade survey, we find that students in small and large schools alike believe that they have caring and involved teachers. Most think their teachers understand them. Only one question on respect produced a significant difference. Students in large schools were less likely to report respect for teachers and administrators than youth from small or intermediate-size schools ($p < .01$). Students in the larger schools were also more likely to acknowledge that they worried about "getting beaten up," compared to students in smaller schools, but this represents a low-priority issue overall.

Up to this point, we have identified three potential explanations for the greater involvement of farm youth in sports, social, and leadership activities, compared to the nonfarm group. They have parents who are (1) better educated and (2) more involved in community life, and (3) they attend small schools that offer greater opportunity for athletics and social roles. But do these factors account for their social prominence and academic achievement?

To answer this question, we designed a two-step regression analysis that predicts total involvement across eighth, tenth, and twelfth grades (appendix table E8.6). The first model includes the contrasts among farm, displaced, and nonfarm families, along with social factors such as gender, parental education, and family residential mobility. The second model adds size of school and the contrasts for parental community ties. Parental education is a significant influence on youth activity only in relation to clubs (beta = .26, $p < .01$); a large school tends to reduce the activity level of youth for sports and, especially, leadership, but the effect is not substantial (beta from −.12 to −.18). The influence of parental involvement is most significant for sports and clubs (figure 8.4). In combination, parental ties and school size account for about a third of the effect of farm status on the activity involvement and leadership of youth.

It is noteworthy that these factors do not explain the greater involvement and leadership of youth from displaced farm families. The prominence of these adolescents in clubs and leadership, compared to nonfarm youth, closely resembles that of farm youth. However, the displaced have more to prove through their accomplishments. They were once "children of farming" and its typically middle-class world, and now they find themselves in another place with parents who no longer make a living off the land. Their aspirations for social recognition appear to be unusually strong.

In all of the analyses to this point, school size does not measure up to the explanatory influence of parental community ties. However, we can also view differences in school size as contextual variations that modify the influence of a family's community involvement. Compared to large schools, small schools offer more social options to young people With these differences in mind, we ask whether parental involvement is more consequential for the involvement of youth in small schools where the options are greater. To address this question, we estimated the effects of parental education, residential change, and parental involvement on youth activity (sports, clubs, leadership) in subgroups defined by small and large schools.

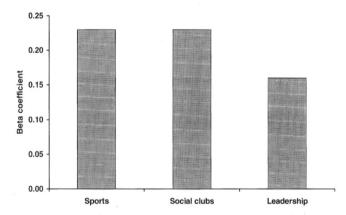

Figure 8.4 Youth Involvement by Parents' Community Ties: Strong versus Weak Ties, in Beta Coefficients

Contrary to expectations, parental civic ties do not matter most for youth involvement in small schools. In large and small schools, socially engaged parents are more likely to have children who are involved in sports, clubs, and leadership responsibilities. Small schools are more likely to have socially engaged parents, in part because they have more farm parents, but parental social ties per se do not matter more if the school is small.

Achieving Competence through Activities

Much like formal work, school and civic activities convey lessons that have relevance for personal growth and life itself. A good many of the adolescents who held paid jobs mentioned some of these lessons—learning to control one's true feelings when dealing with an unpleasant customer or employer; recognizing new strengths and abilities in oneself; and demonstrating to oneself and others the capacity to handle major responsibilities on the job. Skills in managing people were called for in service enterprises, and the imperatives of the job set in motion ways to acquire them. The value of cooperation and teamwork was underscored by the pressures of farm work. Other youth learned something from their jobs about what they did and did not want to do for their life's work.

We can think of these lessons as shedding light on developmental mechanisms in the commonplace world of social activities. Lessons of this kind stand out in the reflections of youth—how to be responsible, how to deal with irritating authority, how to be assertive and stand up for one's self, and the value of hard work and determination. A farm-reared girl claimed that her numerous leadership roles, from student body president to homecoming chair, taught her how to be a leader:

> How to just come out and say things. A lot of times I try to please everybody, but I'm learning that sometimes you can't do that. And it's taught me to be responsible and organized. I was never organized before this, but now I really am.

In much the same way that farm chores and paid work increase a young person's sense of significance to the family, participation in school sports, clubs, and leadership increase their sense of significance, responsibility, and commitment to school and community as a whole. School and civic activities provide an arena for contributing to the welfare of others and achieving success, experiences that may be most critical for adolescents who receive little in the way of support and encouragement at home.

Success with peers and a stronger feeling of self-confidence are clearly relevant outcomes of student activities. Schoolwork and involvement in school social activities are frequently seen as alternative careers,[14] but the incentives, values, and disciplines of student activities have much in common with the discipline of doing well in academics. Indeed, studies show that involved youth are more successful in their academic work.[15] The social maturity expressed in student activities may be recognized by the questions parents ask their sons and daughters, questions that imply the maturity to provide valuable answers or information.

The activity involvement of youth from eighth to twelfth grade is strongly predictive of both academic and social success among Iowa high school seniors (appendix table E8.7), and these activities largely account for the competence advantage of growing up on a farm. Participation in sports and clubs matters more for grades and perceived achievement than leadership (average beta of .22 versus .12), while sports and leadership are instrumental for peer success, more so than clubs (average beta = .29 versus .11). Athletics and student leadership ensure higher visibility in peer culture than the typical range of clubs. This analysis makes adjustments for farm status, parent education, residential change, and child gender.

Far less influenced by student activities are feelings of self-confidence and the reports of parents who ask their children for input, though it is noteworthy that sports make a difference, with an average beta coefficient of .12 ($p < .10$) on both reports. Athletic events are uniquely public events with wide support and appreciation. They are potentially the most affirming experiences for youth in small midwestern communities. Classmates, friends, and family are avid fans of school activities and the participants they know.

These activities also help to explain why the community ties of families make such a "developmental" contribution to the lives of children. Youth activities largely account for the effect of family community ties on school grades and perceived achievement (appendix table E8.8). Both parental civic ties and youth activities make a substantial difference in peer success, but the latter are more consequential, more than doubling the explained variance. Unlike school achievement, success with peers has more to do with these family ties and activities than with the socioeconomic status and mobility of families. Academic achievement is a product of all three influences: the socioeconomic standing of families, their civic engagement, and the activity involvement of students.

So far, we have assessed variations in the achieved status of youth at the end of high school, their influences and correlates. Well-educated parents who are actively engaged in community affairs, and socially active youth in school and community life are important influences, but they do not tell us about sources of developmental gains or declines. Are these factors also influential in the lives of youth who are on track to becoming more competent academically and socially? Are youth activities a general source of *increasing* academic and social competence across the adolescent years?

To address these questions, we included measures of grades, perceived achievement, and peer success in the eighth grade. Since teacher reports on peer success are not available except for the tenth and twelfth grades, we constructed a measure from three interrelated questions asked of mothers for grades 8 and 12 regarding their children's acceptance by classmates, social popularity, and leadership. The twelfth-grade measure has a correlation of .47 with the teacher rating.

To assess growth in competence, we used total levels of social involvement in each of the three domains to predict twelfth-grade competence (grades, perceived achievement, and peer success) after accounting for initial levels of competence in the eighth grade. With this procedure, we investigated the connection between extracurricular activities and twelfth-grade competence by making adjustments for the relation of student activities to initial and stable competence. The results indicate that youth who are consistently more involved in sports and school clubs also show gains in school grades, perceived achievement, and peer competence across the high school years (appendix table E8.9).[16] The effects of extracurricular activity are small, owing to the strong stability of competence over time, yet they are suggestive of a reciprocal process whereby expectations and achievements in the curricular and extracurricular realms of schooling reinforce each other in mutually beneficial ways (figure 8.5).

It is puzzling, in view of these results, that the activity involvement of students is not more highly correlated with their feelings of self-confidence, especially in view of the numerous comments by youth that sports or clubs made a big difference in their sense of personal competence. Once involved in a sport or drama club, a good many adolescents claimed that they gained a greater sense of competence. They discovered many things that they were capable of doing well.

Consistent with this developmental process, a farm boy observed how his experience in 4-H gave him a new sense of competence. "I kind of sat back . . . but when I got into 4-H I started doing presentations and stuff, and became confident with myself. My self-esteem has gone up. I think I've gained a lot of leadership abilities from it." The challenges and demands of a new role (giving presentations, etc.) mobilize efforts to achieve mastery, and success reinforces self-confidence.

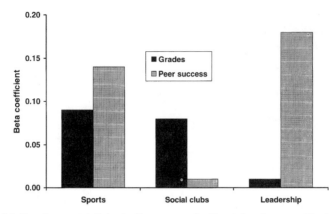

Figure 8.5 Developmental Gains in Competence by Youth Involvement, Grade 8 to 12.
Source: Appendix table E8.9

To explore this developmental change, we focused on adolescents whose self-confidence in the eighth grade placed them below average in the sample. The overall level of self-confidence increased up to the twelfth grade, and thus the original percentage of youth in the below-average group declined to approximately 26 percent of the sample by the end of school. Were the young people who gained more confidence in themselves most likely to have been involved in student activities?

With this question in mind, we divided the adolescents who lacked self-confidence in the eighth grade into two groups: the upper third and the bottom two-thirds on total scores (eighth, tenth, and twelfth grades) for club, sports, and leadership activities. By focusing on the most active students, we identify a group that is most likely to show a notable increase in self-confidence. With adjustments for gender, we find that only student involvement in clubs significantly increased the likelihood of greater self-confidence by the twelfth grade. In a logistic regression, the odds ratio is 1.76, $p < .10$.

Leadership activities seldom recruited students who lacked self-confidence, whereas club and sports activities did attract them. The odds ratio for athletics suggests that it made a positive difference but not a reliable one.[17] Overall, school and community activities emerge as a promotive factor in the development of greater self-confidence among students, along with paid work and earnings.

The modest benefits of social involvement for self-confidence may be partially indebted to a cultural preference for modesty.[18] Socialization for such modesty may be reflected in an unwillingness to check immodest statements about the self. This upbringing may also be coupled with high adult standards for the young. Such standards could endow youth with the impression that "nothing they do will satisfy their parents."

Assuming that social activity and its rewards bolstered the mastery and self-esteem of some youth, we are still faced with the task of explaining the social involvement of youth with low self-esteem. What is the process by which these unlikely candidates become active and acquire a more positive image of self? One path joins opportunities and participation pressures. The need for an actor in a play might be accompanied by peer pressures. Teacher encouragement is another factor. Large, strapping boys who are not trying out for football are likely to encounter intense pressures from peers and coaches.

Turning Points in Youth Activities

The stories young people tell about their personal change through student activities vary from modest individual growth and maturity to a dramatic change in course, both socially and psychologically. Turning points refer to a more pronounced change in course. The change may involve all of the following: a new path, an altered developmental trajectory, and the discovery of new meanings. In these concluding pages we explore some lessons gained from such change, beginning with subjective accounts and concluding with young people who have done better and worse than one would expect.

Turning points have become a source of fascination in the study of lives. Chance events, experiences, and choices at critical periods in life can provide insights regarding the process by which young people overcome the odds and develop into emotionally, socially, and physically healthy adults.[19] Chance events and choices, under the right circumstances, can set in motion a cascade of positive experiences and opportunities that literally change the course of a person's life trajectory. As we have seen, school and community activities, along with the sense of belonging and self-worth they instill, can and often do act as powerful recasting experiences, changing identities, plans, and life courses.

Not everyone who participates in school activities is changed in this manner, but involvement can produce a new vision of self and future. Prominence on the track team, for example, can deepen awareness of personal strengths and prospects. Discovery of a hidden talent or ability might reshape the life chances and outcomes of youth who are at greatest risk. Consider two of the most vivid examples of turning points in our records. Robert is the son of a family that lost its land and livestock during the Great Farm Crisis. Allen, the son of a hard-pressed, middle-class family, lived in a small community of 1,500.

Even now Robert's family continues to suffer financially, and he is very much aware of its plight. "I see a lot of people who can do more things than me because they have the money. And sometimes I'm even a little bitter about it, but you take what you get." His accomplishments by the end of high school completely hide from view the economic difficulties of his family. In the twelfth grade, his list of accomplishments included student council president, National Honor Society president, captain of the school's cross-country team, choir, speech-debate club, and 4-H. We found Robert in our "resilient" group overall at the end of twelfth grade. He was doing better than one would expect, given his family circumstances during the seventh and eighth grade. He was academically and socially resilient, and ranked well above average on feelings of self-confidence.

Why was Robert able to surmount the limitations of his family background and achieve so much by his senior year? The reasons are many—close and supportive grandparents, a loving father and mother, the rewards of a service job, and his social activities. We did not ask him directly about the single most important experience or factor, but he promptly focused on his involvement in the school theater and the support, recognition, and opportunities it provided. Consistent with the dynamics of a control cycle (loss and recovery of control), the door opened to cumulative advantages, with positive experiences reinforcing a positive image of self:

> When I was a sophomore, I went out for my first play, and that opened the door for a lot of things down the road. They picked me out for the part before I even tried out. I was kinda pushed into it, but I liked it. Drama . . . changed my life. It gave me the confidence to speak in front of groups, and then it rolled into music, which rolled into speech, which rolled into getting offices, and all of a sudden I was going to camp, I couldn't believe all the stuff I was doing then. And hopefully next year I'll try some drama down at the university.

When asked as a senior what he considered the best things that had happened to him, he listed three events: student body president, National Honor Society, and, most of all, his first play that was attended by his entire family and many friends.

Allen's route to the top involved much family hardship and a different turning point experience. The farm crisis diminished sales opportunities for his father, and the legacy of hard times continued well into the 1990s. In reflecting upon this experience, Allen stressed some lessons that he had picked up in his family, such as the ethic of hard work. He noted the odds against him and the way hard work had paid off in jobs, school work, and sports. By the twelfth grade, he was doing much better academically and socially than expected (a member of the general resilience group in one of the largest high schools in the study region). Indeed he had been elected senior class president and captain of his baseball and golf teams. He played guard on the football team and was also a member of the band and student council.

These achievements did not come easily and might not have occurred at all were it not for Allen's talent in baseball. He talks about the influential people in his life: his sister who taught him at age six how to field his first ground ball, the encouragement of his father, and most importantly the guidance he received from his best friend's father, the local softball coach. "He was the one who convinced me to go out for baseball. He told me I would be good as a pitcher, and he formed me into a pitcher, and I stuck with it because I love it." Here is how he describes the influence baseball has had on his life:

> Baseball is one of the best things that's ever happened to me. I went through elementary school and junior high and really wasn't the most popular—our school is big on politics. If you don't have the right last name, you're nobody. My freshman year, I didn't get a crack at baseball. I was basically told you're too young, you're not good enough. Beginning my sophomore year I was told the same thing and I worked hard, worked my butt off, and by the fifth game I had a varsity start, and my sophomore year I ended up pitching eight varsity games. My junior year I ended up first team all-conference pitcher, and last year as a junior we were ranked as high as fifth in the state. But we got a little cocky and we got beat. This year we're ranked third in the state. Baseball is probably one of the best things. It's made me want to keep going. Every time I get out on a baseball field, it's my own little world. I feel like I can't do anything wrong out there.
>
> It's made me think of myself as someone who . . . if I go out for something, I don't quit. No matter what it is, even if I hate it. I feel like I've become an overachiever now, because baseball made me achieve something I never thought I could, by being co-captain my junior year. I think it has helped me in my studies because you have to stay eligible. I think it's helped me an awful lot.

When interviewed in the spring of his senior year, Allen was looking forward to attending the University of Iowa, a choice his family could not have afforded without the help of a baseball scholarship. In yet another way, baseball provided a turning point in his life. With these two cases, we find compelling evidence for the power of school and civic activities in shaping the life chances of at-risk youth. Corresponding evidence appears in other lives, such as one farm boy's path to recognition.

The compensatory influence of athletic rewards are expressed in Martin's life as a farm boy whose family has still not fully recovered from the Great Farm Crisis. He talks at length about the alienation he felt and still feels because of his family's crisis and geographic isolation. "Sometimes you feel like an outsider to other people, especially in my case because I live a long way from people." Severe economic hardship also isolated the family from others. "My parent's life has been a huge struggle financially. I think if we had more money things could have changed socially for my brother and me as far as friendships or closeness to other families."

Yet life improved when his track abilities were discovered in a physical education class. The big event occurred during a ten-minute run in which the students were encouraged to go around as many times as possible. Each student was paired with another who would keep time.

> Out of our class I came around the most times and a lot of people were impressed with how I ran. I ran strong and didn't look tired. People . . . asked me if I was going out for track. I hadn't thought much about it, but I decided to just go out and see what I could do. I really liked the coach and I stayed with it.
>
> I think track has given me more self-confidence. My class is really talented as far as sports goes, so it was hard for me to be an up-and-coming football or basketball player. I wouldn't have been good at it. But track was pretty much my niche, and I concentrated on that. It kind of helped me that way.

These cases of individual growth and development reflect a general principle of life-span psychology, that of *selective optimization with compensation.* This principle provides a model of successful development that describes how "individuals and their life environments can manage opportunities for, and limits on, resources at all ages."[20] Through the process of school and community activities, young people select activities in which they do well and optimize these talents so that they compensate for certain limitations. Martin's specialization in track enabled him to achieve excellence, even though he was only average in school work and had little to do with student leadership. Robert specialized in drama, but his development of leadership skills involved him in a wide net of responsibilities in student culture. Specialization is also expressed in Allen's baseball adventures.

These narratives make a case for turning points from the vantage point of youth. Are the testimonials borne out systematically in our quantitative measures of resilience, of youth who are doing far better than expected on academic and social competence? In any predictive model, some people's behaviors are explained rather well, while the behaviors of others deviate too much from this explanation. Some youth, for example, end up doing far better than expected—in the top quartile. Other youth end up doing far worse. Approximately ninety adolescents are in the resilient group. We used logistic regression to determine a youth's likelihood of becoming a member of the resilient category across all indicators, and also for each one.

We focused initially on the "generally" resilient, like Robert and Allen, and their distinctive activities in two types of schools, small and large. These students were resilient on at least three of four developmental outcomes. Youth who did worse on these measures of competence were defined as vulnerable if they were so classified across three of the four outcomes—academic competence, peer success, self-confidence, and advice-giving. The inclusive nature of activities in small schools suggests that sports and club activities may well distinguish between youth who are academically and socially resilient and those who are not. This effect also seems likely in the area of student leadership. Small schools offered more leadership options to young people than larger schools.

Turning points are concentrated among students in the small schools, as expected. In the realm of general resilience (appendix table E8.10), sports clearly played a lead role. Adolescents who participated in school athletics between grades 8 and 12 were significantly more likely to be resilient in their twelfth-grade accomplishments and feelings. Conversely, involvement in sports minimized the likelihood of vulnerability across schools of all sizes (appendix table E8.11). The athletes we have interviewed provide numerous insights into why sports play such a developmental role. Often against great adversity, they forge lasting friendships that become a supportive network. The coaches frequently serve as confidantes and trusted advisors. No other type of activity made such a difference.

When we turn to specific kinds of competencies, three observations emerge. First, school sports are most predictive of resilience in two areas among students from small schools: academic competence and recognition of advice-giving maturity by parents. Second, involvement in clubs matters exclusively in relation to academic success, and mainly in small schools. Students who are doing better than expected on academics are likely to be involved in club activities of one kind or another. Student leadership does not seem to make a difference in academic success or self-confidence. What it does contribute to is peer success in the smaller schools. The socially resilient are likely to be leaders in the smaller high schools.

Resilience suggests an upswing in competence over time. Consistent with that pattern, we find that the club and leadership activities of resilient youth in small schools tend to show an upward trajectory beginning in the eighth grade (figure 8.6). Even in this grade, the generally resilient are far more involved in student leadership and in clubs. This difference markedly expands across the years, further differentiating the resilient from other adolescents. Though not shown, resilient youth are more involved in sports as well, and the usual decline up to the twelfth grade is less pronounced for them. Overall, these adolescents are consistently more involved in leadership, clubs, and sports from junior high or middle school to the end of high school.

If extracurricular activities matter more for resilience in small schools than larger schools, are youth in these schools also more apt to be resilient? And are they also less likely to be vulnerable? Our sample does not include the entire student body of any school, but we find that there is no difference in the percentage of resilient youth between small and large schools. *However, academically vulnerable students, those not achieving as well as expected given their level of intellectual ability and family advantage, are more common in the larger schools.* Involvement in sports becomes less possible for youth in these schools, and yet this involvement lowers the chances for vulnerability. Club involvement also

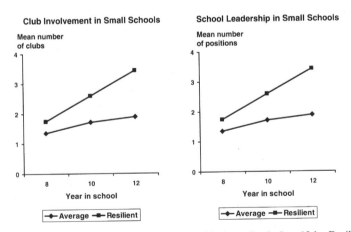

Figure 8.6 Club Involvement and School Leadership from Grade 8 to 12 by Resilient and Other Students in Small Schools

protects against academic vulnerability, whereas school sports and leadership offer such protection in relation to peer success.

Whether viewed in terms of life stories or according to trajectories of resilience and vulnerability, participation in the social activities of school and community can lead to events that change the direction and meaning of life. The experiences of drama, baseball, and track each played a recasting role in changing the lives of Robert, Allen, and Martin. Likewise, many girls described the transforming effect of being involved in Girl Scouts and theater productions. In each of these examples, we find changes along the road to adulthood, in the meaning of this pathway, and in development itself. In words, deeds, and self-definitions, they became different kinds of people.

The concept of resilience also speaks to the issue of turning points. By definition, a resilient student is faring much better in the area of academic competence than predictions from his background would indicate. In their own way, Robert, Allen, and Martin are also faring much better than they and perhaps others would have predicted. The participation experiences of social activities and leadership develop skills of resilience and minimize the risk of doing more poorly than one would expect in terms of family background.

Lessons for Life

Lessons from activities in the daily experiences of young people can be viewed as principles of a civic culture that gives and requires human nurture. In the best version of the democratic tradition, many Iowa parents invest in their communities by participating in local churches, schools, and civic organizations. Those who do this are better educated, often live on farms or have some tie to the land, and are generally stable in residence. The more they participate, the more they invest in their children, directly by example and shared experience, and indirectly through activities that enrich their children's lives.

The children of socially engaged parents are typically involved in school and community activities themselves. In early adolescence through the high school years, these children are more likely to be involved in sports, in clubs, and in leadership roles. Participation opportunities increase for club involvement and for leadership, especially in small schools, while the competition for a place on sports teams becomes more intense over time. Even youth with ordinary talents have more of a chance to participate and lead student organizations in small schools. Farm youth are likely to attend small schools, which partly accounts for their greater social involvement.

Socially engaged parents and children represent a positive force in human development—in academic success and the perception of ability, in peer success, and in the self-confidence and recognized maturity of youth. The athletic, social, and leadership activities of youth account in large part for the effects of parental social ties on the successful development of youth. Even when we take competence into account during early adolescence, subsequent youth activities enhanced academic and social success up to the twelfth grade.

Among youth from disadvantaged backgrounds, both academic and social success have much to do with school and community activities. Youth who are doing better than expected in terms of family background owe much to the developmental benefits of their athletic and club activities. Those at risk typically have little involvement of this kind. From narrative accounts and quantitative evidence, youth participation in social activities produced turning points in personal development and life trajectory. Involvement in social activities can establish pathways out of disadvantage.

Our view of the extracurricular activities of youth is based on a tally of the number of activities they have encountered. Consequently, it does not do justice to the quality of these experiences. Not all school and civic organizations are equally successful in providing youth with opportunities for self-direction, mastery, and connectedness to others.[21] Some Scout troops may be exemplary, for example, while others are barely marginal. A coach for the baseball team may be impossible to get along with, while nearby teams enjoy excellent people in the coaching ranks.

The capacity of the adult sponsor to be an effective mentor and create a climate of support and respect is an attribute that deserves more attention.[22] Information on the qualities of these youth organizations exceeds the resources of the present study, yet, because of the crudeness of our measures, the findings we report may actually underestimate the importance of extracurricular activities for the development of competence.

We come now to the end of our search for pathways to competence that link families in agriculture to the successful development of their young people. The journey has taken us from the importance of strong ties to father in generational continuity among farm families, to the importance of shared work and social activities in farm life, and to the developmental significance of productive roles in the lives of rural Iowans. We turned next to families in the community and their social ties. Grandparents are part of this larger community, and we explored their significance as companions, mentors, and moral influences.

In addition to the family, the local church and school are institutional anchors in rural communities. Parents lead their children into the church through their own religious practice, and children frequently build a social world in its youth group and its peer community. Mothers and fathers also establish a bridge to youth involvement in school and community through their own social activities. Families with ties to the land are actively engaged in local communities, and these networks of social engagement extend across the generations, fostering competence and confidence in each new generation.

Up to this point, we have identified many pathways to success among youth, from parent support and kin involvement to the rewards of social activities and leadership in school. In the next chapter we investigate the extent to which these worlds protect youth from "teenage troubles," such as stealing, heavy drinking, and using drugs. Does success in academics and community activities insulate students from the lure of deviant classmates and their antisocial activities? Academic success may protect youth through the recognition of significant adults as well as through social ties that bind, constrain, and commit.

CHAPTER NINE

Achieving Success, Avoiding Trouble

If I do something wrong, my father hears about it at the coffee
shop next morning.

An Iowa farm youth

In the midst of declining wages and opportunities, a good many Iowa
youth with ties to the land are engaged in rewarding activities. The economic troubles of the region appear to have made little difference in
their behavior and outlook. For example, they are not more likely than
nonfarm youth to be unsuccessful in school and, as this chapter makes
clear, they are more successful in avoiding problem behavior. Indeed,
the evidence suggests that their profile of competence includes academic
and social success, coupled with the avoidance of problem behavior. This
is not an uncommon finding in farming communities,[1] but little is known
about factors that account for success amidst generalized hardship. The
more typical story links hard times to personal demoralization and
failure.

In this chapter, we explore two explanations for the extent to which
rural Iowa youth are avoiding problem behavior. The first centers on
the social fabric or network of families and their children. Families with
ties to the land are characterized by more shared activity across generational lines and by greater involvement in religious, school, and civic
activities. These resources contribute to the effectiveness of informal social control,[2] and, as prior chapters document, they help to explain the
unusual level of academic and social success among youth from agrarian
families. A second explanation focuses on the protective influence of this
accomplishment. Successful young people are more likely to be insulated
from the pressures and incentives of trouble-making peers and their activities. Families with ties to the land may steer their children away from
trouble through a network of social relationships.

As noted at the beginning of this volume, the avoidance of trouble

This chapter was written in collaboration with Lisa S. Matthews.

represents an important dimension of youth competence. A competent young man or woman may be thought of as an individual who has acquired and demonstrated skills that are necessary to attain socially desirable goals, such as success in school. But conventional attainments of this kind can be undermined by adjustment problems that generate negative responses from adults and peers or that threaten the reliability and quality of personal efforts. For these reasons, we assume that youth competence involves skills and dispositions that promote positive outcomes and avoid problem behaviors. In this chapter, we find that the two facets of competence are highly interrelated.

Before considering the adjustment problems of Iowa youth and their prevalence, we briefly survey what we have learned about their lives. Then we relate this set of findings to an analytic framework that links key influences to competence, the achievement of success, and the avoidance of disabling troubles.

Agrarian Culture and Youth Competence

In theory, midwestern families with ties to the land occupy a special relation to resources that can make a positive difference in the lives of children. Some ties to the land, whether from parents who only grew up on a farm or from the part-time and full-time farm family, define a social world with an agrarian lifestyle. This world is distinguished by the valuing of family life and generational continuity over material gain, by a web of intergenerational relationships that join child to parent and grandparent, and by a parental network of social engagement in the community, expressed in contact with and support for the local school, in the active religious participation of parents as congregants and leaders in the local church, and in civic activities of one kind or another. This pattern of activity was associated with family ties to the land, though not exclusively so. Some families with no involvement in agriculture were active in local institutions.

The social involvement of these families carried over to the next generation through the school and community participation of their young people. Active parents have active children, and the smaller the school, the more likely they were to be active as leaders in school government, social clubs, art/drama groups, and athletic teams. This intergenerational continuity also occurred in terms of religious affiliation and leadership. Active parents set in motion an involvement pattern for children that extended through the high school years and often entailed leadership of the church youth group. Another form of activity linked to families in agriculture is productive labor, whether unpaid as a form of exchange for college support in the years ahead, or as paid work from the sale of stock raised from birth. Adolescents who grew up on farms were likely to view their labor and earnings as a contribution to the family enterprise.

Among children who aspire to life on a farm, relations between parents and youth are especially strong, and include shared activity across intergenerational lines in work and community functions. These patterns were notable among fathers, the parents most strongly tied to a tradition of agriculture. Ties to grandparents on the father's side of the family are also distinctively stronger among families in agriculture. In addition to a sense of family contribution, farm youth had a strong perception of themselves as individuals who matter and possess significance in the eyes of others. Compared to nonfarm adolescents, farm youth were more likely to aspire to community leadership, a religious life, and a career not centered on material gain. Overall, these findings characterize family culture with ties to the land as a more communal and spiritual orientation when compared to perspectives centered on individual gain, narcissism, and opportunism. This culture also has significance as a collective world that offers a more resourceful community for all children.

Rural farm children in the study region can be thought of as being socialized in an adult-sponsored regime. Most everything they do is likely to be within the purview of family and other adults known to them. Youth from families engaged in community life were least likely to "hang out" with age-mates after school during the week and on weekends. The contrasting model would be run by peers, a spontaneous peer system that could promote risky behavior involving early sex, drug use, and binge drinking. Significant adults made a difference in steering youth away from such influences. A high school girl noted such influences in explaining the turnaround in her life. "Now that I've been hanging around different people [not "bad influences"], life has been a lot better. I've had really good high school years."

In the study region, young people grow up knowing most people in their community and are in turn known by these people. As a young boy put it, "Everybody knows your business. You can't really do anything because your parents will find out." Or their friends will find out. The pain of this discovery kept another farm boy from doing "anything really stupid." After all, he said, "I know most of the people in the community." Some of these people were civic or community leaders. A senior in high school claimed that "small places" enable people to know and deal with their civic leaders. Most young people in the study actually valued the recognition they had in their community, but they chafed at the informal social control that came with it.

The opportunity to get involved in drinking and drugs was curtailed by the prominence of adults in the lives of Iowa youth. And it was even more limited among farm youth by their distance from peers in town. A teenage girl from an Iowa farm felt that this separation was critical in restricting her contact with drugs and drinking. "I didn't have that pressure of doing that because my friends lived in town and I wasn't with them at all because I couldn't go with them at night." Another youth decided to change her peer group because she discovered that she didn't want to be like them, getting in trouble and not going any place. "I always did want to finish high school without getting pregnant and then go on to college." Observing the "negative side of drugs and alcohol" prompted similar changes in friends for two small-town girls.

An adult-sponsored environment, involving well-educated, committed parents, can also establish a culture of moral standards for youth. This is most evident in the local church and in the community more generally. An Iowa boy from the vicinity of Alden noted the ever-present expectations of accomplishment in his community. "In a small town you are expected to do well, and if you don't, people will notice it a lot more than if you were in a big town. You have to try and succeed or people will look down on you." But in small schools, students also felt they got more help from the teachers who, in turn, were likely to know each student's parents. The activity involvement of youth restricted options for troublemaking. As one boy put it, you "don't have to be excellent" to get involved. "You can just be average and still participate in everything." Small places are thus amplifiers of civic engagement and its multiple benefits for community life.

Considered as a whole, we find much support for the proposition that Iowa families with ties to the land are more likely than nonfarm households to provide young people with important social resources and supports. These resources refer in large part to what we have termed "social capital." For example, significant relationships and social networks played major roles in the academic and social success of youth and in their self-confidence and recognized maturity by parents, as we observed them, especially at the end of high school.

The broad-based community ties of parents and the school activities of youth figured prominently in their academic and social success. Even under conditions of socioeconomic disadvantage, warm ties with parents and closeness to grandparents tended to enhance the self-confidence of youth and the parent's perception that their sons and daughters had the maturity and wisdom to be sources of advice and counsel for them. These findings are consistent with our hypotheses and suggest that family resources have different implications for developmental outcomes. Ties to the community appear to be especially important for success and accomplishments outside the family, while family closeness has special relevance to self-confidence and personal well-being.

These findings strengthen earlier reports on this young generation of Iowans; that parents and families represent an important bridge to opportunity and personal well-being for young people, as expressed in terms of accomplishments, relations with peers, and sense of self.[3] In addition, the key resources that foster these competencies are related to the culture of farming and ties to the land. Competence-promoting resources among these families are entwined with the larger community and extended family. They cannot be reduced to specific parenting practices alone. Families with ties to the land thus confer a special advantage to sons and daughters through social resources, values, and beliefs that facilitate competence. Are there other social factors that aid or undermine this process?

As reported in previous chapters, traditional markers of a family's position in the class structure, such as family income and parents' education, increased life chances and success, even after taking farm background and other resources into account. In addition, family mobility, as indexed by the number of residential moves, played a consistently negative role in children's academic and social success. Residential change represents the antithesis of a farming lifestyle, defined, in part, by enduring ties to a specific locale.

Farm families are identified with a homestead, a plot of ground that may have been in the family for more than a hundred years. Across the generations, family members have been identified with community institutions, with the school, church, government, and newspaper, if any. They tend to be community leaders who involve their own children, through example and action, in the life of the community and its institutions. By contrast, family residential change is concentrated among nonfarm families and contributes to the developmental handicap of their children. They do less work in school, and they are less apt to acquire ties to community institutions.

With these earlier results in mind, we turn to an expanded model that links problem behaviors to limitations in family background, social resources, and behavioral competence. Such resources and competence represent protective influences in this region of declining economic opportunity.

Promoting Success and Avoiding Trouble

In the rural Midwest, we expected the success of youth to reduce the likelihood of adjustment problems, such as delinquent activities and emotional distress, but the topic has not received the attention it deserves. Most studies have *either* investigated conventional competence *or* deviance.[4] To address their interrelationships, we draw upon our knowledge of success among Iowa young people, and connect it to the problematic side of their lives. We do so by drawing upon a theory that links the two worlds—conventional pursuits and problematic outcomes.[5] Before moving to this connection, we consider ways of measuring such outcomes.

Problems of youth adjustment do not exist in isolation; rather, they cluster in ways that define different types of young people. For example, youth who engage in delinquent activities also tend to be more emotionally distressed and more inclined to abuse substances than nondelinquents.[6] There are two general categories of maladjustment, known as externalizing behavior (e.g., delinquency and substance use) and internalizing symptoms (e.g., depression, anxiety, and hostile feelings), but even here we find that the two domains of behavior are intercorrelated.

With these considerations in mind, we developed an index of problem behavior that combined indicators of both kinds of symptoms. One form is reflected in the ability to avoid a wide range of "interrelated" problems that range from emotional depression to interpersonal violence. We are interested in youth *who do not* become more actively involved in such behavior between early adolescence (seventh grade) and the twelfth grade.

To capture important dimensions of externalizing behavior, the index for the seventh and twelfth grades includes two established measures in national samples, one for delinquency and one for substance use. Delinquency refers to above average participation in such activities as theft, vandalism, petty larceny, selling drugs, and violence toward others. Substance use includes above-average use of different types of tobacco, alcohol, and illegal drugs. In addition to these outside-the-home activities, we included a measure on aggression inside the household or family, in this case toward mother. We identified in the seventh and twelfth grades the adolescents who were above average on whether they had gotten angry at, shouted at, or hit their mothers. Last, to measure internalizing symptoms in 1989 and 1994, we identified youth who scored above average on three composited subscales: depression, anxiety, and hostile emotions. These scales have been shown to index feelings of unhappiness, anxiety, and anger among young people in valid and reliable ways. The resulting scores were summed to form an index that ranges from zero to four.[7]

The Analytic Model

Figure 9.1 provides a conceptual map of our approach in the analysis, as informed by the theoretical framework of this project. First we note that family background and ties to the land are linked to a set of resources (path A) that are elements of an agrarian lifestyle in the Midwest—for example, shared activities, close ties to kin, and networks of engagement in the community. In theory and practice, these resources enhance the competence and well-being of youth (path C), as reflected in conventional developmental trajectories. We hypothesize that some influence of family background on the problem behavior of youth occurs through the competencies of youth (defined by paths B and E) and some is expressed through the social resources of families (defined by paths A and D).

Paths C and E extend the early model (see chapter 1) by adding specific hypotheses concerning problem behavior. Conger and Simons suggest that the contingencies of reinforcement or punishment in proximal situations will either promote conventional competence or increase the risk of maladjustment.[8] As the findings in this book attest, the most striking developmental feature of an agrarian lifestyle is the generalized press of parents and grandparents toward constructive activities in the household, farm operation, and broader community. Parents with ties to the land are most likely to (1) foster joint activities in conventional pursuits; (2) reinforce values and behaviors that support collective well-being as much or more than individual aggrandizement; (3) recognize and promote their children's school and church activities that are supportive of the general social order; and (4) receive considerable support from the

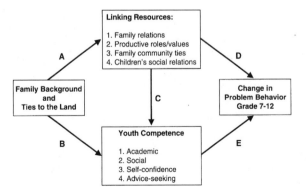

Figure 9.1 Conceptual Model for Problem Behavior

elder generation of grandparents in nurturing socially approved activities by their children.

In theory, these developmental contingencies reduce the attractiveness of illegal activities and the risk of emotional distress (path D of the conceptual model). Moreover, conventional competencies that are fostered by the resources we have identified should also minimize the risk for problem behavior (path E of the model). Academic achievement, social success, self-confidence, and respect by parents are all rewarding states and accomplishments. According to theory, time spent in relation to conventional pursuits will reduce time that is available for deviant or less appealing activities.

In addition, the resulting conventional commitments of success would also reduce the likelihood of problem behavior, according to social control theory.[9] For example, personal experimentation with substances risks discovery, expulsion from school, and threats to the continuation of peer friendships, positive relations with teachers, and a future marked by academic success and a stable job. According to the theoretical reasoning for paths D and E, youth apply an informal calculus to assess the degree of risk for specific actions or behaviors. If certain problem behaviors pose too much of a threat to conventional success and social approval, they will be less appealing and hence more easily avoided. A teenage boy in the study noted that he had "seen a lot of the negative side of things. . . . I want to do the exact opposite of it. I've seen how drugs and alcohol affect people, so I'm not going in that direction."

The conceptual model (figure 9.1) implies that the life ways of families with ties to the land foster successful social relations and valued achievements that establish barriers against problem behaviors. But why does the model emphasize change in behavior (toward greater or less problem behavior up to the twelfth grade) rather than the amount or seriousness of the behavior at a point in time, such as high school? We know from prior work in this study and others that deviant activities and emotional problems increase over the adolescent years, on average.[10] Thus, we are particularly concerned with factors that minimize an increase in such behavior, especially increases that ultimately threaten a successful transition to adult opportunities.

In the following analyses, we estimate change by predicting problem behavior in the twelfth grade from evidence of such behavior and other factors five years earlier, in the seventh grade. We also specifically consider issues of resilience and vulnerability, as in earlier chapters, giving special emphasis to turning points—a change in trajectory from early maladjustment or its absence. Last, we consider how profiles of competencies and problem behavior can themselves be clustered in patterns that reflect an overall pattern of development at the close of the high school years.[11] This final step reminds us that individual and social-contextual attributes produce a developmental configuration that should be considered as a whole, not as separate elements in the course of human development.

Preventing More Problem Behavior in Adolescence

In the model just outlined, we have identified two sets of influences—social resources and conventional forms of youth competence—that in theory restrict or diminish problem behavior as youth move through the teenage years. Both of these influences are associated with families that have ties to the land, but they are also found among families with no such connections.

To put this approach to a test, we established three sets of analyses based on ordinary least squares regression. Along with dimensions of youth competence, from academic to social, the first set (1) is identified by a focus on *family relations,* the second (2) on *grandparent influence,* and the third (3) on *the social ties of parents and youth.* Each set begins by estimating the influence of family background and youth character-istics on problem behavior in the twelfth grade. These factors include parental education, family income, residential change, and farm status, along with a measure of problem behavior in the seventh grade and gender.

Early problem behavior predicts similar behavior in the twelfth grade, but the modest coefficient (betas of .21 to .26) suggests that much change is occurring across the secondary school years. Some young people become less engaged in this lifestyle by the twelfth grade, though early problem behavior clearly remains a risk factor.[12] We are interested in precisely this ameliorative change. What factors increase its likelihood? In table E9.1 (appendix E), the only background factor that makes a difference are well-educated parents (beta = −.11 for both parents, $p < .05$, one-tailed). Residential instability makes no difference, and neither do family income, farm status, or gender.

Three family patterns were introduced in the next model: work with parents, parent identification and warmth, and shared activities with parents. Only maternal identification and warmth significantly reduced the likelihood of increasing problem behavior (beta = −.10), and this influence did not explain the protective effect of education. However, "working with parents" had the opposite effect, slightly increasing the risk of deviance (beta = .09), possibly by accelerating the desire for independence. Some delinquent activities express early claims on adult status, such as precocious sexual acts, drinking, and smoking. Working with parents may involve obligatory pressures that generate resentment and rebellious actions of this kind.

The next and last model in the table introduces modes of adolescent competence. Only two forms contributed to a decline in problem behavior: academic success and self-confidence. We averaged the scores for these competencies across the secondary school years. Both aspects of competence emerged as significant protective factors, lessening an increase in problem behavior across the high school years. As measured in this analysis, adolescent competence (and not family relations) explains the influence of family background, such as education. Earlier analyses also show that parent education and family income, farm status, and family residential change are predictive of academic success across the adolescent years. The results in table E9.1 are consistent with these findings and with theory which asserts that competence decreases the risk of such behavior.

The overall picture, then, centers on the protective influence of academic success and self-confidence for boys as well as girls. A record of academic success is more predictive of the avoidance of problem behavior and its insulation from such temptations over time than any other factor in the study. Even the avoidance of problem behavior in the seventh grade tells us *less* about a youth's prospects for avoiding such activity in subsequent grades. The affectional salience of mother remains a significant factor, but it, too, pales in relation to the potency of academic success. Some of its influence is expressed through the self-confidence and academic achievement of youth.

One explanation for the protective power of academic success comes from its mastery effects on self-competence and the access it provides to other rewarding opportunities from school clubs and plays to teacher recognition. Academic success is more generally part of a cumulative advantage process—each success leads to other successes. Doors open, and one good thing "rolls into another" good thing, as a student leader (in our sample) put it. Robert Merton has referred to this process in terms of the Matthew Principle in the field of science (based on the gospel of St. Matthew).[13] Distinguished scientists gain more in grants and research acclaim, while the less accomplished scientists gain less and may even lose over time the stature they once possessed. In referring to the cumulative direction and outcome of a person's actions, M. Brewster Smith speaks of benign and vicious circles of development. There is, as he points out, much empirical truth to the biblical maxim from St. Matthew, "To him who hath shall be given; from him who hath not shall be taken away even that which he hath."

>Launched on the right trajectory, the person is likely to accumulate successes that strengthen the effectiveness of his orientation toward the world while at the same time he acquires the knowledge and skills that make his further success more probable. His environmental involvements generally lead to gratification and to increased competence and favorable development. Off to a bad start, on the other hand, he soon encounters failures that make him hesitant to try. What to others are challenges appear to him as threats; he becomes preoccupied with defense of his small claims on life at the expense of energies to invest in constructive coping. And he falls increasingly behind his fellows in acquiring the knowledge and skills that are needed for success on those occasions when he does try.[14]

But we know that vicious cycles of threat, withdrawal, and defeat are frequently broken. A bad start in life can be turned around, as we have observed among Iowa young people who lacked confidence in themselves at the beginning of secondary school. Some were presented with an opportunity to demonstrate competence when a school play sought actors. Classmates persuaded one young man to give playmaking a try. He did and then experienced a series of reinforcing experiences that gave him more confidence and opportunities. Another youth found this path of redirection on the baseball team.

Relations with parents, in our first set of analyses, tell us little about youth who manage to avoid problem behavior, particularly when compared to the influence of academic competence. However, ties to grandparents (in the next set) may be a different matter. Young people who were not more involved in problem behavior by high school tended to have strong ties to their living grandparents (see appendix table E9.2). During their senior year, we interviewed their grandparents about relationships with grandchildren and the nature of such activity. The grandparents were asked about the quality of the relationship, their closeness and the companionship, joint involvement in activities (such as school and community events), and the provision of guidance and tangible help.

Two aspects of this intergenerational relationship are negatively associated with more problem behavior among grandchildren by the twelfth grade: a high-quality relationship and shared activities, the strongest correlate. Both factors contribute to adolescent competence, but only shared activities make a significant difference apart from evidence of youth success or competence. Both factors largely account for the influence of family background, such as parental education and family ties to the land. As in the preceding analysis, academic success emerges as the most important dimension of competence for the avoidance of teenage problems, from delinquency to drugs, alcohol abuse, and feelings of emotional depression.

Before turning to the influence of social ties, in the last set of analyses, we need to consider the meaning of grandparent significance. Across the adolescent years, a young person's relationships usually reflect some choice or selection. They choose their friends to some extent on the basis of shared interests and talents, and the latter in turn make a difference in the young person's life, for better or worse.[15] The behavior of parents toward adolescent sons and daughters may actually reflect the actions of these youth as much as their values or social circumstances. Punitive behavior and inconsistent discipline may be the last resort for parents whose teenagers have become "uncontrollable." Likewise, the reported relationship of grandparents to grandchildren may be contingent on the initiative and conduct of the adolescent. An impulsive, ill-tempered, or narcissistic grandchild is not likely to have a supportive relationship with grandparents.

This interpretation may apply to the negative association between the problem behavior of youth and their relation to grandparents, as reported by the grandparents. The easy-going, likable child will have more rewarding relations with grandparents than a troubled child. And this behavior differential is likely to increase across the adolescent years. A "reactive" dynamic is pertinent to our observation that the positive influence of grandparents is frequently coupled with a nurturant family environment (see chapter 6). When family support is missing, grandparent support may be missing as well. The explanation has much to do with the gatekeeper role of the parent generation. Adult sons and daughters are gatekeepers for ongoing, supportive relations between grandparents and grandchildren. Encouragement of such relations is not as likely when the child's own family environment is abusive or neglectful.

With data at only one point in time, we are unable to determine the reciprocal nature of relations between grandparents and grandchildren in the study. It is entirely plausible that young people who had close ties to grandparents were less likely than other youth to become vulnerable to the risk of problem behavior as they moved across the secondary school years. But we could also argue that troubled and at-risk youth were least likely to develop warm relations with their grandparents. It is clear, nevertheless, that warm, nurturant relations with parents, positive ties to grandparents, a sense of self-confidence, and academic success represent a cluster of protective influences in the lives of Iowa young people. All such influences are concentrated in families with ties to the land.

The last set of influences—community involvement—has played a most important developmental role in the lives of Iowa youth up to this point, particularly among those who live in families with some connection to agriculture. Five measures of community involvement were included in our analysis (appendix table E9.3): the community involvement of parents, the religious involvement of youth (attending church and youth group), and involvement in sports, social clubs, and leadership in school. All of these aspects of community involvement increased the likelihood of academic and social success among youth, a key source of protection relative to antisocial influences. Do they have any independent influence in establishing modes of informal social control? Were socially involved youth in this conventional domain less likely to become more involved in antisocial activities across the adolescent years?

With family background in the analysis, these types of social involvements explain very little of the background influence of families (such as education), and they do not carry much direct weight in predicting an increase in problem behavior up through high school. The influence of social involvement is largely indirect, through levels of youth competence.

Two results are worth noting. As expected, adolescents who were actively engaged in a religious community rank lower than other youth on the risk of becoming more involved in problem behavior, although this influence is not statistically reliable. And student leaders are also less apt than nonleaders to engage in problem behavior in adolescence. However, these effects are modest (beta circa $-.10$), and they generally decline with adolescent competencies in the analysis. But involvement in sports and club activities is more predictive of an increase in problem behavior when youth competence is controlled.

The most plausible explanation for the latter result involves the link between academic success and social involvement. When socially involved adolescents also do well in school, they are insulated from the appeal of teenage deviance. By controlling academic competence in the analysis, we remove a key protective feature from school activities of any kind. Under these conditions, social clubs and athletics are more likely to identify youth with delinquent interests or teenage maladjustment—those who are not doing well in their school work and who do not feel self-confident. In other words, athletes include young people who are doing well *and* those who are faring poorly in the classroom. The deviance implications of sports have much to do with membership in the latter group. The same distinction applies to involvement in school clubs.

Two twelfth-grade students illustrate the role of a positive configuration of activities. In thinking about the best things in high school, a male athlete stressed entry into the National Honor Society because, as he put it, "Not everybody gets to be part of it. The state football championship was nice to win as a senior, also." A female classmate cited her busy schedule of activities, from cheerleading and the drill team to student council, homecoming queen, and the National Honor Society. "I kept busy, learned a lot of things, used my talents, and had a lot of fun."

Overall, the results are highly supportive of the problem-behavior model (see Figure 9.1). First, problem behavior appears to be relatively stable across time and represents a risk factor even during early adolescence. Second, family background and farm status produce change in problem behavior only to the extent to which they influenced key family resources—relations with mother and father, ties to grandparents, and the conventional modes of competence. We do not find a direct path between family background and an increase in problem behavior across the adolescent years.

Third, the most protective influence is academic success, considering all factors in the analysis. Interventions that enhance the success experience of youth in school have well-demonstrated possibilities in reducing problem behavior across the adolescent years. Fourth, developmental processes in the problem-behavior model apply to boys and girls in much the same way. We find no gender effects, possibly because behavioral and emotional problems are included in the measure of problem behavior.

Fifth, prior chapters have clearly documented the connections between family background (especially family ties to the land, residential stability, and parental education) and linking resources (such as family relations, mastery experience, etc.) and through these linkages to conventional modes of youth competence. Findings from earlier chapters provided evidence for the path from linking resources to conventional competencies (path C) in the model, and these individual assets are directly associated with a reduced risk for problem behavior (see path E in the model). Direct influences are also evident in the results. For example, mother's identification and warmth directly reduced the likelihood of an increase in problem behavior between the seventh and twelfth grades. This result is consistent with path D in the conceptual model.

Questions of Resilience and Vulnerability

Family influences and individual achievements tend to steer adolescents away from an increasing level of problem behavior through high school. Do they also enable us to identify youth who are doing far better in avoiding trouble than most age-mates from the same background, such as low income and abusive parents? We refer to these young people as resilient. Are such factors negatively predictive of boys and girls who are doing worse than expected, given certain background characteristics? This trajectory reflects increasing vulnerability.

To identify resilient and vulnerable youth on the avoidance of trouble, we followed the same procedures described in chapter 3 for estimating resilience and vulnerability in relation to other domains of competence. Based on selected family and personal characteristics described in chapter 3, we predicted risk for problem behavior in the twelfth grade. Those adolescents who demonstrated less problem behavior than expected from the prediction equation were labeled "resilient," while those youth exceeding expectations for problem behavior were identified as "vulnerable." Specifically, youth who ended up in the upper quartile of residuals from the analysis (who became more problem-oriented than most adolescents, given a certain background) were defined as "vulnerable." At the other extreme on residuals are resilient youth who became much less engaged in problem behavior between early and late adolescence. These young people ended up in the lowest quartile on residuals.

The following analyses were conducted to predict membership in the resilient and vulnerable groups. Earlier problem behavior is controlled to reflect our continuing interest in risk for change in problem behavior. Following the procedures for the regression models, one set of resource variables (e.g., relations with grandparents) was included in each analysis, and all competence variables were included in each analysis. For parsimony, only predictor variables that were statistically significant are included in the appendix tables that report findings from these procedures.

We first consider the role of adolescent competence and relations with father and mother, and then turn to the influence of grandparents and social ties. When measures of competence and family relations are included in the same analysis, any observed effects of family relations are independent of youth competence. This point gains importance when we turn to sources of gains or declines in problem behavior (appendix table E9.4). Self-confidence in early adolescence is most predictive of resilient youth who were likely to do well in school. This success also minimized the risk of vulnerability. The protective significance of academic success needs to be considered when we interpret the role of relations with father.

Warm relations with father are negatively predictive of resilience, and boys who reported working with their fathers were most likely to be vulnerable on problem behavior. This finding tells us that positive relations with father do not contribute to resilience when academic success is controlled and not part of the story. Likewise, the strong contribution of work with father to vulnerability applies to youth who are not particularly achievement-oriented. Beyond these points, the findings suggest that too close a relation with father at a time of growing independence may lead to rebellious actions.

Also contrary to expectations, strong ties to mother did not play an important role in steering youth away from trouble (appendix table E9.5). They did not increase the likelihood of resilience or vulnerability to problem behavior, though boys again stand out as more vulnerable. The latter appear to be more sensitive to family stresses, especially in the early years, compared to girls.[16] As in the case of fathers, youth who work with their mothers were significantly more likely to become vulnerable through the adolescent years. Questions of dependency and maturation most likely play a role in these results.

The only other notable finding involves the consistently potent effect of academic success. Consistent with Smith's developmental cycle of competence,[17] earlier academic success strengthened feelings of efficacy, greater personal investment in school work, and higher aspirations. Success fostered prospects for continued success, establishing expectations of high accomplishment among peers, teachers, and parents.

Grandparents in this region of the rural Midwest live unusually close to their grandchildren, when compared to those in large cities, and we have observed their role in the safety net of Iowa families. At least 60 percent of the adolescents in this study report close relations with grandparents they regard as very significant figures in their lives. What role do grandparents play in steering youth toward resilience and away from vulnerability? Prior analysis suggests that they enable young people to avoid becoming more at risk and vulnerable—not to lose their self-confidence and become less successful over time than predicted by their background. They do not contribute to a youth's resilience, in part because strong ties to parents and grandparents cluster in families. When one type of bond is present, the other is likely to be as well. The presence of effective relations with grandparents depends on the middle "parental generation."

What do we find in relation to problem behavior? Grandparents are more likely to believe that they can make a difference in preventing risky behavior by their grandchildren than that they can influence their academic success,[18] but grandparents have no direct effect on change in problem behavior. Strong ties with grandparents and shared activities do not distinguish youth who become less or more involved in problem behavior over the adolescent years. Nevertheless, interaction with grandparents does foster self-confidence that in turn protects against teenage trouble. Grandparent involvement carries the message that young people matter and provides assurance that life success is possible no matter what the odds may be.

Our last protective influence involves a defining feature of rural farm communities—community involvement. No influence made more of a difference in the academic and social success of Iowa youth than community involvement by parents and their children. Through its web of community ties and informal social control, we had reason to believe that community involvement would lessen the risk of problem behavior. However, we find little evidence of this kind. What matters is the moral valence of community ties—involvement in the church or synagogue has the greatest influence on reducing the risk for problem behavior.[19] Interactions with others in the community and institutional settings encourage conventional behavior when they occur under conditions that support social norms and inhibit social transgressions.

Religious institutions are prime examples of such organizations, particularly in rural communities, and they clearly have the major effect in this study (appendix table E9.6). The more youth report involvement in religious services and the youth group, the less likely they are to be engaged in problem behavior—the resilient (odds ratio = 1.53, $p = .05$). The socializing influence of the youth group is undoubtedly a major factor in this result since it includes like-minded friends and parents who become a core-member moral reference group across the adolescent years. The influence of the religious community is only matched by academic success. On the negative side are community involvement and school activities—both lessen rather than increase the prospects for resilience. They have this effect in part because they promote resilience indirectly, through academic success. Only academic success and gender (being a girl) significantly lessened the chances of becoming "vulnerable."

Considering all factors that make a difference in the likelihood of resilience, three emerge as most prominent: *doing well academically, participation in a religious community,* and *feelings of self-confidence.* As a reflection of positive family influences, these three factors cohere in the lives of a good many youth in the study. The adult and peer community of a rural church establishes and supports standards of accomplishment, service, and moral conduct. A trajectory of vulnerability is concentrated among boys more than among girls, and among youth who work with their parents, compared to those who don't. The vulnerability risk of "working with parents" may be associated with the unwanted prolongation of dependency and rebellious responses to the extension of parental control, or it may reflect the adolescent's perception that adult responsibilities should confer adult privileges, such as the use of alcohol and tobacco.

Putting the Story Together

Drawing on theories of the life course and problem behavior, this inquiry has proposed a set of connections among family attributes, resources, youth competencies, and the risk for teenage trouble, such as heavy drinking and drug use. The approach reveals a chain of events and processes. Thus, family ties to the land, in conjunction with socioeconomic advantage, promote social resources within the family and community. These two facets of the young person's environment, in turn, nurture personal competencies that enable youth to avoid the growing risk for externalizing (e.g., ill-temper) and internalizing problems (e.g., emotional depression) across the years of adolescence.

The resulting story is based on the association of social and individual factors that describe a sample of families and youth in this study. But in this approach we do not see a "configuration or profile of attributes" that depict individuals. Increasingly, human development is represented as systemic change of this configuration over time. According to life-course theory, "the developing individual is viewed as a dynamic whole, not as separate strands, facets, or domains, such as emotion, cognition, and motivation."[20] When we conclude from a multiple regression that one aspect of competence, for example, is more predictive of problem behavior than others, we do not deny the reality that these competencies are intercorrelated. In real life, social resources, personal competencies, and related experiences tend to cluster together in meaningful patterns. Taking these patterns apart may help us to see important mechanisms of development, but putting the elements back together can enable us to achieve a deeper understanding of human functioning. We turn our attention to this task.

In thinking about profiles of competence, we have argued that avoiding troubles may be defined as one component of the competencies that enable youth to make a successful transition to the adult years. In this sense, normative competencies involving academic success, social relations, sense of self-confidence, and advice seeking from parents become elements of a common fabric that includes success in avoiding antisocial behavior and emotional depression. Young people may vary in lawful ways around these modes of competence, reflecting higher levels on some than on others. They fit different profiles.

Presumably, there should be two extreme groups that represent the highest and lowest levels of competence in the sample. The highest level is likely to be defined by a profile of normative competencies and of low scores on problem behavior. The most problematic group would be defined by the opposite profile, low normative competence and high problem behavior. In addition to these types, we are likely to identify groups that vary greatly across the domains of competence. One profile might be defined by social competence and self-confidence, and by lower scores on academic success and problem behavior. In another case, academic competence might be coupled with feelings of inadequacy. Most important, these variations in profiles of competence should be connected to the earlier explanatory variables, from family attributes to social resources.

To investigate these possibilities, we first carried out a cluster analysis on all dimensions of competence, including the avoidance of problem behavior (table 9.1).[21] As expected, a meaningful set of five clusters emerged, including two extreme groups, the most and the least competent youth (group A, "most competent"; and group E, "least competent"). Members of these groups differed significantly on every competence domain.[22] For example, the contrast is particularly striking on grade-point average and perceived academic achievement; the most competent group scored .97 on grade-point average, compared to −1.45 for the least competent youth. On perceived achievement, the range of mean scores varies from 1.24 to −1.31. Compared to the other four clusters, the least competent adolescents ranked at the bottom on average scores for all but one dimension of normative competence and at the top on problem behavior. With the exception of peer competence, the most competent group scored at the top on measures of competence and at the bottom on problem behavior.

Lynn Parsons exemplifies an all-around youth, and her record of accomplishments brings to mind a good many of the young people we met in chapter 8, "Lessons from School." A daughter of socially engaged parents—her mother was a PTA leader and father was a church trustee—Lynn put substantial energy into a number of school activities—academic, social, and athletic. In her senior year, she was the co-captain of the cheerleading and girl's basketball teams. She served in the Student Senate and played an active role in the local unit of the National Honor Society. She sang in the church choir and mentored children in the community. Her favorite group was the National Honor Society. She worked hard to attain an academic record for admission and said her experience with the Honor Society has really made her "determined and confident. It just makes me strive for the best." She most enjoys "the respect" gained from teachers through her affiliation with the Honor Society.

Table 9.1
Profiles of Competence by Competence Dimensions; Comparison of Standardized Means

Competence Dimensions	(a) Most Competent ($N = 85$)	(b) Self-Critical Achievers ($N = 85$)	(c) Socially Recognized ($N = 83$)	(d) At Risk; Socially Ignored ($N = 94$)	(e) Least Competent ($N = 77$)
GPA	.97[bcde]	.50[acde]	−.32[abde]	.14[abce]	−1.45[abcd]
Perceived achievement	1.24[bcde]	.21[acde]	−.19[abe]	−.07[abe]	−1.31[abcd]
Peer success	.60[bce]	.81[cde]	.22[abde]	−.80[abc]	−.82[abd]
Self-confidence	.91[bde]	−.62[acd]	.64[bde]	−.21[abce]	−.74[acd]
Advice-seeking from parents	.88[bde]	−.50[acd]	.80[bde]	−.82[abce]	−.28[acd]
Problem behavior	−.50[bcde]	.05[a]	−.06[a]	.22[a]	.30[a]

Note: All measures of competence were obtained in 1994. Superscripts indicate that a specific mean is significantly different from means for other alphabetically identified groups ($p < .05$): for example, the problem behavior mean of .22 for the socially ignored group is significantly different from the mean of −.50 for group A, the most competent adolescents.

At the other end of the continuum on academic competence is Ruth Hartz, a twelfth-grader from a broken family (mother died) who was held back a year. All of her friends had left school. Now living with a boyfriend, Ruth has little positive to say about school and is not involved in a single social activity. With a record of poor grades, she claims to "hate her principal" and does not "get along with any teachers at that school." She has tried drugs and uses alcohol. Her future is uncertain, but she has a significant grandfather on her mother's side of the family who "understands her love of horses" and seems to understand her. Ruth's work on a horse farm has become the center of her life. She cleans stalls and halters and rides horses for approximately thirty hours per week. Her maternal grandfather is also involved with horses, and she seeks his advice about work-related problems. "He is really big into the horse. He really understands everything." By comparison, her other grandparents "haven't a clue about horses, and my dad thinks it is a waste of time."

The second cluster of adolescents (group B), labeled "self-critical achievers," outperforms all other groups, except the most competent, on academic success. This title reflects a defining feature of their lives— that they are much more competent than they and perhaps their parents think they are. They also have better relations with peers than any other group, although their score is not significantly higher than the mean of the most competent. Their Achilles heel is a low sense of personal confidence. These tendencies toward a negative self-evaluation come at a cost—a higher risk of problem behavior than among the most competent adolescents.

The self-critical achievers resembled the least competent group on a lack of confidence, and their parents appear to share a less positive view of their abilities—they show little tendency to seek their advice or counsel. Lack of affirmation from parents may stem in part from high standards, or it may reflect an inability to offer praise.

We did not seek evidence of critical parents in our surveys and interviews. However, a twelfth-grade boy recalled an event that is relevant. He notes that both parents were critical of the work he did at home. His father, in particular, was hard to satisfy. "My dad is really fussy about the yard, and if it isn't mowed just right, it's not good enough for him. Most people just cut the grass and that's good, but not for him; he's kind of fussy, and it's tough to please him sometimes."

The third cluster (group C), labeled "socially recognized," includes adolescents who are exceptional in social activity and leadership. They are characterized by relatively good social relations and feelings of self-confidence. These adolescents receive high respect from parents, they feel self-confident, and they enjoy positive social relationships with age-mates. They are not academic superstars, but they are relatively secure in their own personal worth and show little risk of behavior problems. Their developmental path to self-esteem and social competence involves social involvement of all kinds, including leadership.

In the fourth cluster (group D), labeled "at-risk; socially ignored," we encounter another opposite group—youth who feel socially ignored. Their ignored status extends rather broadly; they are not recognized and highly valued by significant figures in their life, from teachers and parents to peers. Some of this neglect may come from their lack of accomplishment and distinction. This deficiency may also stem from social neglect. In any case, ignored youth rank lowest of all groups on advice-seeking from their parents, and they match the least competent adolescents on poor relations with peers. Although they also resemble youth engaged in problem behavior, they do fare better on academic success and self-confidence. This suggests that they have the skills to avoid serious maladjustment over time in comparison with the least competent youth.

These groupings of adolescents enable us to understand more fully the meaning of high or low self-confidence. They identify adolescents who appear to have everything going their way and those who are disadvantaged across most areas of life. They also identify academic success and social involvement as pathways to different forms of competence. Profiles distinguishing the five groups have important implications for development into the adult years. Can we predict membership in each profile cluster from the family attributes and social relations we have explored up to this point? The findings in table 9.2 clearly reveal the usefulness of profiles for identifying and linking developmental pathways and outcomes among young people in the rural Midwest. Results in the table are based on the full set of explanatory factors.

With the exception of activities with father, the most competent youth live in a very different world than that of the least competent. The comparison includes family attributes and relations, closeness to grandparents, and community involvement. The most competent youth (1) had families with higher incomes, (2) moved less often, (3) had parents with more education, (4) experienced greater warmth and identification with both parents, (5) had more activities with grandparents and a higher-quality relationship with them, (6) were more religiously engaged and academically successful, and (7) were more involved in school sports, club activities, and student leadership. In all ways, the explanatory variables in the conceptual model powerfully discriminate between youth at greatest and lowest risk of serious problem behavior. And, as before,

Table 9.2
Profiles of Competence by Family/Child Characteristics, Family Relations, Close Relations with Grandparents, and Community Involvement

Predictor Variables	(a) Most Competent ($N = 85$)	(b) Self-Critical Achievers ($N = 85$)	(c) Socially Recognized ($N = 83$)	(d) At Risk; Socially Ignored ($N = 94$)	(e) Least Competent ($N = 77$)
Family/Child characteristics					
Gender (1 = boys, 0 = girls)	−.24[ce]	−.03	.21[a]	−.18[e]	.30[ad]
Per-capita income	.10[e]	.04	.13[e]	.04	−.34[ac]
Moves	−.30[be]	−.04	−.05	.16[a]	.23[a]
Parents' education	.28[e]	.18[e]	.03[e]	.01[e]	−.55[abcd]
Family relations					
Father's id/warmth	.46[bde]	−.24[ac]	.35[bde]	−.40[ac]	−.16[ac]
Activities with father	−.05[b]	.48[acde]	.03[b]	−.25[b]	−.22[b]
Mother's id/warmth	.53[bde]	−.31[acd]	.34[bce]	−.60[abce]	−.18[acd]
Close relations with grandparents					
Relationship quality	.15[e]	.05[e]	.10[e]	.10[e]	−.47[abcd]
Activities	.21[c]	.10[c]	.09	−.05	−.41[ab]
Community involvement					
Youth religion	.34[bde]	.25[e]	−.06[e]	−.07[ab]	−.49[abcd]
School sports	.37[de]	.38[de]	.05[de]	−.38[abc]	−.43[abc]
School activities	.36[ce]	.28[e]	−.10[ab]	.04[e]	−.63[abcd]
School leadership	.41[de]	.26[de]	.16[de]	−.33[abc]	−.52[abc]

Note: All measures of competence were obtained in 1994. Superscripts indicate that a specific mean is significantly different from means for other alphabetically identified groups ($p < .05$); for example, the parents' education mean of .28 for the most competent group is significantly different from the mean of −.55 for group e, the least competent group.

boys are at a greater risk than girls for being in the most troubled, least competent group.

The "all-around" group of adolescents fits a developmental history of cumulative advantage—success opens the door to more success and stronger feelings of self-worth. If only one adult who "truly cares about a child" is enough to make a difference in a young life, these young people have profited from an abundance of people who care, from parents to siblings and relatives, as well as close friends, school staff, the local minister or youth-group leader, and, for many, an employer. The other world of cumulative disadvantage is concentrated among youth who rank on the bottom of competence. This group is disadvantaged in terms of every possible social and economic dimension in the study, from family income to involvement in school sports.

The findings also provide explanations for some earlier mysteries, particularly with regard to family relations. For example, we found evidence that working with a parent can actually increase a youth's risk for problem behavior across adolescence. We proposed at the time that issues of dependency and normal maturation could account for this unexpected outcome. Table 9.2 offers valuable insights along this line. The "self-critical achievers" are much more likely to be involved with their fathers than youth in any other cluster. They also experience relatively low support from and identification with their parents. In combination, these family processes suggest that the parents verbalize a critical view of children's accomplishments, despite their notable achievements in school. Such demanding, critical parenting can be internalized in ways that devalue the self. Frequent association with parents through "obligatory work" would enhance the impact of this critical self-evaluation.

It is noteworthy that many of these young people come from operating farms where "working with parents" is a common expectation. Too many activities with parents at this time of life could expose youth to judgments that are too critical when they need to be gaining a sense of confidence and independence. As one youth noted, "my parents think I can't do anything well." From another perspective, Sonya Salamon (personal letter) suggests that some of the farm influence reflects a socialization norm on personal modesty. Farm youth are likely to be overly modest about their accomplishments. Undoubtedly, both this form of upbringing and high standards with minimal praise would contribute notably to a devaluation of self.

Family relations also tell an important story of the "socially ignored" and "socially recognized" groups. Socially ignored youth report significantly lower identification with and support from their mothers when compared to all other groups. And this distance is mirrored by relations with fathers. Such problematic social relations appear to begin at home, setting in motion difficulties for achieving in school sports, student leadership roles, and school clubs. By comparison, the socially recognized follow a reverse dynamic in their lives. They identify with parents who are relatively warm and supportive, a closeness that bolsters confidence in self and their relations with others outside the family.

Some Reflections

What lessons for young lives can be derived from this pattern of findings? We began by proposing two broad domains of competence, one having to do with culturally valued accomplishments and the other with avoiding behavior problems that carry risks for the successful transition to adulthood. Based on this framework, we sketched a life-course theory of problem behavior (figure 9.1) that drew upon earlier analyses. This work shows that family ties to the land through agriculture and other background characteristics generate important social resources (family relationships, community ties) and culturally valued competencies, such as doing well in academics and getting along with peers. These resources, in turn, have developmental relevance for children's competence. Resources and competencies establish conditions that are supportive of conventional behavior and minimize the risk of emotional distress.

Three empirical themes deserve special note in relation to our findings: (1) the prominence of academic success in minimizing problem behaviors of all kinds, from drug use and drinking to stealing, and interpersonal aggression; (2) the "indirect" protective influence of family and community activities on minimizing teenage troubles—the protection occurs mainly through the competencies of youth; and (3) the role of academic success and religious involvement in placing youth on a resilient trajectory that avoids antisocial activity. Success in conventional activities has long been recognized as a protective influence for children, insulating them from the attractions of a wayward life. Both academic and social success have much to do with a nurturant family with high standards, but the experience of success has its own self-generating dynamic, as we have seen.

Youth who are doing well academically tend to have more rewarding relationships with their parents across the adolescent years, and they are more likely than other age-mates to be recognized by parents as people with good judgment and advice. Academic success generates a sense of academic competence that can generalize to mastery beliefs and expectations.[23] Good students have more access to social opportunities in school, and they are likely to benefit from the positive recognition by teachers and community residents, especially in a small town. For many adolescents, academic success covaries with social success, and the most involved Iowa students generally gained a stronger feeling of self-confidence up to high school. Participation in school clubs and athletics, student leadership and community organizations all contributed to this self-confidence, along with a solid record of academic achievement and good friends.

Academic success also provides a pathway to opportunity after high school, from college to placement in a rewarding career. Access to such pathways generates optimism about the future, a sense of personal worth, and high educational aspirations. It also establishes commitments that minimize exposure to unwise or risky actions that threaten this future, such as precocious sexual activity, pregnancy, and an extramarital birth. This path to future achievement is further defined along the way by friends and social expectations that commit young people to a certain identity and reputation.[24] We find this collective experience to be commonplace in small communities. As one Iowa student put it, "people in this small town expect a lot from us. One must try to do well."

In theory and evidence, academic success and other forms of youth competence represent strong links between family ties to the land and the avoidance of problem behavior. The distinctive resources of these families, such as shared activities and engagement in local communities, play an important developmental role in youth competence, as we have seen in prior chapters. Theory also suggests that these resources could minimize the involvement of youth in problem behavior, perhaps by reducing risky behavior.[25] Loving and supportive parents who remain invested in the lives of their adolescents would diminish the likelihood of their experimentation with problem behavior. Informal social control occurs through family attachment and monitoring.

Family influences of this kind do have direct consequences for children's avoidance of problem behavior. Supportive mothers make an important difference, as do grandparents who are engaged in activities with their grandchildren. But most of this influence is transmitted through the competencies of children. Nurturant families lessen the risk of problem behavior among their children largely because the latter are equipped to be successful in academic work and social activities. One partial exception to this indirect influence is the involvement of youth in a religious community—in religious services and in the youth group's activities: social, service, and religious. Adolescents who are religiously involved were more likely than other youth to show a pattern of increasing avoidance of problem behavior through high school. We refer to this pattern as "a trajectory of resilience." Involved adolescents became significantly less engaged in problem behavior by the end of high school.

This contribution of religious communities has been documented as well in the more dangerous neighborhoods of inner city Philadelphia.[26] A good many black parents in high-risk neighborhoods were successful in placing their children in the protective culture of religious communities. One mother joined the Catholic Church so that her son could attend the parish school and grow up in a culture with moral discipline and high behavioral expectations. Another mother became a member of the Jehovah's Witnesses.

A black youth by the name of Robert lived in an economically disadvantaged neighborhood. His mental health ranked above average, and he was not involved in problem behaviors. Robert's social activities and those of his family were centered on the church. Most of his friends attended the local church, and their joint service and social activities were encouraged by adults in the church. Robert knew most of the local youth, but he did not regard them as friends. This boy's religious upbringing in Philadelphia has many parallels to the lives of Iowa youth.

All of the central themes of this chapter have emerged from our study of variables in a life-course theory of problem behavior, and from a comparison of different "types of adolescents." Each type identifies a group of adolescents with a particular profile of competence. We cluster-analyzed the key developmental outcomes (such as academic success and social competence) and discovered that they identified five differentiated groups: the most competent youth versus the least competent, who were also engaged in problem behavior, along with the socially recognized and ignored, and youth at high risk. The most competent youth scored highest on every dimension of normative competence, and also lowest on problem behavior. This group also displayed the greatest socioeconomic advantage and support from parents.

By contrast, the least competent scored lowest on every dimension of normative competence and highest on problem behavior. These problem youth experienced the greatest socioeconomic deprivation and the fewest social resources, from minimal engagement in the community and poor relations with parents to a relatively difficult family environment. They constitute the most at-risk group in terms of long-term developmental problems. Clearly, the identification of a meaningful profile of incompetence improves our understanding of this subsample with its cumulative problems.

Across the other groups, we discovered that the tie between involvement with parents and risk may have to do with the connection between activities with parents at this life stage and the tendency for parents to be excessively critical. Especially when parents lack warmth and support, a youth's activities with them could diminish self-confidence and promote self-doubts, as in the "self-critical achievers" group. These findings add support for a person-centered approach to developmental inquiry.

Specific types of social relations with parents also tend to play an important role in the lives of youth who were either "socially ignored" or "socially recognized." In particular, the socially recognized group did not perform especially well academically, but they remained confident and socially involved. This pattern appears to be the result of supportive parents who emphasize positive qualities as opposed to negative attributes. Socially ignored youth were unlikely to experience such family life.

With this chapter we complete our empirical journey in the young lives of Iowa youth, from the beginning of secondary school to the end of high school. Our final chapter turns to the theoretical and practical significance of this life story.

Past, Present, and Future

An Iowa farmer from the north central region reflects on his life situation: "Life is changing drastically for me and my family as we seek to find a way to hold on to our family farm in order to pass it on to our children. At times it seems that the American farm dream may no longer be attainable by the time our children are grown. I have been an independent farmer in north-central Iowa for nearly twenty years now. . . . Pam and I have raised our three children and participated in the local school, church, and community projects. Ball games and recitals, harvests, and hogs have been our way of life.

"We deeply value certain social benefits long extolled in our rural communities. . . . We watch out for each others' children and homes and console each other in times of tragedy. . . . We commit time and financial resources to see to it that our children and elderly are well cared for, that our churches serve our congregations thoughtfully, and that our schools provide the best opportunities and educational environments that our communities can provide.

"The structural changes of the hog industry threaten all of the community values that we cherish. Earthen storage basins and open manure lagoons are leaking and contaminating wells and other waters. . . . Social life changes as traditional rural families leave to find new jobs elsewhere and are replaced by underpaid transient laborers working in the large-scale facilities. . . . Newcomers tend to be less involved in local community life through churches and school. Seldom do they own properties that help to ensure proper upkeep of a community."[1]

CHAPTER TEN

Legacies of the Land

When the farmers are gone, "the church will be gone, the bank will be gone. The town will dry up."

Manager, grain elevator

We have followed a group of rural American children from their early adolescent years in an agricultural recession to the end of high school and major life decisions. Some of these young people lived on working farms, while others had parents who were trying to manage the farm and a job in town at the same time. The most visible casualties of the changing agricultural scene were the young people and families who left farming and the family farm. Still other parents had grown up on a farm but left it to find employment in the small towns and cities. Over a fourth had no such "ties to the land" and agriculture. Consistent with expectations, such ties are associated with social experiences that significantly enhance the success and life prospects of young people, even with less opportunity in the rural countryside.

Hard times persist in the study area as the twentieth century comes to an end, despite the booming economies of nearby cities. The profit margin in farming is declining, largely in response to declining prices in global markets and the loss of farm subsidies.[1] Rural wages have also fallen well below those in cities. Pushed by such forces, economic inequality is driving a larger wedge between rural and urban communities. The bright lights of nearby cities look even brighter. Among the young people in this study, very few anticipated a life of farming or even just living on a farm.

Such economic troubles are not uncommon in the rural Midwest. Indeed, most families have managed to cope well with hardship. During the years of this project, for example, the north central region of Iowa has experienced serious drought, two major floods, and periods when there was a dismal market for cattle and grain. The rapid growth of industrial hog operations has produced additional hardship for independent family farmers.

Despite such hardship, Iowans continue to reach out to people in need. During the record-breaking flood of 1993, Tom Brokaw, a television broadcaster, grabbed writer Hugh Sidey by the arm and said, "You'd have been proud of those Iowans. They were just magnificent, helping each other, giving to each other."[2] In this study, we have assumed that such collective resourcefulness is found, most especially, among families with ties to the land. These families are residentially stable, tend to be invested in their communities, and consequently play a key role in social institutions that are important for their children—churches, schools, and civic groups. Good husbandry has such primordial meanings, caring for home, community, and the land.

This final chapter returns to the main themes observed across three generations (grandparent, parent, and child), with emphasis on the younger generation. We begin by considering a key matter of approach, a sequence of ecological niches to capture the variation in family ties to the land. Some families derive most if not all income from farming, while others obtain only a fourth or less of their income from the farm and do not live on the land. Still other parents moved away from farming in adolescence and adulthood. In all of our comparisons, we must keep in mind the generalization limitations of this study. It occupies a specific place and time in the American Midwest, and both features need to be considered.

Our findings tell us about successful pathways through adolescence and into young adulthood. Five themes define these pathways, extending from intergenerational continuities and family connectedness to the power of small worlds. We discuss each theme and conclude with future scenarios that are part of a worldwide pattern, including the continued decline of families on the land and the uncertain future of community life in this part of rural America.

Approaches and Some Alternatives

A common view of rural America depicts a homogeneous world that differs from urban life in many ways, ranging from greater spatial isolation and diminished services to a lower socioeconomic level of living. For years the White House Conferences on Children addressed such inequalities by treating rural populations of children as if there were no internal differences worth noting.[3] Rural children were simply more disadvantaged. Though recent reports claim that rural children do more poorly in education than urban children, they generally ignore important differences among rural families.

We have focused on differences in family ties to agriculture and the land. We refer to this connection in terms of "ties to the land." Such ties are important, we find, because they tell us something about the community and institutional investments of adults and their lives with children. Invested families are engaged in community life, and such engagement tends to promote similar involvement on the part of children, along with feelings of self-confidence, social leadership, and academic excellence.

Families with the strongest ties are engaged in full-time farming, and most of their income is derived from farming. These households are involved in farming as a way of life and a business. In both household and community, children's family activities typically involved substantial interaction with parents. Children are embedded in a web of family relationships that includes grandparents, aunts and uncles, and cousins. Usually family members are available to help out during emergencies of health, finances, or weather.

The next category in proximity to the land includes parents and children who found themselves straddling the world of agriculture and non-farm life. Typically, much less than half of all family income was obtained from farming. Both parents usually held jobs off the land, and the farm work was sometimes completed at night. Children in this family situation thus experienced the lifestyle and disciplines of farming and a more urban environment. For many decades across this century, part-time farming has been seen as a way to keep more families on the land.[4] Indeed, most of the families in this category saw employment off the land as a way to remain involved in farming. But the costs of this life are high, including extraordinary time pressures—not enough time for the marriage, for children, the community, and oneself. As a mother described her marriage during the busiest season, "We live on notes."[5]

Some families grew up on farms and launched their own farms only to encounter the collapse of land values and soaring levels of debt. They eventually had to leave their farms, frequently ending a family legacy, through bankruptcy or sales. This painful transition out of farming usually occurred between the late 1970s and mid-1980s, at a time when the Iowa children were growing up. The emotional imprint of this event was still very strong in the memories of displaced parents and their children. A father recalled feeling "numb up to the sale and then after the sale I was just so depressed."[6] Marriages were often embroiled in conflict and much fault-finding.[7] One of the girls in the study remembers turning to her grandmother for solace and understanding when her parents were so upset by the loss of the farm. No group of families and children ranked higher on emotional distress during the first year of the Iowa study, but we found that most of the children had adapted well to the new situation by their high school years, five years later. Typically, this adaptation reflected their parents' success in finding a new life. However, ties to the land remained a theme in their histories and cultural preferences.

As we move away from proximity to the land, we come to parents who are only connected to agriculture through their childhood. They grew up on a farm and then proceeded to leave this home for other opportunities and places. But they did not leave the study region and maintained frequent visits with family and friends. As a result, the study children from this family background enjoyed many opportunities to be with their grandparents. In all of these ways, the farm childhood of parents continued to influence family life well into their middle years. For the most part, these adults still had the work ethic and social responsibility of their childhood environment, and they remained tied to rural farm influences through relations with parents, relatives, and friends. Indeed, some of their siblings remained involved in farming and they occasionally spent holidays on one of the farms.

The most distant group of families from the land includes all parents who did not grow up on farms or enter farming as adults. They are currently engaged in nonagricultural fields of employment, such as mail carrier, minister, contractor, local bus driver, and high school teacher. We label them the nonfarm group, and they represent the comparison standard for all analyses of the influence of ties to the land. Thus, they were compared with the full- and part-time farm families, and also with the displaced and farm-reared groups.

For the most part, these nonfarm families currently live in agriculturally dependent counties, but they have no direct connection to this line of work. Without ties to the land and farming, they are free to move about, and they do so. These families were by far the most residentially mobile of all households. With fewer ties to kin and community, these families were also more vulnerable to the pressures of economic swings in seeking jobs. As economic conditions worsened in the study region, these families were more prepared to follow the job opportunities.

The social ecology of north central Iowa, then, consists of these "niches" with their social and developmental implications. Thus, the sons and daughters of farm families were subject to the social imperatives of farm routines or chores. The young had responsibilities to fulfill each day, and their successful management tended to enhance feelings of self-confidence. They were also engaged with parents and siblings in family and community activities. This developmental social ecology is not matched by parents who gave up farming or by those who grew up on a farm, but all of these rural ecologies have farming ties that could enrich young lives. From this vantage point, nearly four out of five Iowans in the project have some connection to the land.

Over many decades the transition away from ties to the land has been expressed in a substantial decline of full-time farmers and an increase in farm families who are also engaged in nonfarm employment. With each passing generation, the farms get larger and the number of farmers declines (see chapter 1). Concerning the dryland country of western Kansas, Bair observes that the tractors and combines have gotten bigger over the years, "as have the farms, . . . and the farmers themselves have become almost as scarce as white-tailed jackrabbits."[8] Farm-reared parents in our sample, as one generation off the land, have also declined significantly in the Midwest's population. The grandfathers in this three-generation project are nearly twice as likely as their sons to have farmed. And only a handful of the grandsons have plans of this kind.

The farm crisis accelerated the movement of families off the land, and the increasingly bleak state of commodity prices today has produced another more serious crisis, especially on the High Plains, a tableland of wheat and cattle. In the hardest hit state, North Dakota, estimates show more than 4,000 farmers would leave the land by the end of 1998. By mid-summer of 1998, most commercial establishments in the North Dakota town of Buxton had closed, and a sign on the Buxton elevator told the story, "Times are so tough that even the people who don't intend to pay aren't buying."[9] In the words of the state's agriculture commissioner, a continuation of the crisis will be "emptying out the countryside."[10] In some parts of the High Plains, this "emptying out" has occurred. On a recent journey across the country, Jonathan Raban observed many ruined houses for each surviving ranch: "As far as one could see, the dead had left their stuff lying around, to dissolve back into nature in its own time, at its own pace. A civilization of sorts, its houses, cars, machinery, was fading rapidly off the land."[11]

Iowans have witnessed such times, and we have written about the 1980s Farm Crisis in the experience of families who are part of this study (chapter 1). But the severity of this crisis did not extend to other regions, as we note in chapter 1. Social and economic diversity typifies rural America. However, conditions remain difficult for farming families in the study area. In particular, the oldest members of our study were not optimistic about a return to the better life of the 1960s.

Keeping such ecological variations in mind, we have referred to the study area as a high-risk setting for young people, but it is not the kind of high-risk setting that we see in the Mississippi Delta or in the inner-city "Black Belt" of Chicago and Philadelphia, where drugs and violence flourish.[12] Though socioeconomic conditions and drugs have made life more risk-filled for young people in rural Iowa,[13] they have significant adults in their lives, usually three or more. And schools remain among the best in the country.

From the standpoint of resourcefulness, Iowa families with ties to the land have much in common with the middle class of the Great Depression era.[14] These depression families often suffered heavy losses, but they usually had the resources, inner and social, to rebound from adversity. As hardships have come and gone among Iowa families on the land, they have learned how to make the best of what they have. The "ability to bounce back from adversity" in the farm crisis is plainly evident in the lives of children and parents. But there is another story of hardship and disadvantage. Some of the families were not resourceful, and their children did not succeed in school, either socially or academically.

Over the years many questions have been asked about the people who stay in rural America and those who leave. This is a complicated issue, as we make clear, but it is relevant to our efforts to link involvement in agriculture with the life chances of young people. We know that the process is selective of people who leave disadvantaged regions and communities for lands of greater opportunity. All over the Midwest and highlands, the loss of talented youth to places that offer greater opportunity is a matter of great concern, and this applies to the loss of talented adults as well. Within the Iowa study, we find that young people with the weakest attachments to settling near family and kin tend to have greater ability and ambition than other youth.[15] The least competent are most committed to settling down in the local community. However, we find high levels of competence among young people who want to farm. This survey occurred in the eleventh grade, a time when advanced education was the primary issue.

If we follow the process long enough, "movement off the land" would include two different kinds of people. Some fathers give up farming and take local jobs such as truck driving. A number of the parents who were displaced from the land ended up in jobs of this kind at first, though eventually we find many in a variety of jobs with similar or higher income. Other people give up farming to move to places of greater opportunity. In Iowa this might be the greater metropolitan region of Des Moines or Mason City. These economic areas are close enough for some to commute on a daily basis for the work week and weekend. But what about the parents who have survived *in* farming? Do they differ in any way from the parents who were pushed off the farm—the displaced?

We gave these questions much thought by considering the size and history of the farm, the role of education and managerial style,[16] as well as life histories that produce unstable behavior. As noted in chapters 1 and 2, studies suggest that large and small farms were at risk in the Great Farm Crisis of the 1980s, and that an expansive managerial style increased the risk of heavy indebtedness. Data limitations prevented us from testing these potential influences. However, the personal histories of men reveal little of significance. Men who lost their farms were not characterized as more impulsive, and their early family experience was not more conflicted or unstable. We found no evidence that ties to parents were weaker among men who lost their farms. To make adjustments for income and educational differences, as well as variations in residential change, we included these variables in all analyses.

In any case, the story of how "ties to the land" influenced the development of young people in the study is more than a matter of individual histories—it includes the way of life of each rural economy and not just the individual attributes of each parent. Farming organizes life differently for children than do nonfarm occupations, and growing up on a farm has consequences for skills, social attachments, and values that can persist through life, regardless of whether one leaves or continues in farming. "Ties to the land" are also coupled with a lifestyle that has been fostered over the years by a distinctly Iowan institution, *Wallace's Farmer*. This magazine was founded by Henry Wallace's family, and he served as editor between World War I and the Great Depression years. Many pages of the journal were devoted to helping farmers become more efficient.

The journal also stressed the connection between males and the land. Just before his service in the New Deal as Secretary of Agriculture, Wallace wrote that "the farm boys we want to hold on the farm are those who have real common sense and intelligence, a love of their fellowman and a vision of building up a fine community and a fine national civilization based on agriculture."[17] Consistent with the agrarians of his time, Wallace thought that the vigor of a civilization depended on its being rooted in the soil.

Wallace advocated models of success in rural America, as well as the centrality of work and its ambition, including the value of hard physical labor. He wrote about the appeal of family life on the farm, the importance of family responsibilities in a man's life, and the essential dimension of involved citizenship. Many features of this prescriptive account are reflected in the lives of Iowa youth who have ties to the land—for example, the value of hard work, success, and family connectedness in the community. If he were writing today, Wallace would undoubtedly favor more balance between the roles of men and women on the land.

Iowa is embraced by the heartland of America, but its families from the north central region may not resemble families and youth in other rural places. Little is known about these other places. Much like a town that has been bypassed to make way for a superhighway, rural America has been sadly neglected by the social and behavioral sciences. Poverty has drawn primary attention to the inner city, not to pockets of hard living in rural America. Nevertheless, rural variation is notable from the evidence at hand. Barlett's study of farming in Dodge County, Georgia, does not find the intergenerational continuity that we see in Salamon's study of German farmers in Illinois or in our farm families of German heritage.[18] Despite the absence of comparative inquiry, much can be learned from this study that has relevance to children in other places, rural and urban.

Some additional limitations deserve comment before we turn to the pathways of Iowa youth. First, we have a snapshot of a long-term historical process, that of movement off the land. This snapshot gives us a view of only one age group of Iowa children—those who were born in the mid-1970s and grew up during the Great Farm Crisis. The story might well have differed if we had conducted this study at a different time, the 1940s, 1950s, or 1960s. The fathers of our young people were born in the 1940s and 1950s, and over 40 percent had served in the military, mainly in Vietnam. A significant number of these men lost their farms after acquiring heavy debts. The three generations—grandfather, father, and son—brought different life histories to the farm crisis and were influenced by it accordingly. In theory, "the life course of individuals is embedded in and shaped by the historical times and places they experience over their lifetime."[19]

In addition, the present study was designed to resemble *Children of the Great Depression*[20] in terms of the respondent's age, that of selected seventh-grade students in a number of schools. These children were followed across the secondary school years to young adulthood. To locate enough farm families, we had to survey a large number of schools in the north central region ($N = 34$). Nevertheless, the counties that make up our study region are homogeneous on social and economic factors. The school districts did not vary in ways that would make school contexts relevant to an understanding of human development. Despite all of these considerations, we have the very best option for the question at hand. No data archive on rural generations approximates the richness of the Iowa Youth and Families Project.

Pathways of Resilience for Young Lives

Cycles are common in rural America—from seasons of the year to good and bad times. In a poor agricultural year, people expect next year "to be better." Economic cycles establish vivid historical markers in lives and people's conversations, such as "the flood of 1993"—before and after the great flood. Grandparents in this study experienced the Great Depression and World War II during their early years. Their children were born during the years of postwar prosperity and came of age during the Vietnam era. The sons and daughters who later went into farming did so in an era marked by expansionistic thinking on food production for a soaring world population. Production soon outstripped demand, land values declined precipitously, and farm indebtedness increased significantly.

The study children were born just before the Great Farm Crisis, the late 1970s, and they grew up during the worst years of this decline. One of the fathers in this study was a businessman just off the main street of his small town. In great alarm, he exclaimed, "I have watched business after business after business go out. We've lost industry. There hasn't been anything left unaffected by this" (circa 1989).[21] A tour of the study area during the late 1980s revealed much evidence of decline and personal troubles—the boarded-up storefronts of commercial establishments, going-out-of-business signs, and announcements of "hot lines" for assistance. In planning a study of this economic crisis, we focused on the impact of the general economic downturn on families in the area, and especially on the process by which the decline made a difference in the lives of children. We were also concerned with factors that minimized the adverse effects of hardship.

To address these matters, we launched the Iowa Youth and Families Project in 1989 with 451 families who had a seventh-grade child and a near sibling, all from eight counties in north central Iowa. These seventh-graders were in many respects "Children of the Farm Crisis," born at the end of an era of rural prosperity. The study assumed that heavy indebtedness, low income, unstable work, and income loss collectively increased the emotional distress and marital negativity of the parents by sharply increasing the level of economic pressure—material pressures that stem from reduced expenditures and growing indebtedness. In theory, the mounting emotional distress and marital discord of parents would undermine the nurturant behavior of parents, placing at risk the emotional well-being of children.

In the very first wave of data on boys, we found substantial evidence of these consequences.[22] Objective family deprivations did, in fact, increase the risk of a depressed mood among parents through felt economic pressures. Depressed feelings also significantly heightened the likelihood of marital strife, and consequently increased the risk of harsh behavior by both parents. These behaviors, in turn, undermined the boys' self-confidence, peer acceptance, and school performance. Similar results have been reported for the girls.[23]

These findings show both similarities and differences when compared to results from *Children of the Great Depression,* a study conducted many years ago. In both studies, major economic downturns in the economy influenced the lives of children through family relationships and processes. Variations in family process often made a significant difference, such as when parental marriages remained strong and supportive through the crisis.[24] In the Iowa study, however, the emotions and behaviors of mothers were as significant as those of fathers in linking hardship to adverse developmental outcomes for adolescents. In addition, unlike parents in the Depression study, which found that only previously emotionally unstable fathers were negatively affected by economic stress, Iowa parents with and without a history of behavioral problems or emotional distress became more moody, irritable, and angry in response to economic hardship. Moreover, and contrary to the earlier findings, adolescent girls were as vulnerable as boys to these economic stress processes.

Both studies also tell another story: *that life trajectories are by no means solely determined by socioeconomic disadvantage and subsequent misfortune.* A large number of young people from disadvantaged circumstances ended up doing better than one would predict; they exceeded expectations based on their backgrounds. Extraordinarily high levels of unemployment and hardship during the 1930s led many observers to expect an impaired life among children of the Great Depression. But to an unexpected degree, most of these children followed a trajectory of resilience into the middle years. They ended up doing far better than expected from the vantage point of their beginnings. The resulting challenge from this study was not a continuation of adversity, but rather centered on success in adulthood. *Resilience* is a popular term these days, but it refers most especially to "how people deal with life chances and what they do about their situations."[25] Some young people do very little, even with an advantaged situation. They become more vulnerable to risk, showing a lack of motivation and risky behavior. They lose the advantage of a stable, nurturant home and the advantage of well-educated parents who make a good living.

The Iowa adolescents were also adversely influenced by economic hardship during the 1980s, and consequently we expected to find evidence of continuity into high school. However, we found much evidence of resilience when follow-ups were carried out across the high school years. In the tenth grade, four years after the first data collection, we compared youth in families that had lost their farms with young people on functioning farms.[26] We also considered the level of economic hardship when the study began. The tenth-grade children of displaced families were not more emotionally distressed than other youth, and we were unable to find any substantial evidence of their early prominence on measures of distress. Family relationships also failed to reveal differences between this group and all other youth.

To explain these results, we turned to the social resources of farming families for insight. We knew at the time that some of these families had increased their income over the years; however, some were doing worse. But the historical connection between social resources and family ties to the land seemed to provide a deeper understanding of our results. In life-course theory, linked lives establish a medium for social influence, most especially within families: "Lives are lived interdependently and social-historical influences are expressed through this network of shared relationships."[27] The ideas of social capital offered similar insights on family networks in communities.

When farming families settled the study region in the nineteenth century, they established local churches, schools, civic groups, and governmental bodies. Ties to the land thus entailed an unusual investment in community life. These ties and investments were especially prominent among Midwest families of German heritage.[28] In addition to their social embeddedness, these families were characterized by a distinctive interweaving of the generations in children's lives. The work of the farm brought parents and older children together in shared activities. In these ways, such families offered their children a lifestyle that "money could not buy,"[29] or that the lack of money would not erase.

This view of the family differs from the common focus on parent-child interactions *within* the household,[30] a view that ignores parenting activity beyond the household—in the neighborhood, school, church, and civic groups. For many years, the voluntary organizations and activities of adults were studied with little attention to family processes.[31] To be sure, the ever-changing demands of family life, from marriage to births and the maturation of children, were recognized as altering the constraints on parent participation in the community. But this participation itself was not considered a source of parental effectiveness or as a mode of parental control and social stimulus for children's development.

Parental models of social competence through community activities were largely neglected. This more contextual view of families and children did emerge in the MacArthur Foundation Research Network on Successful Adolescent Development among Youth in High-Risk Settings, as expressed most fully in the Philadelphia study, *Managing to Make It*.[32] Our approach is consistent with this more embedded view of the family within a life-course framework.

If Iowa families on the land establish resourceful pathways for their children, as indicated by theory and research, they seemed likely to do so through strong intergenerational ties with parents and grandparents, productive roles that foster skills and self-confidence, parental networks of social engagement in the community, and the social involvement of children. Some families off the land might well have similar attributes, but we assumed that they were less common in this subgroup. Each type of family resource has relevance to age-graded competencies, such as academic success, social competence, self-confidence, and the avoidance of problem behavior.

Nurturant family relationships are most relevant to academic success, which tends to create future opportunities and raise aspirations. Social competence or success is expressed in positive relations with age-mates, teachers, and parents. Social achievements enhance feelings of competence, which in turn increase prospects for additional accomplishments of this kind. Social appraisals of self-esteem, mastery, and maturity are likely to stem from productive achievements, and they also facilitate them. Finally, as reported in chapter 9, academic and social success limits the appeal of deviant behavior. This appeal is reduced as well by involvement in conventional activities, such as church groups and community organizations.

From the evidence at hand, young people with ties to the land are more successful across all domains than other adolescents. They tend to rank higher on academic performance, social prominence, self-confidence, and the avoidance of problem behavior, other factors being equal. This level of accomplishment has much to do with the social resources of their families. Consider academic and social competence, as expressed in the histories of Iowa youth through high school. This competence is linked to families on the land and their social resources, even with adjustments for parental education, their income, and residential instability.

Parental warmth and supportiveness are important for this level of achievement, and the salience of father is especially prominent among children who aspired to life on the farm. Involvements beyond the household also prove to be influential. Despite hard times, families involved in agriculture are more engaged in community institutions (church, school, and civic associations) than other families, and involved parents tend to have sons and daughters who are socially active in school, church, and community. Such forms of involvement are among the most influential predictors of success and psychological health across the years of secondary school.

Youth with ties to the land were also more involved in productive labor than other young people up to high school, both as chores and as paid work. Earning activities generally increased a sense of mastery up to the years after high school. In addition to this perception of self, workers tended to report that they had become more effective as a result of "lessons on the job," from greater patience and self-control to management skills. Only excessive hours, over twenty per week, were associated with academic difficulty. Productive labor involved farm youth in activities with family members and strengthened the influence of parents in their lives, but it had special significance in the lives of adolescents who had been displaced from their family farms. These young people felt the greatest urgency to become economically self-sufficient and their earnings rose most sharply through high school.

Academic and social success, along with feelings of self-confidence, suggest a path to the adult years that is not jeopardized by problem activities—using drugs, alcohol, sexual promiscuity, delinquent acts. Success nurtures feelings of personal worth and greater ambition, while failure threatens regard for self and may lead to problematic friends and activity. Problem behavior is not as common in this part of rural Iowa as it is in the cities or in urban areas throughout the country, but it is least common among successful youth in school who were involved in a religious community. Leadership responsibilities in school also steered youth away from deviant friends and activities.

Families with ties to the land were unusually successful in nurturing academic and social achievement by their children, in part through their own accomplishments in education, work, and civic leadership. These activities strengthened self-confidence and generally reinforced the protective influence of personal accomplishments. Children's involvement in the church and youth group also ensured a peer group with acceptable moral values and objectives.

What has occurred in the lives of these young people since they left high school in 1994? One year out of high school, we find that most were enrolled in college, either four- or two-year. Nearly three out of five youth from farm families were enrolled in a four-year college, and an additional third were attending two-year schools. Almost half of youth with other agrarian ties were in four-year colleges. This figure is well above that of the nonfarm group at 27 percent. Girls were more likely than boys to be in college, a difference that reflects the lack of occupational opportunity for young women in rural areas.

Four types of influence have special relevance to the unusual achievement of youth with family roots in the land: (1) social and economic resources, (2) the civic involvement of parents and adolescent, (3) academic success and ambition, and (4) gender.[33] We know that families on the land rank high on economic and educational resources compared to other rural households, except professionals. And college-going youth tend to come from high-status households, defined by wealth, a well-educated mother, and the high standing of father's occupation. These factors explain some of the effect of farm origins on college attendance. Equally important are family social ties—the parent's school involvement, residential permanence, and the church and school activities of the adolescent. The educational influence of farm families has much to do with their networks of social involvement.

Last, the college-going superiority of farm families is linked to the academic success of their offspring and their sponsorship of daughters for advanced education. Other things being equal, farm youth do better in school than students with other backgrounds, and this is especially true for girls. Apart from their competence as students, farm girls are unusually successful in pursuing higher education. Some of this success may stem from the lack of good alternatives. Farm boys have the possibility of farming and farm-related occupations to keep them at home. In a familiar story, talented girls seek a life outside the agricultural world, while some able boys still retain the hope of a farm in the not-too-distant future.

Competence in the young adult transition involves the avoidance of trouble, as we have noted in the prior chapter, and success in school has emerged as the most important protective influence. Students who were successful in school were unlikely to be involved in problem behavior, such as heavy drinking, drug use, and antisocial activities. These observations bear upon the risk of pregnancy and childbearing among youth in the Iowa project.[34] According to self-reports, a total of 39 adolescents were involved in a pregnancy up through the end of high school, and 14 decided to keep their children (8 girls and 6 boys). This rate of childbearing is comparable to that of a nationwide sample of white, unmarried women, aged 15–19.

Lack of warmth and involvement by parents during the seventh grade increased the risk of pregnancy in the twelfth grade by increasing contact with deviant peers and the teen's own risk-taking behavior, and also by increasing the prospect of academic trouble. Decisions to keep the child occurred in a context that lacked emotional support from parents and successful young people with a sense of ambition and responsibility. The unpromising life course of these new parents involved non-nurturant parents, the company of deviant peers, and risky behavior.

Midwest Themes of a Rural Adolescence

One of the more enduring features of a young person's childhood in the rural Midwest involves socioeconomics—a family's social position in the class structure. Whether on farms or not, youth from higher-status families have fared better on academic competence and social success, compared to lower-status young people, and they were more likely to go on to a four-year college. Such Midwestern differences were described in great detail over a half century ago in *Elmtown's Youth* by August Hollingshead.[35]

Hollingshead focused on the class structure of a small town and its consequences for youth in different strata, from the lower to the upper middle class. Academic success, social leadership, and persistence in school were associated with the higher social strata. Youth from lower-status families were at greater risk of academic failure, early sexual activity, heavy drinking, and dropping out of school. Youth's access to achievement opportunities and influences was structured in these ways by the social stratification position of families.

Hollingshead also documented the extent to which young people and adults were segregated from each other. This segregation was expressed in schools and churches, workplaces, and social activities in general. Instead of ensuring proper development, as many believed, age segregation turned young people toward themselves and away from the concerns of adult life. By "trying to keep the maturing child ignorant of this world of conflict and contradictions, adults think they are keeping him 'pure.' "[36] Hollingshead also "ignored this world of conflict" by disregarding the historical time of his study, the middle of the Second World War. Most of his older boys were mobilized into the armed forces.

Socioeconomic differences and age segregation remain important social issues today,[37] but they are less characteristic of adolescence in the Iowa region we have studied. This world of adolescence has more to do with the ties that bind Iowans to the land and to each other, both within and between families and social institutions. Coleman refers to these ties as social capital.[38] From the end of the 1980s to 1995, the study families in agriculture have not, as a group, been able to maintain their income, although some recovery was in evidence in 1996 and 1997. More recently, they have been under mounting levels of economic stress and uncertainty, and yet their children are doing remarkably well according to the developmental markers of this project. Even with adjustments for family income, parental education, and residential change, they are doing better than other youth on measures of educational and social success.

Five themes of their adolescence identify influences that have special relevance to successful paths through adolescence. We begin with the "intergenerational investment" of parents who have ties to the land and then explore "family connections" with family members and relatives. A full story of the social embeddedness of families within the larger community is subsumed under the theme of "networks of social engagement." A fourth theme, "mastery experiences," underscores three activities that can generate a sense of personal efficacy: productive labor, academic work, and social activities, including community service. The fifth and concluding theme highlights the "multiple caring adults" who are commonly part of the lives of children in the area, from parents to teachers, coaches, community recreation leaders, and ministers.

Intergenerational Investments

Ties to the land foster a sense of stewardship among families in farming, an attitude of appropriate cultivation, nurture, and conservation. Stewardship may be assured across the years when land remains within the family and is passed down across the generations. In the words of a young farmer, good stewardship means "conserving the soil for generations to come, allowing part of tillable land to be set aside for wildlife, leaving trees to protect the environment, and most of all, sharing some of the land with neighbors."[39] Family continuity in farming is one means of ensuring good stewardship of the land over time. When farming is less a way of life and more a business, such continuity is at risk of business considerations.

Within the German-American heritage of north central Iowa, the transition from one generation to the next is part of an intergenerational investment. Typically the farm is passed along to a son in the younger generation, frequently the eldest son, and with a warning not to value material things too highly. This son is entrusted with care of the land and farm up to the point when he passes the farm along to the next generation. This "turning of the generations" has also been observed by Salamon among German farming communities in the state of Illinois.[40] The Farm Crisis disrupted this process and the intergenerational expectation of good stewardship which leads to passing on land to the young. The emotional trauma of "the lost farm" had much to do with a sense that one had failed prior generations and one's children.

The intergenerational investment of families in this study thus concerns their ties to the land and agrarian stewardship. It is also supported by the strength of lineal ties across the generations. Most of the older generation in this study had some tie to the land—they grew up on farms and over half followed careers in farming. A majority of these older members of the family lived relatively close to their grandchildren and a large number were identified as significant people in their lives. The grandparents had lived through a sobering decline in farming opportunity and embraced their grandchildren's ambitions, whatever they might be.

Literally only a handful of the boys in this study expressed a desire for working a farm. Many more wanted to live on a farm (along with girls in the study) and make a living elsewhere. They were well aware of the hard work and modest living conditions of their parents, and they were not eager to follow in their footsteps. As they left high school for college and work, they encountered more evidence that farming did not have a promising future. Fathers who discussed with us their aspirations for sons generally insisted that they be well aware of the many problems and risks. In October of 1998, ten years after the harsh deprivations of the 1980s, an Iowa State University study found 10 percent of Iowa farmers to be in severe financial trouble, compared to 3 percent the previous year. Experts claim this figure could rise to 33 percent if commodity prices do not improve.[41]

This news might well discourage the few boys who were still planning to return to farming after completing college. However, the real crisis for family continuity will occur when the elderly father wishes to retire from farming and no children are in the wings to take over. In some cases, sons who are in urban jobs may trade their careers for the chance to save the family farm. The full story of intergenerational farming is not played out until this stage of life is reached.

Historically, the male line has been most important for family and intergenerational continuity in farming across the heartland. The prominence of father in the lives of sons and daughters is linked to farming and the patrilineal line. Whether youth think of farming as a livelihood or not, their desire for this lifestyle (to "live on a farm") increased their closeness to father and his closeness to them. They had much to share, and they did so through common projects. Boys and girls were least close to fathers when their aspirations centered on life away from the farm and local community. The strong sentiments of these men about land, home, and community functioned as a primary route to their attachments to sons and daughters. In view of the public visibility of fathers who are depicted as "absent, detached from family, and irresponsible," it is important to underscore the involvement of these rural men and, in many cases, their constructive role as parents.[42]

Whether on a farm or not, *Iowa mothers in the study were more involved than their husbands in preparing children for life in the larger world,* especially through higher education. They were more often than their mates a "bridge to the larger world." On average, they were better educated, and they were more aware of the economic disadvantage of rural living, especially on a farm. At a time when the profit margin was slight or nonexistent, family needs were likely to be subordinated to the survival needs of the farm—paying farm debts for seed, fuel, and so on. Indeed, mounting family economic needs played a major role in the employment of over 80 percent of the mothers. One mother taught school, and another worked as an accountant for a mill. Another mother worked a part-time job at the local library and held a part-time clerk position.

Despite low wages, this money from mothers made an essential difference in family living standards. Daily economic pressures from insufficient income continually reinforced in the minds of these women the escape role of college for sons and especially for daughters. Moreover, disenchantment with family farming, with its cyclical risks of a meager livelihood despite hard work, fueled such aspirations among some women who were still on farms. This disenchantment stemmed in part from an urban background, but arose primarily from the genuine economic uncertainty or hardships of farming. Such risk is especially present for small- to mid-size farms with high debt and few economies of scale in farm production.

Family Connections

Both intergenerational investments and ties to the land have family implications, including a web of connections among members of the immediate and extended family. Typically, bonds across the generations are strong among families on the land, with paternal grandparents living nearby, but they are also strong on the maternal side. Iowa children tend to have significant ties to grandparents when the latter are on good terms with their own children, the parents.

A collective sense of family most frequently appears in the views of young people on farms. This perspective is sustained through the labor of doing things together, work as well as social activities. Farm youth tend to work with parents and siblings, and these joint activities give them a stake in the family and an awareness of its priorities. The young quickly learn that failure to carry their weight means that other family members will have to step in and do their work. A boy in the Iowa study vividly recalled how badly he felt when he came home late to find that his father had taken care of his livestock. On a similar theme, a girl described her feelings of remorse when her hard-working mother had to do chores that she had forgotten about.

When children are connected to other family members through expectations and obligations, they feel counted on to carry out certain responsibilities. Farm youth in particular grow up in a culture where people count on them, beginning at a very young age. They are trusted to meet the commitments they have made about delivering goods or feeding animals. The subjective experience of failing to meet these commitments underscores the importance of being responsible. Stepping into assignments and doing them well produces a feeling of significance, that what one does "matters to people who also matter to them." In these ways, shared activities, especially on farms, represent a learning environment for responsibility and social relationships.

In view of these payoffs, it is noteworthy that shared activities with parents also have negative consequences. Joint activities with parents do not emerge consistently as a positive developmental influence. In part, this reflects the extent to which shared activities accentuate both positive and negative parental practices, such as the constant use of critical replies or evaluations. Critical parents are not easily avoided when they are part of the work team. A devalued sense of personal worth is one likely outcome, as seen in chapter 9. For young people in the teenage years, doing work and social activities with parents may also give rise to negative appraisals by restricting their independence opportunities, whether intentionally or not. In this sense, farm work with father in the teenage years is likely to precipitate tensions over unresolved issues of individual autonomy and responsibility.

Networks of Social Engagement

A third feature of agrarian culture involves networks of social engagement. Much has been said of late about the presumed decline of civic life in the United States.[43] This belief clearly does not fit the lifestyle of Iowa families, and especially those with ties to the land. These farm families are among the most actively engaged in our study. Regardless of education, income, and residential permanence, they are significantly more involved in civic groups, churches, and schools, compared to non-farm households. Their involvement includes leadership roles as well, from choirmaster for the local church to president of the Parent-Teacher Association and director for a local cooperative.

The civic life of farming families has much to do with their long-term investment in local communities. Caring for community institutions is part of the responsibility and stewardship that comes from farm ownership and from the commitment to intergenerational continuity in farming. Healthy schools, churches, and community services make continuity in farming attractive to successive generations. Over fifty years ago, the anthropologist Walter Goldschmidt put such ideas,[44] and others (e.g., farm size) to a test by comparing two farming communities in the San

Joaquin Valley of California; Arvin, a community dominated by large farms and a low rate of family ownership, and Dinuba, a community of small farms with a high level of family ownership.

Goldschmidt focused on the size of farms, though ownership was central as well; the larger the farm, the greater the likelihood of corporate ownership and management. In his words, "the institution of small independent farms is indeed the agent which creates the homogeneous community, both socially and economically democratic."[45] Both farming communities, Dinuba and Arvin, were located in the same agricultural valley and climate zone. Both were equidistant from urban centers and lacked any manufacturing or processing. They were similar in size and agricultural sales. Both communities relied on irrigation and a harvest work force. But substantial differences emerge between the 722 farm operators in Dinuba with an average farm size of 57 acres, and the 133 farm operators in Arvin, with an average farm size of 497 acres. Over three out of four Dinuba farms were operated by owners, compared to only a third of the Arvin farms.

Income inequality was less pronounced in Dinuba. Only a third of the household income earners were farm workers, compared to about two-thirds of the earners in Arvin. Farm workers tended not to own their homes and were typically transient. The farm operators in Arvin were frequently absentee owners, unlike the Dinuba farmers with their permanent residence. The quality of living conditions and sustenance was higher in Dinuba, as might be expected from the large class difference. Arvin's "factories in the fields" consisted of a large plant made up of land, capital, and heavy equipment, manned by a transient labor force of unskilled or semiskilled workers. Power was centralized in the hands of a few families in this community, and the workforce had little investment in the care of community institutions and democratic government. Civic apathy prevailed. Dinuba, by contrast, was far more democratic in terms of citizen participation in town government and schools through community elections.

By all measures, Dinuba had a more lively civic life. The community ranked much higher on the number of civic and social organizations, newspapers, and churches. It also ranked higher on community facilities, such as schools, parks, and libraries. Local businesses were flourishing, compared to a much smaller business sector in Arvin. And the community offered higher quality living through more paved streets, sidewalks, and sewage and garbage disposal. In a statewide effort to assess the status of small farms in central California, the Small Farm Viability Project revisited the two communities in the late 1970s and concluded that "the economic and social gaps have widened. There can be little doubt about the relative effects of farm size and farm ownership on the communities of Arvin and Dinuba."[46]

In Goldschmidt's account, a convergence of historical and environmental factors gave rise to the differences in farm scale between the two communities. These differences, in turn, eventually produced differences in class structure, inequality, quality of life, and civic participation. Within our study region, farms have also become much larger over the past fifty years, and farms under two hundred acres tend to rank higher on economic risk, especially during periods of very low commodity prices—even below cost. But the growth in farm size has also taken the form of family partnership, such as between brothers and between fathers and sons. A comprehensive survey of the issues raised by Goldschmidt's seminal study concludes that mid-size farms emerge with many advantages for farm families and communities.[47] And that "the Midwest context of protection of family farming, state regulation of corporate farming, and history of agrarian populism may offset any deleterious impacts of industrialized farming."

Studies spawned by Goldschmidt's investigation raise serious questions about the social future of rural communities in the Midwest under conditions of widespread industrial farming. As Norah Keating makes clear, food can be produced in ways other than by family farming, such as by corporate farms with resident managers, but "keeping families on the land is essential if we are to maintain agricultural communities."[48] For this reason, agricultural policy and social policy should be considered together. Cost efficiency is not the only objective. For example, the hog and chicken factories of Iowa may satisfy the demands of cost efficiency, but they can damage environmental quality through pollution of the air, water, and soil. And such damage reduces the quality of life for residents, as well as the possibility of other modes of development and settlement in the area by people who are living elsewhere.[49]

Not all Iowa families in the study were engaged in civic life, and the disengaged typically had no connection to the land and agriculture, from childhood to the middle years. Some of the parents with part-time farms were too busy for community life, though in many cases they encouraged their children to take part. Whether coupled with community activity or not, the value parents placed on "being involved in the community" made a difference in the lives of offspring.

Nevertheless, involved parents were more aware of opportunities for their children, and they knew more about the options available to them. These parents were also likely to be perceived by their children as efficacious adults and admirable models. Such emulation linked involved parents and socially active children. No factor was more predictive of students who participate in athletics and other school activities than the community ties of parents. Social engagement, then, is passed down across the generations and so is the practice of leadership. Parents who assumed community leadership roles often had children who aspired to become like them when they grew up.

In this account of social engagement, we have stressed the link between community involvement and ties to the land, between the rural social order and land tenure, as shown many decades ago by the Goldschmidt study. Ownership of the farm may be just as important as size of farm in fostering a rich civic life. Homeowners are typically more involved in community life than people who rent. A second aspect of the theme concerns the relationship between socially involved parents and children. This transmission represents an important part of the story of democratic vitality in small communities. A third aspect of parental engagement takes the form of intergenerational transmission through the role of peers or friends as "allies of the family." Religiously involved parents tend to have children who are also active in the church and youth group. These young people are thus likely to make friends who share the values of their parents.

Entry into a church "youth group" resembled a "rite of passage" for youth in the region, marking greater opportunity for self-direction and autonomy. On Thursday nights the youth group "was just what all your peers were doing," as one student put it. These groups embrace the values and control of parents, defining a social network in which a youth's parents know the parents of his or her "youth group" friends. The peer group thus becomes an ally of the family and community.

Mastery Experiences

Accomplishments typically produce feelings of personal mastery, another distinctive feature of agrarian culture. These achievements include success in academics that creates opportunities for the future; social engagements in worthwhile community and school activities that may entail leadership; and involvement in challenging work, especially when standards of performance must be met. Each of these accomplishments is nurtured by families in agriculture. Their children do better in school than other children in the study area; they are more involved in community and school activities; and they are exposed to more challenging work from the earliest days of childhood.

Children on Iowa farms are assigned tasks or responsibilities at an early age, and they learn that family members are counting on their good work. We frequently encountered the maxim that one should "always do the best you can" in conversations with senior members of the family. This attitude carries over to children's school work as well. Disciplines (hard work, punctuality, careful efforts, and persistence, etc.) that are part of being a member of a "working farm family" undoubtedly contributed to a habit of doing well at school and elsewhere. Nurturant adults with high standards were frequently the parents of children in the local honor society, and such achievement strengthened the support and affirmation they experienced from parents and grandparents.

Social involvement in school clubs, student government, and athletic teams represents one of the more plausible routes to academic success. Involved students feel more attached to school than the disengaged, and we know that they are less likely to leave school early, when compared to the alienated.[50] Efforts to keep youth in school are giving more attention to programs that engage them in social activities. Indeed, we find that involvement in school activities significantly enhanced the self-confidence of some boys and girls by the end of high school, beginning in early adolescence. Improvements in academic achievement are likely to parallel such personal change.

In chapter 4 we encountered a young boy who discovered inner resources on a demanding job. He recalled his first Saturday meeting with the manager of a large stock farm and the "huge list" of jobs to be completed by the end of the day. The list seemed impossible to him. "I can't do that. I'd die if I did that." But he ended up getting everything done well before the day's end: "Now I look at that and I am not afraid to try anything. I'm not afraid because I know that I can do something if I try my hardest." Experiences based on challenges that are mastered can be a resource for life. Sometimes these contrasts are instructive and motivating to the young when they occur in the lives of admired older family members. A young granddaughter found her future more possible through knowledge of what her much loved grandmother was able to manage in her lifetime—great hardships in the 1930s, the childhood loss of her mother and the war death of her husband.

Youth employed on a job seemed to gain much from even the adversities of the work. Three values and skills, in particular, emerged from their comments in an interview. The importance of responsibilities (e.g., to show up on time, to do a careful, thorough job) appears in virtually all of their accounts of work experience. A good many learned to do their work under some adversity, such as when the winter weather was most inclement or when something had to be done on Saturday night, the big night for social activities.

The second type of skill or value involves learning to get along with people one might not like—a social etiquette of relations with employers and customers that involves self-control. Success on the job required living up to the adage that "the customer is always right," no matter how nasty the response. These lessons may generalize to getting along with harsh teachers and obnoxious peers. A third outcome entailed the clarification of goals. Work experience told some youth that they did not want a life based on their current jobs. Other youth discovered how much they enjoyed their work, suggesting a possible career.

Caring Adults in Young Lives

This theme brings us to the fifth and last dimension of agrarian culture, the number of significant adults in the lives of youth in rural Iowa. Caring adults play an important role in the lives of these young people. Even one such adult can make a significant difference, as we have seen among children who have risen above their family and community disadvantages through the guidance and support of a caring person outside the family—a teacher, coach, or neighbor.

The good fortune of most children in this study is that they have many such adults in their lives. Within the family, most have two parents along with two or more grandparents who are living nearby, and even an aunt and uncle or two, plus many cousins. Parents also commonly know a number of their children's friends and parents through involvement in joint activities, such as the local schools, churches, and civic associations. Through such connections emerge social networks in which "almost everyone knows everyone else." In farming, this commonality may also arise through cooperative ventures in the harvest and storage of crops. Of course, not all adults known to youth are significant figures, but many have been counted on to help when needed.

There is a degree of social redundancy in rural networks in the sense that they have a number of people to step into emergency roles if need be. We have also used the phrase *social redundancy* to refer to the family world of youth, especially in relation to grandparents.[51] Parents who have strong ties to their own parents generally encourage them to have frequent contact with their own children. More than half of the young people in this study consider their grandparents to be significant people in their lives. On the farm, the most significant grandparents tend to be the father's parents, and they live relatively close at hand. One boy claimed he saw his grandfather every day on the farm. The mother's side of the family tends to be more prominent among youth who live off the farm, and this is the typical intergenerational pattern for the United States.

In both cases, grandparents who are identified as significant by their grandchildren generally believe that they make an important difference in their lives.[52] Such contacts have also enriched the lives of children in this study, but rarely is this difference independent of parental influence. Some grandparents are effective in preventing youth from "becoming vulnerable" on personal worth, social acceptance, and "getting in trouble." Significant grandparents are typically members of a family in which parents are also emotionally supportive figures in the lives of these children. Families are resourceful in more than one way, just as problem families tend to have more than one problem. Social redundancy, then, refers to a safety system of backup people, whether grandparents or aunts and uncles.

In the rural midwest of north central Iowa, this social redundancy contributes to the social influence of the "small worlds" most young people inhabit across this region, particularly when they live on farms. Family, school, church, and friendship groups are core elements of these worlds. Small worlds require social participation from everyone. There are many jobs to be done, and few people to do them—this applies to the farm family, to the rural church, and the local school. Small worlds are undermanned. Young people in the study noted the rewards of being known by adults in their town, but they also complained about the social control. Consistent with Barker and Gump,[53] we find that small schools provide students with greater opportunity to participate in school activities, particularly those involving leadership, compared to larger schools. From the perspective of adult influence, the teaching staff and parental influence tend to weigh more heavily in the smaller schools. Students also claim to have more access to teachers in such schools.[54]

As noted before, we should not ignore the substantial cost issuing from the social ties, significant others, and perceived integration that young people experience in their small worlds. Strong ties can restrict the pursuit of opportunities in other places as well as initiatives in the local community. A sense of autonomy in the adolescent years may be elusive. In small communities young people are called upon to play important roles that have meaning beyond the self, producing a feeling of personal significance. However, with the social recognition and visibility youth experience in such places comes more effective social control. Clearly, social connections offer both rewards and disadvantages.

The central themes discussed so far depict a social world in which adults are especially prominent and play a leadership role in matters concerning their children. Parents with ties to the land are more likely to be involved in school affairs, civic life, and the local church than are other adults. And ties to the land identify men who play an especially active role in matters of the family. This is a culture that actively promotes the disciplines of adult life in the rearing of children and establishes pathways to adulthood. By contrast, the adult role is diminished when schools are large and underfunded, when churches and other local institutions are weak or nonexistent, when economic conditions are marginal or precarious, and when a large percentage of families are headed by relatively young, single parents. In many cases, this is the portrait of inner-city life in northern metropolitan areas of the United States, as so graphically described by Wilson's *The Truly Disadvantaged.*[55] The spontaneous peer group or street gang tends to rule under such conditions.

Continuity and Change

When we turn the clock back to the end of postwar prosperity, the early 1970s, we find that to an unparalleled degree, America's children were also growing up without adults. They were isolated from adults in school and neighborhood, and time demands restricted their contact with parents. This theme was highlighted by Urie Bronfenbrenner in *Two Worlds of Childhood.*[56] Since then, the picture has shown more continuity than change. Freedman concludes that we have "witnessed the withering away of civil society, of the developmental infrastructure so essential for the nurturance and socialization of future generations."[57] The decline in this account involves a growing disparity between the country as a whole and the impoverished, isolated minority populations of major inner cities. Four years later, Peter Benson notes that today "it is common for a young person not to know well any adults outside of her own family."[58] This isolation could be corrected, he suggests, by promoting intergenerational communities that break down age segregation.

The rural Midwest is characterized by such interage communities, and we have documented them in the north central region of Iowa, especially among families with ties to the land—shared work and social activities among family members, intergenerational ties that bind children to their aunts, uncles, and grandparents, and networks of community engagement that extend across age groups (from school to church and civic associations). In addition, local churches and their young people are en- . gaged in service activities with an intergenerational thrust. Interage communities may be more natural and readily established in rural America, but they are found everywhere.

Consider inner-city Philadelphia, a place far removed from the rural countryside of north central Iowa. On close inspection, effective parents in these two worlds have much in common on practices that encourage success among young people, despite the greater risks of bringing up children amidst the poverty and crime of inner-city neighborhoods. In 1991, a research team collected interview data in Philadelphia from nearly five hundred white and black families of children, ages 11–15, and an older sibling near in age.[59] The poverty rate among neighborhoods ranged from 10 to over 40 percent. Gun violence and drug transactions were common in the most impoverished areas.

The high risks of this part of the city called for special efforts by parents to protect their children from local dangers outside the household. A good many parents minimized the risks of their neighborhood by placing children in a religious community, such as a Catholic parish and school. The Jehovah's Witnesses provided a total community of like-minded peers and adults for one of the most successful black students. As in Iowa, then, both religious and school involvement by parents played an important role in the school and social success of boys and girls. Other Philadelphia parents placed their children with a relative who lived in a safer environment, such as a nearby suburb. Still others made arrangements that would ensure the safety of their children as they walked to and from school. In the most dangerous neighborhoods, parents kept their children inside when gangs roamed the streets.

One of the most distinctive themes of Iowa families with ties to the land is the institutional engagement of parents—as members and leaders of churches, civic organizations, and parent-teacher organizations. A similar pattern of social engagement appears among black and white families in Philadelphia, but it is much less common. Philadelphia mothers were less likely to have the support of a husband and father, and they were less apt to live in areas that offered the civic options that are so common in rural Iowa communities. As Wilson points out, inner-city America is distinguished by the relative absence of commercial institutions, such as banks and grocery stores; dynamic churches; and effective schools.[60] Employment options are less available and attractive as well. Nevertheless, socially engaged parents in Philadelphia made a very significant difference in the lives of their children. The latter were more likely to be socially involved in the school and community, and they also were more successful in school.

Philadelphia youth from inner-city neighborhoods also had less access to the family support, disciplines, and ambitions observed in rural Iowa families. Fathers, in particular, were more prominent in family and community life across rural Iowa communities, when compared to inner-city Philadelphia. Although the design of the Iowa Project called for recruitment of families that included both mothers and fathers, single-parent farm families are quite rare. Rural communities are generally more characterized by strong kinship ties, and this is certainly the case for north central Iowa. Young people in this region were embedded in a proximal world of family support and affirmation, ranging from aunts and uncles to cousins and grandparents. A good many were involved in shared activities with parents, siblings, and older relatives. All of these family bonds tend to be strongest among families with ties to the land.

The children of these families generally flourished despite a lengthy period of hardship in agriculture, and they have done so in large part because of their way of life. At a land grant university in the Midwest, a professor noted that she could readily identify students who had grown up on farms in her classes. "Year in and year out such students sparkle in my class. They are mature, they do not whine, they have a work ethic, they have a civic engagement in the campus community, they respect their parents, and they are open to learning."[61] Assuming that qualities of this kind are common among the sons and daughters of farming families, it is sobering that such families are becoming more scarce each year as the often meager and always uncertain financial returns drive more farm families into heavy debt and bankruptcy.

The historic movement of Midwest families off the land has been viewed in terms of its severe economic cost to communities—the loss of tax-paying residents and consumers. But the cost is multiplied many times over by "the social loss" of these families, since they are the foundation of community institutions. These families are also primary caretakers of the land. As long-standing members of the middle class, they provide leadership for community activities and services. With the loss of each farm family, a community is diminished as a social world with civic vitality and the collective talent for nurturing the young and caring for the old. Critical services erode, involving churches and schools, shops, medical, and recreational facilities. As the manager of a North Dakota grain elevator put it in the epigraph to this chapter, when the farmers go, the "town will dry up."

This decline, with occasional spurts and plateaus, represents a central theme of rural America in the twentieth century. Among other factors, it is encouraged by an agricultural policy on food production (efficiency, high levels) that pays little attention to the support and health of rural communities. The maintenance of healthy agricultural communities requires a policy that enables farming families to remain on the land, particularly those of mid-size and above. With the high costs of rural depopulation at issue, wisdom demands more effective coordination of agricultural *and* social policies. Family-based farms serve a larger purpose than agricultural production in the rural Midwest; they are the core foundation of community life. The same cannot be said of factory farms.

In notable fashion, Iowa families that work the land bring strengths to the lives of their children through ties to family, school, and church. And they have done so despite much adversity from Mother Nature and the market. Though an endangered species, as history suggests, these families are only one segment of a larger mosaic of agrarian influence on young people, including parents who "farm and work off the farm," those who have been displaced from the land, and parents who only have a farm childhood.

Considered as a whole, this mosaic is distinguished by strong bonds across the generations, a community investment in church, school, and civic groups, and a culture of industry, civic responsibility, and care for others. The young rank among the academic and social leaders of their secondary schools.[62] And some might claim that this culture has produced more than its share of good citizens and leaders in government and business, religion, education, and the military. Whatever the course of rural society in the years ahead, we have much to learn from "the way of life" associated with family ties to the land.

The Iowa Youth and Families Project

The Iowa Youth and Families Project was launched in 1989–90 with a sample of 451 two-parent families from eight north central counties of Iowa (see figure 1.2) just north of Des Moines and Ames, the home of Iowa State University. Seven of the eight counties had poverty rates above the state average of 11 percent, and most had lost more than a tenth of their resident population in the 1980s. The counties were selected in terms of their rural farm economy and proximity to the project's home at the Family Research Center in Ames.

To facilitate the recruitment of farm families (they are typically intact) and minimize variations in family structure, the study design called for two-parent families with a seventh-grader and a near sibling (within four years of age). The initial pool of families was defined in terms of seventh-grade students who were enrolled in public and private schools during the fall term of 1989. The seventh-grade criterion provided a match to the sample used in the study *Children of the Great Depression.*[1] This rural sector of the state includes no sizeable minority population, and thus the sample is white. Nearly four out of five eligible families chose to participate in the project.

Patterned after *Children of the Great Depression,* the study viewed the family, its strains, relationships, and adaptations as a set of linkages between the socioeconomic decline across the region and its effects on children and adults. The research plan called for a socially diverse sample with a substantial number of farm and rural nonfarm households, and for the collection of panel data, including videotaped observations in the household, survey forms, and interviews. Following a successful pilot study, a research team carried out the first wave of data collection in the winter of 1989 with a sample of 451 households.

A third of the families were involved in farming, and two-thirds of these men defined themselves primarily as farmers. Their farms generally exceeded four hundred acres, owned and rented, and most were devoted to grain and livestock operations. Thirteen percent of the study families had given up farming as a result of the Great Farm Crisis. The other families had not farmed, though some of the parents had grown up on farms. The typical husband and wife were born shortly after World War II. They married for the first time in 1970 and had three children. Three of five parents have some education beyond high school, and 40 percent of the men served in the military, most during the Vietnam War. The median income for the households in 1988 was approximately $34,000, a figure that matches the median for American families of this size. More than three-fourths of the mothers were gainfully employed, usually full-time.

Data were collected each year from 1989 through 1992 (the tenth year in school of the target child), and then again in 1994, the senior year. Table A.1 shows the number of families for completed/projected waves of data collection beginning with wave 1 of the Iowa Youth and Families Project (IYFP), winter 1989. For the first four waves of data collection, retention rates from the immediately preceding year have ranged from 95 percent (1990) to 99 percent (1992) for IYFP. The average rate of retention is 96 percent. A number of incentives, such as reimbursement and communications (newsletters, cards), have been used to maintain high retention rates. Consistent with other longitudinal studies, parents who remained in the study over time tend to be slightly better educated (an average of .5 years) than the drop-outs. However, we have found no difference in family income or in emotional distress.

Table A.1
Sample Characteristics and Interview Schedule of Iowa Youth and Families Project

	Year					
Sample	1989	1990	1991	1992	1993	1994
N	451	424	407	403	—[a]	413
% of previous N	—	94	96	99	—	102
Average age, target	13	14	15	16	17	18
Average age, mothers	37	38	39	40	41	42
Average age, fathers	39	40	41	42	43	44

[a] No data collection.

Measurements I: Indicators of Competence and Success

Academic Competence

Academic success is divided into the categories of performance, general competence, and the target's sense of competence. "Target" refers to the study adolescent.

Academic Performance ($n = 406, r = .87, .87, .87, .88, .72$)

At each wave, targets and their parents were asked to report the target's current grade-point average (GPA): $A = 11, F = 1$. In Wave F, twenty-eight study children were no longer in school for one reason or another. Four of these were in college and did report a GPA. We have made assignments for the other twenty-four subjects out of school who did NOT report a GPA—either GPA = 0 for drop-outs, or Wave F GPA equal to Wave D GPA for those who finished high school early. We do not use the teachers' reports of GPA because they are not available for Wave F.

General Competence (alpha = $.94, n_f = 391$)

Mother's and teacher's reports were used to construct this scale from Wave F data. Wave D teacher reports were used when Wave F teacher reports were missing. The average correlation between the eight Wave D and F teacher-reported indicators is .516. Also, targets who were out of school had no mother reports, so Wave D reports were used. The items included follow.

Mother Survey

1. In terms of his or her performance in school, would you say your seventh-grader is . . . (1 = a far below average student; 5 = a superior student)
2. Did he or she get a "D" or an "F" in any class on the last grade report? (1 = yes)

3. How well do you think your child keeps up with his or her classes? (1 = is far behind and it will be hard to catch up; 5 = ahead of most classmates in class work)

Teacher Survey

1. Compared to others of his or her age, *how well does this youngster do the following things?* Schoolwork, learning, getting good grades, etc. (1 = worse than most kids; 3 = better than most kids)
2. Compared to typical pupils of the same age . . . How much is he learning? (1 = much less; 7 = much more)
3. How much do you agree or disagree with these statements *about this student's school attitudes or behaviors?* (1 = strongly disagree; 5 = strongly agree)
   - S/he tries hard at school.
   - S/he usually finishes her homework.
   - She does most of her schoolwork without help from others.
   - He is able to do a good job of organizing and planning his schoolwork.
   - Learning school subjects is easy for her.
   - He knows how to study and how to pay attention in class, so he does well in school.

Sense of Competence (alpha = .88, .88, .87, .87, .89; n_f = 398)

This is a measure of how well the target feels that she or he is doing in school, as distinct from reported GPA. The scale includes items for the targets who were out of school. The items include the following.

1. How well do you think you keep up with your schoolwork? (1 = I am very behind, and it will be hard to catch up; 5 = ahead of most classmates in class work)
2. Indicate how much you agree or disagree with these statements about school. (1 = strongly disagree; 5 = strongly agree)
   - I don't do well in school (reversed).
   - I usually finish my homework.
   - I have a high grade-point average.
   - I do well in school, even in hard subjects.
   - My teachers think I am a good student.
   - Other students think I am a good student.

A composite score was created by combining these three constructs. The alpha = .87. The correlations among the three subscales are as follows:

GPA	1.0		
Sense of competence	.74	1.0	
General competence	.76	.57	1.0

Self-Confidence

Self-confidence is composed of two scales based on self-reported information from the target: mastery and self-esteem. These scales are traditionally measured by self-report, so there is no issue of multiple sources of information.

Mastery

This scale is based on the Pearlin mastery scale; the items are available in all waves of data.

- There is really no way I can solve some of the problems I have.
- Sometimes I feel that I'm being pushed around in life.
- I have little control over the things that happen to me.
- I can do about anything that I really set my mind to. (reversed)
- I often feel helpless in dealing with the problems of life.
- What happens to me in the future depends mostly on me. (reversed)
- There is little I can do to change many of the important things in my life. (1 = strongly agree, 5 = strongly disagree).

The correlations among these items are not always good—scattered in the .15 to about .40 range. The alpha reliabilities for the five waves of data are .70, .74, .79, .78, and .82. The fifth item is particularly weakly correlated with other items in the subscale, but deleting it does not increase the alphas in any serious way. Moreover, these results are fairly consistent with findings from the Minneapolis Youth Development Study conducted by Jeylan T. Mortimer, and Michael D. Finch, and the scale is considered standard.

Self-Esteem

This scale is comprised of six items based on the Rosenberg scale; the items are available in all waves of data (1 = strongly agree, 5 = strongly disagree).

1. I feel that I am a person of worth, at least on an equal level with others. (reversed)
2. I feel that I have a number of good qualities. (reversed)
3. All in all, I am inclined to feel that I am a failure.
4. I am able to do things as well as most other people. (reversed)
5. I take a positive attitude toward myself. (reversed)
6. On the whole, I am satisfied with myself. (reversed)

The correlations among these items tend to be good, ranging from about .25 to .75—many correlations are in the .4 or better range. The alpha reliabilities for the five waves of data are .82, .83, .88, .89, and .90.

A *global self-confidence* variable was created by joining the two. The two scales correlate well in the five waves of data: .54, .53, .57, .63, .71.

Advice-Seeking

Advice-seeking items were included in surveys of each parent and the target child—from the parent on how much the target seeks advice, and from the target on how much the parent seeks advice. We focus on the latter on the assumption that parents would not ask an incompetent target child for advice. This scale is comprised of four items that are not part of a standard scale; they were put together based on work done by project staff (Michael Shanahan and Valarie King) on adolescent-parent relationships. The items are available in all waves of data.

1. When mom has a problem to solve, how often does she . . . (1 = always, 7 = never)
   * Listen to your ideas about how to solve problems? (reverse)
   * Consider your ideas for solving the problem? (reverse)
2. During the past month, how often did your mom . . .
   * Ask you for your opinion in an important matter? (reverse)
   * Listen carefully to your point of view? (reverse)

The reliabilities for the respective waves are mother: .77, .81, .86, .86, .89; father: .85, .88, .91, .90, .89. The mother and father scales correlate well: .63, .71, .65, .65, .47 through the waves of data.

Peer Success

This scale is composed of three items (available in Waves D and F) which are not part of a standard scale.

How much do you agree or disagree with the following statements about the student? (1 = strongly agree, 5 = strongly disagree)

   * She is one of the more popular kids in her school. (reversed)
   * She hangs out with the popular kids at school. (reversed)
   * Compared to people the same age, how well does the student . . . make new friends, meet new people, get along with others, etc? (1 = worse than most people, 3 = better than most people) The scale was recoded to match the 1–5 distribution of the first two items (1 = 1, 2 = 3, 3 = 5).

Data in Wave F were available for only about 345 cases. When Wave D information was available but Wave F was not, we also used Wave D data for about 55 cases for a total *n* of approximately 400. How realistic is it to use Wave D data? The correlational stability from D to F (where the data are available for both waves) is as follows: popular kid = .62, hangs out with popular kids = .59, makes new friends = .45 (average = .55).

Once data are used from both waves, the correlations among the created variables are acceptable, ranging from .55 to .77; the alpha reliability is .84.

Problem Behavior

This measure is described in chapter 9.

Measurements II: Other Indicators by Chapter

Chapter 2: Families and the Generations

Antecedents of the grandparent-grandchild relationship, based on the Grandparent Phone Survey, 1994

HS GRADUATE, COLLEGE (1994, one item/three dummy variables)
High school graduate, at least some college, versus less than a high school graduate

GP INCOME (1994, one item)
Categories of income from below $5000 = 1 to $55,000 or more = 9. A dummy variable for those missing on income was also created.

GP AGE (1994, one item)
Age of the grandparent, 51–92

GP HEALTH (1994, one item)
Grandparents' assessment of their own health in general, from poor = 1 to excellent = 4

DISTANCE (1994, one item)
Number of miles grandparent lives from G2 household, capped at 250+

CHURCH INVOLVEMENT (1994, one item)
How often grandparent attends services or listens to religious broadcasts on TV or the radio. 1 = never to 4 = once a week or more. A dummy variable for those missing on this variable was also created.

COMPETENT AS PARENT (1994, one item)
How often the grandparent has felt competent as a parent. 1 = never to 4 = always

PATERNAL SIDE (1994, one item)
Paternal grandparent = 1, Maternal grandparent = 0

GOOD RELATIONSHIP TO ADULT CHILD (1994, one item)
Quality of the relationship with the adult child. 1 = poor to 4 = excellent

GRANDFATHER (1994, one item)
Grandfather = 1, Grandmother = 0

NO. OF GRANDCHILDREN (1994, one item)
Total number of grandchildren (capped at 20 or more)

MALE GRANDCHILD (1994, one item)
Target grandchild is a male = 1 versus a female = 0

Chapter 3: Ties to Family and Land

JOINT ACTIVITIES
Time spent working with parents. (Target; 1992; one item)
1. How much time do you spend on your job with . . . your mother? . . . your father? (1 = no time; 6 = all the time)
Time spent in youth-group activities with parents (Target; 1991; one item)
1. How often do you do any of the following activities with . . . your mother? . . . your father? Participate in youth-group activities together like Scouts, 4-H, or something like that? (1 = never; 4 = often)

FARM PREFERENCE
(Target; 1990, 1991, 1994; one item)
1. How important are the following in choosing where you would like to live? To live on a farm. (1 = not at all important; 5 = very important). Children indicating a score of 3 (somewhat important) or higher in any of the three years of measurement are coded as having a farm preference.

IDENTIFICATION WITH PARENTS
(Target, 1989–94; four items; mother average alpha = .83; father average alpha = .84)
1. When I grow up, I'd like to be like my mother.
2. I have a lot of respect for my father.
3. My mother is the kind of person other people respect.
4. I really enjoy spending time with my father.
(1 = strongly disagree; 5 = strongly agree)

PARENTAL WARMTH
(Target, 1989–94; six items; mother average alpha = .91; father average alpha = .93)
How often does your mom/dad . . .
1. Let you know she/he really cares about you?
2. Act loving and affectionate to you?
3. Let you know she appreciates you, your ideas, or the things you do?
4. Help you do something that is important to you?
5. Have a good laugh with you about something that was funny?

6. Act supportive and understanding to you?
(1 = never; 7 = always)

Chapter 4: Always Work to Do

All measures are presented in the chapter.

Chapter 5: Bridging Family and Community

QUALITY OF SOCIAL NETWORKS

Support from Friends (mother and father, 1989–92, average alpha = .88)
Thirteen-item scale:
1. Other than my wife or children, there are several people that I trust to help solve my problems.
2. My friends really care about me.
3. I feel like I'm not always included by my circle of friends (reverse).
4. There is really no one outside my immediate family who can give me an objective view of how I'm handling problems (reverse).
5. If I needed a place to stay for a week because of an emergency, I could easily find someone who would put me up.
6. If I were sick, I could easily find someone outside my immediate family to help me with my daily chores.
7. There is someone outside my immediate family I can turn to for advice about handling problems with my family.
8. If I needed an emergency loan of $100, there is someone I could get it from.
9. There is someone outside my immediate family I could turn to for advice about making career plans or about changing my job.
10. If I wanted to have lunch with a friend, I could easily find someone to join me.
11. No one I know would throw a birthday party for me (reverse).
12. It would be difficult to find someone outside my immediate family who would lend me their car for a few hours (reverse).
13. My friends appreciate me.
(1 = definitely false to 4 = definitely true)

Support from Kin (mother and father, 1990, average alpha = .68)
Mean of three items, averaged across parents, siblings, aunts, uncles, and cousins:
1. How much do kin make you feel appreciated, loved, or cared for?
2. How much can you depend on kin to be there when you really need them?
3. How much concern or understanding do kin show for your feelings and problems?
(1 = not at all to 4 = a lot)

Conflict with Kin (mother and father, 1990, average alpha = .65)
Mean of two items, averaged across parents, siblings, aunts, uncles, and cousins:
1. How much conflict, tension, or disagreement do you feel there is between you and kin?

2. How critical of you are kin?
(1 = none at all to 4 = a lot)

Contact with Kin (mother and father, 1990)
1. During the past six months, how often did you have contact with kin, either in person, by phone, or by mail?
(0 = no contact to 5 = daily); scores averaged across parents, siblings, aunts, uncles, and cousins

Proximity to Kin (mother and father, 1990)
1. How far do you live from kin?
(0 = more than 250 miles to 5 = live together); scores averaged across parents, siblings, aunts, uncles, and cousins

Joint Family Activities (mother and father, 1991, average alpha = .77)
Seven-item scale:
1. My family takes regular vacations.
2. We always celebrate holidays together.
3. My family usually eats an evening meal together.
4. My family has traditional holidays that always seem to bring us closer to one another.
5. We celebrate birthdays and anniversaries as a family.
6. My family enjoy doing things as a family.
7. We like to have big family reunions or get-togethers.
(1 = strongly disagree to 5 = strongly agree)

COMMUNITY SATISFACTION
Local Economy (mother and father, 1991, average alpha = .78)
Seven-item scale:
1. There have been a lot of business failures in our area.
2. Too many women with children have to work.
3. Businesses and homes are more run down than they used to be.
4. A lot of people are having financial problems in this area.
5. A lot of people are unemployed around here.
6. Most jobs around here pay too little to raise a family.
7. You don't get any benefits like health insurance or vacation time for most jobs in this area.
(1 = strongly agree to 5 = strongly disagree)

Quality of Schools (mother and father, 1991, average alpha = .79)
Three-item scale:
1. I think we have good schools for our children.
2. The schools in our area seem to get worse each year (reverse).
3. Teachers in our area really care about kids.
(1 = strongly disagree to 5 = strongly agree)

Community Support (mother and father, 1991, average alpha = .85)
Four-item scale:
1. The nice thing about this area is everyone is friendly and helpful.

2. People work hard to make this a nice place to live.
3. Churches in this area help people with food, clothing, or shelter when they have financial problems.
4. We don't have the church support we need for people with troubles (reverse).
(1 = strongly disagree to 5 = strongly agree)

PARENTAL INVESTMENT

Awareness of Youth Services (mother and father, average 1990–91, average r = .40)
1. I am very familiar with special activities available to my children in this area.
(1 = strongly disagree to 5 = strongly agree)

Improvement of Youth Services (mother and father, 1990)
1. Have you been involved in efforts to improve services or activities for children or teenagers in your area?
(1 = no to 4 = very involved)

Assist Child in Afterschool Programs (mother and father, 1990)
1. What actions did you take to involve your child in after-school educational programs like music, art, or tutoring in math, and so on?
2. What actions did you take to involve your child in school sports?
Sum of five actions across two questions:
1. Urged child to participate
2. Got information for child
3. Helped child make contact with program
4. Helped pay for program
5. Helped organize or run program with other parents

Parent-Child Youth Group (mother and father, 1991)
1. How often do you participate in youth group activities with child like Scouts or 4-H?
(1 = never to 4 = often)

Parent-Child Volunteer Work (mother and father, 1991)
1. How often do you do volunteer or community work with child?
(1 = never to 4 = often)

Discuss School (mother and father, 1991)
1. How often do you talk about what is going on at school with child?
(1 = never to 4 = often)

Help with Homework (mother and father, 1991)
1. How often do you do homework or a school project with child?
(1 = never to 4 = often)

Know Child's Teachers (mother and father, average 1989 and 1990, average r = .6)
1. Does your spouse know your children's teachers and how well they are doing in school?
(1 = strongly disagree to 5 = strongly agree)

Child Monitoring (child report on mother and father, average 1989–92, average alpha = .74)

Five-item scale:

1. In the course of a day, how often does your mom/dad know where you are?
2. How often does your mom/dad know who you are with when you are away from home?
3. How often does your mom/dad talk with you about what is going on in your life?
4. How often do you have a set time to be home or in bed on weekend nights?
5. How often does your mom/dad know if you came home or were in bed by the set time?

(1 = never to 5 = always)

CHILD'S EXTRAFAMILIAL CONTACTS

Unsupervised Time with Peers (child report, average 1990–92, average r = .44)

1. How many hours do you usually spend each weekday after school doing things with or talking with friends?
2. How many hours do you usually spend during the entire weekend doing things with or talking to friends?

(0 = no time to 7 = more than 6 hours.) Score sums hours after school and on weekends

School Mentors (child report, sum 1989–92)

1. Are there any adults who are not your relatives who you can talk to about your problems or worries? Who are they?

Score = number of teachers, counselors, and coaches

Community Mentors (child report, sum 1989–92)

1. Are there any adults who are not your relatives who you can talk to about your problems or worries? Who are they?

Score = number of neighbors, friends' parents, doctors, and ministers

Older Peer Mentors (child report, sum 1989–92)

1. Are there any adults who are not your relatives who you can talk to about your problems or worries? Who are they?

Score = number of adult friends & friends' adult siblings

Chapter 6: Wisdom of the Ages

Measures of Grandparent-Grandchild Relationship, Based on Grandparent Phone Survey, 1994

GRANDPARENT-GRANDCHILD CONTACT (1994, one item)

1. During the past six months, how often have you seen the target face to face, either in your home or somewhere else?

(1 = not at all to 6 = daily)

ACTIVITIES (1994, three items summed, alpha = .55)

In the past twelve months . . .

1. Did you attend an event in which target was involved, such as a play, sports competition, or a musical event?
2. Did you and target do activities together in the community, such as going to a museum, sports events, or shopping?
3. Did you and target work on projects together, such as repairs, farm tasks, or things around the house?

(1 = no, 2 = yes, once, 3 = yes, more than once)

COMPANION/FRIEND (1994, one item)
1. How often are you a companion and friend to the target?
(1 = never, 2 = sometimes, 3 = often)

EMOTIONAL QUALITY (1994, three items averaged, alpha = .80)
1. How would you describe your current relationship with target?
(1 = poor, 2 = fair, 3 = good, 4 = excellent)
2. How close do you feel to target?
(1 = not at all or not very, 2 = somewhat, 3 = pretty, 4 = very close)
3. How much does target make you feel appreciated, loved, or cared for?
(1 = not at all, 2 = a little, 3 = some, 4 = a lot)

MENTOR (1994, four items summed, alpha = .70)
1. How often do you give advice to the target?
2. How often are you a voice of wisdom and experience for target?
3. How often do you serve as a source of family traditions, stories, and history?
4. Did you talk about your childhood?
(1 = never, 2 = sometimes, 3 = often)

INSTRUMENTAL ASSISTANCE (1994, three items summed, alpha = .42)
1. How often do you help target financially?
2. How often does target have the chance to learn your skills?
3. How often have you served as a resource in helping target find a job?
(1 = never, 2 = sometimes, 3 = often)

Measures of Grandparent-Grandchild Relationship:
Based on Adolescent Questionnaire, 1994

ESPECIALLY CLOSE GRANDPARENT (1994, two items, average r = .67)
1. How much can you depend on your grandparent to be there when you really need him/her?
2. How much does your grandparent make you feel appreciated, loved, or cared for?
(1 = not at all, 2 = a little, 3 = some, 4 = a lot.) Recoded so that scoring a 4 on both items = 1, especially close and 0, otherwise. Created for each living grandparent and then summed across all grandparents to measure having at least one especially close grandparent.

CLOSENESS OF CLOSEST GRANDPARENT (1994, five items averaged, average alpha = .78)
1. How much can you depend on your grandparent to be there when you really need him/her?

2. How much does your grandparent make you feel appreciated, loved, or cared for?
(1 = not at all, 2 = a little, 3 = some, 4 = a lot)
3. How happy are you with your relationship with your grandparent?
(1 = very unhappy, 2 = fairly unhappy, 3 = fairly happy, 4 = very happy)
4. Compared to the other grandchildren, including your brother or sister in the study, how close are you to your grandparent?
(1 = less close than some or most, 2 = about the same, 3 = closer than some, 4 = closer than most)
5. How often does your grandparent help you in important ways by giving you advice or helping you solve problems you may have?
(1 = never, 2 = rarely, 3 = sometimes, 4 = often.) Scale created for each living grandparent, and then the score of the highest scoring grandparent within a family is used as a measure of the closest grandparent.

Chapter 7: Church, Family, and Friends

VALUES
Achievement/Other
How important is it to you . . . [tenth grade]
1. to have a college education?
2. to work hard to get ahead?
3. to be successful in your work or career?
4. to be a religious person?
5. to devote yourself to improving the world or working for some good cause?
6. to have a good marriage?
7. to have close friends?
(1 = not at all important to 5 = extremely important)

Personal Qualities
To what extent do you accept or reject each of the following as a guiding principle in your life? [eighth grade]
1. to be carefree: acting on impulse, doing things at the spur of moment
2. to be considerate: being thoughtful of others' feelings
3. to be polite: being well-mannered
4. to be unselfish: putting the interests of others before your own
5. to be helpful: ready to assist others
(1 = very strongly reject to 7 = very strongly accept)

Things to Be in Adulthood
How important do you think each of the following things will be to you when you are an adult? [ninth grade]
1. friendships
2. participation in community activities
(1 = not at all important to 5 = extremely important)

FRIENDS SAY ACTIVITIES ARE "COOL"

If you had done one of these things, what do you think your friends would say if they knew about it? [ninth grade]

1. You took part in church activities.
2. You took part in school activities like clubs or school dances.
3. You took part in school athletics.
4. You took part in community activities like YMCA, YWCA, Boys club, campfire, 4-H, etc.
5. You worked hard to get good grades in school.

(1 = not cool, 2 = O.K., 3 = cool)

RELATIONS WITH FRIENDS

Would still see friends parents object to

If your parents strongly objected to your friends, what would you do? [tenth grade]

   0 = stop seeing them, going places with them or see them less

   1 = see them secretly or keep seeing, going places with them openly

Closest friends show problem behavior

How much do you agree or disagree with the following statements about your closest friends? [tenth grade]

1. These friends sometimes get in trouble with the police.
2. These friends sometimes break the law.
3. These friends don't get along very well with their parents.
4. These friends don't like school very much.
5. These friends get bad grades in school.

(1 = strongly disagree to 5 = strongly agree.) Average of the five items leads to a 5-point scale (alpha = .73).

Friends outside school are older

Are the kids in your group of friends outside school . . . [tenth grade]

0 = about the same age or younger than you?

1 = mostly or all older than you?

Friends encourage deviant behavior

Sometimes your friends may want you to do things that could get you into trouble at school. How often do your friends encourage you to do the following things? [tenth grade]

  1. do things at school that can get you in trouble
  2. skip school when you are bored or upset
  3. smoke or chew tobacco
  4. use illegal drugs like marijuana
  5. use other drugs to have fun or get high
  6. drink beer, wine, wine coolers, or liquor
  7. destroy or damage someone else's property
  8. get into a fight or get mad at someone
  9. make out
10. have sexual intercourse

11. lie to your parents or teachers
12. shoplift or steal something
13. cheat on a test

(1 = never to 4 = often.) Sum of the thirteen items leads to a thirteen- to forty-eight-point scale (alpha = .89).

Deviant Activities of Friends
During the past twelve months, how many of your close friends have . . . [tenth grade]

1. run away from home?
2. skipped school without an excuse?
3. purposely damaged or destroyed property that did not belong to them?
4. stolen something worth less than $25?
5. stolen something worth more than $25?
6. gone joyriding?
7. hit someone with the idea of hurting them?
8. attacked someone with a weapon or with the idea of seriously hurting them?
9. used a weapon, force, or strong-arm methods to get money or other things from people?
10. used tobacco?
11. used alcohol?
12. used illegal drugs?
13. used prescription drugs for fun or to get high?
14. used inhalants such as solvents, gas, rush, or glue?
15. used nonprescription drugs like Vivarin, NoDoz, or diet aids for fun or to get high?

(0 = none of them, 1 = a few to all of them.) Sum of the fifteen items leads to a 0–14 scale (alpha = .78).

Parent Report of Target on Peer Competence
Two items from mom and two items from dad averaged together

1. Would you agree to disagree that this child is one of the more popular kids in his/her school? (1 = strongly disagree to 5 = strongly agree)
2. Compared to other children of his/her age, how well does the target child get along with other children? (1 = worse, 3 = about the same, 5 = better)

Chapter 8: Lessons from School

All measures are described in the chapter, or in appendix measures for Chapter 2.

Chapter 9: Achieving Success, Avoiding Trouble

All measures are described in the chapter.

Analytic Approach: Identifying Resilient and Vulnerable Youth

In any disadvantaged environment, some young people do far better than one would expect from knowledge of their social and personal circumstances, while others fail to live up to social expectations (Werner and Smith 1982, 1992). The classic example of these two pathways contrasts the academic failures of the son of a successful businessman with the unexpected accomplishments of a boy from a poor family. Children of prosperous families have certain advantages in their schooling and, accordingly, are expected to do better than the offspring of impoverished parents. These expectations are not always realized; the resulting disparities raise questions and require explanation. What factors enable children to exceed behavioral expectations, or ensure that they fail?

We assumed that the academic success of these adolescents would vary according to (1) predivorce factors (such as gender of child, family income, and the education of the mother); (2) social and economic influences (such as economic pressure, negative life events, and frequency of residential moves); (3) personal attributes of the mother, such as emotional depression and antisocial behavior; (4) the social engagement of mother—her civic organizations, church attendance, and PTA attendance; and (5) her socialization.

We find that girls outperform boys on grades, and that children whose mothers have high levels of education rank higher as well. Conversely, economic pressure depresses academic performance, as does the antisocial behavior of children. Countering these influences are the positive effects of parental engagement in the community—in church, school, and civic organizations, as well as parental interest in the child's education. This model leaves much unexplained on academic success—over 70 percent of the variation. A good many children are doing better than expected and some are doing worse.

In statistical terms, the children who are doing better than expected can be identified by their high positive residual scores based on the regression model. Their actual grades are higher than their predicted grades. High negative residuals identify children who are doing much worse than expected. The actual grades of these children are lower than their predicted grades. We graphed all residual scores from the model against the predicted values of academic performance (with its mean set to zero) based on the regression model. Most cases cluster around the center point, [0,0], indicating that a majority of the cases have a predicted academic performance score around their mean level. Differences between the predicted and actual values are close to zero. An example is illustrated in figure D.1.

However, the outlying cases present a challenge. The predictive model does not work well in explaining their achievement or lack of academic success. Consider the youth who is identified on the scatterplot by a capital A. His predicted value of academic success is approximately −2.0, in contrast to the actual value of 4.5, producing a residual score that exceeds 6.5. Achievement of this kind, that exceeds expectations, indicates "resilience." In a similar manner, youth who are performing at lower levels than anticipated can be identified by negative residual scores, as seen in the case of respondent B. We refer to such cases as "vulnerable."

Residual scores thus enable us to identify children who are resilient or vulnerable, given what we know about their family origins and personal attributes. To study these cases, we identified groups of children at the extremes on residuals—the 25 percent of the sample with the largest positive residuals (the resilient), and the same percentage with the largest negative residuals (the vulnerable). Using logistic regression, we asked what factors accounted for why some youth are doing much better than expected (compare resilient with all other cases) and why others are doing worse (compare vulnerable with all other cases). Such factors are selected from variables that did not predict academic success in the primary model.

We followed this procedure in the present study by including indicators of the

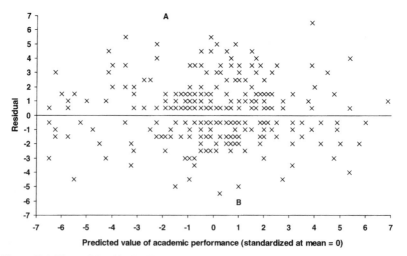

Figure D.1 Plots of Residuals Illustrating Youth with Higher and Lower Performance Scores than Anticipated Based on Regression Model

Table D.1
Residual Analyses for Competence Domains; Correlation and Standardized Regression Coefficients Presented

	Academic Competence		Peer Success		Self-Confidence		Advice-Seeking	
	r	beta	r	beta	r	beta	r	beta
Social and Economic Environment								
Parent's education	.34***	.13***	.18***	.07	.12**	.03	.14**	.06
Family income, logged	.13**	.07*	.12**	.07	.09+	.07	.07	.05
Debts/assets	-.19***	-.01	-.10*	.02	-.06	.03	-.03	.08+
Residential moves	-.23***	-.07+	-.18***	-.10*	-.17***	-.11*	-.16***	-.11*
Parents' unstable work	-.19***	-.05	-.16***	-.08	-.09+	-.01	-.11*	-.03
Family and Parenting Resources								
Parental depression	-.17***	-.07+	-.12*	-.06	-.14**	-.09+	-.05	.04
Marital hostility	-.15**	.03	-.10*	.02	-.11*	.02	-.16***	-.07
Inconsistent parenting	-.13**	.01	-.01	.07	-.18***	-.12**	-.14**	-.08
Harsh parenting	-.32***	-.19***	-.19***	-.13**	-.23***	-.18***	-.33***	-.29***
Ability								
Iowa test score	.64***	.54***	.32***	.25***	.19***	.10*	.13**	.04
N	424		402		422		424	
R^2	.49		.16		.12		.15	

Note: All outcome measures taken from grade 12 (1994); parent's education (mom's ed*dad's ed) is measured at grade 7 (1989); all other measures based on data from seventh through tenth grades.
+ $p < .10$; *$p < .05$; **$p < .01$; ***$p < .001$

socioeconomic environment (parental education—a multiplicative index, family income logged, the debt-asset index, residential moves of family, and parents' unstable work), family and parenting resources (parental depression, marital hostility, inconsistent parenting, and harsh parenting), and the child's ability—the Iowa Test of Basic Skills, an achievement test score. Scores for all of these measures, except parental education, were averaged across four years—1989–92. Each measure is described in detail at the end of this account. Four developmental outcomes from the twelfth grade were used in the analysis (see table D.1), as described earlier: academic competence, social success, self-confidence, and perceived advice-seeking by parents (an average score for both parents).

Academic success is predicted by residentially stable families of high status, by parents who do not employ punitive discipline, and by youth who have scored well on the Iowa achievement test. Similar factors predict the social success and acceptance of youth, though not as effectively. Self-confidence and the perception that parents value and use their advice are mainly a product of a nurturant family environment. Harsh, inconsistent parenting predicts low self-confidence and advice-seeking. We first identified "resilient" and "vulnerable" youth from residuals on each outcome, and then formed "overall" groups for youth who were resilient or vulnerable on at least three of the four measures. These groups are used in chapters 3 through 8, where we ask how the resourcefulness of families made a difference in the lives of Iowa young people.

APPENDIX E

Tables

Table E1.1
Comparison of Study Region with Other Areas on Selected Indicators of
Economic Change, 1977–92

| Indicator and Area | 1977 | Percentage of 1977 Total | | |
		1982	1987	1992
Housing Units Authorized by Building Permits				
Study region	1,176	19	6	19
Des Moines, MSA	4,192	23	56	81
Midwest	402,700	32	70	64
South Atlantic	291,166	86	151	101
Retail Sales (in 1992 dollars)				
Study region	1,492,603	85	77	74
Des Moines, MSA	3,277,390	99	102	126
Midwest	456,313,602	88	98	103
South Atlantic	262,585,713	100	128	136

Sources: U.S. Census Bureau, "Housing Units Authorized by Building Permits"; U.S.
Census Bureau, Census of Agriculture; and Sales & Marketing Management Magazine,
Survey of Buying Power.

Table E2.1
Parents' Characteristics by Current Farming Status

Variables	Men			Women		
	Farm $N = 123$	Nonfarm $N = 149$	Probability Level	Farm $N = 75$	Nonfarm $N = 125$	Probability Level
Age at marriage ($\bar{X}$)	23.3	22.8		21.4	20.7	
Age at first birth ($\bar{X}$)	25.6	24.7		23.9	23.3	
Education						
% HS grad	99.2	97.3		98.7	99.2	
% college grad	21.9	26.2		26.7	17.6	
Relative education						
% wife more	36.6	24.8	*	36.0	24.8	
% husband more	24.6	34.2		22.7	36.0	*
Economic status						
Wife employed	85.4	86.6		82.7	90.4	
Median income, 1989	40,100	37,450		39,750	37,050	
Kin proximity (% <25 miles from):						
Mother	84.0	59.2	***	76.2	51.3	***
Father	86.2	63.5	***	72.2	52.0	**
Mother-in-law	62.0	54.9		89.5	50.5	***
Father-in-law	60.5	53.4		92.6	50.7	***
Kin contact (% weekly contact with):						
Mother	82.3	57.8	***	80.0	65.1	*
Father	84.5	62.8	***	70.4	56.7	
Mother-in-law	37.0	40.6		64.9	37.6	***
Father-in-law	39.5	38.1		68.5	37.8	***

$*p < .05; **p < .01; ***p < .001$

Table E2.2
Paternal Grandparents' Reports of Role in Grandchildren's Lives by Farm
Status: Regression Coefficients in Standard Form

	Paternal Grandparents' Role in Grandchildren's Lives					
Ecological Niche	Contact Frequency	Quality Relations	Activity Support	Companion, Doing Things Together	Mentor, Teacher	Assistance, Tangible
Full-time	.45**	.24**	.18**	.19**	.26**	.20**
Part-time	.17**	.18**	.11+	.13*	.20**	.24**
Displaced	.14*	.19**	.04	.01	.13*	.17**
Farm-reared	.14*	.27**	.03	.12*	.15*	.11+
N	337	337	337	334	319	325

Models included controls for grandparent's age, gender, education, income, and health,
with nonfarm as reference category.
$^+p < .10$; $^*p < .05$; $^{**}p < .01$

Table E2.3
Sibling Relations in Farm and Nonfarm Families

	Farm Status		
Indicators of Relations to Sibling	Nonfarm $\overline{X}$ (N)	Farm[a] $\overline{X}$ (N)	Level of Significance
Satisfied with relationship, 1989			
Sisters	3.24 (94)	3.35 (37)	
Mixed-gender	3.19 (143)	3.22 (65)	
Brothers	3.16 (81)	3.45 (31)	$p < .05$
Total	3.20	3.31	
Admires sibling, 1989[b]			
Sisters	2.92 (94)	2.93 (37)	
Mixed-gender	2.50 (143)	2.69 (65)	
Brothers	2.52 (81)	2.89 (31)	$p < .05$
Total	2.74	2.80	
Cares about sibling, 1990			
Sisters	4.17 (85)	4.45 (35)	
Mixed-gender	3.89 (136)	3.89 (60)	
Brothers	3.41 (74)	4.20 (28)	$p < .01$
Total	3.85	4.12	$p < .10$

[a]Includes full- and part-time farm.
[b]Four 5-point items were averaged to form an "admire" scale (alpha = .85). They include "admire sib," "can count on sib," "look up to sib," "sib gives good avice." The
"cares about sib" scale includes three correlated items: "let sib know you care," "act
loving toward sib," "let sib know you appreciate him/her" (alpha = .91).

Table E2.4

Parents' Civic, Church, and School Involvement by Farm Status: Means
Adjusted for Average Annual Income and Parental Education

Involvement	Full-Time Farmers	Farm Ties[a]	Nonfarm	Significant Differences
Fathers				
Civic involvement	8.17	7.58	6.52	Full-time vs. others: $F = 1.61$
				Nonfarm vs. others: $F = 2.28$
Civic leadership	2.03	1.56	1.36	Full-time vs. others: $F = 9.04$**
				Nonfarm vs. others: $F = 5.08$*
Church attendance	3.60	3.21	2.64	Full-time vs. others: $F = 23.24$***
				Nonfarm vs. others: $F = 29.94$***
PTA attendance	4.04	3.88	3.63	Full-time vs. others: $F = 5.50$*
				Nonfarm vs. others: $F = 7.36$**
Mothers				
Civic involvement	8.89	7.32	5.96	Full-time vs. others: $F = 9.52$**
				Nonfarm vs. others: $F = 8.46$**
Civic leadership	1.97	1.70	1.41	Full-time vs. others: $F = 4.99$*
				Nonfarm vs. others: $F = 5.11$*
Church attendance	3.83	3.57	2.79	Full-time vs. others: $F = 28.31$***
				Nonfarm vs. others: $F = 55.13$***
PTA attendance	4.04	3.88	3.63	Full-time vs. others: $F = 5.50$*
				Nonfarm vs. others: $F = 7.36$**
N	82	259	83	

[a]Includes part-time farm, displaced, and farm-reared parents.

*$p < .05$; **$p < .01$; ***$p < .001$

Table E2.5
Parents' Reports of Children's Materialism in Relation to Farm Status,
Income, and Parents' Education: Metric Regression Coefficients, 1990

| | Children's Materialism[a] Reported by Parents | | | |
| | Mother's Report | | Father's Report | |
Social Factors	I	II	I	II
Farm Status				
Full-time farm family[b]	−.39**	−.33**	−.31**	−.28*
Part-time/displaced	−.22*	−.19[+]	−.27*	−.24*
Farm-reared	−.18[+]	−.16	−.18[+]	−.17
Social Factors				
Parent stresses well-paid job				
(1 = low, 5 = high)		.07		.06
Education, parent		−.05*		−.01
Family income		−.48		−1.18[+]
Adjusted R^2	.02	.03	.01	.02

$N = 418$
[a]Children's Materialism Scale: "children never happy with amount of money we have,"
"children never satisfied with things we buy them," "children think money grows on
trees." Alpha, Mom = .86; alpha, Dad = .79. High score = materialistic.
[b]Nonfarm category used as references in this and other comparisons.
[+]$p < .10$; *$p < .05$; **$p < .01$

Table E3.1
Relationship of Family Ties, Future Plans, and Activities with Father in
Means and Percentages

| | Works with Father (1992) | | | | Social Activity with Father (1991) | | | |
| | Total | | Farm Youth[a] | | Total | | Farm Youth[a] | |
Future Plans, Family Ties	Yes	No	Yes	No	Yes	No	Yes	No
Aspires to farm,	22	06***	41	04***	19	05***	21	05***
% (boys only)	(23)	(173)	(12)	(98)	(48)	(148)	(23)	(87)
Wants to live on	62	43	92	57*	59	41	83	55
farm, %	(39)	(385)	(12)	(98)	(71)	(353)	(23)	(87)
Identifies with	4.16	4.00	4.55	4.01[+]	4.11	4.00	4.41	3.97[+]
father, $\bar{X}$	(39)	(368)	(12)	(89)	(71)	(336)	(23)	(78)
Warmth of	5.36	5.13	5.92	5.19*	5.38	5.10**	5.71	5.15**
father, $\bar{X}$	(39)	(368)	(12)	(89)	(71)	(336)	(23)	(78)

[a]Farm youth come from full-time and part-time farm families.
[+]$p < .10$; *$p < .05$; **$p < .01$; ***$p < .001$

Table E3.2
Adolescents' Academic and Social Competence by Farm Status, Residential Preference, and Gender. Means Adjusted for Parent's Education, Residential Moves, and Income; Boys/Girls (Cell Size), F-statistic for Significant Gender Differences within Groups

Competence and (Number)	Farm[a]		Nonfarm		Significant group difference
	Farm Preference A	Nonfarm Preference B	Farm Preference C	Nonfarm Preference D	
Academic	.01	.27	−.22	.08	A > C: $F = 3.56^+$
competence	(67)	(43)	(121)	(193)	A < B: $F = 2.71^+$
(424)					C < D: $F = 10.00^{**}$
By gender:	−.20/.21	.12/.41	−.43/−.03	−.04/.18	
boys/girls	(36/31)	(17/26)	(64/57)	(79/114)	
	$F = 4.28^*$		$F = 7.52^{**}$	$F = 3.61^+$	
Peer success (402)	3.73	3.96	3.38	3.64	A > C: $F = 5.31^*$
	(59)	(42)	(116)	(187)	C < D: $F = 5.34^*$
By gender:	3.48/3.98	4.05/3.90	3.45/3.30	3.58/3.68	
boys/girls	(30/29)	(16/26)	(62/54)	(77/110)	
	$F = 4.24^*$				
Self-confidence	3.91	4.46	3.96	4.09	C < D: $F = 3.59^+$
(422)	(67)	(43)	(120)	(193)	A < D: $F = 4.60^*$
By gender:	3.91/3.92	4.81/4.11	3.94/3.99	4.17/4.06	
boys/girls	(36/31)	(17/26)	(64/56)	(79/114)	
Advice-seeking,	4.94	3.82	4.72	4.98	A > B: $F = 4.64^*$
father (422)	(66)	(40)	(120)	(193)	C < D: $F = 3.77^*$
					B < D: $F = 7.22^{**}$
By gender:	4.90/5.00	4.07/3.68	4.82/4.63	5.03/4.92	
boys/girls	(35/31)	(15/25)	(63/57)	(79/114)	

[a]Farm group includes full- and part-time farm families; nonfarm includes all others.
$^+p < .10$; $^*p < .05$; $^{**}p < .01$; $^{***}p < .001$

Table E3.3
Antecedents of Academic and Peer Success by Residential Preference; Regression Coefficients in Standard Form

	Academic Competence				Peer Success			
			Farm				Farm	
Antecedent by Year	Bivariate	Total	Preference	Other	Bivariate	Total	Preference	Other
Socioeconomic Status								
Farm family[a] (1989–94)	.23***	.15*	.32**	.15*	.22***	.14*	.29*	.10
Displaced farm family (1989–94)	.11+	.06	.23**	.03	.08	.05	.17	.01
Farm reared (1989–94)	.17**	.12+	.23*	.08	.15*	.12+	.24*	.05
Parents' education (1989)	.33***	.26***	.17*	.31***	.18***	.08	–.02	.10
Average annual income (1989–94)	.21***	.10*	.12	.10	.23***	.19***	.22*	.17*
Residential moves (1989–92)	–.20***	–.13**	–.08	–.15*	–.15**	–.10+	–.16*	–.04
Relationship with Father								
Paternal identification/warmth (1991–92)	.13**	.04	.08	.02	.15**	.12*	.12	.13+
Inconsistent parenting (1989–92)[b]	–.12*	–.11*	–.22**	.01	–.01	.03	.02	.06
Time spent working with him (1992)[b]	–.06	–.08+	–.05	–.11+	.01	–.02	.03	–.07
Youth activities with him (1991)	.03	.02	.04	.04	.06	.04	.03	.11
Other								
Boy	–.19***	–.17***	–.22**	–.08	–.03	–.04	–.06	–.01
N		392	175	217		379	169	210
R^2		.21	.28	.21		.12	.18	.11

[a]Farm group includes full- and part-time farm families; nonfarm family is the reference category.
[b]The only significant differences ($p < .05$) by farm preference involve "inconsistent parenting" and work time with father in relation to academic competence.

$+p < .10$; $*p < .05$; $**p < .01$; $***p < .001$

Table E3.4

Antecedents of Self-Confidence and Paternal Advice-Seeking; Regression
Coefficients in Standard Form

Antecedents and Date	Self-Confidence		Advice-Seeking, Father	
	Bivariate	Total	Bivariate	Total
Socioeconomic Status				
Farm family[a] (1989–94)	.00	−.06	.02	−.06
Displaced farm family (1989–94)	.08	.10	.01	.04
Farm-reared (1989–94)	.06	−.01	.07	−.04
Parents' education (1989)	.13**	.03	.15**	.07
Average annual income (1989–94)	.05	.02	−.01	−.06
Residential moves (1989–92)	−.15**	−.12*	−.16***	−.14**
Farm as Residential Preference	−.11*	−.06	−.04	−.31
Parenting and Family Relations				
Paternal identification/warmth (1991–92)	.25***	.25***	.48***	.46***
Farm preference * paternal identification/warmth (1991–92)	−.08	−.07	.01	.21
Inconsistent parenting, father (1989–92)	−.17**	−.13*	−.10*	.00
Time spent working with father (1992)	.03	.02	.02	−.02
Youth activities with father (1991)	.02	.01	.04	−.03
Other				
Boy	.02	.04	.07	.09
N		390		390
R^2		.13		.28

[a]Farm group includes full- and part-time farm families; nonfarm family is reference category.

$*p < .05; **p < .01; ***p < .001$

Table E3.5

Relations with Father in Youth Resilience and Vulnerability, Residual Group Analyses: Odds Ratios from Logistic Regressions

Variables	Academic Competence		Peer Success	
	Resilient	Vulnerable	Resilient	Vulnerable
Boy (=1)	.72	1.54	.76	.58
Residential preference (1990, 1991, 1994)	.82	.99	.83	1.04
Paternal identification/warmth (1991–92)	.79	.86	1.18	.88
Time spent working with father (1992)	.74$^+$	1.22$^+$	1.05	1.23*
Youth activities with father (1991)	1.04	.95	1.11	1.11
N	392	392	379	379
$-2 \operatorname{Log}(L)$, df = 8	13.93	9.72	6.35	9.97

	Self-Confidence		Advice-Seeking	
	Resilient	Vulnerable	Resilient	Vulnerable
Boy (=1)	1.43	.68	.93	.63$^+$
Residential preference (1990, 1991, 1994)	.85	1.16	.90	1.09
Paternal identification/warmth (1991–92)	1.56**	.76*	2.28***	.52***
Time spent working with father (1992)	.95	1.04	1.11	1.24$^+$
Youth activities with father (1991)	.99	1.03	.91	.91
N	390	390	392	392
$-2 \operatorname{Log}(L)$, df = 8	18.37	7.54	34.80	32.81

Note: Farm family status controlled.

$^+p < .10$; $*p < .05$; $**p < .01$; $***p < .001$

Table E4.1
Chore Time and Annual Earnings by Grade Level, Farm Status, and Gender:
Means over Time, Repeated Measures Analysis

Chore Time and Earnings	N	Grade				
		7[a]	8	9	10	12
Chore Time (Hours/Week)						
Farm[b]						
Boys	38	—	11.13	7.71	8.39	8.95
Girls	49	—	9.31	8.41	8.47	9.55
Nonfarm						
Boys	124	—	9.12	8.69	7.47	8.35
Girls	135	—	9.27	8.29	8.38	8.14
Significant differences	Grade: $F = 7.31$***					
Annual Earnings Reported in 1988 Dollars						
Farm[a]						
Boys	38	$425.74	$665.49	$854.34	$1305.37	$2473.03
Girls	49	222.20	368.68	545.51	596.83	1766.22
Nonfarm						
Boys	124	286.01	529.82	760.42	1255.79	3386.60
Girls	134	207.37	311.72	408.67	692.27	2316.00
Significant differences	Gender: $F = 28.96$***; Grade: $F = 165.06$***; Grade * Gender: $F = 4.94$***; Grade * Farm: $F = 6.88$***					

[a]Data on chores not available for seventh grade.
[b]Includes full-time and part-time.
*$p < .05$; **$p < .01$; ***$p < .001$

Table E4.2
Youth Reporting Earning More or Doing More Chores in Response
to Family Need (Proportions)

Responses to Need	N	Grade 7	Grade 8	Grade 9	Grade 10
Performed More Chores					
Farm[a]					
Boys	38	.63	.42	.21	.21
Girls	52	.58	.48	.38	.29
Nonfarm					
Boys	132	.52	.53	.28	.24
Girls	151	.53	.47	.36	.42
Significant effects	Grade: $F = 80.38$***; Gender: $F = 2.91$[+];				
	Grade * Gender: $F = 8.55$**				
Earned More					
Farm[a]					
Boys	38	.55	.50	.53	.45
Girls	52	.67	.73	.67	.73
Nonfarm					
Boys	133	.61	.63	.53	.65
Girls	151	.68	.69	.68	.73
Significant effects	Grade: $F = 7.00$[+]; Gender: $F = 10.86$**				

[a]Includes full-time and part-time.
[+]$p < .10$; *$p < .05$; **$p < .01$; ***$p < .001$

Table E4.3
Adolescent Earnings (1988 Dollars) and Weekly Chores over Time by Social
Factors: Random Effects Generalized Least Squares Regression

Social Factors	Chore Time and Earnings Trajectories: Generalized Least Squares Regression with Random Effects		Doing More Chores/ Earning More: Logistic Regression with Huber Standard Errors	
	Chore Time (hrs/wk)	Earnings (1988 dollars)	More Chores	Earns More
Intercept	−8.77***	−5757.90***		
Age	−.20**	428.49***	.70***	1.02
Gender (boy = 1, girl = 0)	−.26	364.61***	.74*	.60***
Farm[a]	.70[+]	9.09	1.03	.83
Debt-to-asset ratio	.16	68.90**	1.16*	1.04
Household size	.49**	−16.33	1.24**	1.23**
Hours mother works	.02**	.19	1.02***	1.01
Overall R^2	.03	.31	.05	.02
N	2024	2024	1585	1586

[a]Includes full-time and part-time.
[+]$p < .10$; *$p < .05$; **$p < .01$; ***$p < .001$

Table E4.4
Personal Mastery and Perceived Achievement of Youth in Relation
to Earnings, Age, and Gender: A Generalized Least Squares Regression
with Random Effects[a]

Social Factors	Mastery	Perceived Achievement
Intercept	1.85***	4.28***
Age	.12***	−.08**
Gender	−.05	.01
Farm[b]	−.08	.05
Earnings (logged)	.27***	−.06
Age * earnings	−.02**	.01
Gender * earnings	.01	−.02
Overall R^2	.03	.13

$N = 418$

[a]Statistical controls of farm status, family income, parental education, residential moves, and residential preference.

[b]Includes full-time and part-time.

**$p < .01$; ***$p < .001$

Table E5.1
Demographic Differences among Families with Weak, Average, and Strong
Community Ties: Odds Ratios from Multinomial Logistic Regressions

| Demographic Factors | Family Group Comparisons | | |
	Average vs. Weak	Strong vs. Weak	Strong vs. Average
Mother's education	1.34**	1.78**	1.32**
Father's education	1.32**	1.53**	1.16*
Mother's age	1.06	1.16[+]	1.10
Father's age	.96	.91	.95
Per capita income average 1989–92	1.04	1.10	1.05
Mother's work hours[a]	.85	.72*	.84
Father's work hours[a]	.92	.94	1.02
Time in community[a]	1.06**	1.07**	1.01
$\chi^2 (16) = 95.28, p < .001$			

$N = 404$

[a]Average 1989–92.

*$p < .05$; **$p < .01$

Table E5.2
Geographic Differences among Families with Weak, Average, and Strong
Community Ties: Odds Ratios from Multinomial Logistic Regressions

Geographic Factors, 1991	Family Group Comparisons		
	Average vs. Weak	Strong vs. Weak	Strong vs. Average
Farm status (full-time = 1)	4.73**	5.87**	1.24
Distance to work			
Mother	.98	.96*	.98
Father	.99	.95*	.96*
Distance to hospitals	.98	1.02	1.04*
Distance to shopping	1.02	1.02	1.00
Distance to school	.94+	.91+	.97
χ^2 (12) = 39.21, p < .001			
N = 360			

+p < .10; *p < .05; **p < .01

Table E5.3
Quality of Parents' Social Networks by Strength of Community Ties: Odds Ratios from Multinomial Logistic Regressions

Network Quality	Mothers			Fathers		
	Average vs. Weak	Strong vs. Weak	Strong vs. Average	Average vs. Weak	Strong vs. Weak	Strong vs. Average
Support from friends, avg 1989–92	2.00+	3.03*	1.52	.92	1.26	1.36
Kin support, 1990	1.44	1.14	.79	1.47+	1.28	.87
Kin conflict, 1990	.69+	.59*	.85	.48**	.65	1.36
Kin contact, 1990	1.04	1.95+	1.88*	2.79**	2.72**	.97
Proximity to kin, 1990	.87	.69	.80	1.03	.80	.78
Joint family activities, 1991	2.61**	5.57**	2.13**	2.60**	6.88**	2.65**

Mother model: χ^2 (12) = 63.36, $p < .001$; $N = 384$
Father model: χ^2 (12) = 67.05, $p < .001$; $N = 384$

+$p < .10$; *$p < .05$; **$p < .01$

Table E5.4
Parents' Community Satisfaction by Strength of Community Ties, in Means
Adjusted for Parent Education and Length of Time in Community, 1991

Community Indicators		Weak Mean	Average Mean	Strong Mean	Planned Comparisons	
					Weak vs. Average	Weak vs. Strong
Local economy	Mother	2.64	2.88	3.05	$F = 11.52**$	$F = 17.59**$
	Father	2.81	2.94	2.93	$F = 3.65*$	$F = 1.75$
Quality of schools	Mother	3.75	3.87	4.07	$F = 2.42$	$F = 9.77**$
	Father	3.61	3.80	4.05	$F = 6.90**$	$F = 20.06**$
Community support	Mother	3.54	3.76	3.95	$F = 12.17**$	$F = 24.09**$
	Father	3.45	3.69	3.78	$F = 20.14**$	$F = 20.28**$
N		91	224	69		

$*p < .05; **p < .01$

Table E5.5
Twelfth Graders' Competence by Social Status and Strength of Community
Ties: in Standardized Regression Coefficients

Predictors	School Grades		Perceived Achievement		Peer Success	
	1	2	1	2	1	2
Social Status						
Farm (full- and part-time)	.21**	.16*	.07	.04	.21**	.11
Displaced farm	.10	.08	.01	.01	.05	.01
Farm-reared	.18**	.13**	.06	.03	.12+	.03
Parent education	.31**	.24**	.29**	.25**	.16*	.08
Boy (=1)	−.17**	−.17**	−.16**	−.16**	−.03	−.02
Community Ties						
Strong vs. weak		.20**		.12*		.25**
Average vs. weak		.15**		.07		.31**
R^2	.16	.18	.12	.13	.06	.12
N		404		403		387

Note: Nonfarm status is the reference category for farm groups.
$+p < .10; *p < .05; **p < .01$

Table E5.6
Parents' Involvement in Youth Programs by Strength of Community Ties, in Means Adjusted for Parent Education and Length of Time in Community

Program Involvement		Weak Mean	Average Mean	Strong Mean	Planned Comparisons	
					Weak vs. Average	Weak vs. Strong
Awareness of	Mother	3.66	3.82	4.03	$F = 5.48*$	$F = 15.41**$
programs, 1990	Father	3.43	3.79	3.87	$F = 28.84**$	$F = 23.66**$
Improvement of	Mother	1.67	1.93	2.23	$F = 6.72**$	$F = 16.53**$
programs, 1990	Father	1.55	1.90	2.39	$F = 10.17**$	$F = 33.18**$
Assists child in	Mother	1.29	1.71	2.29	$F = 5.48*$	$F = 15.41**$
programs, 1990	Father	1.36	1.76	2.23	$F = 3.39^+$	$F = 9.13**$
Volunteer work	Mother	4.44	4.85	5.23	$F = 18.05**$	$F = 37.86**$
with child, 1991	Father	4.56	4.84	5.09	$F = 9.99**$	$F = 19.61**$
Youth group with	Mother	4.69	5.26	5.64	$F = 22.05**$	$F = 34.21**$
child, 1991	Father	4.60	5.23	5.48	$F = 32.99**$	$F = 35.45**$
N		91	224	69		

$^+p < .10; *p < .05; **p < .01$

Table E5.7
Parents' Investment in Child's Education by Strength of Community Ties, in Means Adjusted for Parent Education

Parental Investment		Weak Mean	Average Mean	Strong Mean	Planned Comparisons	
					Weak vs. Average	Weak vs. Strong
Child monitoring,	Mother	3.77	3.82	3.99	$F = .62$	$F = 7.29**$
average 1989–92	Father	3.41	3.51	3.61	$F = 1.74$	$F = 4.15*$
Discusses school,	Mother	6.61	6.75	6.78	$F = 6.08*$	$F = 4.68*$
1991	Father	6.06	6.34	6.49	$F = 13.15**$	$F = 17.37**$
Helps with home-	Mother	5.54	5.55	5.58	$F = .04$	$F = .08$
work, 1991	Father	5.31	5.52	5.39	$F = 5.82*$	$F = .48$
Knows teachers,	Mother	3.12	3.08	3.06	$F = 1.51$	$F = 1.50$
average 1989–90	Father	2.99	3.10	3.00	$F = 5.38*$	$F = .04$
N		91	224	69		

$*p < .05; **p < .01$

Table E5.8
Community Ties and Father's Investment in Activities of Socially Resilient and Vulnerable Youth: Odds Ratios from Logistic Regressions

	Resilience		Vulnerability	
Predictors	Model 1	Model 2	Model 1	Model 2
Boy (=1)	.71	.71	.58*	.57*
Community Ties				
Strong vs. weak	2.12*	1.48	.49*	.60
Average vs. weak	2.51**	2.10*	.28**	.32**
Father Investment				
Child monitoring, average 1989–92		.99		.83
Assists child in programs, 1990		1.24**		.74**
Discusses school with child, 1991		1.71*		.86
Youth group with child, 1991		1.10		.95
−2 log likelihood	438.92	389.80	426.49	380.93
N resilient = 93				
N vulnerable = 93				

*$p < .05$; **$p < .01$

Table E5.9
Extrafamilial Contacts of Resilient and Vulnerable Youth, Academic and Self-Confidence Domains: Odds Ratios from Logistic Regressions

	Academic Achievement		Self-Confidence	
Predictors	Resilience	Vulnerability	Resilience	Vulnerability
Boy (=1)	.58*	1.50+	1.34	.77
Time with peers, average 1990–92	.96*	1.06**	1.00	.97
School mentors, sum 1989–92	1.17**	.83**	1.20**	.91
Community mentors, sum 1989–92	.93	1.14	1.39**	1.00
Older peer mentors, sum 1989–92	1.07	1.10	1.04	.86
N resilient or vulnerable	101	100	102	99

*$p < .05$; **$p < .01$

Table E6.1

Grandparents' Beliefs about Grandparenthood

Statements	Percent Agreeing
I want to influence others	68.5
Grandchildren carry on the family line	91.0
I can achieve immortality through grandchildren	89.5
I want grandchildren involved in my life	87.1
I want to feel needed and helpful	95.7
Grandchildren belong to me	77.4

Table E6.2

Grandparents' Reports of Dimensions of Intergenerational Relationships and Their Antecedents: Regression Coefficients in Standard Form, 1994

Grandparent Characteristics	Association				Task-Orientation	
	Contact	Activity	Companion	Quality	Mentor	Help
Social Status						
Full-time farm	-.05	.03	.02	.002	-.08	.01
Farm ties	-.06	.02	.01	-.01	.02	.02
Side of family (1 = paternal; 0 = maternal)	-.22**	-.04	-.14*	-.20**	-.24**	-.19**
High school grad (vs. <HS)	-.09*	-.03	-.08+	-.06	-.00	-.07
College (vs. <HS)	-.07*	.05	-.11*	-.07	.06	-.03
Income (1 = <$5,000; 9 = $55,000 or more)	.001	.08	.09+	.07	.04	.17**
Gender (1 = grandfather; 0 = grandmother)	.06+	-.03	-.07+	-.09**	-.10*	.01
Grandparent age (51–92)	-.08**	-.08*	-.03	.01	-.02	.00
Grandparent health, self-assessed (1 = poor; 4 = excellent)	.04	.06	.03	.07*	-.03	-.00
Distance from child (miles from G2 household, capped at 250+)	-.58**	-.18**	-.13**	-.07+	-.12**	-.10*
Life History						
Church involvement (attending church; religious TV/radio programs) (1 = never; 4 = weekly or more)	.07+	.16**	.15**	.07+	.08	.17**
Competent as parent, self-ranked (1 = never; 4 = always)	.03	.00	.09*	.11**	.08*	.02
Good relations with adult child (1 = poor; 4 = excellent)	.11**	.17**	.19**	.37**	.21**	.07*
No. of grandchildren (total; capped at 20 or more)	-.08**	-.15**	-.15**	-.08*	-.06	-.13**
Grandchild gender (1 = boy; 0 = girl)	.11**	-.01	.03	.03	.07*	.01
Interactions						
Paternal * full-time	.22**	.03	.07	.12*	.20**	.10+
Paternal * farm ties	.19**	.00	.06	.24**	.14*	.13+
R^2	.44	.15	.15	.24	.14	.10
N	751	751	746	752	709	733

Note: Dummy variables created for missing information on grandparents' income and church involvement.

+ $p < .10$; * $p < .05$; ** $p < .01$

Table E6.3
Grandparental Influence on Grandchild's Twelfth-Grade Competence;
Regression Coefficients in Standard Form

	Grade Point Average		Perceived Achievement		Peer Success	
	Model 1	Model 2	Model 1	Model 2	Model 1	Model 2
Full-time farm	.07	.18**	.08	.08	.15*	.15*
Farm ties	.14*	.13*	.05	.05	.10	.10
Parental education	.32**	.32**	.32**	.30**	.12*	.11*
Boy (=1)	−.23**	−.22**	−.17**	−.16**	−.05	−.04
Closest grandparent, 1994 (=1)	.05	.04	.12*	.08+	.04	.01
Parental warmth, 1994		.05		.17**		.15**
N	384	384	384	384	383	383
R^2	.19	.19	.16	.18	.04	.06

	Self-Confidence		Advice-Seeking by Mothers		Advice-Seeking by Fathers	
	Model 1	Model 2	Model 1	Model 2	Model 1	Model 2
Full-time farm	.01	.01	.07	.07	−.03	−.04
Farm ties	.05	.04	.05	.03	.01	−.02
Parental education	.11*	.06	.09+	.03	.14**	.07+
Boy (=1)	.03	.07+	−.02	.04	.08+	.15**
Closest grandparent, 1994 (=1)	.14**	.04	.14**	.004	.12*	−.01
Parental warmth, 1994		.49**		.67**		.70**
N	382	382	383	383	382	382
R^2	.03	.26	.03	.45	.04	.50

$+p < .10$; $*p < .05$; $**p < .01$

Table E6.4

Family Influences on Youth Resilience and Vulnerability, Overall
Twelfth-Grade Competence in Residual Group Analyses: Odds Ratios
from Logistic Regressions

	Resilient		Vulnerable	
Factors	Model 1	Model 2	Model 1	Model 2
Full-time farm	1.19	1.12	.85	.90
Farm ties	2.26	2.27	.89	1.01
Boy (=1)	.40*	.57	.33*	.28*
Closest grandparent, 1994	1.22	.78	.42**	.50*
Parental warmth, 1994		3.99**		.41**
N	384	384	384	384

$*p < .05; **p < .01$

Table E6.5

Linking Grandparents to Resilience and Vulnerability: Models Predicting Residual Groups by Grandchild's Relationship to Closest Grandparent: Odds Ratios from Logistic Regressions, 1994

| | Academics | | | | Peer Success | | | |
| | Resilient | | Vulnerable | | Resilient | | Vulnerable | |
Variables	Model 1	Model 2	Model 1	Model 2	Model 1	Model 2	Model 1	Model 2
Full-time farm	.94	.94	.80	.80	1.32	1.34	.82	.82
Farm ties	1.08	1.08	.84	.85	1.13	1.11	.85	.85
Boy (=1)	.62*	.62*	1.59+	1.55+	.69	.72	.71	.70
Closest grandparent	1.38	1.38	.66*	.69+	1.03	.97	.80	.81
Parental warmth		.98		.87		1.19		.99
N	384	384	384	384	363	363	383	383

| | Self-Confidence | | | | Advice-Seeking | | | |
| | Resilient | | Vulnerable | | Resilient | | Vulnerable | |
	Model 1	Model 2	Model 1	Model 2	Model 1	Model 2	Model 1	Model 2
Full-time farm	.66	.63	.92	.93	1.25	1.37	1.01	1.12
Farm ties	.96	.89	.94	1.02	.99	.92	.80	.90
Boy (=1)	1.50+	2.14**	.87	.76	1.03	2.04*	.56*	.33**
Closest grandparent	1.25	.91	.62**	.75	1.36	.82	.59**	.76
Parental warmth		2.77**		.46**		6.90**		.17
N	382	382	382	382	384	384	384	384

+$p < .10$; *$p < .05$; **$p < .01$

Table E6.6
Twelfth-Graders' Ranking above Grand Mean on Prosocial Competence
in Three Family Systems, in Percentages

Indicators in Twelfth Grade	1 No Close Grandparent + Low Parent Warmth $N = 33$	2 Have Close Grandparent + Low Parent Warmth $N = 18$	3 Have Close Grandparent + High Parent Warmth $N = 73$
Academic Competence			
Grade point average	48	56	66
Perceived achievement	33	40	73
Social Competence			
Peer success	44	56	64
Advice-seeking: mothers	12	22	90
Advice-seeking: fathers	3	00	85
Self-confidence	12	6	75

Note: Groups 1 and 3 differ significantly on all outcomes ($p < .10$). Groups 2 and 3 differ significantly on all outcomes except GPA and peer competence. Groups 1 and 2 are not significantly different on any outcome.

Table E7.1
Religious Involvement of Youth by Farm Status, Social/Economic Factors, and Parents' Social Activities: Regression Coefficients in Standard Form, 1990–94

Variables	Model 1: Bivariate	Model 2: Multivariate	Model 3: Multivariate
Farm Status			
Full-time	.43**	.39**	.16**
Farm ties	.34**	.31**	.11*
Social/Economic Factors			
Parental education	.28**	.25**	.06
Income, 1989 (per capita, logged)	−.01	−.03	.02
Residential move, 1989–94	−.12*	−.05	−.01
Boy (=1)	−.14**	−.14**	−.13**
Parents' Social Activities			
Religious involvement, 1989–94	.71**		.63**
Civic ties, 1989–94	.37**		.03
R^2		.21	.54
$N = 416$			

Notes: Parent's religious involvement = average of each parent's average church attendance across 1989–94. Civic ties = average of each parent's nonreligious organization involvement across 1989–94.
*$p < .05$; **$p < .01$

Table E7.2
Indicators of Adolescent Competence by Initial Competence, Religious Involvement, and Change by Twelfth Grade: Regression Coefficients in Standard Form

| | | Indicators of Adolescent Competence | | | | | |
| | | | | | | Advice-Seeking | |
Models[a]	Grades	Perceived Achievement	Peer Success	Self-Confidence		Mother	Father
1. Effects of Religious Change							
Religious changes, grades 8–12	.26**	.20**	.21**	.10+		.11*	.16**
Religious involvement, grade 8[b]	.19**	.06	.21**	.05		.11+	.08
2. Religious and Developmental Gain							
Religious changes, grades 8–12	.10**	.14**	.04	.08+		.05	.12**
Competence, grade 8[c]	.73**	.54**	.60**	.47**		.48**	.48**
3. Religious and Developmental Gain							
Religious changes, grades 8–12	.11**	.13**	.04	.08		.06	.14**
Religious involvement, grade 8	.02	–.02	–.01	.01		.05	.04
Competence, grade 8	.72**	.54**	.60**	.47**		.48**	.48**

[a]Farm status, parental education, and adolescent gender controlled.

[b]Changes in religious involvement refer to differences in scores for grades 8–12.

[c]Since teacher ratings of peer success are available only in grade 12, we relied on a parent index for grades 8 and 12 to estimate developmental change. The index represents the average of four 5-point items asked of mother and father (the same two for each parent). One item asked about peer friendships, one about peer leadership. The twelfth-grade index is correlated .46 with the teacher index.

+$p < .10$; * $p < .05$; ** $p < .01$

Table E7.3

Influence of Linking Religious Involvement on Resilient and Vulnerable
Youth: Odds Ratios from Logistic Regressions

Developmental Indicators	Resilient (High Residual Scores)	Vulnerable (Low Residual Scores)
Academic Competence		
Increasing religious involvement, grades 8–12	1.65**	.63**
Religious involvement, grade 8	1.12	.90
Peer Success		
Increasing religious involvement	1.66**	.72*
Religious involvement, grade 8	1.31	.86
Self-Confidence		
Increasing religious involvement	1.27+	.87
Religious involvement, grade 8	1.41*	1.05
Advice Giving		
Increasing religious involvement	1.43*	.80
Religious involvement, grade 8	1.04	.72*
General Model		
Increasing religious involvement	1.81*	.71
Religious involvement, grade 8	.94	.84

$^+p < .10$; $^*p < .05$; $^{**}p < .01$

Table E8.1
Youth Activities

School Sports

Boys	*Girls*	*Both*
football	volleyball	basketball
baseball	softball	cross country
wrestling	cheerleading	track
		golf
		tennis

School/Civic Clubs and Activities

National Honor Society	band	Future Farmers of America
quiz bowl	choir	Future Teachers of America
speech/debate club	drama club	Future Homemakers of America
science/math fair	orchestra	Future Business Leaders/
community food pantry	Scouts	Distributive Education Clubs of
language club	dance club	America
yearbook/newspaper staff	art club	SADD/Students Against Drunk
model United Nations	4-H	Driving
library/office helper	shop club	DARE/Just Say No club
county council		Junior American Legion
		hospital/nursing home volunteer

School Leadership

student council	homecoming committee
class officer	homecoming queen candidate
club officer	prom committee
sports team captain	school standards committee

Table E8.2

Youth Involvement Patterns by Farm, Displaced, and Nonfarm Status, in Means Adjusted for Parent Education and Residential Mobility

Activities (N)		8th	10th	12th	Significant Effects
School Sports					
Farm (88)	Girls	2.84	2.06	1.80	Farm: $F = 6.18$*, Farm > Nonfarm
	Boys	3.10	2.75	2.31	Gender: $F = 6.04$*, Boys > Girls
Displaced (66)	Girls	2.39	1.68	1.53	Time: $F = 9.15$**, linear
	Boys	2.63	2.13	1.98	$F = 6.69$*, curvilinear
Nonfarm (206)	Girls	2.56	1.81	1.57	
	Boys	2.64	2.13	1.79	
School/Civic Clubs					
Farm (88)	Girls	1.86	2.37	3.02	Farm: $F = 3.92$*, Farm > Nonfarm
	Boys	1.31	1.52	1.71	Gender: $F = 39.09$**, Girls > Boys
Displaced (66)	Girls	1.86	2.60	2.91	Time: $F = 3.15$*, linear
	Boys	1.18	1.52	1.70	
Nonfarm (206)	Girls	1.49	2.23	2.55	Time * Gender: $F = 6.39$**
	Boys	1.20	1.19	1.25	
School Leadership					
Farm (88)	Girls	.70	.46	.90	Farm: $F = 3.86$*, Farm > Nonfarm
	Boys	.91	.65	1.28	$F = 4.35$*, Displaced > Nonfarm
Displaced (66)	Girls	.66	.71	1.22	Time: $F = 13.22$**, linear
	Boys	.79	.75	1.01	$F = 21.69$**, curvilinear
Nonfarm (206)	Girls	.55	.44	.77	
	Boys	.70	.51	.74	

*$p < .05$; **$p < .01$

Table E8.3

Youth Involvement Patterns by Family Community Ties, in Means Adjusted for Parent Education and Residential Mobility

Activities (N)		8th	10th	12th	Significant Effects
School Sports					
Weak ties (87)		2.22	1.40	1.10	Ties: $F = 17.30$**, Weak < Strong
					$F = 24.24$**, Weak < Avg.
Average ties (207)		2.75	2.26	1.99	Ties * Time: $F = 3.52$**
Strong ties (66)		3.00	2.33	2.02	
School/Civic Clubs					
Weak ties (87)	Girls	1.28	1.61	1.92	Ties: $F = 19.05$**, Weak < Strong
	Boys	1.06	.90	1.26	$F = 8.43$**, Weak < Avg.
Average ties (207)	Girls	1.83	2.52	2.90	Ties * Gender: $F = 4.15$*
	Boys	1.13	1.13	1.24	Ties * Time: $F = 3.40$*
Strong ties (66)	Girls	1.59	2.66	3.31	
	Boys	1.66	2.31	2.08	
School Leadership					
Weak ties (87)		.72	.37	.61	Ties: $F = 6.00$**, Weak < Strong
					Ties * Time: $F = 3.84$*
Average ties (207)		.64	.53	.95	
Strong ties (66)		.79	.81	1.14	

*$p < .05$; **$p < .01$

Table E8.4

Youth Involvement Patterns by Size of School, in Means Adjusted for Parent Education and Residential Mobility

Youth Activities	8th	10th	12th	Significant Effects
School Sports				
Small schools $N = 111$	2.81	2.19	1.94	Size: $F = 4.99^*$, Small > Large
Medium schools $N = 128$	2.76	2.08	1.77	
Large schools $N = 121$	2.42	1.85	1.60	
School/Civic Clubs				
Small schools $N = 111$	1.52	2.03	2.38	Size: $F = 3.87^*$, Small > Large
				Size * Time: $F = 5.25^*$
Medium schools $N = 128$	1.42	1.93	2.32	
Large schools $N = 121$	1.47	1.67	1.76	
School Leadership				
Small schools $N = 111$	.83	.74	1.18	Size: $F = 16.54^{**}$, Small > Large
				$F = 3.99^*$, Small > Medium
Medium schools $N = 128$	.70	.55	.90	
Large schools $N = 121$	.52	.34	.65	

$^*p < .05; ^{**}p < .01$

Table E8.5

Eighth Graders' Time Allocation and Perceptions of Teachers
and Classmates by Size of School, in Means

Time Allocation and Perceptions of Teachers and Classmates	Average Size of School, Eighth Grade			Statistics
	Small (S) <30 $\overline{X}$	Medium (M) 30–69 $\overline{X}$	Large (L) 70+ $\overline{X}$	
Allocation of Time[a]				
Weekdays, $\overline{X}$ hours				
Schoolwork	2.77	2.71	2.49	$S > L$**
				$M > L$*
Friends	3.15	3.37	3.66	$S < L$**
School activities	2.94	3.22	3.21	
Weekends, $\overline{X}$ hours				
Schoolwork	2.86	2.61	2.48	$S > L$**
				$S > M$*
Friends	4.65	4.89	5.42	$S < L$**
				$M < L$*
School activities	2.35	2.51	2.64	
Perceptions of Teachers[b]				
Care about students	3.94	4.01	3.96	
Spend extra time helping	3.90	4.01	3.81	
Students respect teachers, administration	3.27	3.29	3.02	$S, M > L$*
Teacher understands problems	3.56	3.64	3.61	
Perception of Classmates[b]				
Worry about getting beaten up	1.33	1.42	1.57	$S < L$*
Sports more important than grades	2.35	2.27	2.43	
Worry about getting picked on, teased	2.30	2.39	2.38	

[a]Time allocated to family does not vary by size of school.
[b]Scored on scale of 5 to 1.
*$p < .05$; **$p < .01$

Table E8.6

Youth Involvement Patterns by Farm Status, School Size, and Family Community Ties: Regression Coefficients in Standard Form

Predictors	Sports		Clubs		Leadership	
	I	II	I	II	I	II
Social Factors						
Parent education	.07	.01	.33**	.26**	.09$^+$	.06
Residential moves, sum 1988–93	−.08	−.03	−.14**	−.11*	−.09	−.05
Gender						
Boy (=1)	.09	.11*	−.33**	−.33**	.06	.07
Farm Status						
Farm	.13*	.08	.10*	.07	.11*	.07
Displaced farm	−.03	−.03	.08$^+$	.09$^+$	.11*	.12*
Social Resources						
School size		−.12*		−.03		−.18**
Strong vs. weak ties		.23**		.23**		.16*
Average vs. weak ties		.27**		.16**		.07
Adjusted R^2	.05	.11	.27	.31	.04	.09
$N = 360$						

Note: Farm-reared and nonfarm families are the reference category for farm status.

$^+p < .10$; $*p < .05$; $**p < .01$

Table E8.7
Twelfth Graders' Competence by Farm Status, Social Factors, and Youth Activities: Regression Coefficients in Standard Form

Predictors	School Grades		Perceived Achievement		Peer Success		Self-Confidence		Advice-Seeking by Parents	
	I	II	I	II	I	II	I	II	I	II
Farm Status										
Farm	.07	.01	.01	-.04	.10+	.02	-.11*	-.13*	-.07	-.10+
Displaced farm	.02	-.01	.01	-.02	-.01	-.04	.03	.02	-.04	-.05
Social Factors										
Parent education	.30**	.19**	.28**	.19**	.16*	.07	.13*	.10+	.11*	.09
Residential moves, sum 1988–93	-.17**	-.10*	-.14**	-.08+	-.11*	-.06	-.08	-.06	-.12*	-.11+
Boy (=1)	-.19**	-.13*	-.18**	-.12*	-.04	-.04	.01	.01	.01	.01
Activities										
School sports, sum 1990–94		.22**		.15**		.30**		.12+		.13*
School/civic clubs, sum 1990–94		.28**		.23**		.11*		.02		.03
School leadership, sum 1990–94		.12*		.12*		.27**		.08		.06
Adjusted R^2	.17	.32	.13	.22	.05	.30	.02	.04	.02	.04
N	360		359		354		358		360	

+$p < .10$; *$p < .05$; **$p < .01$

Table E8.8

Twelfth Graders' Competence by Social Factors, Family Community Ties, and Youth Activities: Regression Coefficients in Standard Form

Predictors	School Grades		Perceived Achievement		Peer Success	
	I	II	I	II	I	II
Social Factors						
Parent education	.24**	.17**	.24**	.18**	.08	.04
Residential moves, sum 1988–93	−.15**	−.10*	−.12*	−.08	−.09+	−.05
Boy (=1)	−.19**	−.13**	−.18**	−.12*	−.03	−.03
Family Community Ties						
Strong vs weak	.22**	.08	.13*	.01	.28**	.15*
Average vs weak	.19**	.08	.07	−.02	.34**	.24**
Youth Activities						
School sports, sum 1990–94		.20**		.15**		.25**
School/civic clubs, sum 1990–94		.26**		.22**		.07
School leadership, sum 1990–94		.12*		.11*		.28**
R^2	.21	.34	.15	.23	.13	.34
N	360		359		354	

$^+p < .10;\ *p < .05;\ **p < .01$

Table E8.9

Change in Competence from Eighth to Twelfth Grade by School
and Community Activities: Regression Coefficients in Standard Form

| Predictors | Twelfth-Grade Competence | | |
| | School Grades | Perceived Achievement | Peer Success |
	beta	beta	beta
Eighth-grade competence	.68**	.48**	.49**
Social Factors			
Parent education	.07*	.11*	−.01
Residential moves, sum 1988–93	−.11**	−.10*	.02
Boy (=1)	−.09**	−.11*	.09*
Youth Activities			
School sports, sum 1990–94	.09*	.07	.14**
School/civic clubs, sum 1990–94	.08*	.10*	−.01
School leadership, sum 1990–94	.01	.05	.18**
R^2	.66	.41	.44
N	360	359	359

$*p < .05; **p < .01$

Table E8.10
Youth Activities as Predictors of Resilience in Small and Large Schools: Odds Ratios from Logistic Regressions

Predictors	Academic Competence		Peer Success		Self-Confidence		Advice-Seeking Parents	
	Small School	Large School	Small School	Large School	Small School	Large School	Small School	Large School
School sports, sum 1990–94	1.08+	1.03	1.05	1.10*	1.04	1.05	1.13*	1.04
School/civic clubs, sum 1990–94	1.10**	.99	1.02	.96	.98	.95	1.01	.98
Student leadership, sum 1990–94	.93	1.03	1.30**	1.07	1.13	1.01	1.01	.89
No. of resilient youth	44	46	53	41	43	49	42	53

+p < .10; *p < .05; **p < .01

Table E8.11

Youth Activities as Predictors of Vulnerability: Odds Ratios
from Logistic Regressions

Predictors	Academic Competence	Peer Success	Self-Confidence	Advice-Seeking, Parents
School sports, sum 1990–94	.91**	.88**	.96	.94*
School/civic clubs, sum 1990–94	.95*	1.01	1.01	.98
Student leadership, sum 1990–94	.97	.82**	1.00	.99
N	360	354	358	360

$*p < .05; **p < .01$

Table E9.1

Increase in Problem Behavior (Grade 7–12) by Family/Child Background,
Family Relations, and Youth Competence: Regression Coefficients
in Standard Form

Predictor variables	Father			Mother		
	1	2	3	1	2	3
Family/Child Background						
Parent's education (mean)	−.11*	−.10*	−.02	−.11*	−.10*	−.02
Per capita income (1989–92, 1994)	−.04	−.04	−.02	−.04	−.02	.00
Moves (1989–92, 1994)	.02	.01	−.03	.01	.01	−.03
Farm status (high = farm)	−.01	−.01	−.03	−.01	−.01	−.02
Problem behavior (1989)	.26*	.24*	.21*	.26*	.23*	.20*
Gender (1 = boys, 0 = girls)	−.02	−.03	−.06	−.01	−.01	−.04
Family Relations						
Work with parent (1992)		.11*	.09*		.08	.09*
Parent's Id/warmth (1989–94)		−.06	.02		−.16*	−.10*
Activities with parent (1991)		−.01	−.03		.00	.00
Youth Competence (1989–92, 1994)						
Academic competence			−.23*			−.25*
Peer competence			.07			.09
Advice-seeking			−.09			−.06
Self-confidence			−.13*			−.10*
Adjusted R^2	.07	.07	.14	.07	.09	.15

Note: measures over multiple years are means.

$*p < .05$, one-tailed test

Table E9.2

Increase in Problem Behavior (Grade 7–12) by Family/Child Background, Relations with Grandparents, and Youth Competence: Regression Coefficients in Standard Form

Predictor variables	1	2	3
Family Child Characteristics			
Parent's education (mean)	−.13*	−.07	.01
Per capita income (1989–92, 1994)	−.04	−.04	−.02
Moves (1989–92, 1994)	.04	.04	.02
Farm status (high = farm)	−.09	−.06	−.02
Problem behavior (1989)	.27*	.25*	.23*
Gender (1 = boys, 0 = girls)	−.07	−.09	−.04
Close Relations with Grandparents (1994)			
Close grandparent		.00	.06
Grandparent is companion		.06	.07
Contact with grandparent		.16*	.11
Relationship quality		−.12*	−.08
Activities with grandparent		−.20*	−.19*
Instrumental help		.04	.04
Guidance from grandparent		.07	.05
Youth Competence (1989–92, 1994)			
Academic competence			−.23*
Peer competence			.09
Advice-seeking			−.10
Self-confidence			−.09
Adjusted R^2	.13	.15	.20

Note: Measures over multiple years are means.

*$p < .05$, one-tailed test

Table E9.3
Increase in Problem Behavior (Grade 7–12) by Family/Child Background,
Community Involvement, and Youth Competence: Regression Coefficients
in Standard Form

Predictor variables	1	2	3
Family/Child Characteristics			
Parent's education (mean)	−.12*	−.10	−.04
Per capita income (1989–92, 1994)	−.04	.04	−.01
Moves (1989–92, 1994)	.02	.02	−.02
Farm status (high = farm)	−.01	.01	−.02
Problem behavior (1989)	.25*	.25*	.21*
Gender (1 = boys, 0 = girls)	−.01	.00	−.02
Community Involvement			
Family community involvement (1989–92)		.01	.00
Youth religion (1990–92, 1994)		−.09	−.07
School sports (1990–94)		.00	.04
School activities (1990–94)		.05	.11*
School leadership		−.10*	−.06
Youth Competence (1989–92, 1994)			
Academic competence			−.25*
Peer competence			.08
Advice-seeking			−.10*
Self-confidence			−.11*
Adjusted R^2	.07	.07	.14

Note: Measures over multiple years are means.
*$p < .05$, one-tailed test

Table E9.4
Youth Resilience and Vulnerability on Problem Behavior in Residual Group
Analyses, I: Odds Ratios from Logistic Regressions

Predictor variables[a]	Resilience	Vulnerability
Gender (1 = boys, 0 = girls)	1.53	1.38
Work with father	.90	1.45*
Father's Id/warmth	.69*	1.23
Academic competence	1.27	.64*
Self-confidence	1.62[+]	.85
N	342	342
−2 log (L), (df):	21.74 (10)	39.17 (10)

[a]Farm status and earlier problem behavior included in analysis as controls.
[+]$p < .10$; *$p < .05$

Table E9.5

Youth Resilience and Vulnerability on Problem Behavior in Residual Group Analyses, II: Odds Ratios from Logistic Regressions

Predictor variables[a]	Resilience	Vulnerability
Gender (1 = boys, 0 = girls)	1.28	1.64*
Work with father	.92	1.47*
Academic competence	1.36*	.58*
N	347	347
$-2 \log (L)$, (df):	15.30 (10)	38.62 (10)

[a]Farm status and earlier problem behavior included in analysis as controls.
*$p < .05$

Table E9.6

Youth Resilience and Vulnerability on Problem Behavior in Residual Group Analyses, III: Odds Ratios from Logistic Regressions

Predictor variables[a]	Resilience	Vulnerability
Gender (1 = boys, 0 = girls)	1.29	1.76*
Community involvement (parent)	.82*	.98
Religious involvement (youth)	1.53*	.85
School activities	.94+	1.03
Academic competence	1.54*	.61*
N	366	366
$-2 \log (L)$, (df):	15.30 (10)	38.62 (10)

[a]Earlier problem behavior included in analysis as a control.
+$p < .10$; *$p < .05$

NOTES

Full facts of publication (subtitles, names of publishers, etc.) are given only for works not listed in the bibliography. Sources for chapter epigraphs from published works are identified in unnumbered notes following the chapter heading.

Chapter One

The chapter epigraph is from an article by David M. Shribman in the *Des Moines Register,* 27 January 1996.

1. A statistical account of this dramatic flow of population out of agriculture is provided by Donald Bogue's *The Population of the United States.* Glen V. Fuguitt, David L. Brown, and Calvin L. Beale show regional variations on the general theme in their book, *Rural and Small Town America.* A local picture of population decline is documented by Jane Adams in *The Transformation of Rural Life*—a colorful historical analysis of a poor agricultural region, Union County, IL, from the late nineteenth century to the present. Depopulation of the Great Plains is most striking and has caught the eye of journalists such as John Margolis ("The Reopening of the Frontier").

2. The single most important source of information on the growing inequality between rural and urban America is the Rural Sociological Society Task Force on Persistent Rural Poverty report, *Persistent Poverty in Rural America.* See also Daniel T. Lichter, Gail M. Johnston, and Diane K. McLaughlin, "Changing Linkages between Work and Poverty in Rural America," and Linda M. Lobao's survey of regional variations in economic inequality, *Locality and Inequality.*

3. A historical record of the farm crisis in Iowa is documented by Mark Friedberger's *Shake-Out.* Paul Lasley's chapter, "Rural Economic and Social Trends," offers a statistical account of the economic and social consequences for the study region. Stephen H. Murdock and F. Larry Leistritz, in *The Farm Financial Crisis,* provide a more comprehensive account of the economic decline.

A survey of farm-couple adaptations to the economic crisis, based on a multistate sample from the U.S. Midwest, was carried out in 1989: Paul Lasley,

F. Larry Leistritz, Linda M. Lobao, and Katherine Meyer, *Beyond the Amber Waves of Grain.* The study traces economic hardship to political action by focusing on household strategies and processes. See also Katherine Meyer and Linda Lobao, "Farm Couples and Crisis Politics," as well as Linda M. Lobao and Katherine Meyer, "Consumption Patterns, Hardship, and Stress among Farm Households."

4. Rand D. Conger and Glen H. Elder Jr., in collaboration with Frederick O. Lorenz, Ronald L. Simons, and Les B. Whitbeck, *Families in Troubled Times,* 89. An April 1992 editorial in the *Iowa Falls Times Citizen,* a newspaper in the study region, sums up the impact: "Rural Iowa has been damaged the most by changing economic winds. While not broken, the rural fiber has been stretched until vacant store fronts, lost jobs, dwindling population, and decaying small towns dot the rural scene" (Conger and Elder, 5).

5. John W. Bennett, in association with Seena B. Kohl and Geraldine Binion, *Of Time and the Enterprise.*

6. Such expectations are common in writings on the role of independent farmers in American democracy and economic success, from Thomas Jefferson to one of Iowa's most famous citizens, Henry A. Wallace; see Richard S. Kirkendall, *Second Thoughts on the Agricultural Revolution;* more generally, see Richard Hofstadter, *The Age of Reform,* 23–30. Empirical outcomes of this kind emerged from our first monographic study of Iowa children in the project region (see Conger and Elder, *Families in Troubled Times*), and they correspond with findings from Sonya Salamon's ethnographic study of Illinois farm families, *Prairie Patrimony,* and from a Kentucky study of farm families, based on intensive interviews (Lorraine Garkovich, Janet L. Bokemeier, and Barbara Foote, *Harvest of Hope*).

7. The central role of farm families in the collective life of rural communities and populations has been documented by John W. Bennett ("Natural and Social Science: Historical Background," and *Of Time and the Enterprise*) and by Salamon's enlightening study of farm families with different ancestral roots (*Prairie Patrimony*). She notes that families of German origin were more committed to intergenerational continuity than families of English origin, and they were more engaged in community affairs. Networks of civic engagement observed in farming communities are central to the existence and effectiveness of democratic government (Francis Fukuyama, *Trust;* Robert D. Putnam, *Making Democracy Work*) and to the vitality of economic life.

8. James S. Coleman's theoretical elaboration of social capital is presented in "Social Capital in the Creation of Human Capital"; in his theoretical treatise on rational choice, *Foundations of Social Theory;* and in his discussion of youth unemployment, "Social Capital, Human Capital, and Investment in Youth"; as well as in accounts of the achievement success of Catholic students (James S. Coleman and Thomas Hoffer, *Public and Private High Schools*). In the present study, social capital theory usefully underscores the resourceful dimension of social relationships, though it is important to note that relationships also constrain and involve a certain price or cost. Thus, the availability of social support represents a resource, but it comes with a certain price in the present or future.

9. Salamon, *Prairie Patrimony.*

10. Gilbert Courtland Fite, *American Farmers,* 243.

11. James S. Coleman, "The Rational Reconstruction of Society."

12. Lobao, *Locality and Inequality,* 192. The pioneering study of industrial farming is Walter Rochs Goldschmidt, *As You Sow,* originally published by Harcourt, Brace in 1947. Mark Friedberger's comparison of Central Valley farming in California and Iowa family farming leads to some analysis of the costs of industrialized farming *(Farm Families and Change in Twentieth-Century America).*

13. Friedberger, *Farm Families and Change.*

14. Life-course theory emerged in the 1960s around concepts of development, a socially patterned, age-graded life course, and sensitivity to the impact of ongoing social changes; see Glen H. Elder Jr., "Time, Human Agency, and Social Change," "The Life Course Paradigm," and "The Life Course and Human Development."

Four paradigmatic principles are worth special note: human lives in time and place; the role of human agency in constructing the life course; the temporal variations of events and transitions across the life span; and the embeddedness of the life course in which multiple lives are linked. Time and place distinctions are central to this study, and we view parents and children as agents of their own lives or life courses, making as well as using social capital through social relationships. Social capital distinctions speak most directly to the embeddedness concept and to the timing of new transitions and departures. Very much related to life-course theory is Urie Bronfenbrenner's *Ecology of Human Development.* See also his "Ecological Systems Theory," and Urie Bronfenbrenner and Stephen J. Ceci, "Nature-Nurture Reconceptualized in Developmental Perspective."

15. A study using the first wave of data on families was published as Conger and Elder, *Families in Troubled Times* in 1994. The design of this study has much in common with Elder's study of families and children during the Great Depression (Glen H. Elder Jr., *Children of the Great Depression*). Both studies view the family as a bridge between macroeconomic change and the experience of children; and as a potential source of children's resilience.

16. The general program of the MacArthur Foundation Research Network on Successful Adolescent Development among Youth in High-Risk Settings is described by Richard Jessor in "Successful Adolescent Development among Youth in High-Risk Settings."

17. The early papers from this research documented the adverse effect of economic hardship and pressures on marital relations (Rand D. Conger, Glen H. Elder Jr., Frederick O. Lorenz, Katherine J. Conger, Ronald L. Simons, Les B. Whitbeck, Shirley Huck, and Janet N. Melby, "Linking Economic Hardship to Marital Quality and Instability"), the effect of hardship on adolescent behavior through marital hostility (Glen H. Elder Jr., Rand D. Conger, E. Michael Foster, and Monika Ardelt, "Families under Economic Pressure"), and the complex pathways between hardship and the competence of youth (Rand D. Conger, Katherine J. Conger, Glen H. Elder Jr., Frederick O. Lorenz, Ronald L. Simons, and Les B. Whitbeck, "A Family Process Model of Economic Hardship and Ad-

justment of Early Adolescent Boys," and "Family Economic Stress and Adjustment of Early Adolescent Girls."

18. See note 15.

19. A Task Force Report on Persistent Rural Poverty (see note 2) recently
concluded that the social and economic well-being of rural America had deterio-
rated significantly between the early 1970s and the late 1980s. Over this period,
unemployment rates increased more in rural America and wages declined more
drastically. The working poor are more common in rural America, and the most
disadvantaged groups include the racial and ethnic minorities, the elderly,
women, and children.

20. Peggy F. Barlett, *American Dreams, Rural Realities.* For an account of the
severity of the farm crisis in the western prairies of Canada, see Jerome Martin's
anthology of reports, *Alternative Futures for Prairie Agricultural Communities.*

21. This section is drawn from Conger and Elder, *Families in Troubled Times,*
chapters 4 and 5.

22. Barlett, *American Dreams,* 138.

23. Frederick O. Lorenz and Janet N. Melby, "Analyzing Family Stress and
Adaptation."

24. Lorenz and Melby, "Analyzing Family Stress."

25. Charles M. Super and Sara Harkness ("The Developmental Niche: A Conceptualization at the Interface of Child and Culture") propose the term *developmental niche* to represent the interrelation of three factors: the physical and social settings of the child, the customs of child rearing and child care, and the
psychology of the caretakers. For our purposes, each ecological niche is defined
by a different configuration of family history and culture, occupation, and household economy. Physical setting shapes the constraints, options, and situational
imperatives in family life and the experience of the younger generation. From
this perspective, the greatest contrast occurs between the family world of full-
time farming and that of nonfarm households in which neither parent grew up
on a farm (hence grandparents of the child lack involvement in farming) or
farmed as an adult.

26. William J. Weston *(Education and the American Family: A Research Syn-
thesis)* assembles much evidence on the academic influence of family relations
in children's lives; and the powerful implications of parental involvement and
social capital are demonstrated by Barbara Schneider and James S. Coleman in
Parents, Their Children, and School. Parent involvement (James P. Comer and
Norris M. Haynes, "Parent Involvement in Schools") is central to Comer's theory of children's achievement.

27. A great many insightful biographies and autobiographies provide rich accounts of these overlapping worlds (such as Kathleen Norris, *Dakota*). A valuable source is the ethnography conducted by Sonya Salamon, *Prairie Patrimony.*
The county or state fair (Leslie Mina Prosterman, *Ordinary Life, Festival Days*)
brings most of these worlds together—church, school, community, and family.
Churches run services and food places, school classes come on particular days,
and farm families are on display everywhere, from the produce displays to the

barns where children show their animals. Thirty years ago, Roger G. Barker and Paul V. Gump (*Big School, Small School*) assessed the developmental implications of schools of different sizes. Most of the intellectual concern regarding the social and psychological implications of size of place has centered on the growth end of the continuum. What happens when communities grow? See Clyde S. Fischer's excellent essay on this topic, "The Subcultural Theory of Urbanism."

28. Coleman and Hoffer, *Public and Private High Schools.*

29. Coleman, *Foundations of Social Theory,* 593.

30. Sponsored by the MacArthur Foundation Research Network on Successful Adolescent Development among Youth in High-Risk Settings, the Philadelphia Family Management Study (Frank F. Furstenberg Jr., Thomas D. Cook, Jacquelynne Eccles, Glen H. Elder Jr., and Arnold Sameroff, *Managing to Make It*) has developed an elaborate approach to in-house and out-of-house strategies. The link between a sense of parental efficacy and family management strategies is documented by a recent study (Glen H. Elder Jr., Jacquelynne S. Eccles, Monika Ardelt, and Sarah Lord, "Inner-City Parents under Economic Pressure.")

31. Garkovich, Bokemeier, and Foote, *Harvest of Hope,* 32.

32. Jessor, "Successful Adolescent Development."

33. Elijah Anderson, *Streetwise.*

34. Michael Rutter, "Transitions and Turning Points in Developmental Psychopathology."

35. An earlier example of the conceptual exercise of linking family status to children's lives is provided by Glen H. Elder Jr., ed., *Linking Social Structure and Personality* and by his *Children of the Great Depression.*

36. Salamon, *Prairie Patrimony.*

37. Bennett, "Natural and Social Science," 204. See also Bennett's *Of Time and the Enterprise,* John Hutson's account of English farms in the 1980s ("Fathers and Sons"), and Gasson and colleagues' review of the farm as a family business enterprise (Ruth Gasson, Graham Crow, Andrew Errington, John Hutson, Terry Marsden, and D. Michael Winter, "The Farm as a Family Business").

38. See Salamon, *Prairie Patrimony,* 102.

39. See Glen H. Elder Jr., E. Michael Foster, and Monika Ardelt, "Children in the Household Economy," in *Families in Troubled Times,* edited by Conger and Elder, 144. A shortage of men to succeed retiring farmers has prompted some to advertise for young apprentices in the farming business.

40. Women have always played important economic and labor roles on the family farm, but only recently have their contributions been documented; see Wava G. Haney and Jane B. Knowles, eds., *Women and Farming,* and Rachel Ann Rosenfeld, *Farm Women.* In Iowa, husbands and fathers typically run the farm.

41. In one of the very first studies of how American agriculture structures grandchild-grandparent relations, Valarie King and Glen H. Elder Jr. ("American Children View Their Grandparents") show that the patrilineal connection is strongest for farm boys and girls. Boys and girls are closer to their paternal relatives, in part because they live closer.

42. Elder, Foster, and Ardelt, "Children in the Household Economy." See also chapter 3 of Garkovich, Bokemeier, and Foote's account of growing up on a farm, *Harvest of Hope.*

43. Salamon, *Prairie Patrimony,* 53.

44. Ibid., 52.

45. See Viviana A. Zelizer, *Pricing the Priceless Child.*

46. David M. Shribman, "Iowa: A Civic Place," *Des Moines Register,* 27 January 1996.

47. Lasley, "Rural Economic and Social Trends." A technical account of the farm crisis is presented by Murdock and Leistritz, *Farm Financial Crisis.* See also Lasley et al., *Beyond the Amber Waves.*

48. Glen H. Elder Jr., Elizabeth B. Robertson, and E. Michael Foster, "Survival, Loss, and Adaptation," in *Families in Troubled Times,* edited by Conger and Elder, 106. A Kentucky farmer (Garkovich, Bokemeier, and Foote, *Harvest of Hope*) observed that "you just have to roll with the tide, I suppose. You either have to learn to live with it or get out" (45).

49. A more general account of the strategy of off-farm employment is provided by Max J. Pfeffer and Jess Gilbert ("Gender and Off-Farm Employment in Two Farming Systems"). One of the Iowa couples describes a typical day in this way: "The daily schedule is really rough on our lives because we both get up early in the morning and go all day and then come home at night and go over and do chores. In the summer I try to do my own field work and that kind of thing" (Conger and Elder, *Families in Troubled Times,* 117). See Peggy F. Barlett's thoughtful assessment of the growth of part-time farming, "Part-Time Farming." In his later years, Henry A. Wallace (Secretary of Agriculture under Franklin D. Roosevelt in the 1930s) advocated part-time farming as a way to curb the drastic decline of the farm population. See Kirkendall, *Second Thoughts on the Agricultural Revolution.*

50. Elder, Foster, and Ardelt, "Children in the Household Economy." Bonnie L. Barber and Janice M. Lyons observe similar patterns among children of broken families ("Family Processes and Adolescent Adjustment in Intact and Remarried Families").

51. See Lasley, "Rural Economic and Social Trends," 58.

52. See Barlett, *American Dreams.*

53. See Elder, Robertson, and Foster, "Survival, Loss, and Adaptation."

54. Donald A. Hansen and Reuben Hill ("Families under Stress," 803) refer to the social standards that made middle-class families especially vulnerable to status loss. Paul C. Rosenblatt *(Farming Is in Our Blood)* also makes reference to deep-seated values of self-support and self-direction in farming communities that made it difficult for hard-pressed families to seek help from others.

55. See Rosenblatt, *Farming Is in Our Blood.*

56. See Elder, *Children of the Great Depression.*

57. Ibid., 15.

58. Ibid.

59. Repeated contacts with families and children over time are thought to make them different from other families and children. Whether this is the case

or not, all of the families in this study have been exposed to the same research conditions or treatments. If these conditions make families different, the effect would mainly lessen chances for replication.

Chapter Two

The chapter epigraph is from Garkovich, Bokemeier, and Foote, *Harvest of Hope*, 48.

1. Garkovich, Bokemeier, and Foote, *Harvest of Hope*, 48. One Kentucky farmer they interviewed concluded that "a farm is the best place in the world for a child to grow up. They have a lot of advantages. They learn the sense of responsibility for one thing. They don't have a lot of idle time with nothing to do; there's always something for them to do" (61). Idealized views of farm life and the rural countryside as a place "to bring up children" are commonplace in the Iowa sample. Gill Valentine has investigated the process by which such imaginings are constructed in a rural community in England ("A Safe Place to Grow Up?").

The other side of the safe-haven image of rural farm life is the extraordinarily high accident rate. In general, agriculture is among the most hazardous industries in the United States (Michael D. Schulman, Christian T. Evensen, Carol W. Runyan, Lisa R. Cohen, and Kathleen A. Dunn, "Farm Work Is Dangerous for Teens"). Boys are most likely to have farm jobs in adolescence and were at highest risk of injuries in this North Carolina study.

2. In an open-ended interview during the twelfth grade, Iowa youth from farms were most likely to cite the following advantages of living on a farm and in the rural countryside: the freedom and beauty of the open space, privacy, the appeal of wildlife and nature, and the acquisition of practical skills. Small-town young people cited friendliness and safety as primary advantages of their locale. As disadvantages, youth from the farm and open countryside cited the distance and transportation challenge, while town youth stressed the lack of things to do, the prevalence of gossip, and the disadvantages of a more sheltered life.

3. Friedberger, *Farm Families and Change*, 133.

4. Thomas A. Lyson, "Pathways into Production Agriculture."

5. Salamon, *Prairie Patrimony*, 52.

6. Barlett, *American Dreams*.

7. Four elements of family structure were included in the analysis: number of brothers, birth order, standard of living, and father-son age difference. Information on the adult status of the grandfather came from educational level, evidence of unemployment, farm involvement (from ownership to work on other farm), and years farming. Recollections of family by G2s were obtained on marital conflict, hostility, depression, parental rejection, and harsh parenting. Significant differences between men who entered farming and those who entered nonfarm employment were obtained on number of brothers, standard of living, education, unemployment, farm involvement, years farming, and marital conflict. See tables 3 and 4, pp. 316–17 in Glen H. Elder, Jr., Elizabeth B. Robertson, and Rand D. Conger, "Fathers and Sons in Rural America."

8. Historically, entry into farming is expressed through generational collaboration and succession. Thus, 85 percent of the fathers of men in farming as of 1989 owned their farms, compared to 48 percent of the fathers of nonfarm men. These men in the G2 generation were nearly twice as likely to have fathers who were still farming when compared to the nonfarm men: 64 versus 33 percent. By comparison, fathers who worked on other farms were concentrated in the lives of nonfarm men. See Elder, Robertson, and Conger, "Fathers and Sons in Rural America," table 2, 315.

9. Salamon, *Prairie Patrimony.*

10. Friedberger, *Farm Families and Change.*

11. Donald J. Hernandez, *America's Children.*

12. Deborah Fink writes that "daily provisioning of the household, typically with small egg-and-cream enterprises and home production for the family's consumption, was the farm wife's work" into the first half of the twentieth century (67). This quotation comes from *Agrarian Women: Wives and Mothers in Rural Nebraska, 1880–1940,* though it applies to Iowa farm life as well. See Deborah Fink, *Open Country, Iowa.* See also Mareena Wright, "Holding up Their Half of the Sky."

13. King and Elder, "American Children View Their Grandparents."

14. In 1990, we asked respondents if they agreed or disagreed with this statement: "I have a lot of chores to do in my family's business or on my family's farm" (see Glen H. Elder Jr., Valarie King, and Rand D. Conger, "Intergenerational Continuity and Change"). Responses ranged from 1 (strongly disagree) to 5 (strongly agree). We also asked adolescents who were working about working for their parents (1992): "Do you work for your parents?" (0 = no, 1 = yes). Information on joint work with parents was obtained by asking, "How much time do you spend on your job with your father, mother?" (asked only of adolescents who were currently working). On shared community activity, we asked, "How often do you and your father, mother, participate in young group activities together like Scouts, 4-H, or something like that?"

15. Perception of mother's and father's warmth was measured by the following statements asked about in the 1990 follow-up: "Lets you know she/he really cares about you"; "acts loving and affectionate to you"; "lets you know she appreciates you, your ideas, or the things you do"; "helps you do something that is important to you"; "has a good laugh with you about something that was funny"; "acts supportive and understanding to you." Responses range from 1 (never) to 7 (always). The alpha coefficient for mother and father averages .92. Identification with mother and father was measured by the following statements presented in the 1990 follow-up: "When I grow up, I'd like to be like my mother, father"; "I have a lot of respect for my mother, father"; "My mother, father is the kind of person other people respect," and "I really enjoy spending time with my mother, father." Response categories range from 1 (strongly agree) to 5 (strongly disagree). The alpha coefficient for mother and father averages .84. The effect of farm status on father identification is .20 ($p < .05$) for boys and girls (with parental education and income controlled). This effect drops to a beta

coefficient of .11 for mother identification among boys and girls. The coefficients on perceived warmth tend to be weaker.

16. See Conger and Elder, *Families in Troubled Times,* 119–21. In reply to her husband, a displaced farmer, a wife observed that "the farm still influences us today because you don't like it here and you want to go back. Yet we left there to have a better life. It is hard for the kids and me because we don't understand why you want to go back" (120).

17. This analysis across four years of the Iowa Youth and Families Project uses latent growth curve models to assess the interplay of three trajectories for each husband and wife: depressed feelings, negative events, and family income. The analysis estimates level and rate of change for each trajectory. Thus, the most depressed group in the entire sample during 1988 consisted of the wives of men who lost their farms—the displaced. Four years later, their mental outlook had improved dramatically (large rate of change), reflecting a much improved economic situation. See Frederick O. Lorenz, Glen H. Elder Jr. K. A. S. Wickrama, Wan-Ning Bao, and Rand D. Conger, "After Farming."

18. Partnership is one expression of this norm among farm couples. We asked mothers and fathers in the study who makes important decisions. Most of them claimed they made decisions together. In the reports of mothers, 18 percent of the women on farms said that their husbands made such decisions, in contrast to 8 percent among nonfarm women. When the husbands were asked about major decisions on spending, a fourth of the farmers said they made the decisions, compared to 15 percent of the nonfarm men. All of these reports were made in 1991.

19. To avoid identification, the case is a composite of farm families.

20. Robert Wuthnow has studied the functional significance of small groups or assemblages in American communities and portrays them in much the way Nancy Ammerman views religious congregations. See his *Acts of Compassion* and *Sharing the Journey.*

21. Nancy Tatom Ammerman, *Congregation and Community,* 360.

22. Ibid., 370.

23. Classification of Community Ties Groups:

Step 1: Families assigned a score of 0, 1, or 2 on each of four involvement indexes for 1989–92:

1. Civic Membership
   a. Both parents in lower third = 0
   b. One or both parents in middle third = 1
   c. Both parents in upper third = 2
2. Civic Leadership
   a. Neither parent served leadership role = 0
   b. One parent served leadership role = 1
   c. Both parents served leadership role = 2
3. Church Attendance
   a. Both parents attend church less than once a week = 0
   b. One or both parents attend church once a week = 1
   c. Both parents attend church at least once a week = 2

4. PTA Attendance
   a. Child disagrees that parents attend PTA events often = 0
   b. Child agrees somewhat that parents attend PTA events often = 1
   c. Child strongly agrees that parents attend PTA events often = 2

Step 2: Total score across four indexes, averaged from 1989–92, used to identify families as follows.

   Weak Ties, total score 0–2 ($N = 97$)
   Average Ties, total score 3–5 ($N = 236$)
   Strong Ties, total score 6–8 ($N = 71$)

24. Shmuel Noah Eisenstadt, *From Generation to Generation.*
25. Urie Bronfenbrenner, *Two Worlds of Childhood.*
26. Ibid., 95.
27. Salamon, *Prairie Patrimony.*
28. Conger and Elder, *Families in Troubled Times,* 114.
29. See Ronald Inglehart's three monographs on this value transition: *The Silent Revolution, Culture Shift in Advanced Industrial Society,* and Paul R. Abramson and Ronald Inglehart, *Value Change in Global Perspective.*
30. Arthur L. Stinchcombe, *Rebellion in a High School.*

Chapter Three

1. Salamon, *Prairie Patrimony,* 45.
2. Garkovich, Bokemeier, and Foote (*Harvest of Hope,* 70) note that disaffection from a career in production agriculture extends even to national officers of the Future Farmers of America. In 1986, none of the twelve national officers was committed to such a career. In their study of Kentucky farm families, they found that many parents were steering their children away from this occupation. The sentiment of a successful farmer in their study area is widely shared among Iowa parents in the present study. "Like I said, if they want to farm, I'll try to do all I can to help them farm. But as for a preference, I've seen both sides and they'd probably be better off not farming. Farming was about the only choice I had. It is a hard way of life. We've talked to our kids about better ways of living" (70–71).
3. The lessons from this historical record are being learned again in the former territory of East Germany. Reunification of East and West Germany set in motion efforts to replace collective farms with independent farmers, recruited in part from the young. An ongoing study in Northern Germany has found that the children of nonfarm families have no interest in the hard work, low pay, and insecurity of farming. See Artur Meier, "Report of the Mecklenberg Study." See also Elder and Meier, "Troubled Times."
4. See Elder, Robertson, and Conger, "Fathers and Sons in Rural America." Intergenerational succession in farming takes most of a lifetime and depends on a working relationship with the father over this period. In Iowa, the median age of farmers when they signed over their farms to sons was in the mid-60s.
5. Historically, out-migration streams from rural areas generally recruit the

most able and ambitious young people. We find that even in the seventh grade there are notable differences of this kind between children who want to farm and those who prefer a different life. For example, mean scores on the Iowa Test of Basic Skills for these two groups are significantly different ($p < .01$).

6. Urie Bronfenbrenner and Pamela M. Morris, "The Ecology of Developmental Processes."

7. Herbert Quick, 1913, as quoted in Fink, *Agrarian Women,* 156.

8. Conger and Elder, *Families in Troubled Times,* 120.

9. The mean scores for mothers' satisfaction with farming as a way of life in the farm-oriented and other-oriented groups are 3.48 vs. 2.93, $F = 13.5$, $p < .001$; for satisfaction with farming as a way to make a living, 2.73 vs. 2.24, $F = 6.86$, $p < .01$; and for willingness to get out of farming, if given the chance, 2.07 vs. 2.50, $F = 4.68$, $p < .05$. The average difference between means of spouses is .39 for the mothers of farm youth who plan to leave, compared to .07 for the farm-oriented group.

10. However, the degree of value agreement is surprisingly weak. The value of being a community leader shows agreement only between youth and their fathers. And this figure is slightly stronger among farm youth who plan to leave home than among adolescents who plan to live on a farm (with father, .21 and .26). Correlations with mother are weaker. It is noteworthy that the leadership of fathers makes more of a difference than the civic leadership of mothers in the value youth place on community leadership (Christopher G. Chan and Glen H. Elder Jr., "The Reproduction of Social Capital"). On the other two values, concordance occurs mainly with mothers: an average r for the farm-oriented group of .30 versus .14 for the other group.

11. Seymour Martin Lipset and Reinhard Bendix, *Social Mobility in Industrial Society.*

12. These analyses were carried out in terms of aspirations that were reported in the eighth and eleventh grades, 1991 and 1993. At the time, the last wave of data available for analysis was reported in the eleventh grade. Temporal patterns were identified on the importance of parents, relatives, community, and life on a farm for residence in the adult years (responses yes or no). Some youth remained stable in response, while others changed in either direction—the factor became more or less important. Multinomial logistic regressions identified significant predictors of three groups: stay important, become important, become unimportant. The reference category was "stay unimportant" (Glen H. Elder Jr., Valarie King, and Rand D. Conger, "Attachment to Place and Migration Prospects"; "Intergenerational Continuity and Change in Rural Lives."

13. Roberta G. Simmons and Dale A. Blyth, *Moving into Adolescence.*

14. John Hagan, Ross MacMillan, and Blair Wheaton, "New Kid in Town."

15. From p. 421 in Norman Garmezy, "Resiliency and Vulnerability to Adverse Developmental Outcomes Associated with Poverty." For pioneering work on these issues, see Werner and Smith, *Vulnerable, but Invincible,* and *Overcoming the Odds.*

16. The study of behavioral continuity from early childhood into adolescence and the adult years focuses on the process by which early disadvantage is carried

forward across the years. Thus, poverty is reproduced in the lives of children who grow up in poverty. The central question addresses the mechanisms of this reproduction. Jay MacLeod's powerful enthnography, *Ain't No Makin' It,* illustrates this perspective on the perpetuation of disadvantage. Presumably some youth in MacLeod's population did escape, but they are not the central theme.

By contrast, the study of resilience investigates factors that enable youth to rise above the limitations of their background. Examples include some "children of the Great Depression" who grew up in the midst of family hardship but nevertheless managed to succeed in education, business, and family (Elder, *Children of the Great Depression*). The conceptual and empirical works of Werner and Smith (1982, 1992) and Masten and Garmezy (Ann S. Masten and Norman Garmezy, "Risk, Vulnerability, and Protective Factors in Developmental Psychopathology"; Ann S. Masten, Karin M. Best, and Norman Garmezy, "Resilience and Development: Contributions from the Study of Children Who Overcome Adversity") is important, along with that of Michael Rutter (*Studies of Psychosocial Risk: The Power of Longitudinal Data; "Transitions and Turning Points"*) and others (Suniya S. Luthar and Edward Zigler, "Vulnerability and Competence"; Suniya S. Luthar, Carol H. Doernberger, and Edward Zigler, "Resilience Is Not a Unidimensional Construct").

17. Elder, *Children of the Great Depression,* chapter 4.

Chapter Four

1. Awareness that others are depending on one's actions teaches the valuable lesson of citizenship and responsibility in an interdependent world. Morris Rosenberg and B. Claire McCullough ("Mattering") found that adolescents who realize that they are depended on acquire a heightened sense of mattering or importance.

2. The comparison involves a sample of adolescents in St. Paul, MN, and the Iowa Youth and Families sample. In the tenth grade, St. Paul youth were two and a half times as likely to spend their money on records, tapes, sports equipment, and so on, while Iowa adolescents were three times more apt to give money to the family. The latter were also more likely to place their earnings in savings. See Michael J. Shanahan, Glen H. Elder Jr., Margaret Burchinal, and Rand D. Conger, "Adolescent Earnings and Relationships with Parents," 114.

3. See Garkovich, Bokemeier, and Foote, *Harvest of Hope,* 63. In their Kentucky farm family study, Garkovich and associates note that "for many farm parents an essential part of the advantage of growing up on a farm is learning responsibility and the value of work. When you grow up on a farm you have freedom, but the freedom is balanced by responsibilities; there are many opportunities to play and as many opportunities to contribute in important ways to the work of the farm" (60). See also Salamon, *Prairie Patrimony,* chapter 2.

4. See p. 2185 in Michael J. Shanahan, Glen H. Elder Jr., Margaret Burchinal, and Rand D. Conger, "Adolescent Paid Labor and Relationships with Parents." This study of the Iowa Youth and Families Project sample found that boys earn more than girls up to high school and gain more in earnings over the middle

school years. Boys in rural areas also earn more than their counterparts in the city.

5. Stinchcombe *(Rebellion in a High School)* identified these claims as expressions of rebellion to adult authority in a high school. Ellen Greenberger and Laurence Steinberg *(When Teenagers Work)* document the negative consequences of adolescent work, the promotion of "pseudomaturity." The more adolescents worked, the higher their risk of antisocial behavior and academic failure, though one might conclude that students in academic trouble sought employment as an alternative life style. Greenberger and Steinberg suggest that low-quality service jobs tend to induct youth into a subterranean youth culture.

6. Stanley Rachman, "The Concept of Required Helpfulness."

7. McHale and associates found that the developmental consequences of household work for children cast helpful behaviors as maturity demands. See Susan M. McHale, Todd W. Bartko, Ann C. Crouter, and Maureen Perry-Jenkins, "Children's Housework and Psychosocial Functioning."

8. Elder, *Children of the Great Depression.*

9. Albert Bandura, *Self-Efficacy.*

10. Elder, *Children of the Great Depression,* chapter 4.

11. Elder, Robertson, and Foster, "Survival, Loss, and Adaptation."

12. Elder, *Children of the Great Depression.*

13. Anthony S. Bryk, and Stephen W. Raudenbush, *Hierarchical Linear Models.*

14. Shanahan et al., "Adolescent Earnings."

15. Bandura, *Self-Efficacy.*

16. Shanahan et al., "Adolescent Earnings."

17. Ibid.

18. Bronfenbrenner and Morris. "The Ecology of Developmental Processes."

19. Erving Goffman, *The Presentation of Self in Everyday Life.*

20. Little attention has been given to the role of early work experience in developing skills of emotion management. Psychologists have written extensively on this dimension of self-control (see Jutta Heckhausen, *Developmental Regulation in Adulthood*), and sociologists have stressed the situational properties of this process. Emotion management requires an understanding of the "feeling rules" (Arlie Russell Hochschild, "Emotion Work, Feeling Rules, and Social Structure") that govern situations, such as consumer relations in a retail store. Productive labor among youth in this region of Iowa provided opportunities to learn such rules and develop ways of complying with them. Obnoxious customers sorely tried the patience of many youth in the study, and some expressed pleasure with their ability to manage the situation.

21. Cited on p. 12 of Richard S. Kirkendall's, "Reflections of a Revolutionary on a Revolution."

Chapter Five

1. Coleman discusses both of these mechanisms in his socialization theory of social capital (see "Social Capital in the Creation of Human Capital," and Cole-

man and Hoffer, *Public and Private High Schools*). Within the MacArthur Network on adolescence, a Philadelphia study suggests that social capital can make a difference in child socialization through family management processes (see Furstenberg et al., *Managing to Make It*). We shall put this mediational model to a test in this chapter.

2. Socialization studies (John A. Clausen, ed., *Socialization and Society*) have traditionally focused on processes within households. Sociological studies have shown these processes are influenced by historical change (Elder, *Children of the Great Depression*), income loss and chronic hardship (Conger and Elder, *Families in Troubled Times*), and parental work characteristics, such as the complexity of work. In a longitudinal study based on the National Longitudinal Study of Youth, Toby L. Parcel and Elizabeth G. Menaghan ("Early Parental Work, Family Social Capital, and Early Childhood Outcomes"; see also their "Family Social Capital and Children's Behavior Problems") found that the occupational complexity of mothers' work influence the cognitive and social outcomes of children by interacting with her social resources and employment attributes.

The distinctive feature of our approach to Iowa families involves the connection between what goes on inside families and the involvement of parents and children in community and school organizations. Community involvement can empower parents in ways that make a notable difference in the lives of children. Another example of this approach can be found in the Philadelphia study of the MacArthur Network on Adolescents in High-Risk Settings (see Furstenberg et al., *Managing to Make It*).

3. See Laurence Steinberg, Sanford Dornbusch, and B. Bradford Brown, "Ethnic Differences in Adolescent Achievement." Peers are most likely to represent extensions of family values in adult-sponsored regimes, as illustrated by the social worlds of families with ties to the land.

4. Mark S. Granovetter, "Strength of Weak Ties."

5. Salamon, *Prairie Patrimony*.

6. Ibid., 67.

7. Ibid., 74.

8. Ibid., 239.

9. Parents who gain knowledge and insight regarding community institutions are likely to feel more efficacious as parents (Elder, Eccles, Ardelt, and Lord, "Inner-city Parents under Economic Pressure"; Furstenberg et al., *Managing to Make It*), but a sense of personal efficacy often prompts initiatives that provide greater knowledge (see Bandura, *Self-Efficacy*).

10. See Glen H. Elder Jr., "Adolescence in Historical Perspective"; and Laurence Steinberg, "Autonomy, Conflict, and Harmony in the Family Relationship." Autonomy comes early to children of farming families in the sense that they are expected to play responsible roles within a framework of interdependence. A Kentucky farm boy observed (Garkovich, Bokemeier, and Foote, *Harvest of Hope*) that one becomes "more independent a little bit younger on the farm. You learn to use your judgment a little quicker" (61). This point applies even though farm youth operate under parental authority and supervision. Au-

thority must be delegated in far-flung operations on a farm. Farm youth have something akin to a partnership with their fathers.

11. Time pressure is a common theme in accounts of American life, from Staffan Burenstam Linder's *The Harried Leisure Class* to Arlie Russell Hochschild's recent book *(The Time Bind)*.

12. See also Joyce Epstein, "Perspectives and Previews on Research and Policy for School, Family, and Community Partnerships"; Frank F. Furstenberg Jr. and Mary E. Hughes, "Social Capital and Successful Development among At-Risk Youth"; and Furstenburg et al., *Managing to Make It*.

13. For mother and father, effective child monitoring is concentrated among families with strong community ties (contrast between weak and strong ties is significant at .05). In addition, parents who are involved in the community tend to discuss school more frequently with their children (a difference significant at the .05 level for mother and father). Socially engaged parents are not more likely than isolated parents to know their children's teachers, and they are not more likely to help them on matters of homework.

14. Epstein, "Perspectives and Previews."

15. Regarding the prediction of grades, the only statistically significant influences beyond community ties and socioeconomic factors are father discusses school (beta = .09, $p < .10$), unsupervised time with peers (beta = $-.20$, $p < .01$), and school mentors (beta = 11, $p < .05$). For perceived achievement, the same factors emerge as statistically significant. As for social success, only a father who assists a child in programs is predictive (beta = .19, $p < .01$). The explained variance is .23 on grades, .19 on perceived achievement, and .16 on social success.

16. These include Epstein, "Perspectives and Previews," and Robert J. Sampson, "Family Management and Child Development: Insights from Social Disorganization Theory." An example of this is the influence of neighborhood properties on children. The effect of neighborhood disadvantage varies by outcome according to the developmental stage of children, and it may also vary in degree (personal communication, Delbert Elliott, MacArthur Network meeting, Boulder, CO, 8 July 1997).

17. Coleman and Hoffer, *Public and Private High Schools*.

18. Alan Peshkin, *Growing up American*.

19. Though encouragement seems to make a difference in youths' social activity among isolated families, this may not produce the same level of community awareness and parental effectiveness (see Anne C. Fletcher, Glen H. Elder Jr., and Debra Mekos, "Parental Influences on Adolescent Involvement in Community Activities."

20. See the Philadelphia monograph in the MacArthur program, Furstenberg et al., *Managing to Make It*.

21. Hillary Rodham Clinton, *It Takes a Village*.

22. For example, Coleman and Hoffer, *Public and Private High Schools*, found that the benefits of attending Catholic schools, with their array of social resources, were greatest for children who were at risk of school failure. Some evidence of this effect appears in our findings on academic success and self-

confidence. In particular, youth with greater access to school and community mentors for guidance felt more self-confident than one might expect from knowledge of their family background. The total sample, however, shows no evidence of this effect.

Chapter Six

The chapter epigraph is from Margaret Mead, "Grandparents as Educators," 70.

1. Margaret Mead, "Grandparents as Educators," 70.

2. A hundred years ago only one out of fifty children had four living grandparents when they reached age fifteen. See Andrew J. Cherlin and Frank F. Furstenberg Jr., *The New American Grandparent.* By the late 1970s, three out of four older Americans had assumed the role of grandparenthood (Joan F. Robertson, "Grandparenting in an Era of Rapid Change"). This suggests that most contemporary Americans will get to know their grandchildren and even watch them develop into adulthood. Conversely, most young children will grow up with access to grandparents (see Peter Uhlenberg and James B. Kirby, "Grandparenthood over Time").

3. We use the grandparent interviews in this section because they allow us to look at a greater variety of information that is only available in this data set. To bring out the special circumstances of youth from single-parent households, we drew upon qualitative material from interviews with the grandparents of such children, even though they are part of another study on single parents. Of the 424 families in this study, 396 had complete information from the adolescents on all of their grandparents. The remaining 28 adolescents were no longer in high school and received a somewhat different version of the twelfth-grade questionnaire. Unfortunately, the set of questions about grandparents was not a part of their version. For the purposes of this chapter, these 28 adolescents were omitted from the analyses based on the grandchild reports. The remaining 396 adolescents provided information on all of their grandparents, 1,103 of whom were still living and 720 of whom participated in the telephone interviews. The telephone interviews also include an additional 49 respondents who were grandparents of the 28 adolescents no longer in high school. The analyses based on the grandparent reports come from these 769 grandparents.

4. Peter Uhlenberg and Bradley G. Hammill, "Frequency of Grandparent Contact with Grandchild Sets."

5. Christine A. Johnson, Les B. Whitbeck, and Dan Hoyt, "An Investigation of the Influence of Grandchild Personality on the Quality of the Grandparent-Grandchild Relationship."

6. See Roseann Giarrusso, Michael Stallings, and Vern L. Bengtson ("The 'International Stake' Hypothesis Revisited") for their examination of the developmental stakes phenomenon—that the elder generation has more invested in a successful relationship and consequently tends to inflate sentiment toward children. The latter have more at stake in differentiating self from parents and generally express less positive views.

7. Though children become more peer-oriented as they move through the adolescent years, this shift away from parents is generally selective. Peers are sought for counsel on matters of social life, for example, whereas parents typically remain most salient as guides on matters of the future, education, work, and family (see Steinberg, "Autonomy, Conflict, and Harmony in the Family Relationship"). Especially in the middle class, parents are more knowledgeable and consequential for the future. A similar pattern of selectivity appears in the relative importance of grandparents and peers on significant matters. Grandparents are likely to be the unchallenged experts on the family and family traditions, and they are sought out for advice on this topic. Religion and morality are part of this expertise. Close friends have greater relevance on problems concerning boy and girl friends.

8. Chrystal C. Ramirez-Barranti, "The Grandparent/Grandchild Relationship."

9. Gunhild O. Hagestad, "Continuity and Connectedness."

10. Arthur Kornhaber and Kenneth L. Woodward, *Grandparents, Grandchildren.*

11. One of the more compelling accounts of grandparent care as a last resort is provided by a Los Angeles study conducted by sociologist Linda Burton. Burton interviewed members of forty-one female lineages from urban, multigenerational, black families. Each lineage included the new mother, grandmother, and great-grandmother. Eighteen of these lineage units were defined as "early" transitions. The age ranges of respondents in these early lineages were 11–18 for the young mothers, 25–38 for the grandmothers, and 46–57 for the great-grandmothers. The remaining lineage units were classified as "on-time" transitions. The age ranges for mothers, grandmothers, and great-grandmothers were 21–26, 42–57, and 60–73, respectively.

Evidence from this study shows that the transition to motherhood was welcomed by the majority of members in the on-time lineages—the new mothers, grandmothers, and great-grandmothers. This was not the case for the early transition group. The new adolescent mothers typically expected their mothers to assume the important care of their children, but four of five did not experience such help. The vast majority of their own mothers refused to assume an active grandparent role. Grandmothers in the early-transition lineage, having been teenage mothers themselves in most cases, were collaborators in their own off-time dilemma. Through their daughters' decision to have children, they were involuntarily propelled into roles that they did not expect or desire at that point in their lives. As one mother put it, "being a grandmother is the one thing I can do without right now. I just wish that my daughter could have waited. I would have had more time to help her later. . . . But now I got too many other things to do with my own life and raising another baby even if it is my own grandchild ain't one of them" (Glen H. Elder Jr., Avshalom Caspi, and Linda M. Burton, "Adolescent Transitions in Developmental Perspective," 159). See Linda M. Burton and Vern L. Bengtson, "Black Grandmothers."

12. A majority of the small number of studies that have directly tried to assess the influence of grandparents have found positive effects. Greater grandparent

involvement has been linked to grandchildren's secure attachment as infants and young children (Susan B. Crockenberg, "Infant Irritability, Mother Responsiveness, and Social Support Influences on the Security of Infant-Mother Attachment"; see also Ellen A. Farber and Byron Egeland, "Invulnerability among Abused and Neglected Children"; Barbara J. Myers, Patricia A. Jarvis, and Gary L. Creasey, "Infants' Behavior with Their Mothers and Grandmothers"; and Angela M. Tomlin and Richard H. Passman, "Grandmothers' Responsibility in Raising Two-Year-Olds Facilitates Their Grandchildren's Adaptive Behavior"). Grandparent involvement has also been linked to scores on mental and physical development scales (Norma Radin, Daphna Oyserman, and Rita Benn, "Grandfathers, Teen Mothers and Children under Two"; Barbara R. Tinsley and Ross D. Parke, "Grandparents as Interactive and Social Support Agents for Families with Young Infants"). The involvement of grandparents has also been reported to be beneficial for children of divorce. Such children show fewer behavior problems and better coping skills (E. Mavis Hetherington, "Coping with Family Transitions: Winners, Losers, and Survivors"; E. Mavis Hetherington, Margaret Stanley-Hagan, and Edward R. Anderson, "Marital Transitions: A Child's Perspective"; Judith S. Wallerstein and Joan Berlin Kelly, *Surviving the Break-Up*).

13. Cherlin and Furstenberg, *New American Grandparent.*

14. The analyses in this section were also examined by substituting the dichotomous measure of having at least one close grandparent. No differences emerged for the analyses predicting twelfth-grade outcomes and only a few differences appeared for the residual analyses. However, the dichotomous measure showed somewhat stronger effects (more likely to attain statistical significance) than the continuous measure in model 1. But after adding parental warmth in model 2, the results were similarly nonsignificant for both measures of closeness to grandparents. The similarity of results indicates a general robustness of the findings, regardless of the way significant grandparents are identified.

Chapter Seven

1. In the prairie country of western Canada, Norah C. Keating ("The Future of the Farm Family in Prairie Agricultural Communities") observes that "the church remains the centre of the community, encouraging a similarity of basic values and a strong religious faith among community members" (71). Examples of parental use of religious communities to insulate children from drugs and violence come from the Philadelphia study of the MacArthur Foundation Research Network on Successful Adolescent Development among Youth in High-Risk Settings. Black mothers report joining a Catholic parish and Jehovah's Witnesses congregation to ensure a desirable peer community for their children. This protective strategy also includes sending children to suburban areas. See Furstenberg et al., *Managing to Make It.* See also Darwin L. Thomas and Gwendolyn C. Henry, "The Religion and Family Connection"; and Howard M. Bahr and Bruce A. Chadwick, "Religion and Family in Middletown, USA."

2. There is a resemblance here to the culture of respect for elders in Japanese households (see Robert John Smith, *Japanese Society*). To shed light on grand-

parenting among grandchildren in two-parent and one-parent households, we draw on interviews with grandparents in both kinds of situations.

3. Rodney Stark, *Sociology,* 190. For a more detailed account of the religious communities thesis, see Stark, "Religion as Context."

4. Evidence on the reduced risk of drug and alcohol abuse comes from Peter L. Benson, Michael J. Donahue, and Joseph A. Erickson, "Adolescence and Religion: A Review of the Literature from 1970 to 1986"; David Brownfield and Ann Marie Sorenson,"Religion and Drug Use among Adolescents"; John E. Donovan, Richard Jessor, and Frances M. Costa, "Adolescent Health Behavior and Conventionality-Unconventionality"; William Alex McIntosh, Starla D. Fitch, J. Branton Wilson, and Kenneth L. Nyberg, "The Effect of Mainstream Religious Social Controls on Adolescent Drug Use in Rural Areas"; and Patricia B. Sutker, "Adolescent Drug and Alcohol Behaviors."

A lowered risk of problem behavior and emotional depression, and greater academic success are documented by Benson, Donahue, and Erickson, "Adolescence and Religion"; Anthony S. Bryk, Valerie E. Lee, and Peter B. Holland, *Catholic Schools and the Common Good;* Richard Jessor and Shirley L. Jessor, *Problem Behavior and Psychosocial Development;* and Loyd S. Wright, Christopher J. Frost, and Stephen J. Wisecarver, "Church Attendance, Meaningfulness of Religion, and Depressive Symptomology among Adolescents." Religious involvement and beliefs are part of a dimension of conventionality-unconventionality in Jessor's problem behavior theory. For recent applications, see especially Frances M. Costa, Richard Jessor, J. Dennis Fortenberry, and John E. Donovan, "Psychosocial Conventionality."

5. See Ellen L. Idler, "Religious Involvement and the Health of the Elderly." See also Michael J. Donahue and Peter L. Benson, "Religion and the Well-Being of Adolescents."

6. Darren Edward Sherkat, "Religious Socialization and the Family." See also Alfred Darnell and Darren Edward Sherkat, "The Impact of Protestant Fundamentalism on Educational Attainment."

7. For a general statistical report on this topic, see H. Paul Chalfant and Peter L. Heller, "Rural/Urban versus Regional Differences in Religiosity." Claude Fischer's *To Dwell among Friends,* an early study of networks, shows the extent to which social networks are developed within congregations. See also Wade Clark Roof and William McKinney, *American Mainline Religion;* also Rodney Stark and William Sims Bainbridge, *The Future of Religion.*

8. Church attendance was scored $0 =$ none, $1 =$ some, and $2 =$ frequent; involvement in church activities was scored $1 =$ involved, $0 =$ not involved.

9. Evidence on religious inheritance is not consistent, owing partly to different ways of collecting the data. When data are collected from parents and youth on their respective religiosity, the intergenerational link is clearly present (Scott M. Myers, "An Interactive Model of Religiosity Inheritance"; see also Fern K. Willits and Donald M. Crider, "Church Attendance and Traditional Religious Beliefs in Adolescence and Young Adulthood." No study has tested the religiosity of kin and sibling context. A good many rural Iowa families are embedded in a context of religiosity, but presumably other families are not. Does this differ-

ence in religious context actually make a difference in the religious participation of youth? Do religious communities foster in-group solidarity and social intolerance? We find no evidence of this in the data at hand.

10. The five-point "respect" item is correlated .14, $p < .01$ for mother and only .09, $p < .10$ for father. Coefficients range from .17 to .21 on the "others respect" item, all $p < .01$. The correlation with "not seeing friends objected to by parents" is .22, $p < .01$. A similar correlation coefficient, though negative in direction, was obtained on "time spent with friends."

11. Religious involvement is correlated .19 and .14 for college goal and career success ($p < .01$). Involved youth were more interested in a life that would enable them to improve the world (.16, $p < .01$); become a religious person (.50, $p < .01$); and achieve a good marriage (.10, $p < .10$).

12. Mavis Grovenia Sanders, "Breaking the Cycle of Reproduction: The Effect of Communities, Families, and Schools on the Academic Achievement of Urban African-American Youth," Ph.D. diss., Stanford University, 1995.

13. Iowa youth who became more active in the youth group between grades 7 and 10 were not predicted by the increasing religious involvement of parents. However, research on the same sample indicates that Iowa youth who become more religious "in belief" over this time period were likely to be identified with their parents and to become more identified over time. Their parents are religious in beliefs and generally became more so over the four-year period. The adolescents were also likely to describe themselves as "born again" (Valarie King, Glen H. Elder Jr., and Les B. Whitbeck, "Religious Involvement among Rural Youth.")

14. Darnell and Sherkat, "The Impact of Protestant Fundamentalism."

15. Salamon, *Prairie Patrimony.*

16. Ammerman, *Congregation and Community.*

17. Gary Schwartz examines the moral climates of communities in *Beyond Conformity or Rebellion: Youth and Authority in America* (1987). He observes that the "ways in which local authorities selectively define, interpret, and apply the rules reflect that community's conception of what is good, desirable, or necessary for youth" (13).

Chapter Eight

1. Georg Simmel's observations *(The Sociology of Georg Simmel)* on the social interactive effects of group size have been documented by humanists (Norris, *Dakota*) and by empirical studies (Barker and Gump, *Big School, Small School*). In her essay on South Dakota life, Norris observed that "there are far fewer people than jobs to fill" (79). She notes that "in the small towns on the plains . . . there are so few people for so many jobs that we tend to call on whoever seems the most likely to do the job well. This has its bad side, as capable people can find that they are doing too much. It can also lead to mediocrity. . . . But sometimes miracles occur. Sometimes people rise to the occasion and do well more than they believe they can do at all" (118).

2. Norris, *Dakota,* 79.

3. The best single reference to the research literature on this developmental process is Bandura, *Self-Efficacy.* In the Great Depression, successful efforts by young people to earn money typically raised their sense of personal efficacy (Elder, *Children of the Great Depression,* chapter 4). Similar findings are reported in chapter 4 of this volume. The rate of increase in feelings of personal mastery is associated with the rate of earnings growth. Social involvement also forms more rewarding identities, a point empirically developed by Milbrey W. McLaughlin ("Embedded Identities"). Other research links activity involvement to achievement and self-fulfillment (see Mihaly Csikszentmihalyi and Douglas A. Kleiber, "Leisure and Self-Actualization"; Jacquelynne S. Eccles and Bonnie Barber, "Adolescents' Activity Involvement"; Reed Larson, "Youth Organizations, Hobbies, and Sports as Developmental Contexts"; Joseph L. Mahoney and Robert B. Cairns, "Do Extracurricular Activities Protect against Early School Dropout?" For a general account of peer culture, see B. Bradford Brown's thoughtful overview ("Peer Groups and Peer Cultures").

Another type of developmental experience is associated with community service. Most of the youth groups were engaged in community service, but our surveys did not inquire about specific projects. James Youniss and Miranda Yates *(Community Service and Social Responsibility in Youth)* have produced an insightful account of student learning from a class community project. See also Miranda Yates and James Youniss, "A Developmental Perspective on Community Service in Adolescence"; and Stephen F. Hamilton and L. Mickey Frenzel, "The Impact of Volunteer Experience on Adolescent Social Development."

4. Elder, "The Life Course and Human Development."

5. Bandura, *Self-Efficacy.*

6. Elder, *Children of the Great Depression.*

7. Ibid., 147.

8. Ibid., 144.

9. David A. Kinney, "From Nerds to Normals."

10. David R. Reynolds, "Rural Education."

11. Barker and Gump, *Big School, Small School.*

12. D. Stanley Eitzen, "Athletics in the Status System of Male Adolescents."

13. Peshkin, *Growing Up American;* Salamon, *Prairie Patrimony.*

14. James S. Coleman, with the assistance of John W. C. Johnstone and Kurt Jonassohn, *The Adolescent Society.*

15. Schneider and Coleman, *Parents, Their Children, and Schools.*

16. Mahoney and Cairns ("Do Extracurricular Activities Protect?") found that early student involvement in extracurricular activities significantly reduced the risk of leaving school. In a study of Swedish youth from early childhood to adulthood, Joseph L. Mahoney ("Community Engagement and Adolescent Adjustment") found that social engagement increased educational attainment, lowered arrest rates during adolescence, and decreased criminal offending into adulthood. Eccles and Barber ("Adolescents' Activity Involvement") report corresponding results from their Michigan longitudinal sample. See also Schneider and Coleman, *Parents, Their Children, and Schools.*

17. This result for sports involvement may reflect the heterogeneity of athletes

on prosocial and problem behavior, as reported by Eccles and Barber in "Adolescents' Activity Involvement." Some of the athletes in their study were heavy drinkers.

18. Salamon (personal communication, September 1997) suggests that farm youth in particular may be socialized for modesty about personal accomplishments. "In my experience [these] people are socialized not to brag, not to make much of being better than others."

19. Rutter, "Transitions and Turning Points." See also Clausen, *American Lives;* and Werner and Smith, *Vulnerable but Invincible,* and *Overcoming the Odds.*

20. Michael Marsiske, Frieder R. Lang, Paul B. Baltes, and Margret M. Baltes, "Selective Optimization with Compensation."

21. Carnegie Council on Adolescent Development, Task Force on Youth Development and Community Programs, *A Matter of Time.*

22. Milbrey W. McLaughlin, Merita A. Irby, and Juliet Langman, *Urban Sanctuaries.*

Chapter Nine

1. Delbert S. Elliott, David Huizinga, and Scott Menard *(Multiple Problem Youth)* report that "earlier and more recent self-report studies all indicate that we should expect higher prevalence and offending rates in urban areas than in suburban or rural areas" (45). Rates of marijuana and alcohol use also tend to be highest in the large cities. Nothing is said about plausible explanatory processes, although social control has great relevance. As one boy in a small village observed, "If you do anything in town, everybody knows about it. You're the talk of the town for a little bit."

2. Michael R. Gottfredson and Travis Hirschi, *A General Theory of Crime.*

3. For example, an analysis of boys based on the first wave of data from the Iowa Youth and Families Project found that nurturant and involved parenting increased the boys' self-confidence, peer acceptance, and school performance (Conger et al., "A Family Process Model"). Similar results have been reported for the girls (Conger et al., "Family Economic Stress"; see also Conger and Elder, *Families in Troubled Times.* Other analyses have extended these findings across time (e.g., Katherine Jewsbury Conger, Rand D. Conger, and Laura V. Scaramella, "Parents, Siblings, Psychological Control, and Adolescent Adjustment"; Rand D. Conger and Martha A. Rueter, "Siblings, Parents, and Peers: A Longitudinal Study of Social Influences in Adolescent Risk for Alcohol Use and Abuse"; Janet N. Melby and Rand D. Conger, "Parental Behaviors and Adolescent Academic Performance."

4. Mary Ellen Colten and Susan Gore, eds., *Adolescent Stress.*

5. Rand D. Conger and Ronald L. Simons, "Life-Course Contingencies in the Development of Adolescent Antisocial Behavior."

6. Richard Jessor, John Edward Donovan, and Frances Marie Costa *(Beyond Adolescence)* show that delinquent activities and distressed feelings covary in the lives of young people. Dante Cicchetti and Sheree L. Toth *(Internalizing and*

Externalizing Expressions of Dysfunction), along with others (Xiaojia Ge, Karin M. Best, Rand D. Conger, and Ronald L. Simons, "Parenting Behaviors and the Occurrence and Co-occurrence of Adolescent Depressive Symptoms and Conduct Problems"), report a correlation between externalizing and internalizing symptoms.

7. Elliott and associates, in *Multiple Problem Youth,* constructed the delinquency and substance use scales for use in a national study of adolescents. Their average alpha coefficients are .86 and .78 in the Iowa Youth and Families Project. Aboveaverage values on each scale were scored 1, and other values 0. The three-item measure of aggression toward mother has an average alpha coefficient of .72. The depression, hostility, and anxiety subscales come from the SCL-90 inventory (Leonard R. Derogatis, *SCL-90-R: Administration, Scoring, and Procedures Manual-II for the R[evised] Version and Other Instruments of the Psychopathology Rating Scale Series).* The problem behavior index thus has scores that range from 0 to 4.

8. Conger and Simons, "Life-Course Contingencies."

9. Gottfredson and Hirschi, *General Theory of Crime.*

10. The rise in emotional problems across early adolescence is documented by Xiaojia Ge, Frederick O. Lorenz, Rand D. Conger, Glen H. Elder Jr., and Ronald L. Simons ("Trajectories of Stressful Life Events and Depressive Symptoms during Adolescence"), and by Terrie E. Moffitt ("Adolescence-Limited and Life-Course-Persistent Antisocial Behavior"), who refers to this surge in deviance as "adolescence-limited," in contrast to the persistence of early onset deviance. See also Laura Scaramella, Rand D. Conger, and Ronald L. Simons, "Parental Protective Influences and Gender-Specific Increases in Adolescent Developmental Problems," on these developmental patterns.

11. David Magnusson and Håkan Stattin ("Person-Context Interaction Theories") refer to this form of analysis as person-centered, in contrast to variable-centered. In their view, person-centered analysis is more consistent with the holistic and systemic nature of human development. This perspective represents a central theme of the new developmental science (see Robert B. Cairns, Glen H. Elder Jr., and E. Jane Costello, eds., *Developmental Science).*

12. Lee N. Robins and Michael Rutter *(Straight and Devious Pathways from Childhood to Adulthood)* assembled reports from a variety of longitudinal studies that document continuities in antisocial behavior up to the middle years of adulthood (see also Conger and Simons, "Life-Course Contingencies," and Moffitt, "Adolescent-Limited and Life-Course-Persistent Antisocial Behavior"). Robins and Rutter also report evidence of turnarounds in behavior. Most problem children do not become problem adults.

13. Robert K. Merton, "The Matthew Effect in Science, pt. 2, Cumulative Advantage and the Symbolism of Intellectual Property."

14. M. Brewster Smith, "Competence and Socialization"; see p. 277.

15. Denise Bystryn Kandel, "Homophily, Selection, and Socialization in Adolescent Friendship Pairs."

16. Gordon T. Harold and Rand D. Conger, "Marital Conflict and Adolescent Distress."

17. Smith, "Competence and Socialization."

18. Valarie King and Glen H. Elder Jr., "Perceived Self-Efficacy and Grand-parenting."

19. See chapter 7; see also Conger and Simons, "Life-Course Contingencies."

20. Elder, "The Life Course and Human Development," 952. Magnusson (with Stattin, "Person-Context Interaction Theories") has been the most vigorous proponent of this perspective, though it is a dominant theme in the new developmental science (Robert B. Cairns and Beverley D. Cairns, *Lifelines and Risks;* Cairns, Elder, and Costello, *Developmental Science*).

21. Several steps were followed to determine the final set of clusters. First, a principal components analysis was performed on the clustering variables. Second, four clear outliers were identified and omitted from further consideration through a trimming procedure available in the SAS clustering program. Ward's method was used for the cluster analysis, using principal component scores with a cubic clustering criterion. We used ANOVA to determine mean differences on background, resource, and competence measures for members of different clusters.

22. These clusters closely resemble groups obtained in a cluster analysis of inner-city Philadelphia youth, ages 11–14 (Furstenberg et al., *Managing to Make It*). Supported by the MacArthur Foundation Research Network on Successful Adolescent Development among Youth in High-Risk Settings (Jessor, "Successful Adolescent Development among Youth in High-Risk Settings"), this project defined adolescent competence in terms of both prosocial behavior and the avoidance of antisocial behavior. Four clusters emerged from the analysis: all-around competence, social competence, at-risk youth, and delinquent youth.

23. Bandura, *Self-Efficacy.*

24. See Howard S. Becker, "Notes on the Concept of Commitment."

25. Jessor, "Successful Adolescent Development."

26. Furstenberg et al., *Managing to Make It.*

Part Three

1. Jim Braun with Pam Braun, an Iowa farmer and his family in the north central region. In *Pigs, Profits, and Rural Communities,* edited by Kendall M. Thu and E. Paul Durrenberger (Albany: State University of New York Press, 1998), 39, 50–51.

Chapter Ten

The chapter epigraph is from Kerry Rice, manager of the grain elevator at Buxton, North Dakota, quoted in Pam Belluck, "A New Kind of Farm Crisis Pummels the Northern Plains," 17.

1. Across the years of this study, families that continued in farming are not doing as well today as they were in 1988. This decline may not apply to other states, as Sonya Salamon makes clear (personal communication, November 1998). A contributing factor in Iowa is reduced farm exports, stemming from

the worldwide economic crisis. In the midst of a record year for corn in the state of Iowa, the price of corn had dropped to a twelve-year low by the end of August 1998 to nearly $1.50 per bushel (John McCormick, "Corn Price Takes a Plunge"). Export demand for agricultural equipment has also declined sharply in 1998. In addition to these adverse economic trends, estimates suggest that the 1996 Freedom to Farm Act will reduce federal subsidies for an average Iowa farm from $42,672 in 1996 to $14,277 in 1998 (see George Antham, "Here's How New Ag Law Affects Iowa Farm Income"). The adverse effect of this reduction is due in large part to the poor market for farm commodities. Reports also show a decline in the value of farm land.

2. Hugh Sidey, "Introduction: Iowa's Language," 16.

3. White House Conferences on Children and Youth were typically held at the beginning of each decade during the first seventy years of this century. Key publications include the following: Mid-Century White House Conference on Children and Youth (1950: Washington, DC), *Children and Youth at the Midcentury.* White House Conference on Child Health and Protection (1930: Washington, DC), *White House Conference, 1930;* White House Conference on Children (1970: Washington, DC), *World of Children;* White House Conference on Children and Youth (1960: Washington, DC), *Conference Proceedings, March 27–April 2, 1960;* White House Conference on Children in a Democracy (1939–1940: Washington, DC), *Final Report, January 18–20, 1940;* White House Conference on Families (1980, a Research Project), *The 1980 White House Conference on Families, a Research Project;* The educational disadvantages of rural populations are reported by Glen H. Elder Jr., "The Achievement Orientations and Career Patterns of Rural Youth"; William H. Sewell, "Community of Residence and College Plans"; and Mark H. Smith, Lionel J. Beaulieu, and Ann Seraphine, "Social Capital, Place of Residence, and College Attendance."

4. See Kirkendall on Henry A. Wallace's advocacy of part-time farming as a way to keep families on the land: "Reflections of a Revolutionary on a Revolution." See also Kirkendall, *Second Thoughts on the Agricultural Revolution.* See also Barlett's analysis of part-time farm families *(American Dreams).*

5. Conger and Elder, *Families in Troubled Times,* 81. Time pressures are prominent in rural farm households, and especially when mothers hold full-time jobs in the community.

6. Ibid., 88. Another one-time farmer observed that it was difficult "to lose something that's been in one's family, for generations, to watch others come in and pick it up and take it over. Things you've worked hard to preserve and carry on, to see that crushed and gone."

7. Conger and Elder, *Families in Troubled Times,* chapter 9; and Rand D. Conger, Xiaojia Ge, Glen H. Elder Jr., Frederick O. Lorenz, and Ronald L. Simons., "Economic Stress, Coercive Family Process, and Developmental Problems of Adolescents."

8. Bruce Bair, *Good Land,* 36.

9. Belluck, "A New Kind of Farm Crisis Pummels the Northern Plains," 17.

10. Ibid., 1

11. Jonathan Raban, *Bad Land,* 8.

12. Wilson, William J., *The Truly Disadvantaged.*

13. Methamphetamine use has increased in rural areas of Iowa, especially among the disadvantaged ("Meth Isn't Equal Opportunity," *Des Moines Register,* 26 December 1998, 1).

14. Elder, *Children of the Great Depression.*

15. Elder, King, and Conger, "Attachment to Place."

16. Barlett, *American Dreams.*

17. Glenda Riley and Richard S. Kirkendall, "Henry A. Wallace and the Mystique of the Farm Male, 1921–1933."

18. Barlett, *American Dreams;* Salamon, *Prairie Patrimony.*

19. See the four core principles of life-course theory in Glen H. Elder Jr., "The Life Course as Developmental Theory." See also chapter 11, "Beyond *Children of the Great Depression*" in Elder's *Children of the Great Depression,* Twenty-Fifth Anniversary Edition, Boulder, CO: Westview Press, 1999.

20. Elder, *Children of the Great Depression.*

21. Conger and Elder, *Families in Troubled Times,* 89.

22. See Conger et al., "A Family Process Model."

23. See Conger et al., "Family Economic Stress."

24. See Conger, Rueter, and Elder, "Couple Resilience to Economic Pressure."

25. Michael Rutter, "Resilience in the Face of Adversity."

26. See Glen H. Elder Jr. and Debra Mekos, "The Farm Crisis and Its Persistent Effects on Adolescents."

27. Elder, *Children of the Great Depression,* 1999, 307.

28. Salamon, *Prairie Patrimony.*

29. Susan E. Mayer, *What Money Can't Buy.*

30. Eleanor E. Maccoby and John A. Martin, "Socialization in the Context of the Family."

31. For a portrait of this earlier period, see Harold Christensen, ed., *Handbook of Marriage and the Family.* Studies of the dual careers of families emerged in the 1960s by relating family and work roles over time, and some of this research linked work, family, and leisure histories (see Harold Wilensky, "Orderly Careers and Social Participation").

32. A key figure in this reconceptualization of family life and parenting is Frank Furstenberg at the University of Pennsylvania. Furstenberg directed the Philadelphia Study of inner-city families, now published as Furstenberg et al., *Managing to Make It.*

33. This follow-up is based only on the first year after high school (see Raymond R. Swisher, Glen H. Elder Jr., and Rand D. Conger, "Rural Ecologies and Higher Education"). We have just obtained data from the 1997 follow-up, three years after high school, and we find that the general pattern of results has not changed.

34. See Laura V. Scaramella, Rand D. Conger, Ronald L. Simons, and Les B. Whitbeck, "Predicting Risk for Pregnancy by Late Adolescence." A more

recent follow-up on the antecedents of teenage pregnancies and childbirth has not yet been completed.

35. August de Belmont Hollingshead, *Elmtown's Youth.*

36. Ibid., 108.

37. See Peter Benson, *All Kids Are Our Kids.* He concludes that "literally every program and institution is organized to meet age-specific needs at the expense of the richness of intergenerational community" (11). See also Marc Freedman, *The Kindness of Strangers.*

38. Coleman, "Social Capital in the Creation of Human Capital."

39. Darrel Buschkoetter, "To the Viewer: The Farmer's Wife," a David Sutherland Production, PBS Frontline, p. 1; website: http://www.pbs.org/wgbh/pages/frontline/shows/farmerswife.

40. Salamon, *Prairie Patrimony.*

41. From the States News Service, Ames, Iowa, 1 October 1998.

42. See Alan Booth and Ann C. Crouter, eds., *Men in Families.*

43. Many explanations have been offered for this presumed decline (Robert D. Putnam, "The Strange Disappearance of Civic America"), including the growth of television viewing, and the observation itself has been questioned. In farming communities of the Midwest, networks of engagement and a sense of connectedness undoubtedly owe much to the attachments of families to the land. These attachments strengthen residential permanence and rootedness, a sense of place and stewardship concerning this place. Not surprisingly, the most residentially mobile families in the sample also have the weakest ties to community institutions.

All of this bears upon Alan Ehrenhalt's astute observations (Alan Ehrenhalt, *The Lost City*) concerning a decline of community in Chicago neighborhoods. In *The Lost City*, we encounter a description of remarkably communal neighborhoods as of 1957 and then a very different scene in the hyper-individualistic 1990s, over thirty years later. Ehrenhalt attributes the decline of community to the individualistic dynamics of the marketplace and the growth of unlimited choice. As he put its, "Chicagoans have repealed a bargain over the past 40 years, a bargain in which they accepted a 'whole network of restrictions' for communities that offered a good living, were stable and reasonably safe" (270). Likewise, Iowans in past decades made a bargain in which they established abiding attachments to the land that made possible enduring communities and their networks of relationships. Contemporary forces are unraveling this way of life, from the declining profit margin for commodities to the growth of industrialized farming.

44. See Goldschmidt, *As You Sow.* For more contemporary studies of farm size and industrialized farms, see Linda M. Lobao, Michael D. Schulman, and Louis E. Swanson, "Still Going: Recent Debates on the Goldschmidt Hypothesis"; E. Paul Durrenberger and Kendall M. Thu, "The Expansion of Large-Scale Hog Farming in Iowa," and "The Industrialization of Swine Production in the United States."

45. Goldschmidt, *As You Sow,* 306.

46. See Lobao, *Locality and Inequality.*

47. Goldschmidt, *As You Sow,* 191. The role of farm size and ownership in the civic life of these two communities shows some parallels in Mills and Ulmer's comparison of civic welfare in small business and large corporation communities. They identify greater income inequality and civic vacuum in big business cities. Wives of small businessmen were active in the civic culture, unlike the wives of executives in the big business cities. See C. Wright Mills and Melville J. Ulmer, "Small Business and Civic Welfare."

48. Keating, "The Future of the Farm Family."

49. Thu and Durrenberger, *Pigs, Politics, and Rural Communities.*

50. Alan Booth and Judith F. Dunn, eds., *Family-School Links.*

51. Benson, in *All Kids Are Our Kids,* argues for a "certain amount of redundancy of exposure to developmental assets—support should come from parents, grandparents, teachers, coaches, church" (96).

52. King and Elder, "American Children View Their Grandparents."

53. Barker and Gump, *Big School, Small School.* See also John Modell, "School Organization and the Ironies of Social Research."

54. Based on his national survey of youth and communities, Benson (*All Kids Are Our Kids,* 90–91) concludes with a proposal that describes conditions that are most commonly met in small communities. "Every young person should have several sustained relationships with dozens of adults in neighborhoods, religious institutions, teams, organizations, and schools. These relationships should include adults of all ages, from young adults to senior citizens, who can be 'elders' and 'grandparents' to young people."

55. Wilson, *Truly Disadvantaged.*

56. Bronfenbrenner, *Two Worlds of Childhood.*

57. Freedman, *Kindness of Strangers,* 40.

58. Benson, *All Kids Are Our Kids,* 2.

59. See Furstenberg et al., *Managing to Make It.* A recent retrospective study of high-achieving African-American youth obtained results on the process of achievement that resemble findings from the Philadelphia study on parental academic engagement, nurturance, and especially community connectedness. See Kenneth I. Maton, Freeman A. Hrabowski III, and Geoffrey L. Greif, "Preparing the Way."

60. Wilson, *Truly Disadvantaged.*

61. Sonya Salamon, commentary on the book in manuscript form, September 1997; written review, p. 2. As Salamon pointed out, the lifestyle of family-based businesses more generally (such as small, family-run stores, etc.), may have similar beneficial effects on children who have valued roles to play.

62. Superior educational attainment is not uncommon in the history of Iowa. As Goldin and Katz (forthcoming) show in their historical study, Iowa was one of the leading states on the growth of secondary education in 1910 and 1928 assessments. They document the role of social capital, particularly in small towns, as a primary factor in this growth and in the educational accomplishments of Iowa's young people today (Goldin and Katz, "Human Capital and Social Capital"; see also Braatz and Putnam, "Families, Communities, and Education in America."

Appendix A

1. Glen H. Elder Jr., *Children of the Great Depression: Social Change in Life Experience* (Chicago: University of Chicago Press, 1974). This volume has been reprinted by Westview Press in a special 1999 twenty-fifth anniversary edition with a new foreword and concluding chapter, "Beyond *Children of the Great Depression.*"

SELECTED BIBLIOGRAPHY

This bibliography includes only works cited in the text and notes that bear most directly upon the study, its findings, and their implications. Needless to say, no restricted bibliography can do justice to the full corpus of work on rural America.

Abramson, Paul R., and Ronald Inglehart. *Value Change in Global Perspective.* Ann Arbor: University of Michigan Press, 1995.

Adams, Jane H. *The Transformation of Rural Life: Southern Illinois, 1890–1990.* Studies in Rural Culture. Chapel Hill: University of North Carolina Press, 1994.

Ammerman, Nancy Tatom. *Congregation and Community.* New Brunswick, NJ: Rutgers University Press, 1997.

Anderson, Elijah. *Streetwise: Race, Class, and Change in an Urban Community.* Chicago: University of Chicago Press, 1990.

Antham, George. "Here's How New Ag Law Affects Iowa Farm Income." *Des Moines Register,* 17 August 1998.

Bahr, Howard M., and Bruce A. Chadwick. "Religion and Family in Middletown, USA." *Journal of Marriage and the Family* 47 (1985): 407–14.

Bair, Bruce. *Good Land: My Life as a Farm Boy.* South Royalton, VT: Steerforth Press, 1997.

Bandura, Albert. *Self-Efficacy: The Exercise of Control.* New York: W. H. Freeman, 1997.

Barber, Bonnie L., and Janice M. Lyons. "Family Processes and Adolescent Adjustment in Intact and Remarried Families." *Journal of Youth and Adolescence* 23 (1994): 421–36.

Barker, Roger G., and Paul V. Gump. *Big School, Small School: High School Size and Student Behavior.* Stanford, CA: Stanford University Press, 1964.

Barlett, Peggy F. "Part-Time Farming: Saving the Farm or Saving the Lifestyle?" *Rural Sociology* 51 (1986): 289–313.

———. *American Dreams, Rural Realities: Family Farms in Crisis.* Studies in Rural Culture. Chapel Hill: University of North Carolina Press, 1993.

Becker, Howard S. "Notes on the Concept of Commitment." *American Journal of Sociology* 66 (1961): 32–40.

Belluck, Pam. "A New Kind of Farm Crisis Pummels the Northern Plains." *New York Times,* 19 July 1998: National, 1, 17.

Bennett, John W. "Natural and Social Science: Historical Background." In *Social Sciences, Interdisciplinary Research, and the U.S. Man and the Biosphere Secretariat,* edited by Ervin H. Zube. Washington, DC: U.S. Man and the Biosphere Secretariat, Department of State, 1980.

Bennett, John W., in association with Seena B. Kohl and Geraldine Binion. *Of Time and the Enterprise: North American Family Farm Management in a Context of Resource Marginality: Based on a Decade of Research in the Province of Saskatchewan, Canada.* Minneapolis: University of Minnesota Press, 1982.

Benson, Peter L. *All Kids Are Our Kids: What Communities Must Do to Raise Caring and Responsible Children and Adolescents.* San Francisco: Jossey-Bass, 1997.

Benson, Peter L., Michael J. Donahue, and Joseph A. Erickson. "Adolescence and Religion: A Review of the Literature from 1970 to 1986." *Research in the Social Scientific Study of Religion* 1 (1989): 153–81.

Bogue, Donald J. *The Population of the United States: Historical Trends and Future Projections.* New York: Free Press, 1985.

Booth, Alan, and Ann C. Crouter, eds. *Men in Families: When Do They Get Involved? What Difference Does It Make?* Mahwah, NJ: Erlbaum, 1997.

Booth, Alan, and Judith F. Dunn, eds. *Family-School Links: How Do They Affect Educational Outcomes?* Mahwah, NJ: Erlbaum, 1996.

Braatz, Jay, and Robert D. Putnam. "Families, Communities, and Education in America: Exploring the Evidence." Harvard University Working Paper (July, 1997).

Bronfenbrenner, Urie. *Two Worlds of Childhood: U.S. and U.S.S.R.* New York: Russell Sage, 1970.

———. *The Ecology of Human Development: Experiments by Nature and Design.* Cambridge: Harvard University Press, 1979.

———. "Ecological Systems Theory." In *Six Theories of Child Development: Revised Formulations and Current Issues,* edited by Ross Vasta, 1643–47. Greenwich, CT: JAI Press, 1989.

Bronfenbrenner, Urie, and Stephen J. Ceci. "Nature-Nurture Reconceptualized in Developmental Perspective: A Bioecological Model." *Psychological Reviews* 101 (1994): 568–86.

Bronfenbrenner, Urie, and Pamela M. Morris. "The Ecology of Developmental Processes." In *Handbook of Child Psychology,* edited by William Damon. Vol. 1. *Theoretical Models of Human Development,* edited by Richard M. Lerner, 993–1028. New York: Wiley, 1998.

Brown, B. Bradford. "Peer Groups and Peer Cultures." In *At the Threshold: The Developing Adolescent,* edited by S. Shirley Feldman and Glen R. Elliott, 171–96. Cambridge: Harvard University Press, 1990.

Brownfield, David, and Ann Marie Sorenson. "Religion and Drug Use among

Adolescents: A Social Support Conceptualization and Interpretation." *Deviant Behavior: An Interdisciplinary Journal* 12 (1991): 259–76.

Bryk, Anthony S., and Stephen W. Raudenbush. *Hierarchical Linear Models: Applications and Data Analysis Methods.* Advanced Quantitative Techniques in the Social Sciences, no. 1. Newbury Park, CA: Sage, 1992.

Bryk, Anthony S., Valerie E. Lee, and Peter B. Holland. *Catholic Schools and the Common Good.* Cambridge: Harvard University Press, 1993.

Burton, Linda M., and Vern L. Bengtson. "Black Grandmothers: Issues of Timing and Continuity of Roles." In *Grandparenthood,* edited by Vern L. Bengtson and Joan F. Robertson, 61–77. Beverly Hills, CA: Sage, 1985.

Cairns, Robert B., and Beverley D. Cairns. *Lifelines and Risks: Pathways of Youth in Our Time.* Cambridge: Cambridge University Press, 1994.

Cairns, Robert B., Glen H. Elder Jr., and E. Jane Costello, eds. *Developmental Science.* Cambridge Studies in Social and Emotional Development. New York: Cambridge University Press, 1996.

Carnegie Council on Adolescent Development. Task Force on Youth Development and Community Programs. *A Matter of Time: Risk and Opportunity in the Nonschool Hours.* Washington, DC: Carnegie Council on Adolescent Development, 1992.

Chalfant, H. Paul, and Peter L. Heller. "Rural/Urban versus Regional Differences in Religiosity." *Review of Religious Research* 33 (1991): 76–86.

Chan, Christopher G., and Glen H. Elder Jr. "The Reproduction of Social Capital: An Intergenerational Perspective on Rural Society." Paper presented at the annual meeting of the American Sociological Association, New York. August 1996.

Cherlin, Andrew J., and Frank F. Furstenberg Jr. *The New American Grandparent: A Place in the Family, a Life Apart.* New York: Basic Books, 1986.

Christensen, Harold T., ed. *Handbook of Marriage and the Family.* Chicago: Rand McNally, 1964.

Cicchetti, Dante, and Sheree L. Toth, eds. 1991. *Internalizing and Externalizing Expressions of Dysfunction.* Rochester Symposium on Developmental Psychopathology, vol. 5. Hillsdale, NJ: Erlbaum, 1991.

Clausen, John A., ed. *Socialization and Society.* Boston: Little, Brown, 1968.

Clausen, John A. *American Lives: Looking Back at the Children of the Great Depression.* New York: Free Press, 1993.

Clinton, Hillary Rodham. *It Takes a Village: And Other Lessons Children Teach Us.* New York: Simon & Schuster, 1996.

Coleman, James S. "Social Capital in the Creation of Human Capital." *American Journal of Sociology* 94 (1988): S94–S120.

———. *Foundations of Social Theory.* Cambridge: Harvard University Press, 1990.

———. "The Rational Reconstruction of Society: 1992 Presidential Address." *American Sociological Review* 58 (1993): 1–15.

———. "Social Capital, Human Capital, and Investment in Youth." In *Youth Unemployment and Society,* edited by Anne C. Petersen and Jeylan T. Mortimer, 34–50. New York: Cambridge University Press, 1994.

Coleman, James S., with the assistance of John W. C. Johnstone and Kurt Jonassohn. *The Adolescent Society: The Social Life of the Teenager and Its Impact on Education.* New York: Free Press of Glencoe, 1961.

Coleman, James S., and Thomas Hoffer. *Public and Private High Schools: The Impact of Communities.* New York: Basic Books, 1987.

Colten, Mary Ellen, and Susan Gore, eds. *Adolescent Stress: Causes and Consequences.* Social Institutions and Social Change. New York: Aldine de Gruyter, 1991.

Comer, James P., and Norris M. Haynes. "Parent Involvement in Schools: An Ecological Approach." *The Elementary School Journal* 91 (1991): 271–77.

Conger, Katherine Jewsbury, Rand D. Conger, and Laura V. Scaramella. "Parents, Siblings, Psychological Control, and Adolescent Adjustment." *Journal of Adolescent Research,* 12 (1997): 113–38.

Conger, Rand D., and Glen H. Elder Jr. in collaboration with Frederick O. Lorenz, Ronald L. Simons, and Les B. Whitbeck. *Families in Troubled Times: Adapting to Change in Rural America.* Social Institutions and Social Change. Hawthorne, NY: Aldine de Gruyter, 1994.

Conger, Rand D. and Martha A. Rueter. "Siblings, Parents, and Peers: a Longitudinal Study of Social Influences in Adolescent Risk for Alcohol Use and Abuse." In *Sibling Relationships: Their Causes and Consequences,* edited by Gene H. Brody, 1–30. Vol. 10 of *Advances in Applied Developmental Psychology.* Norwood, NJ: Ablex Publishing, 1996.

Conger, Rand D., and Ronald L. Simons. "Life-Course Contingencies in the Development of Adolescent Antisocial Behavior: A Matching Law Approach." In *Developmental Theories of Crime and Delinquency,* edited by Terence P. Thornberry, 55–99. Vol. 7 of *Advances in Criminological Theory.* New Brunswick, NJ: Transaction Publishers, 1997.

Conger, Rand D., Martha A. Rueter, and Glen H. Elder Jr., "Couple Resilience to Economic Pressure." *Journal of Personality and Social Psychology* 76 (1999): 54–71.

Conger, Rand D., Katherine J. Conger, Glen H. Elder Jr., Frederick O. Lorenz, Ronald L. Simons, and Les B. Whitbeck. "A Family Process Model of Economic Hardship and Adjustment of Early Adolescent Boys." *Child Development* 63 (1992): 526–41.

———. "Family Economic Stress and Adjustment of Early Adolescent Girls." *Developmental Psychology* 29 (1993): 206–19.

Conger, Rand D., Glen H. Elder Jr., Frederick O. Lorenz, Katherine J. Conger, Ronald L. Simons, Les B. Whitbeck, Shirley Huck, and Janet N. Melby. "Linking Economic Hardship to Marital Quality and Instability." *Journal of Marriage and the Family* 52 (1990): 643–56.

Conger, Rand D., Xiaojia Ge, Glen H. Elder Jr., Frederick O. Lorenz, and Ronald L. Simons, "Economic Stress, Coercive Family Process, and Developmental Problems of Adolescents." *Child Development* 65 (1994): 541–561.

Costa, Frances M., Richard Jessor, J. Dennis Fortenberry, and John E. Donovan. "Psychosocial Conventionality: Health Orientation, and Contraceptive Use in Adolescence." *Journal of Adolescent Health* 18 (1996): 404–16.

Crockenberg, Susan B. "Infant Irritability, Mother Responsiveness, and Social Support Influences on the Security of Infant-Mother Attachment." *Child Development* 52 (1981): 857–65.

Csikszentmihalyi, Mihaly, and Douglas A. Kleiber. "Leisure and Self-Actualization." In *Benefits of Leisure,* edited by B. L. Driver, Perry J. Brown, and George L. Peterson, 91–102. State College, PA: Venture, 1991.

Darnell, Alfred, and Darren Edward Sherkat. "The Impact of Protestant Fundamentalism on Educational Attainment." *American Sociological Review* 62 (1997): 306–15.

Derogatis, Leonard R. *SCL-90-R: Administration, Scoring, and Procedures Manual-II for the R[evised] Version and Other Instruments of the Psychopathology Rating Scale Series.* 2d ed. Towson, MD: Clinic Psychometric Research, 1983.

Donahue, Michael J., and Peter L. Benson. "Religion and the Well-Being of Adolescents." *Journal of Social Issues* 51 (1995): 145–60.

Donovan, John E., Richard Jessor, and Frances M. Costa. "Adolescent Health Behavior and Conventionality-Unconventionality: An Extension of Problem-Behavior Theory." *Health Psychology* 10 (1991): 52–61.

Durrenberger, E. Paul, and Kendall M. Thu. "The Expansion of Large-Scale Hog Farming in Iowa: The Applicability of Goldschmidt's Findings Fifty Years Later." *Human Organization* 55 (1996): 409–415.

———. "The Industrialization of Swine Production in the United States: An Overview." *Culture and Agriculture* 18 (1996): 19–22.

Eccles, Jacquelynne S., and Bonnie Barber. "Adolescents' Activity Involvement: Predictors and Longitudinal Consequence." Symposium paper presented at the biennial meeting of the Society for Research in Child Development, Indianapolis, April 1995.

Ehrenhalt, Alan. *The Lost City: The Forgotten Virtues of Community in America.* New York: Basic Books, 1995.

Eisenstadt, Shmuel Noah. *From Generation to Generation: Age Groups and Social Structure.* Glencoe, IL: Free Press, 1956.

Eitzen, D. Stanley. "Athletics in the Status System of Male Adolescents: A Replication of Coleman's *The Adolescent Society.*" *Adolescence* 10 (1975): 267–76.

Elder, Glen H. Jr. "The Achievement Orientations and Career Patterns of Rural Youth." *Sociology of Education* 37 (1963): 30–58.

———. *Children of the Great Depression: Social Change in Life Experience.* Chicago: University of Chicago Press, 1974.

———. *Children of the Great Depression: Social Change in Life Experience.* 25th Anniversary Edition, enlarged. Boulder, CO: Westview Press, 1999.

———. "Adolescence in Historical Perspective." In *Handbook of Adolescent Psychology,* edited by Joseph Adelson, 3–46. Wiley Series on Personality Processes. New York: Wiley, 1980.

———. "Time, Human Agency, and Social Change: Perspectives on the Life Course." *Social Psychology Quarterly* 57 (1994): 4–15.

———. "The Life Course Paradigm: Social Change and Individual Development." In *Examining Lives in Context: Perspectives on the Ecology of Human*

Development, edited by Phyllis Moen, Glen H. Elder Jr., and Kurt Lüscher, with the assistance of Heather E. Quick, 101–39. APA Science Volumes. Washington, DC: American Psychological Association, 1995.

———. "The Life Course and Human Development." In *Handbook of Child Psychology,* edited by William Damon. Vol. 1. *Theoretical Models of Human Development,* edited by Richard M. Lerner, 939–91. New York: Wiley, 1998.

———. "The Life Course as Developmental Theory." *Child Development* 69 (1998): 1–12.

———, ed. *Linking Social Structure and Personality.* Sage Contemporary Social Science Issues, no. 12. Beverly Hills, CA: Sage, 1973.

Elder, Glen H., Jr., and Artur Meier. " 'Troubled Times?': Bildung und Status- passagen von Landjugendlichen. Ein Interkultureller und Historicher Ver- gleich." *Berliner Journal Für Soziologie* 7 (1997): 289–305.

Elder, Glen H. Jr., and Debra Mekos. "The Farm Crisis and Its Persistent Effects on Adolescents." Paper presented at the American Psychological Association, Toronto, Canada, August 1993.

Elder, Glen H. Jr., Avshalom Caspi, and Linda M. Burton. "Adolescent Transi- tions in Developmental Perspective: Sociological and Historical Insights." In *Development During the Transition to Adolescence,* edited by Megan R. Gun- nar and W. Andrew Collins, 151–79. Hillsdale, NJ: Erlbaum. 1988.

Elder, Glen H. Jr., Rand D. Conger, E. Michael Foster, and Monika Ardelt. "Families under Economic Pressure." *Journal of Family Issues* 31 (1992): 5–37.

Elder, Glen H. Jr., Jacquelynne S. Eccles, Monika Ardelt, and Sarah Lord. "Inner-City Parents under Economic Pressure: Perspectives on the Strategies of Parenting." *Journal of Marriage and the Family* 57 (1995): 771–84.

Elder, Glen H. Jr., E. Michael Foster, and Monika Ardelt. "Children in the Household Economy." In *Families in Troubled Times: Adapting to Change in Rural America,* edited by Rand D. Conger and Glen H. Elder Jr., 127–46. Hawthorne, NY: Aldine de Gruyter, 1994.

Elder, Glen H. Jr., Valarie King, and Rand D. Conger. "Attachment to Place and Migration Prospects: A Developmental Perspective." *Journal of Research on Adolescence* 6 (1996): 397–425.

———. "Intergenerational Continuity and Change in Rural Lives: Historical and Developmental Insights." *International Journal of Behavioral Development* 19 (1996): 433–55.

Elder, Glen H. Jr., Elizabeth B. Robertson, and Rand D. Conger. "Fathers and Sons in Rural America: Occupational Choice and Intergenerational Ties across the Life Course." In *Aging and Generational Relations over the Life Course: A Historical and Cross-Cultural Perspective,* edited by Tamara K. Har- even, 294–325. Berlin: Walter de Gruyter, 1996.

Elder, Glen H. Jr., Elizabeth B. Robertson, and E. Michael Foster. "Survival, Loss, and Adaptation: A Perspective on Farm Families." In *Families in Trou- bled Times: Adapting to Change in Rural America,* edited by Rand D. Conger and Glen H. Elder Jr., 105–26. Hawthorne, NY: Aldine de Gruyter, 1994.

Elliott, Delbert S., David Huizinga, and Scott Menard. *Multiple Problem Youth:*

Delinquency, Substance Use, and Mental Health Problems. Research in Crimi-
nology. New York: Springer-Verlag, 1989.

Epstein, Joyce. "Perspectives and Previews on Research and Policy for School,
Family, and Community Partnerships." In *Family-School Links: How Do
They Affect Educational Outcomes?* edited by Alan Booth and Judith F. Dunn,
209–46. Mahwah, NJ: Erlbaum, 1996.

Farber, Ellen A., and Byron Egeland. "Invulnerability among Abused and Neglected Children." In *The Invulnerable Child,* edited by E. James Anthony
and Bertram J. Cohler, 253–88. The Guilford Psychiatry Series. New York:
Guilford Press, 1987.

Fink, Deborah. *Open Country, Iowa: Rural Women, Tradition, and Change.*
SUNY Series in the Anthropology of Work. Albany, NY: State University of
New York Press, 1986.

———. *Agrarian Women: Wives and Mothers in Rural Nebraska, 1880–1940.*
Studies in Rural Culture. Chapel Hill: University of North Carolina Press,
1992.

Fischer, Claude S. "The Subcultural Theory of Urbanism: A Twentieth-Year
Assessment." *American Journal of Sociology* 101 (1995): 543–77.

———. *To Dwell among Friends: Personal Networks in Town and City.* Chicago:
University of Chicago Press, 1982.

Fite, Gilbert Courtland. *American Farmers: The New Minority.* Minorities in
Modern America. Bloomington: Indiana University Press, 1981.

Fletcher, Anne C., Glen H. Elder Jr., and Debra Mekos. "Parental Influences
on Adolescent Involvement in Community Activities." *Journal of Research
on Adolescence.* In press.

Freedman, Marc. *The Kindness of Strangers: Adult Mentors, Urban Youth, and
the New Voluntarism.* San Francisco: Jossey-Bass, 1993.

Friedberger, Mark. *Farm Families and Change in Twentieth-Century America.*
Lexington: University Press of Kentucky, 1988.

———. *Shake-Out: Iowa Farm Families in the 1980s.* Lexington: University Press
of Kentucky, 1989.

Fuguitt, Glenn V., David L. Brown, and Calvin L. Beale, assisted by Max J.
Pfeffer, Robert M. Jenkins, and Daniel T. Lichter. *Rural and Small-Town
America.* The Population of the United States in the 1980s. New York: Russell
Sage Foundation, 1989.

Fukuyama, Francis. *Trust: The Social Virtues and the Creation of Prosperity.* New
York: Free Press, 1995.

Furstenberg, Frank F. Jr., and Mary Elizabeth Hughes. "Social Capital and Successful Development among At-Risk Youth." *Journal of Marriage and the
Family* 57 (1995): 580–92.

Furstenberg, Frank F. Jr., Thomas D. Cook, Jacquelynne Eccles, Glen H. Elder
Jr., and Arnold Sameroff. *Managing to Make It: Urban Families and Adolescent Success.* Chicago: University of Chicago Press, 1999.

Garkovich, Lorraine, Janet L. Bokemeier, and Barbara Foote. 1995. *Harvest of
Hope: Family Farming/Farming Families.* Lexington: University Press of Kentucky, 1995.

Garmezy, Norman. "Resiliency and Vulnerability to Adverse Developmental Outcomes Associated with Poverty." *American Behavioral Scientist* 34 (1991): 416–30.

Gasson, Ruth, Graham Crow, Andrew Errington, John Hutson, Terry Marsden, and D. Michael Winter. "The Farm as a Family Business: A Review." *Journal of Agricultural Economics* 39 (1988): 1–41.

Ge, Xiaojia, Karin M. Best, Rand D. Conger, and Ronald L. Simons. "Parenting Behaviors and the Occurrence and Co-occurrence of Adolescent Depressive Symptoms and Conduct Problems." *Developmental Psychology* 32 [1996]: 717–31.

Ge, Xiaojia, Frederick O. Lorenz, Rand D. Conger, Glen H. Elder Jr., and Ronald L. Simons. "Trajectories of Stressful Life Events and Depressive Symptoms during Adolescence." *Developmental Psychology* 30 [1994]: 467–83.

Giarrusso, Roseann, Michael Stallings, and Vern L. Bengtson. "The 'International Stake' Hypothesis Revisited: Parent-Child Differences in Perceptions of Relationships Twenty Years Later." In *Adult Intergenerational Relations: Effects of Societal Change,* edited by Vern L. Bengtson, F. Warner Schaie, and Linda M. Burton, 227–96. New York: Springer, 1995.

Goffman, Erving. *The Presentation of Self in Everyday Life.* Garden City, NY: Doubleday, 1959.

Goldin, Claudia, and Lawrence F. Katz. "Human Capital and Social Capital: The Rise of Secondary Schooling in America." *Journal of Interdisciplinary History* 29 (1999): 683–86.

Goldschmidt, Walter Rochs. *As You Sow: Three Studies in the Social Consequences of Agribusiness.* Montclair, NJ: Allanheld, Osmun, 1978. Originally published in 1947 by Harcourt Brace.

Gottfredson, Michael R., and Travis Hirschi. *A General Theory of Crime.* Stanford, CA: Stanford University Press, 1990.

Granovetter, Mark S. "Strength of Weak Ties." *American Journal of Sociology* 78 (1973): 1360–80.

Greenberger, Ellen, and Laurence Steinberg. *When Teenagers Work: The Psychological and Social Costs of Adolescent Employment.* New York: Basic Books, 1986.

Hagan, John, Ross MacMillan, and Blair Wheaton. "New Kid in Town: Social Capital and the Life-Course Effects of Family Migration on Children." *American Sociological Review* 61 (1996): 368–85.

Hagestad, Gunhild O. "Continuity and Connectedness." In *Grandparenthood,* edited by Vern L. Bengtson and Joan F. Robertson, 31–48. Sage Focus Editions, vol. 74. Beverly Hills, CA: Sage, 1985.

Hamilton, Stephen F., and L. Mickey Frenzel. "The Impact of Volunteer Experience on Adolescent Social Development." *Journal of Adolescent Research* 3 (1988): 65–80.

Haney, Wava G., and Jane B. Knowles, eds. *Women and Farming: Changing Roles and Changing Structures.* Rural Studies Series. Boulder, CO: Westview Press, 1988.

Hansen, Donald A., and Reuben Hill. "Families under Stress." In *Handbook of Marriage and the Family,* edited by Harold T. Christensen, 782–819. Rand McNally Sociology Series. Chicago: Rand McNally, 1964.

Harold, Gordon T., and Rand D. Conger. "Marital Conflict and Adolescent Distress: The Role of Adolescent Awareness." *Child Development* 68 (1997): 333–50.

Heckhausen, Jutta. *Developmental Regulation in Adulthood: Age-Normative and Sociostructural Constraints as Adaptive Challenges.* New York: Cambridge University Press, 1998

Hernandez, Donald J. *America's Children: Resources from Family, Government, and the Economy.* The Population of the United States in the 1980s. New York: Russell Sage Foundation, 1993.

Hetherington, E. Mavis. "Coping with Family Transitions: Winners, Losers, and Survivors." *Child Development* 60 (1989): 1–14.

Hetherington, E. Mavis, Margaret Stanley-Hagan, and Edward R. Anderson. "Marital Transitions: A Child's Perspective." *American Psychologist* 44 (1989): 303–12.

Hochschild, Arlie Russell. "Emotion Work, Feeling Rules, and Social Structure." *American Journal of Sociology* 85 (1979): 551–75.

———. *The Time Bind: When Work Becomes Home and Home Becomes Work.* New York: Metropolitan Books, 1997.

Hofstadter, Richard. *The Age of Reform: From Bryan to F. D. R.* New York: Knopf, 1955.

Hollingshead, August De Belmont. *Elmtown's Youth, the Impact of Social Classes on Adolescents.* New York: Wiley. 1949.

Hutson, John. "Fathers and Sons: Family Farms, Family Businesses, and the Farming Industry." *Sociology* 21 (1987): 215–29.

Idler, Ellen L. "Religious Involvement and the Health of the Elderly: Some Hypotheses and an Initial Test." *Social Forces* 66 (1987): 226–38.

Inglehart, Ronald. *The Silent Revolution: Changing Values and Political Styles among Western Publics.* Princeton, NJ: Princeton University Press, 1977.

———. *Culture Shift in Advanced Industrial Society.* Princeton, NJ: Princeton University Press, 1990.

Jessor, Richard. "Successful Adolescent Development among Youth in High-Risk Settings." *American Psychologist* 48 (1993): 117–26.

Jessor, Richard, and Shirley L. Jessor. *Problem Behavior and Psychosocial Development: A Longitudinal Study of Youth.* New York: Academic Press, 1977.

Jessor, Richard, John Edward Donovan, and Frances Marie Costa. *Beyond Adolescence: Problem Behavior and Young Adult Development.* Cambridge: Cambridge University Press, 1991.

Johnson, Christine A., Les B. Whitbeck, and Dan Hoyt. "An Investigation of the Influence of Grandchild Personality on the Quality of the Grandparent-Grandchild Relationship." Ames, IA: Family Research Center, 1996.

Kandel, Denise Bystryn. "Homophily, Selection, and Socialization in Adolescent Friendship Pairs." *American Journal of Sociology* 84 (1978): 427–436.

Keating, Norah C. "The Future of the Farm Family in Prairie Agricultural Communities." In *Alternative Futures for Prairie Agricultural Communities,* edited by Jerome Martin, 53–84. Edmonton, Alberta, Canada: Faculty of Extension, University of Alberta, 1991.

King, Valarie, and Glen H. Elder Jr. "American Children View Their Grandparents: Linked Lives across Three Rural Generations." *Journal of Marriage and the Family* 57 (1995): 165–78.

———. "Perceived Self-Efficacy and Grandparenting." *Journal of Gerontology: Social Sciences* 53B (1998): S249–57.

King, Valarie, Glen H. Elder Jr., and Les B. Whitbeck. "Religious Involvement among Rural Youth: An Ecological and Life Course Perspective." *Journal of Research on Adolescence* 7 (1997): 431–456.

Kinney, David A. "From Nerds to Normals: The Recovery of Identity among Adolescents from Middle School to High School." *Sociology of Education* 66 (1993): 21–40.

Kirkendall, Richard Stewart. "Reflections of a Revolutionary on a Revolution." *Journal of the West* 31 (no. 4, 1992): 8–14.

———. *Second Thoughts on the Agricultural Revolution: Henry A. Wallace in His Last Years.* Henry A. Wallace Annual Lecture, Agricultural Science, Technology, and Public Policy. Greenbelt, MD: Henry A. Wallace Institute for Alternative Agriculture, 1997.

Kornhaber, Arthur, and Kenneth L. Woodward. *Grandparents, Grandchildren: The Vital Connection.* Garden City, NY: Anchor Press/Doubleday, 1981.

Larson, Reed. "Youth Organizations, Hobbies, and Sports as Developmental Contexts." In *Adolescence in Context: The Interplay of Family, School, Peers, and Work in Adjustment,* edited by Rainer K. Silbereisen and Eberhard Todt, 46–65. New York: Springer-Verlag, 1994.

Lasley, Paul. "Rural Economic and Social Trends." In *Families in Troubled Times: Adapting to Change in Rural America,* edited by Rand D. Conger and Glen H. Elder Jr., 57–78. Hawthorne, NY: Aldine de Gruyter, 1994.

Lasley, Paul, F. Larry Leistritz, Linda M. Lobao, and Katherine Meyer. *Beyond the Amber Waves of Grain: An Examination of Social and Economic Restructuring in the Heartland.* Rural Studies Series. Boulder, CO: Westview Press, 1995.

Lichter, Daniel T., Gail M. Johnston, and Diane K. McLaughlin. "Changing Linkages between Work and Poverty in Rural America." *Rural Sociology* 59 (1994): 395–415.

Linder, Staffan Burenstam. *The Harried Leisure Class.* New York: Columbia University Press, 1970.

Lipset, Seymour Martin, and Reinhard Bendix. *Social Mobility in Industrial Society.* Berkeley: University of California Press, 1959.

Lobao, Linda M. *Locality and Inequality: Farm and Industry Structure and Socioeconomic Conditions.* SUNY Series on the New Inequalities. Albany: State University of New York Press, 1990.

Lobao, Linda M., and Katherine Meyer. "Consumption Patterns, Hardship, and Stress among Farm Households." In *Household Strategies,* edited by Daniel

C. Clay and Harry K. Schwarzweller, 191–209. Research in Rural Sociology and Development, vol. 5. Greenwich, CT: JAI Press, 1991.

Lobao, Linda M., Michael D. Schulman, and Louis E. Swanson. "Still Going: Recent Debates on the Goldschmidt Hypothesis." *Rural Sociology* 58 (1993): 277–288.

Lorenz, Frederick O., and Janet N. Melby. "Analyzing Family Stress and Adaptation: Methods of Study." In *Families in Troubled Times: Adapting to Change in Rural America,* edited by Rand D. Conger and Glen H. Elder Jr., 21–54. Hawthorne, NY: Aldine de Gruyter, 1994.

Lorenz, Frederick O., Glen H. Elder, Jr., K. A. S. Wickrama, Wan-Ning Bao, and Rand D. Conger. "After Farming: Trajectories of Emotional Health of Farm, Non-farm, and Displaced Farm Couples." In press.

Luthar, Suniya S., and Edward Zigler. "Vulnerability and Competence: A Review of Research on Resilience in Childhood." *American Journal of Orthopsychiatry* 61 (1991): 6–22.

Luthar, Suniya S., Carol H. Doernberger, and Edward Zigler. "Resilience Is Not a Unidimensional Construct: Insights from a Prospective Study of Inner-City Adolescents." *Development and Psychopathology* 5 (1993): 703–17.

Lyson, Thomas A. "Pathways into Production Agriculture: The Structuring of Farm Recruitment in the United States." In *Focus on Agriculture,* edited by Harry K. Schwarzweller, 79–103. Research in Rural Sociology and Development, vol. 1. Greenwich, CT: JAI Press, 1984.

Maccoby, Eleanor E., and John A. Martin. "Socialization in the Context of the Family: Parent-Child Interaction." In *Handbook of Child Psychology,* edited by Paul H. Mussen. Vol. 4. *Socialization, Personality, and Social Development,* edited by E. Mavis Hetherington, 1–101. 4th ed. New York: Wiley, 1983.

MacLeod, Jay. *Ain't No Makin' It: Leveled Aspirations in a Low-Income Neighborhood.* Boulder, CO: Westview Press, 1987.

Magnusson, David, and Håkan Stattin."Person-Context Interaction Theories." In *Handbook of Child Psychology,* edited by William Damon. Vol. 1. *Theoretical Modes of Human Development,* edited by Richard M. Lerner, 685–759. 5th ed. New York: Wiley, 1998.

Mahoney, Joseph L. "Community Engagement and Adolescent Adjustment: Patterns of Parenting and Prevention." Paper presented at 15th biennial meeting of the International Society for the Study of Behavioral Development, Berne, Switzerland, 4 July 1998.

Mahoney, Joseph L., and Robert B. Cairns. "Do Extracurricular Activities Protect against Early School Dropout?" *Developmental Psychology* 33 (1997): 241–53.

Margolis, John. "The Reopening of the Frontier." *New York Times Magazine,* 15 October 1995, 51–57.

Marsiske, Michael, Frieder R. Lang, Paul B. Baltes, and Margret M. Baltes. "Selective Optimization with Compensation: Life-Span Perspectives on Successful Human Development." In *Compensating for Psychological Deficits and Declines: Managing Losses and Promoting Gains,* edited by Roger A. Dixon and Lars Bäckman, 35–79. Mahwah, NJ: Erlbaum, 1995.

Martin, Jerome. *Alternative Futures for Prairie Agricultural Communities.* Edmonton, Alberta, Canada: Faculty of Extension, University of Alberta, 1991.

Masten, Ann S., and Norman Garmezy. "Risk, Vulnerability, and Protective Factors in Developmental Psychopathology." In *Advances in Clinical Child Psychology,* vol. 8, edited by Benjamin B. Lahey and Alan E. Kazdin, 1–52. New York: Plenum Press, 1985.

Masten, Ann S., Karin M. Best, and Norman Garmezy. "Resilience and Development: Contributions from the Study of Children Who Overcome Adversity." *Development and Psychopathology* 2 (1990): 425–44.

Maton, Kenneth I., Freeman A. Hrabowski III, and Geoffrey L. Greif. "Preparing the Way: A Qualitative Study of High-Achieving African American Males and the Role of the Family." *American Journal of Community Psychology* 26 (1998): 639–668.

Mayer, Susan E. *What Money Can't Buy: Family Income and Children's Life Changes.* Cambridge: Harvard University Press, 1997.

McCormick, John. "Corn Price Takes a Plunge." *Des Moines Register,* 29 August 1998.

McHale, Susan M., Todd W. Bartko, Ann C. Crouter, and Maureen Perry-Jenkins. "Children's Housework and Psychosocial Functioning: The Mediating Effects of Parents' Sex-Role Behaviors and Attitudes." *Child Development* 61 (1990): 1413–26.

McIntosh, William Alex, Starla D. Fitch, J. Branton Wilson, and Kenneth L. Nyberg. "The Effect of Mainstream Religious Social Controls on Adolescent Drug Use in Rural Areas." *Review of Religious Research* 23 (1981): 54–75.

McLaughlin, Milbrey W. "Embedded Identities: Enabling Balance in Urban Contexts." In *Identity and Inner-City Youth: Beyond Ethnicity and Gender,* edited by Shirley Brice Heath and Milbrey W. Mclaughlin, 36–68. New York: Teachers College Press, 1993.

McLaughlin, Milbrey W., Merita A. Irby, and Juliet Langman. *Urban Sanctuaries: Neighborhood Organizations in the Lives and Futures of Inner-city Youth.* San Francisco: Jossey-Bass, 1994.

Mead, Margaret. "Grandparents as Educators." In *The Family as Educator,* edited by Hope Jenson Leichter, 66–75. New York: Teachers College Press, 1974.

Meier, Artur. "Report of the Mecklenburg Study." Berlin: Humboldt University, 1995.

Melby, Janet N., and Rand D. Conger. "Parental Behaviors and Adolescent Academic Performance: A Longitudinal Analysis." *Journal of Research on Adolescence* 6 (1996): 113–37.

Merton, Robert K. 1988. "The Matthew Effect in Science, pt. 2: Cumulative Advantage and the Symbolism of Intellectual Property." *Isis* 79 (1988): 606–23.

Meyer, Katherine, and Linda Lobao. "Farm Couples and Crisis Politics: The Importance of Household, Spouse, and Gender in Responding to Economic Decline." *Journal of Marriage and the Family* 59 (1997): 204–18.

Mid-Century White House Conference on Children and Youth (1950: Washington, DC). *Children and Youth at the Midcentury: A Chart Book.* Raleigh, NC: Health Publications Institute, 1951.

Mills, C. Wright, and Melville J. Ulmer. "Small Business and Civic Welfare." In *The Structure of Community Power,* edited by Michael Aiken and Paul E. Mott, 124–155. New York: Random House, 1970. Originally published in 1946.

Modell, John. "School Organization and the Ironies of Social Research: Rethinking a Classic Study of Children in Their Schools." Mimeo report, Brown University, November 1998.

Moffitt, Terrie E. "Adolescence-Limited and Life-Course-Persistent Antisocial Behavior: A Developmental Taxonomy." *Psychological Review* 100 (1993): 674–701.

Murdock, Stephen H., and F. Larry Leistritz, eds. *The Farm Financial Crisis: Socioeconomic Dimensions and Implications for Producers and Rural Areas.* Westview Special Studies in Agricultural Science and Policy. Boulder, CO: Westview Press, 1988.

Myers, Barbara J., Patricia A. Jarvis, and Gary L. Creasey. "Infants' Behavior with Their Mothers and Grandmothers." *Infant Behavior and Development* 10 (1987): 245–59.

Myers, Scott M. "An Interactive Model of Religiosity Inheritance: The Importance of Family Context." *American Sociological Review* 61 (1996): 858–66.

Norris, Kathleen. *Dakota: A Spiritual Geography.* New York: Ticknor and Fields, 1993.

Parcel, Toby L., and Elizabeth G. Menaghan. "Early Parental Work, Family Social Capital, and Early Childhood Outcomes." *American Journal of Sociology* 99 (1994): 972–1009.

———. "Family Social Capital and Children's Behavior Problems." *Social Psychology Quarterly* 56 (1993): 120–35.

Peshkin, Alan. *Growing Up American: Schooling and the Survival of Community.* Chicago: University of Chicago Press, 1978.

Pfeffer, Max J., and Jess Gilbert. "Gender and Off-Farm Employment in Two Farming Systems: Responses to Farm Crisis in the Cornbelt and the Mississippi Delta." *The Sociological Quarterly* 32 (1991): 593–610.

Prosterman, Leslie Mina. *Ordinary Life, Festival Days: Aesthetics in the Midwestern County Fair.* Washington, DC: Smithsonian Institution Press, 1995.

Putnam, Robert D. *Making Democracy Work: Civic Traditions in Modern Italy.* Princeton, NJ: Princeton University Press, 1993.

———. "The Strange Disappearance of Civic America." *The American Prospect* 24 (1996): 34–48.

Raban, Jonathan. *Bad Land: An American Romance.* New York: Pantheon, 1996.

Rachman, Stanley. "The Concept of Required Helpfulness." *Behavior Research and Therapy* 17 (1979): 1–6.

Radin, Norma, Daphna Oyserman, and Rita Benn. "Grandfathers, Teen Mothers, and Children under Two." In *The Psychology of Grandparenthood: An*

International Perspective, edited by Peter K. Smith, 85–99. International Library of Psychology. London: Routledge, 1991.

Ramirez-Barranti, Chrystal C. "The Grandparent/Grandchild Relationship: Family Resource in an Era of Voluntary Bonds." *Family Relations* 34 (1985): 343–52.

Reynolds, David R. "Rural Education: Decentering the Consolidation Debate." In *The Changing American Countryside: Rural People and Places,* edited by Emery N. Castle, 451–80. Lawrence: University Press of Kansas, 1995.

Riley, Glenda, and Richard S. Kirkendall. "Henry A. Wallace and the Mystique of the Farm Male, 1921–1933." *Annals of Iowa* 48, nos. 1–2 (1985): 32–55.

Robertson, Joan F. "Grandparenting in an Era of Rapid Change." In *Handbook of Aging and the Family,* edited by Rosemary Blieszner and Victoria Hilkevitch Bedford, 243–60. Westport, CT: Greenwood Press, 1995.

Robins, Lee N., and Michael Rutter, eds. *Straight and Devious Pathways from Childhood to Adulthood.* Cambridge: Cambridge University Press, 1990.

Roof, Wade Clark, and William McKinney. *American Mainline Religion: Its Changing Shape and Future.* New Brunswick, NJ: Rutgers University Press, 1987.

Rosenberg, Morris, and B. Claire McCullough. "Mattering: Inferred Significance and Mental Health among Adolescents." *Research in Community and Mental Health* 2 (1981): 163–82.

Rosenblatt, Paul C. *Farming Is in Our Blood: Farm Families in Economic Crisis.* Ames, IA: Iowa State University Press, 1990.

Rosenfeld, Rachel Ann. *Farm Women: Farm and Family in the United States.* Chapel Hill: University of North Carolina Press, 1985.

Rural Sociological Society Task Force on Persistent Rural Poverty. *Persistent Poverty in Rural America.* Rural Studies Series of the Rural Sociological Society. Boulder, CO: Westview Press, 1993.

Rutter, Michael. "Resilience in the Face of Adversity: Protective Factors and Resistance to Psychiatric Disorder." *British Journal of Psychiatry* 147 (1985): 598–611.

———. "Transitions and Turning Points in Developmental Psychopathology: As Applied to the Age Span between Childhood and Mid-adulthood." *International Journal of Behavioral Development* 19 (1996): 603–26.

———, ed. *Studies of Psychosocial Risk: The Power of Longitudinal Data.* Cambridge: Cambridge University Press, 1988.

Salamon, Sonya. *Prairie Patrimony: Family, Farming, and Community in the Midwest.* Studies in Rural Culture. Chapel Hill: University of North Carolina Press, 1992.

Sampson, Robert J. "Family Management and Child Development: Insights from Social Disorganization Theory." In *Facts, Frameworks, and Forecasts: Advances in Criminological Theory,* vol. 3, edited by Joan McCord, 63–93. New Brunswick, NJ: Transaction Books, 1992.

Sanders, Mavis Grovenia. "Breaking the Cycle of Reproduction: The Effect of

Communities, Families, and Schools on the Academic Achievement of Urban
African-American Youth." Ph.D. diss. Stanford University, 1995.

Scaramella, Laura V., Rand D. Conger, and Ronald L. Simons. "Parental Protective Influences and Gender-Specific Increases in Adolescent Developmental
Problems." *Journal of Research on Adolescence* 9 (1999): 111–141.

Scaramella, Laura V., Rand D. Conger, Ronald L. Simons, and Les B. Whitbeck.
"Predicting Risk for Pregnancy by Late Adolescence: A Social Contextual
Perspective." *Developmental Psychology* 34 (1998): 1233–45.

Schneider, Barbara, and James S. Coleman. *Parents, Their Children, and
Schools.* Boulder, CO: Westview Press, 1993.

Schulman, Michael D., Christian T. Evensen, Carol W. Runyan, Lisa R. Cohen,
and Kathleen A. Dunn. "Farm Work Is Dangerous for Teens: Agricultural
Hazards and Injuries among North Carolina Teens." *The Journal of Rural
Health* 13 (1997): 295–305.

Schwartz, Gary. *Beyond Conformity or Rebellion: Youth and Authority in
America.* Chicago: University of Chicago Press, 1987.

Sewell, William H. "Community of Residence and College Plans." *American
Sociological Review* 29 (1964): 24–38.

Shanahan, Michael J., Glen H. Elder Jr., Margaret Burchinal, and Rand D.
Conger. "Adolescent Earnings and Relationships with Parents: The Work-
Family Nexus in Urban and Rural Ecologies." In *Adolescents, Work, and
Family: An Intergenerational and Developmental Analysis,* edited by Jeylan
T. Mortimer and Michael D. Finch, 97–128. Understanding Families, vol. 6.
Thousand Oaks, CA: Sage, 1996.

———. "Adolescent Paid Labor and Relationships with Parents: Early Work-
Family Linkages." *Child Development* 67 (1996): 2183–2200.

Sherkat, Darren Edward. "Religious Socialization and the Family: An Examination of Religious Influence on the Family over the Life Course." Ph.D. diss.
Duke University, 1991.

Shribman, David M. "Iowa: A Civic Place." *Des Moines Register,* 27 January 1996.

Sidey, Hugh. "Introduction: Iowa's Language." *Iowa: a Celebration of Language,
People, and Purpose, Iowa Sesquicentennial Commission.* Des Moines, IA:
Meredith Publishing Services, 1995.

Simmel, Georg. *The Sociology of Georg Simmel,* translated and edited by Kurt
H. Wolff. Glencoe, IL: Free Press, 1950.

Simmons, Roberta G., and Dale A. Blyth. *Moving into Adolescence: The Impact
of Pubertal Change and School Context.* Social Institutions and Social Change.
New York: Aldine de Gruyter, 1987.

Smith, M. Brewster. "Competence and Socialization." In *Socialization and Society,* edited by John A. Clausen, 270–320. Boston: Little, Brown, 1968.

Smith, Mark H., Lionel J. Beaulieu, and Ann Seraphine. "Social Capital, Place
of Residence, and College Attendance." *Rural Sociology* 60 (1995): 363–80.

Smith, Robert John. *Japanese Society: Tradition, Self, and the Social Order.*
Lewis Henry Morgan Lecture Series, 1980. New York: Cambridge University
Press, 1985.

Stark, Rodney. *Sociology.* 3rd ed. Belmont, CA: Wadsworth, 1989.

Stark, Rodney. "Religion as Context: Hellfire and Delinquency One More Time." *Sociology of Religion* 57 (1996): 163–173.

Stark, Rodney, and William Sims Bainbridge. *The Future of Religion: Secularization, Revival, and Cult Formation.* Berkeley: University of California Press, 1985.

Steinberg, Laurence. "Autonomy, Conflict, and Harmony in the Family Relationship." In *At the Threshold: The Developing Adolescent,* edited by S. Shirley Feldman and Glen R. Elliott, 225–76. Cambridge: Harvard University Press, 1990.

Steinberg, Laurence, Sanford M. Dornbusch, and B. Bradford Brown. "Ethnic Differences in Adolescent Achievement: An Ecological Perspective." *American Psychologist* 47 (1992): 723–29.

Stinchcombe, Arthur L. *Rebellion in a High School.* Chicago: Quadrangle Books, 1964.

Super, Charles M., and Sara Harkness. "The Developmental Niche: A Conceptualization at the Interface of Child and Culture." In *Life-Span Development: A Diversity Reader,* edited by Richard A. Pierce and Michael A. Black, 61–77. Dubuque, IA: Kendall/Hunt, 1993.

Sutker, Patricia B. "Adolescent Drug and Alcohol Behaviors." In *Review of Human Development,* edited by Tiffany M. Field, Aletha Huston, Herbert C. Quay, Lillian Troll, and Gordon E. Finley, 356–80. A Wiley-Interscience Publication. New York: Wiley, 1982.

Swisher, Raymond R., Glen H. Elder Jr., and Rand D. Conger. "Rural Ecologies and Higher Education: Sources of Achievement in a Declining Region." Chapel Hill: Carolina Population Center, the University of North Carolina at Chapel Hill, 1998.

Thomas, Darwin L., and Gwendolyn C. Henry. "The Religion and Family Connection: Increasing Dialogue in the Social Sciences." In *The Religion and Family Connection: Social Service Perspectives,* edited by Darwin L. Thomas, 3–23. Religious Studies Center Specialized Monograph Series, vol. 3. Provo, UT: Religious Studies Center, Brigham Young University, 1988.

Thu, Kendall M., and E. Paul Durrenberger, eds. *Pigs, Politics, and Rural Communities.* Albany, NY: State University of New York Press, 1998.

Tinsley, Barbara R., and Ross D. Parke. "Grandparents as Interactive and Social Support Agents for Families with Young Infants." *International Journal of Aging and Human Development* 25 (1987): 259–77.

Tomlin, Angela M., and Richard H. Passman. "Grandmothers' Responsibility in Raising Two-Year-Olds Facilitates Their Grandchildren's Adaptive Behavior: A Preliminary Intrafamilial Investigation of Mothers' and Maternal Grandmothers' Effects." *Psychology and Aging* 4 (1989): 119–21.

Uhlenberg, Peter, and Bradley G. Hammill. "Frequency of Grandparent Contact with Grandchild Sets: Six Factors That Make a Difference." *The Gerontologist* 38 (1998): 276–85.

Uhlenberg, Peter, and James B. Kirby. "Grandparenthood over Time: Historical and Demographic Trends." In *Handbook on Grandparenthood,* edited by

Maximiliane E. Szinovacz, 23–39. Westport, CT: Greenwood Publishing Group, 1998.

Valentine, Gill. "A Safe Place to Grow Up? Parenting, Perceptions of Children's Safety, and the Rural Idyll." *Journal of Rural Studies* 13 (1997): 137–48.

Wallerstein, Judith S., and Joan Berlin Kelly. *Surviving the Break-Up: How Children and Parents Cope with Divorce.* New York: Basic Books, 1980.

Werner, Emmy E., and Ruth S. Smith. *Vulnerable but Invincible: A Longitudinal Study of Resilient Children and Youth.* New York: McGraw-Hill, 1982.

Werner, Emmy E., and Ruth S. Smith. *Overcoming the Odds: High-Risk Children from Birth to Adulthood.* Ithaca, NY: Cornell University Press, 1992

Weston, William J., ed. 1989. *Education and the American Family: A Research Systhesis.* New York: New York University Press, 1989.

Wilensky, Harold L. "Orderly Careers and Social Participation: The Impact of Work History on Social Integration in the Middle Mass." *American Sociological Review* 26 (1961): 521–39.

Willits, Fern K., and Donald M. Crider. "Church Attendance and Traditional Religious Beliefs in Adolescence and Young Adulthood: A Panel Study." *Review of Religious Research* 31 (1989): 68–81.

White House Conference on Child Health and Protection (1930: Washington, DC). *White House Conference, 1930: Addresses and Abstracts of Committee Reports.* New York: Century Co., 1931.

White House Conference on Children (1970: Washington, DC). *World of Children: Films from the 1970 White House Conference on Children.* Washington, DC: U.S. Government Printing Office, 1970.

White House Conference on Children and Youth (1960: Washington, DC). *Conference Proceedings, March 27–April 2, 1960.* Washington, DC: U.S. Government Printing Office, 1960.

White House Conference on Children in a Democracy (1939–1940: Washington, DC). *Final Report, January 18–20, 1940.* Washington, DC: U.S. Government Printing Office, 1940.

White House Conference on Families (1980, a Research Project). *The 1980 White House Conference on Families, a Research Project: The Concerns, Conclusions, Plans for Implementation: States and Territories of the United States of America.* Beverly Hills, CA: Lan Jordan Institute of Counseling and Psychotherapy, 1981.

Wilson, William J. *The Truly Disadvantaged: The Inner City, the Underclass, and Public Policy.* Chicago: University of Chicago Press, 1987.

Wright, Loyd S., Christopher J. Frost, and Stephen J. Wisecarver. "Church Attendance, Meaningfulness of Religion, and Depressive Symptomology among Adolescents." *Journal of Youth and Adolescence* 22 (1993): 559–68.

Wright, Mareena McKinley. "Holding up Their Half of the Sky: Rural Women and Their Work." Ph.D. diss. University of North Carolina at Chapel Hill, 1992.

Wuthnow, Robert. *Acts of Compassion: Caring for Others and Helping Ourselves.* Princeton, NJ: Princeton University Press, 1991.

———. *Sharing the Journey: Support Groups and America's New Quest for Com-*

munity. New York: Free Press; Toronto: Maxwell Macmillan Canada; New York: Maxwell Macmillan International, 1994.

Yates, Miranda, and James Youniss. "A Developmental Perspective on Community Service in Adolescence." *Social Development* 5 (1996): 85–111.

Youniss, James, and Miranda Yates. *Community Service and Social Responsibility in Youth.* Chicago: University of Chicago Press, 1997.

Zelizer, Viviana A. *Pricing the Priceless Child: The Changing Social Value of Children.* New York: Basic Books, 1985.

INDEX

Locators in boldface refer to pages with tables or graphs.